Writing the History of Emotions

WRITING HISTORY

The Writing History series publishes accessible overviews of particular fields in history, focusing on the practical application of theory in historical writing. Books in the series succinctly explain central concepts to demonstrate the ways in which they have informed effective historical writing. They analyse key historical texts and their producers within their institutional arrangement, and as part of a wider social discourse. The series' holistic approach means students benefit from an enhanced understanding of how to negotiate the contours of successful historical writing.

Series editors: Stefan Berger (Ruhr University Bochum, Germany), Heiko Feldner (Cardiff University, UK) and Kevin Passmore (Cardiff University, UK)

Published:
Writing Medieval History, edited by Nancy F. Partner
Writing Early Modern History, edited by Garthine Walker
Writing Contemporary History, edited by Robert Gildea and Anne Simonin
Writing Gender History (second edition), Laura Lee Downs
Writing Postcolonial History, Rochona Majumdar
Writing the Holocaust, edited by Jean-Marc Dreyfus and Daniel Langton
Writing the History of Memory, edited by Stefan Berger and Bill Niven
Writing Material Culture History, edited by Anne Gerritsen and Giorgio Riello
Writing History (third edition), edited by Stefan Berger, Heiko Feldner and Kevin Passmore
Writing Transnational History, Fiona Paisley
Writing Visual Histories, edited by Florence Grant and Ludmilla Jordanova
Writing Material Culture History (second edition), edited by Anne Gerritsen and Giorgio Riello

Forthcoming:
Writing Queer History, edited by Matt Cook
Writing Gender History (third edition), Laura Lee Downs
Writing Conceptual Histories, edited by Pasi Ihalainen and Jani Marjane

Writing the History of Emotions

Concepts and Practices, Economies and Politics

UTE FREVERT

BLOOMSBURY ACADEMIC
LONDON • NEW YORK • OXFORD • NEW DELHI • SYDNEY

BLOOMSBURY ACADEMIC
Bloomsbury Publishing Plc
50 Bedford Square, London, WC1B 3DP, UK
1385 Broadway, New York, NY 10018, USA
29 Earlsfort Terrace, Dublin 2, Ireland

BLOOMSBURY, BLOOMSBURY ACADEMIC and the Diana logo
are trademarks of Bloomsbury Publishing Plc

First published in Great Britain 2024

Copyright © Ute Frevert, 2024

Ute Frevert has asserted her right under the Copyright,
Designs and Patents Act, 1988, to be identified as Author of this work.

For legal purposes the Acknowledgements on p. vii constitute an
extension of this copyright page.

Cover image © Dariia / Adobe Stock
Background: Witthaya Prasongsin / Getty Images

All rights reserved. No part of this publication may be reproduced or transmitted
in any form or by any means, electronic or mechanical, including photocopying,
recording, or any information storage or retrieval system, without prior
permission in writing from the publishers.

Bloomsbury Publishing Plc does not have any control over, or responsibility
for, any third-party websites referred to or in this book. All internet addresses given
in this book were correct at the time of going to press. The author and publisher
regret any inconvenience caused if addresses have changed or sites have
ceased to exist, but can accept no responsibility for any such changes.

A catalogue record for this book is available from the British Library.

A catalog record for this book is available from the Library of Congress.

ISBN:	HB:	978-1-3503-4588-1
	PB:	978-1-3503-4587-4
	ePDF:	978-1-3503-4589-8
	eBook:	978-1-3503-4590-4

Typeset by Integra Software Services Pvt. Ltd.
Printed and bound in Great Britain

To find out more about our authors and books visit www.bloomsbury.com
and sign up for our newsletters.

CONTENTS

Acknowledgements vii

Introduction 1

1 Affects, Passions and Emotions: Historical Experiences and Historiographical Approaches 11

PART ONE Emotional Concepts and Practices 37

2 Trust Talk and Trust Work 39
3 Practising Honour: Social, Gender and Legal Perspectives 63
4 Honour and Shame in International Relations 89
5 Shame and Shaming in Modern History 117
6 Historicizing Empathy 139

PART TWO Emotional Economies of Capitalism 165

7 Capitalist Cold? Bringing Emotions Back In 167
8 How Does *Homo Oeconomicus* Cope with Emotions? 187
9 Greed and Avarice: Feelings about Money 201
10 *Hans in Luck*, or the Emotional Economy of Happiness in the Modern Age 219
11 Emotions and Material Culture: Say It with Flowers 241

PART THREE Politics of Emotion 257

12 Emotional Politics in Europe's Long Nineteenth Century 259
13 Love and Hate, Faith and Despair under National Socialism 281
14 Emotional Styles and Political Cultures in East and West Germany 307

Name Index 326

ACKNOWLEDGEMENTS

Most chapters of this book have been researched and written at the Max Planck Institute for Human Development in Berlin, at its Center for the History of Emotions, which I founded in early 2008. I am grateful to the Max Planck Society for generously giving me the opportunity to start a new field of historical enquiry and explore it together with a growing group of junior scholars. Writing the history of emotions is by no means an individual enterprise. My own work has greatly benefited from our team's wide-ranging historical expertise and intellectual creativity. It has also benefited from the research assistance and editorial skills of Dr Kerstin Singer. The late Christina Becher, Daniela Petrosino and Emma C. Lawson have helped me to turn my English-language texts into readable prose. Last, but not least, I thank Stefan Berger and his colleagues for accepting the book for publication in their Bloomsbury series.

Introduction

Since the turn of the millennium, emotions have become major issues in public debate and scientific research. Some scholars have gone so far as to consider the contemporary period an age of 'affectivism', while others proclaim that an 'emotional turn' has taken place across disciplines.[1]

Historians, too, have increasingly put emotions on their agenda. In 2008, two research centres were established in Berlin and London, both focusing on the modern history of emotions;[2] other networks study medieval and early modern emotions.[3] Workshops and conferences were organized worldwide and, in 2015, the 22nd International Congress of Historical Sciences in Jinan, China, honoured the history of emotions as one of four major themes. Important professional journals have disseminated the new approach to broader audiences through forum discussions;[4] academic presses have set up book series in the emerging field and commissioned edited volumes in

---

[1] Daniel Dukes et al., 'The Rise of Affectivism', *Nature Human Behaviour* 5 (2021): 816–20, https://doi.org/10.1038/s41562-021-01130-8.
[2] See their websites: https://www.mpib-berlin.mpg.de/research/research-centers/history-of-emotions; https://projects.history.qmul.ac.uk/emotions/. See also the 2014 interim report, Ute Frevert, 'The Modern History of Emotions: A Research Center in Berlin', *Cuadernos de Historia Contemporánea* 36 (2014): 31–55, https://doi.org/10.5209/rev_CHCO.2014.v36.46681.
[3] Between 2011 and 2017, an Australian Research Council Centre of Excellence focused on the History of Emotions in Europe from 1100 to 1800. Scholars from the Université de Québec and the Université d'Aix-Marseille have founded the network EMMA on the history of medieval emotions, http://emma.hypotheses.org.
[4] Nicole Eustace, Eugenia Lean, Julie Livingston, Jan Plamper, William M. Reddy and Barbara H. Rosenwein, '*AHR* Conversation: The Historical Study of Emotions', *The American Historical Review* 117, no. 5 (2012): 1487–531, https://doi.org/10.1093/ahr/117.5.1487; Frank Biess, Alon Confino, Ute Frevert, Uffa Jensen, Lyndal Roper and Daniela Saxer, 'Forum: History of Emotions', *German History* 28, no. 1 (2010): 67–80, https://doi.org/10.1093/gerhis/ghp108.

order to familiarize readers with current scholarship.⁵ Furthermore, new journals have dedicated themselves to publishing articles on the history of emotions: *Passions in Context* (established in 2010) and *Emotions: History, Culture, Society* (published, since 2017, by the Society for the History of Emotions).

At universities, the history of emotions has met with curiosity and growing enthusiasm among students and younger scholars. With more classes and seminars offered, the need for textbooks and research guides became clear. Teachers and students can now draw from a considerable number of introductory materials, including overviews and source books.⁶ This book is therefore not rooted in pedagogy but rather presents primary and substantive research that has been carried out over the last two decades. As a scholar who has shaped the history of emotions both institutionally (through the Berlin Center) and individually (through numerous books and articles), I thought it useful and, hopefully, helpful to reframe some of this work and make it accessible to a broader readership.

At the beginning was ... Günther Anders

The book starts with a more general evaluation of the field as it has developed up to this point, paying regard to earlier attempts and approaches but also trying to explain why the topic gained prominence only around the turn of the millennium. I myself became interested in emotions in the 1990s, after reading Günther Anders's short piece on 'To love, yesterday' (*Lieben gestern*), published in 1986. A philosopher (and Hannah Arendt's first husband), Anders decided to edit some of his diary entries from the late 1940s, when he had been living in New York before eventually returning to Europe with his second wife, after seventeen years of exile, in 1950.

One day in March 1948, seven 'monstrous' boxes and barrels, full of European memorabilia, were delivered to his tiny apartment. His parents, eminent psychologists William and Clara Stern, had packed the boxes

---

⁵See, e.g., the Bloomsbury series *A Cultural History of the Emotions*, ed. Susan Broomhall, Jane W. Davidson and Andrew Lynch, 6 vols (covering historical periods from antiquity to the postmodern age); *The Routledge History of Emotions in the Modern World*, ed. Katie Barclay and Peter N. Stearns (London: Routledge, 2023); *Histoire des émotions*, ed. Alain Corbin, Jean-Jacques Courtine and Georges Vigarello, 3 vols (Paris: Seuil, 2016–17).

⁶Susan J. Matt and Peter Stearns, eds, *Doing Emotions History* (Urbana: University of Illinois Press, 2014); Jan Plamper, *The History of Emotions: An Introduction* (Oxford: Oxford University Press, 2015); Rob Boddice, *The History of Emotions* (Manchester: Manchester University Press, 2018); Barbara Rosenwein and Riccardo Cristiani, *What Is the History of Emotions?* (Cambridge: Polity Press, 2018); Katie Barclay, *The History of Emotions: A Student Guide to Methods and Sources* (London: Red Globe Press, 2020); Katie Barclay, Sharon Crozier-De Rosa and Peter Stearns, eds, *Sources for the History of Emotions: A Guide* (London: Routledge, 2020).

before leaving Hamburg for Durham, North Carolina, in 1934. Out of familial piety – his father had passed away in 1938, his mother only recently – Günther took stock of the many letters, diaries, photos, school and health reports covering the lives of his parents, aunts and uncles and grandparents. At first he disliked the fact that these were all 'dead assets', *Totenpost*, and he burnt most of the documents. Yet he took care to peruse the material. In particular, his grandmother's correspondence from the 1880s caught his attention. All the letters were written by married women friends, and all talked, abundantly, of love. This prompted Anders to conclude, somewhat prematurely, that love was the main topic, the 'core theme' of nineteenth-century European society and literature, and that it seemed to be a female monopoly, as well as a substitute for redemption.

In his diary until 1949, Anders continuously contrasted former cultures of love with his own times, which he deemed careless, slack, inattentive, ungraceful and witless in matters of romance. Throughout, he repeatedly wondered about the historicity of love, and he tried his hand at a few explanations for love's loss of prominence and importance. Reading those observations half a century later, I could not help but be struck by the approach. In my professional career as a social and gender historian I had read and written widely about marriage and family life since the late eighteenth century. But I had never thought about emotions proper. Romantic love, in my account, had figured as a lofty ideal invented by a few hotheads around 1800 in order to challenge the traditional structure of marital relationships. It fitted the needs and signature of a modern society based on individual autonomy and gender hierarchy perfectly. Now this German philosopher was inviting me to look at love as an emotion, and, even more, to conceive of it as an emotion that changed over time.

I immediately grasped the novelty of what Anders was attempting. I knew that he was right in stating that 'tomorrow's historians should write history as the history of emotions'.[7] And I decided to take up the challenge, slowly but steadily. In 1996, I began to give lectures and write articles on the topic, and I developed a large, collaborative research project on the history of trust. Tracing sources and earlier secondary literature, I became aware that there had indeed been forerunners (their work will be discussed in Chapter 1). The historical profession as it emerged during the nineteenth century had not altogether neglected the topic.[8] But it had, time and again, pushed emotions to the margins without crediting them with much weight or impact. Apparently, emotions did not fit the agenda of a historiography

---

[7] Günther Anders, *Lieben gestern: Notizen zur Geschichte des Fühlens* (Munich: C.H. Beck, 1986), 10, *passim*; Günther Anders, *Die Totenpost*, ed. Alexander Knopf (Göttingen: Wallstein, 2022).
[8] As to nineteenth-century inroads into the history of emotions, see Uffa Jensen and Daniel Morat, eds, *Rationalisierungen des Gefühls: Zum Verhältnis von Wissenschaft und Emotionen 1880–1930* (Munich: Fink, 2008).

that was primarily interested in how great men, great ideas and great nations ruled the world. When the agenda shifted after the Second World War, the picture did not change much. The new brand of social or societal history proved to be as indifferent to emotions as the older contingent of political and state historians. Things only really started to change once cultural history became more prominent and influential in the 1990s.

The new emotional tide was not restricted to historians. Literary scholars had discovered emotions far earlier and faster, and cultural theorists soon picked up the topic too. 'Affect' – rather than 'emotion' – developed into their key concept and fuelled a great deal of intellectual creativity, especially in British and US universities. In Chapter 1, I will explain, though, why I prefer to talk about emotions and feelings rather than affects. The main reason, in a nutshell, is that I consider emotions to be deeply cultured and learnt activities, whereas affect is usually thought to be more ephemeral, unwitting, hard to nail down. Cultural studies see affects as 'visceral forces beneath, alongside, or generally *other than* conscious knowing', as 'vital forces insisting beyond emotion'.[9] Such epistemological differences open up different research trajectories as well as different methodologies. It is not by accident that historians tend to focus on emotions rather than affect, while philosophers and cognitive scientists prefer things the other way round.

Emotional concepts and practices: trust, honour, shame, empathy

Focusing on emotions that are culturally shaped and socially acquired then led me to single out some for further historical scrutiny. My first choice was trust (Chapter 2). Trust had become, in recent years and decades, a real buzzword in public discourse and advertisement, and I wondered why. Trust was also on the minds of psychologists, sociologists, economists and political scientists, so I could draw on a large conceptual toolbox. Yet I quickly discovered that those tools seemed overly functionalistic. They tended to emphasize the instrumental value of trust while neglecting its emotional character. Among social scientists in particular, trust is widely conceived of as an attitude that enables human cooperation and allows social actors to pursue goals that they would be unlikely to accomplish without it.

But trust, it seemed to me, was more than a cognitive phenomenon. It was reducible neither to a thought or conviction nor to a belief or wish. It had a strong evaluative component, as most emotions do. Trust did not strike people out of the blue; it had to be learnt, built and nurtured. Again, this

---

[9]Gregory J. Seigworth and Melissa Gregg, 'An Inventory of Shimmers', in *The Affect Theory Reader*, ed. Gregory J. Seigworth and Melissa Gregg (Durham, NC: Duke University Press, 2010), 1.

applied to many other emotions. Trust also came with an expressive body language: its mimics and gestures clearly differed from those of distrust. Furthermore, it contained a phenomenal element: a trusting person felt different from a distrusting one. Last but not least, the feeling of trust had an activating force. Trust did something to those who trusted and were trusted; it let them behave in a certain way and engage in direct communication and transactions. Trust was unthinkable without being exercised.[10]

In order to historicize trust as an emotional practice dependent on specific experiences and expectations, I consulted eighteenth- and nineteenth-century lexical texts. They defined trust in similar terms and explained who should trust (or distrust) whom for what reasons and under which circumstances. This not only helped me to draw up a social map of trusting relationships, it also made me aware that the nineteenth century, in particular, had been very eager to expand those relationships. A myriad of new composite words testified to the urgent desire to put trust at the core of social interaction and communication, be it in the economy, in politics, between teachers and students, husbands and wives, parents and children.

What to make of this? How does 'trust talk' connect to 'trust work', to social practices of trust and distrust, then and now? What does the infatuation with trust tell us about actual experiences? Why do modern people put so much effort into framing these experiences in terms of mutual trust, instead of relying, as earlier generations did, on trust in God and God alone? Asking such questions not only connects the history of emotions with the history of societies and their respective institutions and social groups, it also invites us to consider the relationship between language and feelings.

This relationship is both complex and complicated. Language reflects experience, but it also shapes and constructs experience. Naming and framing emotions is constitutive of experiencing emotions.[11] As long as people cannot find a word for what they are feeling, they will be at a loss as to what this feeling is about. Bodily signs and expressions do not really help to identify an emotional state. You might cry out of joy or grief, distress or elation. You might shiver because you are afraid or because you sense the joy of anticipation. A person who blushes and feels her heart rate accelerate might be experiencing rage or shame. Other emotional states that can be discerned via fMRI technology might go completely unnoticed by the person under examination. What one feels has a lot to do with how one names, labels and addresses those feelings through mimics, gestures, sounds

---

[10] In this, I agree with the philosopher Martin Hartmann, *Die Praxis des Vertrauens* (Berlin: Suhrkamp, 2011). I disagree, however, with his argument that trust is not an emotion but an evaluative attitude (151–71).

[11] As to the interpretative grid that language imposes on feelings, see Anna Wierzbicka, *Emotions across Languages and Cultures: Diversity and Universals* (Cambridge: Cambridge University Press, 1999), 24–31. The author pays particular attention to different languages and how they frame emotions.

and, above all, words.¹² Once you define the emotion by giving it a name, things fall into place: you know what is happening to you, you can evaluate your emotional experience, and you can act upon it in a transformative way.

This said, trust talk easily translates into trust work, or the work invested in social relationships in order to make them function smoothly to the benefit of all concerned. Most of this work happens in institutions like the family, religious congregations, the workplace, social clubs and many others. Making individuals able and willing to engage in trust work (which is risky) requires institutional settings that frame mutual expectations and sanction those who disobey them. The stronger such institutions are – and many argue that they have become stronger and more numerous in modern times – the greater the possibility and propensity of men and women, children and adults to enter into trusting relations. In this sense, we can describe trust as a modern emotion whose reputation increased considerably after 1800.

Other feelings fared less well in the historical 'economy of emotions', that is, in the flow and exchange, traffic and trade of emotions in relations between individuals and among collectives. The term can be traced back to the Scottish philosopher Francis Hutcheson and his 1728 essay 'on the nature and conduct of the passions and affections' (he did not, *nota bene*, write the word 'emotion', which at that time was not yet in use).¹³ For him, as for other thinkers of the Enlightenment, it was most important to keep passions, affections and desires, public as well as private, in a 'just *Ballance and Oeconomy* which would constitute the most happy State of each Person, and promote the greatest Good in the whole'. Individual happiness and the common good were imagined as two sides of the same coin – you could not have one without the other. Just as societies relied on certain passions and desires (like honour, ambition or pity), individual men and women harboured personal feelings that often, but not always, made them happy. Here, Hutcheson proved to be a truly modern intellectual who thought highly of the human capacity for self-control and self-guidance. 'Since we have some considerable *Power* over our Desires', he stated, mankind would ultimately be able to incorporate them into an appropriate 'Oeconomy'.¹⁴

Hutcheson did not mention trust in 1728, but he did write abundantly about honour, which figured prominently in the emotional economy of his time. Yet it largely ceased to do so in the second half of the twentieth

---

¹²The composer and conductor Leonard Bernstein argued the inverse and considered music far more important in 'naming' emotions. See his televised lecture from 18 January 1958, in which he claimed that musical movement 'can tell us more about the way we feel than a million words can', https://leonardbernstein.com/lectures/television-scripts/young-peoples-concerts/what-does-music-mean (accessed 7 March 2023). The jury is still out.
¹³Thomas Dixon, *From Passions to Emotions: The Creation of a Secular Psychological Category* (Cambridge: Cambridge University Press, 2003).
¹⁴Francis Hutcheson, *An Essay on the Nature and Conduct of the Passions and Affections, with Illustrations on the Moral Sense*, ed. Aaron Garrett (Indianapolis: Liberty Fund, 2002), 47.

century, at least in Western societies. In 1970, sociologist Peter Berger noted that honour truly was a thing of the past. Among Americans, only 'obsolete classes such as military officers and ethnic grandmothers' still knew, felt and observed its rules and practices.[15] Why was this the case? How had an emotion like honour come to sink into oblivion, why was it no longer able to elicit strong feelings, either positive or negative? Once more, this question points to the historicity of emotions and their changing place and status in certain parts of the world. An emotion that, during the nineteenth and early twentieth century, had carried great weight and was decisive in matters of life and death had fallen out of fashion, lost its meaning and cohesion. This can be observed on various levels: Chapter 3 looks at honour through the lens of social, gender and legal history, while Chapter 4 explores honour – and its opposite, shame – in international relations, particularly in times of conflict and war.

Interestingly, shame has had a different trajectory. While honour no longer finds itself on the contemporary map of emotions, shame and humiliation do. With the emergence of social media and internet-based shaming platforms, we can even conclude that the power of shame has increased in recent years. This is despite the many attempts to delegitimize public shaming and discredit humiliating practices as indecent and uncivilized. Chapter 5 investigates the resistance to shame and shaming as it developed during the modern period. It also tries to explain the current renaissance of public shaming by analysing the functions and communication of shame, drawing on different politics of shaming. While European societies have abolished official shame sanctions carried out in public, the US still practises them as an element of legal punishment. In China, the politics of humiliation are part and parcel of a top-down strategy to control and regulate the population.

Although shame is an individual and self-conscious emotion that can be elicited by a person's reflection on their own shortcomings, it is, in most cases, induced by social pressure and the public gaze. This is commonly known in present-day China and in the US. It was also familiar to Europeans well into the nineteenth century. Putting defendants on the pillory or flogging them in public seemed far more efficient than throwing them into prison or beating them behind closed doors. When shame sanctions began to draw criticism after 1800, empathy was in large part responsible. Especially with regard to capital punishment, citizens complained about the excessive violence that was on public display and left, as they argued, a dangerous mark on the many thousands of onlookers. Instead of pitying the person subjected to brutal violence, people seemed to enjoy the spectacle and feel good in the safety of the crowd. Pedagogues and educators took offence to such behaviour, which to them appeared disgusting and inhuman. Humanity, as

---

[15]Peter Berger, 'On the Obsolescence of the Concept of Honor', *European Journal of Sociology* 11, no. 2 (1970): 339–47, quote 339.

they saw it, should also reign in the 'theatre of horror', and empathy was to serve as an important mediator (Chapter 6).

Yet they did not speak of empathy when they described the emotions citizens were meant to feel at sites of cruelty. Instead, they used words like pity and compassion, which for many were at the heart of modern civilization. In 1759, Adam Smith had elaborated in great detail on sympathy, or fellow-feeling, as a major component of a society whose cohesion could not rest on the principle of self-love alone. Although he later praised such self-love as the main propellant of capitalism, he was well aware that other emotions were needed in order to make capitalism work. Simply put, it had to be embedded in a culture of human sympathy that extended far and wide, starting with family and neighbours and reaching out to distant countries and populations.[16] Such fellow-feeling was at the root of some of the most powerful social movements that emerged in the late eighteenth century and after, above all the struggle against slavery, as well as many other humanitarian initiatives that continue to this very day.

Returning to the question of lost and found emotions, of emotions that gained currency during the modern period versus those that were shed in transformation, empathy is clearly on the winning side.[17] At the same time, there have been and are limits to empathy. Those limits are usually not due to individual deficiencies or pathologies, but to societal or group pressure, antagonism and prejudice. The latter are learnt through imitation or group affiliation, and they erect powerful barriers against helping or supporting others in need. In her 2016 book *Strangers in Their Own Land*, sociologist Arlie Hochschild wrote about the 'empathy walls' that right-wingers in the US have erected over the years against people 'who hold different beliefs or whose childhood is rooted in different circumstances'.[18] In this setting, empathy is in short supply or solely includes those with shared beliefs and ways of life. Seen against the background of deep political cleavages within and beyond national societies, however, empathy is in high demand, and we might learn something from historical strategies to teach it.

Emotional economies of capitalism

While Adam Smith had claimed sympathy (what has, since the early twentieth century, been called empathy) to be a major pillar, next to self-love, of a modern capitalist society, later critics often accused capitalism

---

[16] Adam Smith, *The Theory of Moral Sentiments* (Amherst: Prometheus, [1759] 2000).
[17] Ute Frevert, *Emotions in History – Lost and Found* (Budapest: Central European University Press, 2011).
[18] Arlie Russell Hochschild, *Strangers in Their Own Land: Anger and Mourning on the American Right* (New York: The New Press, 2016), 5–8; Aleida Assmann and Ines Detmers, eds, *Empathy and Its Limits* (Basingstoke: Palgrave, 2016).

of being emotionally cold and uncaring. Around 1900, sociologist Max Weber went even further in suggesting that capitalism had in fact outlawed 'irrational' emotions from economic life and relegated them to a marginal position – an argument that is critically evaluated in Chapter 7.

In a similar vein, albeit without inherent criticism, twentieth-century economists constructed the capitalist actor as one who simply followed rational calculation and self-maximizing goals. How the artificial figure of *homo oeconomicus* came into being is analysed in Chapter 8, as is the ongoing struggle to furnish him with passions, preferences and animal spirits. Chapter 9 engages more specifically with feelings about money, tracing the dynamic history of greed and avarice. Their antidote can be seen in the hero of the popular fairy tale *Hans in Luck*. Hans knows neither greed nor avarice, and he has nothing in common with the modern capitalist subject who seeks to amass riches and invest them carefully in order to become even richer. Hans does quite the opposite, and he is happy as a result. He experiences joy in trading valuable against less valuable objects and ultimately finds peace in not owning anything and discarding his remaining possessions. How does this tale from the early nineteenth century relate to the advent of capitalism (Chapter 10)? Does it foreshadow the widespread criticism and multiple acts of resistance that would follow? And what does it say about emotional objects – objects that become imbued with intense feelings of joy and happiness, in Hans's case animals and stones?

For others, flowers are such objects. The production and export of flowers has become a multi-billion-dollar business led by the Netherlands, Columbia, Ecuador and Kenya. Among the importing countries, the US and Germany stand out; measured by per capita consumption, Germans love flowers even more than Americans. Such love has been nurtured over many decades, even centuries, and is sustained by powerful advertising campaigns which emphasize flowers as envoys of love, care, affection, appreciation, regret, remorse, grief and gratitude. Chapter 11 looks at this flowery language of emotions from a historical viewpoint and highlights the various sites and circumstances where, and when, flowers were prone to speak it. In addition, the chapter analyses how capitalism commodified emotions by attaching them to objects that were bought and sold as alleged representations or symbols of personal feelings.

Emotional politics

With Chapter 12, the book moves in yet another direction and enters the field of politics. Beginning in the nineteenth century, we follow the multiple attempts of rulers to forge strong emotional relationships with their subjects or citizens. In an age of increasing political participation, bonds of love, fidelity and trust seemed ever more important. At the same time, they were challenged by revolutionary and protest movements. As emotions proved to be genuinely unstable, huge efforts were made to buttress them against the omnipresent threat of defection and dissolution.

Those efforts were not confined to monarchies. Totalitarian regimes, as Chapter 13 shows, were especially eager to influence and channel people's emotions, and used innovative techniques to make them feel part of a unified whole. Democracies also enlisted emotions to reach out to citizens and mobilize them for their own good. Unlike dictatorships, though, they neither aimed for nor achieved emotional consonance. Chapter 14 explores various sorts of emotional politics as they have been articulated since the end of the Second World War. It includes emotional styles from above and below, acted out by professional politicians and engaged citizens. Appealing to emotions is not only a top-down affair. People have often used it as a bottom-up strategy: addressing feelings of despair, fear and anger is meant to force authorities into changing things for the better and altering the course of politics. The youth movement Fridays for Future serves as a recent example, and there have been many predecessors.

Emotional politics, emotional economies, emotional concepts and practices – these are the categories that structure the book. Theoretical questions are discussed in each and every chapter: the distinction between affects and emotions, the role of language, the impact of institutions, social and gender differentiation. Methodological issues are likewise addressed throughout, above all the choice of sources and their respective significance. In terms of timeframe, the chapters mostly cover the modern period, from the eighteenth to the twentieth (and sometimes twenty-first) centuries. The geographical scope does not live up to contemporary demands to write, at all costs, global history. As my own expertise is in European history, I have picked most of my case studies from this region, with a major focus on Central and Western Europe. Some of the material has been published before, but thoroughly revised, rewritten, shortened or broadened for this book.

CHAPTER ONE

Affects, Passions and Emotions: Historical Experiences and Historiographical Approaches

Emotions – or rather affects, passions, desires, feelings and sentiments as they were called up until the twentieth century – have long captured the attention of writers and readers alike. From early antiquity to late modernity, they have been observed, described and analysed in various types of texts. The oldest work of Western literature, Homer's epic poem the *Iliad*, opened with the rage of the Greek hero Achilles and the actions to which it led. Ancient philosophers took a more systematic approach and underscored the phenomenology and communicative function of emotions. Medical doctors tried to assess their effect on people's health and well-being; moreover, they sought to explain the physiological processes that gave rise to or dampened emotions. Legal theory and practice made assumptions about how emotions affected behaviour and prompted people to commit crimes and misdemeanours, and they wondered whether emotions counted as mitigating factors that might justify milder sentences. Church officials, theologians and pious people, meanwhile, actively defined the set of emotions and emotional practices that they believed needed to be felt, experienced and demonstrated before, during and after religious services or while contemplating sacred paintings, texts and spaces.

Over the centuries, societies thus accumulated knowledge through written texts and oral communication, immaterial objects and visual representations about what emotions do and how they do it. They also tried to distinguish

---

This chapter is a revised and expanded version of my contribution 'Affect Theory and History of Emotions', in *Bloomsbury History: Theory and Method Articles* (London: Bloomsbury, 2021), available online: http://dx.doi.org/10.5040/9781350970878.069.

positive from negative affect and strained to arrive at sound judgements regarding which kinds of emotions were healthy and desirable and which were detrimental to a person or group. Although some of this knowledge might have since been lost, historians have been able to uncover a wealth of information about how past societies handled emotions.

An issue of continuous discussion and controversy has been the intensity and degree of emotional fervour that particular societies or social groups found acceptable or necessary. During the modern period, this debate engaged broader parts of the population and numerous societal institutions. In the last decades of the eighteenth century, middle-class men and women set themselves apart from the nobility by emphasizing their own sense of compassion and empathy, which they saw lacking in cold-hearted aristocrats. Romantic authors, for their part, found middle-class life far too disciplined and felt that it left little room for individual creativity or passionate feelings. In 1829, the British historian Thomas Carlyle called his times 'the Mechanical Age' or the 'Age of Machinery, in every outward and inward sense of that word', lamenting that 'men are grown mechanical in head and in heart, as well as in hand', governed 'by rule and calculated contrivance'.[1]

Modernity: disenchantment versus enchantment

Less than a century later, the term and phenomenon of 'rationalization' began to make discursive waves. Among its most influential analysts was the German sociologist Max Weber, who considered it the defining feature of modern societies. As members of market-based classes, he argued, people had become accustomed to acting instrumentally, carefully calculating means and ends. Rather than following culturally defined habits and moral duties, they tailored their behaviour to further their own economic, political or social interests. They learned to control their passions, restrain their impulses and channel their energy in the most promising direction. Rationalization was thus accompanied by a new level of self-reflection and self-evaluation that also included an awareness of other people's interests, strategies and conduct. It was advanced by the institutionalization of rules and norms which rendered individual behaviour uniform, regular, continuous and thus transparent and predictable to others. According to Weber, a major force behind rationalization was capitalism, aided by bureaucratic state administration.[2]

---

[1]Thomas Carlyle, 'Signs of the Times', in *Scottish and Other Miscellanies* (London: Dent & Sons, 1923), 223–45, here 226, 228.
[2]Max Weber, 'Religious Rejections of the World and Their Directions', in *From Max Weber: Essays in Sociology*, ed. Hans Heinrich Gerth and Charles Wright Mills (London: Paul, 1946), 331–43.

Reading Weber, the question immediately arises: what about the other side? What was lost, overcome, suspended as the world became more 'rational' and 'intellectual' (and less 'emotional', 'irrational' or 'enchanted')? What was rationalization good and, possibly, bad for? Weber conceived of rationalization in a non-normative way. He did not judge the movement away from custom, tradition and 'affective behaviour' towards purposefully planned and shrewdly calculated action. But he did think, somewhat mournfully, that there were only a few spheres such as art, love and religion that could escape the 'iron cage' of instrumental rationality and furnish affective motives and experiences.

The alleged triumph of rationalization and intellectualization in a 'disenchanted world' was commented on intensively at the beginning of the twentieth century. According to its digital archive, while the London *Times* mentioned rationalization only twice throughout the entire nineteenth century, that number jumped to 1,200 during the 1920s. In 1935, the Dutch historian Johan Huizinga crowned 'mechanization and organization' the two mighty 'gods of our time' (the German translation used 'rationalization' rather than mechanization). These gods had generated global networks of cooperation, communication and technical precision. Yet, somewhat paradoxically, they had also produced a new type of human being: one less controlled and 'more puerile, more susceptible to reactions of feeling', to a degree that neared madness and brutality. The advent of such humans was heralded and applauded by the new brand of vitalism, which found an eager audience beginning around 1900. Opposing the reign of positivism and rationality, vitalism praised the immediacy of human experience and the creativity of intuition. As Huizinga saw it, this 'life-philosophy' let myth and magic dominate *logos*, or, in Weber's terms, privileged enchantment over disenchantment.[3]

Lebensphilosophie was not simply a school of thought with a few intellectual, post-Nietzschean proponents. In Continental Europe, it captured a powerful mood that had become institutionalized through a great number of reform movements and associations. Most of them were highly critical of contemporary society. Leaving the city and hiking in the countryside, wearing comfortable, often hand-made clothes, preparing healthy food, exposing one's bare skin to the sun and air – all this spoke to a widely felt need to distance oneself from a lifestyle that seemed overly mechanical and bereft of 'spirit' and deep feeling. Such movements were found all along the political spectrum. On the left, they were deemed anti-capitalist and on the right, they signified a longing for an organic way of life that prized community over individualism. In some extreme right-wing circles, followers adopted racist language and practised violent exclusion.

---

[3]Johan Huizinga, *In the Shadow of Tomorrow: A Diagnosis of the Modern Distemper* (Providence: Preservation Books, [Dutch Orig. 1935] 2019), 151–2.

Huizinga's French colleague Lucien Febvre noted this development in the late 1930s. In an attempt to convince fellow historians to take emotions seriously, he cited examples from his own area of expertise, namely, late medieval and early modern history. But he also referred, with urgency, to contemporary experiences, to 'our own history', which was witnessing 'perpetual sentimental resurgences and resurrections':

> We have revivals of the cult of blood, red blood, in its most animal primitive aspects and the cult of the basic forces within us which reveals our lassitude, domestic animals that we are, crushed and beaten down by the frenzied noise and energy of the thousands of machines that obsess us. To compensate, we have the revival of a sort of cult of Mother Earth in whose lap it is so pleasant in the evenings to stretch our weary limbs as if we were her child. No less universal is the revival of a sort of cult of the fostering, healing sun – nudism and camping, frantic immersions in the air and water. We know the exaltation of primitive feelings, going together with a rude dislocation of aim and purpose and the exaltation of cruelty at the expense of love, animal behaviour at the expense of culture, but always animal behaviour that is circumscribed and felt to be superior to culture.[4]

Such feelings and behaviour, according to Febvre, 'will tomorrow have finally made our universe into a stinking pit of corpses'. Although the historian alluded to the universality of 'primitive feelings' and talked, inclusively, of 'we' and 'us', he primarily focused on European fascism. In his view, Germany's National Socialism had ushered in a veritable 'revolution' of 'sensibility and sentimentality', a huge 'social change' of 'morally-accepted affective reactions'.[5]

Interestingly, Febvre interpreted this 'revival' of 'basic forces within us' as compensation for modern experiences that Weber or Huizinga would have subsumed under the categories of rationalization and organization. In dramatic, even pathetic terms, he imagined humankind enslaved and dominated by industrial work and machines that imposed their unrelenting noise and pace onto the bodies and minds of those whom they had 'crushed' and brought under their control. The various vitalistic 'cults' served as an emotional escape from that control, a cry for freedom and excess, a shelter that promised healing and consolation.

Febvre, like so many of his contemporaries, was torn. On the one hand, he empathized with people's quest for refuge from the modern obsession with

---

[4]Lucien Febvre, 'Sensibility and History: How to Reconstitute the Emotional Life of the Past', in *A New Kind of History and Other Essays*, ed. Peter Burke (New York: Harper & Row, 1973), 12–26, here 26.

[5]Jan Plamper, *The History of Emotions: An Introduction* (Oxford: Oxford University Press, 2015), 42–3. See Chapter 13 in this volume.

uniformity, regularity, discipline and speed. On the other hand, he detested what he called 'primitive' or 'animal behaviour'. He saw love superseded by cruelty and hatred, and feared for 'culture' and its capacity to pacify human brutality and violence. Such ambivalence prompted him to thoroughly distrust unilinear, progressive visions of human development and instead explore historical patterns of recurrence and resurgence.

Emotional progress or regression to 'primitivism'?

The belief in progress entertained by many historians and sociologists of the late nineteenth and early twentieth centuries, including Weber, was also embraced by Johan Huizinga in his seminal work *The Waning of the Middle Ages*, which Febvre studied and quoted. Huizinga described the late medieval period as one of exuberance and passionate feelings; 'the most naïve joy' had reigned side by side with 'pride, anger, and covetousness'.[6] After the Reformation, he argued, this emotional culture began to be contained and quietened. Huizinga published the book in 1919, right after the First World War, and it became an immediate hit with those interested in cultural history. Just as Max Weber's work on early capitalism and the religious spirit of Calvinism had done, it narrated European history as the steady forward march of rationalization and organization.

The tale of progress was elaborated further by sociologist Norbert Elias in his analysis of the *Civilizing Process*. First published in 1939, Elias's book deliberately linked sociological and psychological developments to argue that state-building in early modern Europe went hand in hand with the establishment of stricter norms of self-control. Since the state monopolized physical violence, citizen–subjects could form societies whose members engaged in peaceful competition. Faced with increasing social differentiation and rising levels of interdependence, societies were eager to manage and fine-tune human behaviour. In the process, people's affective apparatuses gradually changed to incorporate more restrained modes of conduct and interaction. Instead of giving in to spontaneous desires and strong affects, human beings learned to hold back, think twice and reflect on the consequences of their actions. Elias borrowed from Weber in calling this 'rationalization' and attributed its origins to the European nobility, whose members transformed themselves from fierce warriors and brash knights into polite and polished courtiers from the sixteenth century onwards.

During that transformation, the 'thresholds of repugnance' were decisively lowered. Habits such as spitting, defecating and cursing in public,

---

[6]Johan Huizinga, *The Waning of the Middle Ages* (New York: Dover Publications, 2007), 18.

which had in earlier times been considered normal and acceptable, were now looked upon as utterly despicable and shameful. As the fear of losing face, reputation and honour before one's peers grew, shame became a central regulator of human drives and appetites. It helped people internalize social demands by translating them into individual psychic constraints. The early modern period thus saw shame and embarrassment expand to encompass ever more modes of behaviour and social strata.

Writing in the 1930s, Elias's intention was not to cast an overly optimistic light on what he identified as a European process of civilization and rationalization. Although he criticized psychoanalysis for its lack of historical and social understanding, he nevertheless borrowed from Sigmund Freud's language of 'drives' and 'super-ego'. Behind the intensifying sensitivity towards shame, he argued, lay the ubiquity of fear: fear of social degradation, of someone else's superiority, of one's own vulnerability and defencelessness. Those fears were kept in check by the state and its monopoly on violence, which enabled the pacification of social interaction and communication. But, as Elias added, this particular arrangement was open to change, and the hitherto productive tension between fear and shame might be reversed. Near the end of his book, he remarked:

> At present we are so accustomed to the existence of these more stable monopolies of force and the greater predictability of violence resulting from them, that we scarcely see their importance for the structure of our conduct and our personality. We scarcely realize how quickly what we call our 'reason,' this relatively farsighted and differentiated steering of our conduct, with its high degree of affect-control, would crumble or collapse if the anxiety-inducing tensions within and around us changed.[7]

Elias was born into a German-Jewish family and left his home country in 1933. He wrote the *Civilizing Process* in British exile and published it in Switzerland in 1939, the year of the German attack on Poland that started the Second World War. With this in mind, these final sentences seem to lack political acumen. Although the author had by that point witnessed how a state intentionally incited citizens to lose control of their affects, he evidently could not imagine that 'reason' might collapse altogether and give way to an upsurge of anxieties and the breakdown of decency in German politics and society. The narrative of progressive civilization and rationalization was too powerful and had too much to offer for it to be questioned. It took Elias another twenty years to acknowledge that civilization could break down and regress, and indeed had done so under the Nazi regime.[8]

---

[7]Norbert Elias, *The Civilizing Process: Sociogenetic and Psychogenetic Investigation* (Oxford: Blackwell, 2000), 441.
[8]Norbert Elias, *The Germans: Power Struggles and the Development of Habitus in the Nineteenth and Twentieth Centuries* (New York: Columbia University Press, 1996), 299–402.

As we can see here and in many other cases, 'rationalization' was not just an analytical concept; it also served as a cultural and political pacifier. For Weber, Huizinga, Febvre and Elias, becoming rational meant becoming predictable, controlled and readable. While they might have deplored some of its shortcomings, they ultimately shared the positive view of rationalization as a civilizing force. As much as Weber revelled in art and eroticism as counter-currents to the rational world of bureaucracy and economy, he did not want to see that world succumb to 'affective behaviour' and passionate excess. In a similar vein, Febvre wanted 'culture' to be protected from 'primitive' cults and was deeply suspicious of the 'contagious' emotions that swept through and undermined responsible politics. Elias likewise left no doubt that he preferred the apparent clarity and predictability of reason over the 'fog' of affects and the 'haze' of fears. Writing both as professional academics and as citizens committed to liberal democracy, their aim was to restrict emotions to the private sphere of family and friendship, arts and sports, while walling off political deliberation and decision-making.

This seemed even more important in the age of participatory politics and mass mobilization. During the nineteenth century, many European countries had installed parliamentary or semi-parliamentary systems of political representation. Citizens – all male in those days – cast their votes in general elections and different parties vied for consent and sympathy. The political mass market, as historian Hans Rosenberg called it, completely changed the rules of politics, which had hitherto been handled by social elites.[9] Electoral campaigns became edgier, involving polarizing language, attacks on opponents and passionate appeals to potential followers. Newspapers took sides and fanned the flames of ideological strife. Journalists joined the ranks of political activists and deployed media power to rally support behind certain candidates and pillory others.

These developments were aggravated in times of economic crisis, as the end of the 1920s pointedly demonstrated. Emotional politics rapidly accrued value, both in liberal democracies and totalitarian countries of both communist and fascist stripes. Fanaticism, once criticized as the ugly remnant of religious wars, metamorphosed into a widely applauded characteristic of citizens who knew how to distinguish between friend and foe and keep the enemy at bay.[10]

---

[9] Hans Rosenberg, *Große Depression und Bismarckzeit* (Frankfurt: Ullstein, 1976), 18; James Retallack, 'The Authoritarian State and the Political Mass Market', in *Imperial Germany Revisited*, ed. Sven Oliver Müller and Cornelius Torp (New York: Berghahn, 2011), 83–96; Ute Frevert and Kerstin Maria Pahl, 'Introducing Political Feelings: Participatory Politics, Institutions, and Emotional Templates', in Ute Frevert et al., *Feeling Political: Emotions and Institutions since 1789* (Cham: Palgrave Macmillan, 2022), 1–26, https://doi.org/10.1007/978-3-030-89858-8_1. See Chapter 12 in this volume.

[10] See Chapters 13 and 14 in this volume.

It is therefore no surprise that scholars such as Elias, Huizinga and Febvre found it difficult to make sense of what they were witnessing in their own societies and neighbouring countries. They needed help, and Febvre thought he might get it from his fellow historians by turning towards a history of sensibilities. At least this is what he asked them to do and what he himself embarked on during his first post-war lectures on '*honneur et patrie*' (honour and fatherland), concepts that both Vichy France and Charles de Gaulle's Free France had used as emotional catchphrases and mobilizing slogans after 1940.[11]

Mentalities, experience, emotionologies

Several scholars followed Febvre's lead, though in small numbers and without great impact. They included the historians of the Annales School, who focused on the history of mentalities and increasingly integrated senses, sentiments and sensibilities into their analyses.[12] On the other side of the Atlantic, cultural historian Peter Gay, in his five-volume analysis of the 'bourgeois experience from Victoria to Freud', likewise homed in on the 'education of the senses'.[13] Covering the long nineteenth century and drawing on a wide range of primary sources from Europe and North America, he scrutinized sexual desire, the tender passions of love, the cultivation of hatred, aesthetic tastes and people's energetic attempts to discover the secret life of the self. Indebted to a psychoanalytical framework, Gay put emotions (or, in Freudian language, drives) centre stage and explored their effect on people's *Lebensführung*, or life conduct. At the same time, he took them as given, as an anthropological essence of humanity, timeless and ubiquitous.

While Gay was more interested in the emotional experience of individuals than in normative prescriptions and regulations, Carol and Peter Stearns embarked on the project of unravelling 'emotionologies', 'the attitudes or standards that a society, or a definable group within a society, maintains toward basic emotions and their appropriate expression'.[14] With a firm footing in social and gender history, they articulated this approach in multiple volumes about American emotional standards as they evolved

---

[11]Febvre, Sensibility and History; Lucien Febvre, '*Honneur et patrie*': *Une enquête sur le sentiment d'honneur et l'attachement à la patrie* (Paris: Perrin, 1996).
[12]Alain Corbin, *Time, Desire and Horror: Towards a History of the Senses* (Cambridge: Polity Press, 1995); Jean-Louis Flandrin, *Families in Former Times: Kinship, Household and Sexuality* (Cambridge: Cambridge University Press, 1979); Hans Medick and David Warren Sabean, eds, *Interest and Emotion: Essays on the Study of Family and Kinship* (Cambridge: Cambridge University Press, 1984).
[13]Peter Gay, *The Bourgeois Experience: From Victoria to Freud* (New York: Oxford University Press, 1984–98).
[14]Peter N. Stearns and Carol Z. Stearns, 'Emotionology: Clarifying the History of Emotions and Emotional Standards', *American Historical Review* 90, no. 4 (1985): 813–36, here 813.

during the modern period, ranging from jealousy to fear and anger, from parents' anxiety about child-rearing to coolness as a distinct twentieth-century emotional style.

Both Gay's and the Stearns's studies remained individual enterprises that did not start broader disciplinary trends. At best, they were considered useful additions to social history, which flourished after the 1960s. Not even *Alltagsgeschichte*, the history of everyday life and ordinary people, paid attention to how emotions shaped the everyday and vice versa. Although emotions played a prominent role in the political activism and counterculture of the 1980s, they did not loom large in history departments. Neither social historians nor followers of post-structuralist theory and the linguistic turn were prepared to address them. To the former, they seemed to lack social force and institutional embeddedness. To the latter, they were beyond the scope of narrative plotting and linguistically difficult to pin down. It took the profoundly unsettling insights of post-colonial theorizing and the radical idea of cultural relativism to finally spur interest in the history of emotions. Reading anthropological studies which, rightly or wrongly, asserted that other cultures' emotional concepts and practices did not conform to those of the West, historians felt encouraged to study emotions in a decidedly non-essentialist way.

Meanwhile, the burgeoning field of neuroscience, assisted by newly available technologies of neuroimaging, was ushering in insights into emotions. Rather than confirming the European tradition of strictly distinguishing between rational thinking and apparently irrational feeling, lab experiments delineated the close connection and interaction between the two. After the long devaluation of emotions under the supremacy of reason, such findings served to ennoble emotions by investing them with cognitive meaning, and, conversely, to emphasize how reasoning was intimately tied to emotional experience.

Cultural influences

Grasping the more recent curiosity about the history of emotions necessitates, however, looking beyond developments in science and the humanities. Historiography does not just draw inspiration from scholarly disciplines. As with Febvre, it is also influenced by, and takes account of, experiences that are part and parcel of historians' own contemporary culture.

That culture has long been intensely enamoured with emotions. Starting with the therapeutic turn of the 1960s and the obsession with the self, emotions were placed front and centre, in self-help literature as well as in the numerous therapeutic cures for body and mind.[15] New social movements

---

[15] Eva Illouz, *Saving the Modern Soul: Therapy, Emotions and the Culture of Self-Help* (Berkeley: University of California Press, 2008).

discovered and valorized emotions, invoking them to mobilize people while also seeking to emancipate emotions from 'repressive' forces such as religion, social mores and capitalism. This fitted with the perception of emotions as basic, authentic and non-negotiable. It did not take long for consumer societies and advertising industries to capitalize on this as a unique selling point. Products sold better if they were candy-coated with positive emotions, and vendors did better if they tapped into clients' emotions.[16]

This was what 'emotional intelligence', or EI, meant. In 1990, two New England psychologists wrote a paper about how, in the late 1970s, they had measured people's ability to 'perceive emotion, integrate emotion to facilitate thought, understand emotions and to regulate emotions to promote personal growth'.[17] Hidden in scientific journals, their research saw a surge of interest once it was popularized in the form of didactic advice. In 1995, science journalist Daniel Goleman published his book on EI, which was soon translated into forty languages and sold millions of copies. His success prompted him to set up counselling agencies and training labs that became multi-billion-dollar enterprises. Emotional intelligence was no longer about 'personal growth' but about increased sales figures and leadership skills. It has since been incorporated into management techniques and is used by human resources staff all over the world.[18]

It is also utilized by commercial enterprises, especially advertising. An abundant feature of fast-growing consumer societies, advertising has been closely linked to psychological research since its very inception in the early twentieth century. Selling goods is synonymous with selling emotions: this is the mantra that governs the world of Don Draper and his more or less inventive successors. Some advertising campaigns, such as Benetton's, invade emotional landscapes in an unusual and surprising manner.[19] Others take a more direct approach by labelling goods themselves 'emotion' (as happens with cars, salads, cosmetics, cat food and so forth).

A more sophisticated and far-reaching current approach is to use affective computing. While digital media companies such as Netflix and Amazon access real-time consumer sentiment by closely monitoring people's individual choices and preferences, the MIT Media Lab and its spin-offs go a step further by training computers to recognize human emotions. These new technologies are not just about improving the 'human affective experience with technology', as MIT's website informs us. They also aim to

---

[16]See Chapter 7 in this volume.
[17]Peter Salovey and John D. Mayer, 'Emotional Intelligence', *Imagination, Cognition and Personality* 9, no. 3 (1990): 185–211.
[18]Illouz, *Saving*, ch. 6.
[19]Eilidh Nuala Duffy, 'Benetton's Most Controversial Campaigns', *British Vogue*, 8 December 2017, https://www.vogue.co.uk/gallery/benettons-best-advertising-campaigns (accessed 10 February 2023).

make computers emotionally intelligent, offering new inroads into people's feelings that can (and will) be used by commercial interests.

In addition to online businesses, there are many more institutions that appeal to or instrumentalize people's emotions. In political culture, emotions abound, with politicians grieving, embracing each other, giving enthusiastic speeches and eliciting feelings of pride or disdain. Television, YouTube and social media amplify this. Media, though, do not simply pass on messages between sender and receiver. Mediation is fraught with emotional content. Personal interest stories pervade newspapers, blogs and TV programmes. CNN anchorman Anderson Cooper was appointed the face of 'emo-journalism' when he impassionedly covered Hurricane Katrina in 2005, and he has stuck to this new designation ever since. Emo-journalism invokes and engages viewers' emotions, as well as confronting the audience with other people's feelings and tapping into their ability to empathize. If viewership ratings and sales figures mean anything, the public seems to like it.

'Private' emotions have thus been converted into emotions felt and communicated in public, expressed in a language that is collectively framed, recognizable and understood. Social media sites such as Facebook act as powerful intermediaries: individual users put their emotions on public display and invite 'friends' to witness and share them. Since 1982, emoticons and smileys added to individual emails and instant messages have made use of a simple emotional language that is highly formalized and widely applied.

Psychological approaches

What does this mean for those who study emotions and emotional politics in the humanities and social sciences? How do they approach what they observe in contemporary life, and how do they connect current issues and phenomena to long-term changes and developments?

Approaches differ across disciplines. Literary and media studies often employ a model of emotional behaviour borrowed from affect studies. Historians tend to privilege other conceptual tools and methodologies. So, what is it exactly that attracts some and repels others?

All approaches to emotion in the humanities and social sciences borrow heavily from psychology. Replacing philosophers as the long-term monopolists on thinking about and describing emotions, psychologists took the reins around 1900, but they never spoke with a single voice. Each attempt to conceptualize emotions met with harsh criticism. Even basic definitions were and are highly contested. In 2007, psychologist Carroll E. Izard confirmed that 'there is no consensus on a definition of the term *emotion*, and theorists and researchers use it in ways that imply different processes, meanings, and functions'.[20]

Among the diverse approaches within the fields of psychology and neuroscience, two major strands stand out. One places an emphasis on visceral processes through which emotions are generated and expressed, while the other focuses on emotions as cognitive phenomena. The first classifies emotions, and particularly basic emotions such as sadness, fear, joy, surprise, anger and disgust, as 'natural kinds' that are biologically inherent. The second points to the close interplay between emotions, appraisals and higher order cognition.

This controversy started back in the 1880s, when the James-Lange theory first found approval but was then panned for putting too much weight on physiological states, as exemplified by William James's famous quote: 'We feel sorry because we cry, angry because we strike, afraid because we tremble'.[21] During the 1960s, experimental psychologists Stanley Schachter and Jerome Singer supplemented the James-Lange theory with a cognitive component that added context and meaning to the bodily state of excitation. Cognition here exerted

> a steering function. Cognitions arising from the immediate situation as interpreted by past experience provide the framework within which one understands and labels his feelings. It is the cognition which determines whether the state of physiological arousal will be labeled as 'anger,' 'joy,' 'fear,' or whatever.[22]

Their colleague Silvan Tomkins, meanwhile, singled out an 'affect system' that motivated human beings to act in distinctive ways. By focusing on affect rather than on drives, Tomkins sought to distance himself from the then-fashionable Freudian school of psychoanalysis. He understood affects as

> sets of muscle and glandular responses located in the face and also widely distributed through the body, which generate sensory feedback which is inherently either 'acceptable' or 'unacceptable.' These organized sets of responses are triggered at subcortical centers where specific 'programs' for each distinct affect are stored. These programs are innately endowed and have been genetically inherited.[23]

---

[20]Carroll E. Izard, 'Basic Emotions, Natural Kinds, Emotion Schemas, and a New Paradigm', *Perspectives on Psychological Science* 2, no. 3 (2007): 260–80, here 260.
[21]William James, *The Principles of Psychology*, vol. 2 (New York: Cosimo, 2007), 450.
[22]Stanley Schachter and Jerome E. Singer, 'Cognitive, Social, and Physiological Determinants of Emotional State', *Psychological Review* 69, no. 5 (1962): 379–99, here 380.
[23]Silvan S. Tomkins, 'Affects: Primary Motives of Man', *Humanitas* 3, no. 3 (1968): 321–45, this and the following quote 325–6.

Thus, affects were not learned. And like drives, they did not depend on specified objects: 'There is literally no kind of object which has not been linked to one or another of the affects.' Their 'innate plasticity' permitted 'the investment of any type of affect in any type of activity or object, which makes possible the great varieties of human personalities and societies'.

Affect, in Tomkins's view, was characterized by its biological-genetic origin in human (and nonhuman) brains that stored programmes through which each affect could be triggered and acted out, mostly in the form of mimics and other bodily behaviours: 'When we become aware of these facial and/or visceral responses we are aware of our affects. We may respond with these affects, however, without becoming aware of the feedback from them'.[24] Awareness and consciousness were not seen as an integral part of the affect programme, which set it apart from the Schachter-Singer model. Instead, affect and cognition allegedly inhabited two separate spheres of the brain, with affect preceding cognition by the famous half-second.[25]

Tomkins counted eight innate affects: three he deemed 'positive' and five 'negative'. The positive ones were interest/excitement, enjoyment/joy and surprise/startle; the negative distress/anguish, fear/terror, shame/humiliation, contempt/disgust and anger/rage. Each affect was identified through its facial response. Paul Ekman borrowed the concept and tried to prove its universality, eventually coming up with six, and later seven, affects that he claimed were shared by all human beings regardless of age, gender or nationality. Different cultural backgrounds might play a role in singling out different objects that elicited certain affects, he asserted. But the affects themselves were basically invariable and firmly installed in every person's neural system.

Tomkins's theory did not garner much immediate attention during the 1960s. Yet it lived on in the work of his students Ekman, Izard and Virginia Demos, all of whom gained prominence in the decades to come. They did not necessarily adopt his language (both Ekman and Izard preferred the more established term 'emotion' over affect). But they all conceived of (basic) emotions as a natural 'set of neural, bodily/expressive, and feeling/motivational components generated rapidly, automatically, and nonconsciously'. The emotion 'preempts consciousness and tends to drive a rather narrowly focused stereotypical response strategy to achieve an adaptive advantage'.[26] Emotions were thus considered 'a feeling that motivates, organizes, and guides perception, thought, and action'.[27]

Some psychologists distinguish between 'feeling' and 'emotion' and use 'feeling' to describe a 'consciously detected change in feeling that has

---

[24]Ibid., 327.
[25]Ruth Leys, *The Ascent of Affect: Genealogy and Critique* (Chicago: University of Chicago Press, 2017), 324–49.
[26]Izard, 'Basic Emotions', 261–2.
[27]Carroll E. Izard, *The Psychology of Emotions* (New York: Plenum, 1991), 14.

sensory qualities', while reserving 'emotion' for 'a symbolic appraisal of the feeling, often semantic in form': namely, words that interpret or label the feeling.[28] Neuroscientists either borrow the distinction or turn it upside down. Antonio Damasio speaks of emotions when he addresses the physical patterns of bodily sensations, but he discusses the symbolic, linguistic dimension using the term 'feeling'.[29] Lisa Feldman Barrett, in contrast, consistently writes 'emotion' when presenting her 'theory of constructed emotion' and argues that emotions – generated in the brain – 'are in fact made and not triggered'.[30]

Affect theory

That contention is questioned by those who subscribe to what is now called affect theory, which has burgeoned in the humanities since around 2000. After a strong commitment to theories of cultural relativism and social constructionism during the 1980s, scholars in philosophy and literary studies turned to affect as a new – or rather, old – concept to make sense of human individualities and activities. This turn could not have been more radical, because affect theory contradicts everything that cultural relativism and social constructionism stand for. The latter share the assumption that facts and meanings are created and established through social interaction and convention, while affect theory presupposes a biological given. Affects, in this view, are not artefacts but natural facts that remain beyond the individual's control. They are not learned but inherited, innate and hardwired. They do something to the person, rather than being informed and shaped by the person themselves or by their environment. They do not follow the person's intentions and objectives but lead a dynamic life of their own.

Philosopher Brian Massumi describes affect as 'irreducibly bodily and autonomic', independent of consciousness and deliberate control. Inspired by French philosopher Gilles Deleuze, Massumi defines it as a 'prepersonal intensity corresponding to the passage from one experiential state of the body to another and implying an augmentation or diminution in that body's capacity to act'. Affect thus appears as an experience of unqualified intensity

---

[28]Jerome Kagan, *What Is Emotion? History, Measures, and Meanings* (New Haven: Yale University Press, 2007), 23.
[29]Antonio Damasio, *Looking for Spinoza: Joy, Sorrow, and the Feeling Brain* (Orlando: Harcourt, 2003).
[30]Lisa Feldman Barrett, *How Emotions Are Made: The Secret Life of the Brain* (New York: Houghton Mifflin Harcourt, 2017), xiii.

that precedes will and perception. It is unformed and unstructured, which sets it apart from both 'feelings' and 'emotions'.[31]

In a similar vein, the literary scholar Eve Kosofsky Sedgwick adopted the Tomkins-Ekman paradigm of basic emotions and introduced it to literary theory and criticism. She, too, found there was something to be gained from a distinctly non-cognitive notion of affect. What seemed particularly attractive was its emphasis on the body and its affective performance.[32] Post-structuralism's infatuation with language had largely left out the body, because it was considered pre-linguistic and pre-cultural. For feminists, reference to the body had been a long-standing taboo since it was equated with biology and women's supposed 'nature'. After two centuries of being tied to that nature and how it determined women's lives and options, feminists of the 1970s and 1980s felt liberated by theories that either ignored the body and its materiality altogether or reduced it to a socially constructed artefact.

Others, however, objected to what they criticized as a theoretical straitjacket and discovered the body as a site of resistance and autonomy. To conceive of affects as unintentional, uncontrollable and autonomous, and to see the body (and face) as the material through which affects made themselves known seemed a novel and productive approach. Affects were heralded as forces that might resist and transcend social structures; their intensity was seen to harbour the potential to cut through social conventions and agreements and prompt people to act in ways that were unpredictable, non-conformist and thus possibly revolutionary and life-changing. Affect, as Massumi suggested, 'holds a key to rethinking postmodern power after ideology' and is 'central to an understanding of our information- and image-based late capitalist culture, in which so-called master narratives are perceived to have foundered'.[33]

Cultural theorists also thought that affects relieved individuals from the constraints of acting in line with their roles as members of larger groups and institutions. If affects struck people independently of who they were and what their intentions and 'ideologies' – beliefs, convictions, interests – appeared to be, they created a singular experience that made everyone different. This, in a paradoxical way, reinstitutionalized a sense of individuality that had seemingly become lost in and because of theories that stressed social agreements, group identities and the social construction of reality. Reclaiming individuality through the power of affect could be

---

[31] Brian Massumi, 'Notes on the Translation', in *A Thousand Plateaus: Capitalism and Schizophrenia*, ed. Gilles Deleuze and Félix Guattari (New York: Continuum Massumi, 1987), xvi–xix, here xvii; Brian Massumi, *Parables for the Virtual: Movement, Affect, Sensation* (Durham, NC: Duke University Press, 2002), 23–45.
[32] Eve Kosofsky Sedgwick and Adam Frank, *Shame and Its Sisters: A Silvan Tomkins Reader* (Durham, NC: Duke University Press, 1995), 1–28.
[33] Massumi, *Parables*, 42, 27.

imagined as an act of resistance, creativity and radical autonomy – and as a political statement.

In many ways, this statement recalls the main propositions of *Lebensphilosophie* as it was developed by Friedrich Nietzsche, Henri Bergson and others around 1900. Both Deleuze and Massumi borrowed from that philosophy. Even if history does not repeat itself, it seems necessary to point out analogies and unexpected consequences. To applaud biologically determined 'affect systems' and 'affect programmes' and acknowledge them as a means to potentially change the course of history is to endorse a notion of political activism that privileges spontaneity over organization, individuality over community and undiluted affect over directive emotion.

For historians of knowledge, this theoretical move is part of an epistemological tendency to imbue emotions, affects and passions with an autonomous agency that 'overwhelms', 'grips', 'steers' and 'compels' people to do certain things or refrain from doing them.[34] To some extent, it is reminiscent of ancient beliefs about emotions as demons that take possession of a person and do harm. But demons usually knew what they were doing and why, while affects in the postmodern sense perform non-ideological, chaotic, anarchic work. The fact that both concepts are highly speculative and can hardly be sustained by empirical evidence speaks to the viewpoint that they are, in themselves, highly ideological and serve a (political) purpose, rather than describing the world as it is.

Historical assumptions and methodologies

Where does this leave historians of emotions? What sort of assumptions do they hold and how do they lend evidence to what they assume and contend? By profession, historians are – or should be – less prone to imagining the world is as they would like it to be. Their sources and methods oblige them to stay on the ground rather than venture into the heavens. At the same time, they do bring their own concepts and visions to their sources and make the latter speak to the former. The questions they ask and the methods through which they try to find answers are influenced by their own times and what they witness as inhabitants of the contemporary world. The stories that they tell about the past depend on how they see the present and what they envision for the future. Still, they do encounter what the historian Reinhart Koselleck famously called the 'veto of the sources': it is virtually impossible for them to subsume the source material under theoretical propositions that would violate and distort the voices of the past. Since each and every source has to be checked against others, it is essential to formulate readings that do justice to all of them.

---

[34]Leys, *Ascent of Affect*.

Overall, historians consider emotions to be human artefacts that are deeply embedded in culture and thus open to historical change. Even if they are hardwired in the brain and coordinated with physiological processes in the body, they are first and foremost shaped by culture. Culture starts with an agreement about language: emotions are not only symbolically represented in and through language, language also gives them social and personal meaning, credence and weight. Language – which does not stop at words but includes gestures, mimicry, sounds and bodily postures – also allows emotions to be communicated to and shared by others.

Without language, emotions would be unknown to the person who experiences them. Even if someone initially cannot make sense of what they feel, they usually try to name their feeling in order to act with and upon it. Through language, they can distinguish the shades and intensities and even directions of feeling. Wrath feels different to rage or scorn or indignation; love feels different to affection or reverence. Hatred can burn and boil, but it can also simmer or lie dormant. Each culture has, over many centuries and generations, established repertoires of emotion in more or less nuanced and differentiated forms, and each culture has invested those emotions with meaning and moral judgement. Those meanings and judgements are by no means static but undergo changes through time, space and social attribution.

Such observations and assumptions can hardly be reconciled with affect theory, which presupposes that 'affect systems' and 'programmes' work unconsciously, individually and without orientation. At the same time, cultural framing does leave room for individual agency, experience and spontaneity. Change often occurs when people no longer accept conventional ways of living with emotions and start articulating new 'emotional styles' or 'regimes'.[35] William Reddy thus aimed to detect the emotional 'escapes' sought out by French citizens who had lived through the 1789 Revolution and the following turmoil, while Joachim Häberlen and others found new emotional intensities, experiments, knowledge and productivity among the '68ers and the next generation. The countercultural 'desire for emotions' unleashed new codes and practices of intimacy and authenticity that gradually seeped through other social strata and institutions and left an imprint on society and culture at large.[36]

Here, as everywhere, there was close intertwining between people feeling and 'doing' emotions, new or old, and knowledge systems, which provided them with clues as to how to interpret and act out their desires and longings. Contemporary psychotherapy began to play a powerful role in producing

---

[35] Benno Gammerl, 'Emotional Styles: Concepts and Challenges', *Rethinking History* 16, no. 2 (2012): 161–75; William M. Reddy, *The Navigation of Feeling: A Framework for the History of Emotions* (Cambridge: Cambridge University Press, 2001).
[36] Joachim Häberlen, *The Emotional Politics of the Alternative Left: West Germany, 1968–1984* (Cambridge: Cambridge University Press, 2018), 271.

and disseminating such knowledge in the 1960s.[37] Discovering emotions as authentic, interior, subjective, undiluted, untainted and resistant to societal pressures served the goal of honouring them as true markers of individuality and anti-capitalist spirit. Affect theory was already around before they had a name for it.

Emotion knowledge

For historians of emotions, this is a classic case to study in order to uncover links between social practices, knowledge systems and belief structures. Yet their work is not confined to contemporary history. From the very start, it included attempts to reconstruct a genealogy of emotion terms and concepts and how these were used, as well as for which purposes.[38] Somewhat surprisingly, earlier vocabularies of feeling proved to be far more varied than those of today.

Philosophical lexicons that began to be published in the 1730s defined affects as motions and movements within the body and soul, whereas passions were seen as strong desires or appetites that weighed on a person and made them suffer. For Immanuel Kant, who greatly influenced German- and French-speaking philosophers and psychologists up until the early twentieth century, affects were short-lived sensory perceptions that tended to overwhelm the person and disable rational will. As a 'surprise through sensation', they derailed the 'mind's composure'. As 'drunkenness', they left no room for reflection and immobilized 'dominion over oneself'. However, this was all limited to a 'momentary', 'stormy and transitory' phase. By contrast, passions were thought to be akin to a long-term and persistent addiction, or, to use a favourite metaphor, 'like a river that digs itself deeper and deeper into its bed'. Passion 'takes its time and reflects' and is 'always connected' with a person's 'reason'. For Kant, this made it 'without exception *evil*' because the impassioned person did not allow genuine reason to prevail but instead became a slave to her or his appetites.[39]

When such definitions entered encyclopaedias, they were made known to a broader public. Encyclopaedias as they appeared in the eighteenth century and became popular in the nineteenth offered knowledge and information to non-experts. They reached an ever-growing readership that was educated and wished to be educated further. They accumulated and structured knowledge

---

[37]Illouz, *Saving*.
[38]Thomas Dixon, *From Passions to Emotions: The Creation of a Secular Psychological Category* (Cambridge: Cambridge University Press, 2003); Ute Frevert et al., *Emotional Lexicons: Continuity and Change in the Vocabulary of Feeling 1700–2000* (Oxford: Oxford University Press, 2014).
[39]Immanuel Kant, *Anthropology from a Pragmatic Point of View*, ed. Robert Louden (Cambridge: Cambridge University Press, [Germ. Orig. 1798], 2006), 150, 165–7.

from various disciplines that would otherwise be restricted to scholars of that discipline only. But they also had an important standardizing function: presenting definitions, distinguishing the essential from the nonessential and making judgements. In this way, they were a significant educational medium and rendered normative prescriptions for public use.

It therefore mattered what kind of information and judgement these sources of knowledge conveyed. The shift in the relevant vocabulary from affect and passion to emotion – which had been considered of French origin and translated, very generally and negatively, as a 'disturbance of the mind' – reflected a change in disciplinary power as much as in sense-making. Knowing what emotions were supposed to be, how they worked and how they were valued influenced the way people felt and thought about their feelings. Expert opinions provide great sources for intellectual history. Social and cultural historians, though, need media that reach out to broader sections of society and have an impact on how they interpret and practise emotions.[40]

Lexicons and encyclopaedias are by no means the only sources to tap into national, language-based repertoires of emotion knowledge. Ego-documents offer more personalized insights into how people understood and expressed their affects, passions, desires, longings, appetites and emotions, and they might even reflect different, conflicting usages and their respective pros and cons. Legal texts and court cases provide evidence of how emotion arguments could either ameliorate or aggravate judicial sentencing and how, when and why this changed over the course of time.[41] In some cases, it is possible to trace the impact of certain concepts; for instance, that of Gustave Le Bon's 1895 psychology of the crowd on emotional politics under Italian fascism and German National Socialism.[42]

Emotional concepts and social context

Another approach to analysing the history of emotions has been to unearth the contextual history of particular emotions such as anger, fear, shame, honour and empathy.[43] Context here refers to time, space and social interaction. Different from phenomenologists, historians are interested in the culturally and historically specific work emotions do and how they do it in certain institutional, situational and spatial settings. They inquire

---

[40]Plamper, *History of Emotions*, 173–8.
[41]Laura Kounine, ed., 'Special Section: Law and Emotions', *Journal of Social History* 52, no. 2 (2017): 219–312.
[42]See Chapter 13 in this volume.
[43]Katie Barclay and Peter N. Stearns, eds, *The Routledge History of Emotions in the Modern World* (London: Routledge, 2023), part I; Ute Frevert, *The Power of Emotions: A History of Germany from 1900 to the Present* (Cambridge: Cambridge University Press, 2023).

into when, why and how societies or social groups engaged in publicly humiliating people, and if and under which circumstances those practices induced feelings of shame.[44] They trace the history of empathy during the modern period, delineating its limits while probing its development into a culture of humanitarian intervention closely connected to demands for human rights.[45] They investigate the causes, experiences and explanations of fear as it was felt in eighteenth-century Peru and California as well as in contemporary Russian and Indian cities, in the English-speaking world during the long twentieth century, or in Germany after 1945.[46] Other historians focus on anger and how it was used and performed in medieval societies and beyond.[47] Honour and the rituals of aggressive self-assertion in various societies and time periods have been analysed,[48] and so too have emotions such as love and jealousy, envy and homesickness, religious enthusiasm as well as changing feelings about technology or illnesses like cancer.[49]

---

[44]Ute Frevert, *The Politics of Humiliation: A Modern History* (Oxford: Oxford University Press, 2020).

[45]Susan Lanzoni, *Empathy: A History* (New Haven: Yale University Press, 2018); Aleida Assmann and Ines Detmers, eds, *Empathy and Its Limits* (Basingstoke: Palgrave Macmillan, 2016); Lynn Hunt, *Inventing Human Rights: A History* (New York: Norton & Co., 2007).

[46]Joanna Bourke, *Fear: A Cultural History* (Emeryville: Shoemaker & Hoard, 2006); Michael Laffan and Max Weiss, eds, *Facing Fear: The History of an Emotion in Global Perspective* (Princeton: Princeton University Press, 2012); Peter N. Stearns, *American Fear: The Causes and Consequences of High Anxiety* (New York: Routledge, 2006); Frank Biess, *German Angst: Fear and Democracy in the Federal Republic of Germany* (Oxford: Oxford University Press, 2020).

[47]Barbara H. Rosenwein, *Emotional Communities in the Early Middle Ages* (Ithaca, NY: Cornell University Press, 2006); Barbara H. Rosenwein, *Anger: The Conflicted History of an Emotion* (New Haven: Yale University Press, 2020).

[48]Ute Frevert, *Emotions in History – Lost and Found* (Budapest: Central European University Press, 2011); Robert A. Nye, *Masculinity and Male Codes of Honor in Modern France* (New York: Oxford University Press, 1993); William M. Reddy, *The Invisible Code: Honor and Sentiment in Postrevolutionary France, 1815–1848* (Berkeley: University of California Press, 1997).

[49]William M. Reddy, *The Making of Romantic Love: Longing and Sexuality in Europe, South Asia and Japan, 900-1200 CE* (Chicago: University of Chicago Press, 2012); Barbara H. Rosenwein, *Love: A History in Five Fantasies* (Cambridge: Polity Press, 2021); Sally Holloway, *The Game of Love in Georgian England: Courtship, Emotions, and Material Culture* (Oxford: Oxford University Press, 2019); Mark Seymour, *Emotional Arenas: Life, Love, and Death in 1870s Italy* (Oxford: Oxford University Press, 2020); Niamh Cullen, *Love, Honour, and Jealousy: An Intimate History of the Italian Economic Miracle* (Oxford: Oxford University Press, 2019); Susan J. Matt, *Keeping up with the Joneses: Envy in American Consumer Society, 1890–1930* (Philadelphia: University of Pennsylvania Press, 2003); Susan J. Matt, *Homesickness: An American History* (New York: Oxford University Press, 2011); Monique Scheer, *Enthusiasm: Emotional Practices of Conviction in Modern Germany* (Oxford: Oxford University Press, 2020); Luke Fernandez and Susan J. Matt, *Bored, Lonely, Angry, Stupid: Changing Feelings about Technology, from the Telegraph to Twitter* (Cambridge, MA: Harvard University Press, 2019); Bettina Hitzer, *The History of Cancer and Emotions in Twentieth-Century Germany* (Oxford: Oxford University Press, 2022).

The list could go on and on, thanks to the veritable explosion of research in the history of emotions over the last two decades. Some of it has come from literary studies that analyse literary texts while situating them in the environment in which they were produced. As early as the 1970s, scholars were exploring what they called the 'age of sensibility' in the second half of the eighteenth century, a period that saw an upsurge of novels which elicited strong empathetic emotions in their readers.[50] Romanticism and the love of nature have likewise received a great deal of attention in this field, as have the cultural concepts of distance and distancing that emerged after the First World War.[51] Historians of science have conducted important studies that shed light on how different disciplines gathered and structured information on emotions and thus contributed to producing emotion knowledge that was then implemented by various social, economic and political actors.[52]

For historians, it remains a major challenge not only to trace how emotion knowledge was formed in certain disciplines but also to investigate how it entered social, economic and political practice. Conversely, they explore how that practice influenced the manner in which the sciences approached and conceptualized what emotions do. By way of distinguishing between various emotional styles favoured or shunned by democratic, semi-democratic or undemocratic societies, they study the techniques through which governments, parties, social movements, media, companies, entrepreneurs or humanitarian organizations try to elicit, manipulate and instrumentalize certain emotions for certain ends. They find out who distributed emotional messages and how these messages circulated and were received by individuals and groups. They investigate the role of institutions in creating emotional scripts and incentivizing their members to follow those scripts. In this regard, the history of emotions clarifies how emotions enter into and influence power structures and how they are themselves moulded by those structures. In short, what emotions do in and to history is not at all enigmatic. Historians can analyse it in the same way they unearth the social role of ideas, ideologies and concepts, drawing on similar sources and methodologies while doing so.

---

[50]G.J. Barker-Benfield, *The Culture of Sensibility: Sex and Society in Eighteenth-Century Britain* (Chicago: University of Chicago Press, 1992); John Mullan, *Sentiment and Sociability: The Language of Feeling in the Eighteenth Century* (Oxford: Clarendon Press, 1988).
[51]Iain McCalman, ed., *An Oxford Companion to the Romantic Age* (Oxford: Oxford University Press, 2009); Helmut Lethen, *Cool Conduct: The Culture of Distance in Weimar Germany* (Berkeley: University of California Press, 2002).
[52]Frank Biess and Daniel M. Gross, eds, *Science and Emotions after 1945: A Transatlantic Perspective* (Chicago: University of Chicago Press, 2014); Otniel E. Dror et al., eds, 'History of Science and the Emotions', *Osiris* 31 (2016): 1–257; Lanzoni, *Empathy*; Jan Plamper and Benjamin Lazier, eds, *Fear across the Disciplines* (Pittsburgh: University of Pittsburgh Press, 2012).

It is equally important to observe how emotions were formed in a person's head, heart and body. To be sure, historians cannot use fMRIs, hand out questionnaires or engage in participant observation, as their test subjects are no longer alive. They do have access, however, to what people thought and did, as long as those people left traces. Ego-documents usually convey detailed information about the process of emotions' formation, both intellectually and viscerally. Take the letter of a 32-year-old man who in 1758 wrote to his close friend in the midst of the Seven Years War that was ravaging central Europe. The men were living in different places, one in Berlin, the other in a city a short distance away that was occupied by French troops. The Berliner's 'whole heart' was bleeding, he wrote, and he 'trembled' out of fear for his friend. Yet he had not wept until this very moment, when 'a tear falls down on my hand'. The effect as he described it was twofold: his heart lightened, and his compassion and fear – which he had already expressed through words – were validated and strengthened by the tear that had evidently been caused by the intensity of writing about his feelings.[53]

This source is one of many that allow historians to analyse how emotions worked and what work they were doing. Emotional politics were not invented in the present but have been around for a long time. They have also never been restricted to democracies; pre– and undemocratic regimes have made use of them as well, though in different forms and with different techniques. At the same time, emotional politics not only emanate from governments or abstract institutions like religion, law, schools or the economy.[54] They were and are generated by ordinary people in their daily lives. Even if they do not know it, men and women follow emotional rules and templates.[55] The aforementioned Berliner knew only too well that it was not enough to put his feelings into words; actions had to follow, tears were necessary to prove and corroborate what he had verbally expressed. This was not undirected, unintentional, autonomous affect, but a culturally defined emotional programme that had been internalized by the letter-writer.

Such programmes, different in every facet from Tomkins's innate and genetically inherited 'affect programs', depended on societal scripts. Clearly, those scripts were never homogenous or free of doubt. A tear in 1758 could have had multiple meanings, and might even have been a false tear. Only contextual knowledge helps to clarify what it was actually about. A century later, however, the tear would not have fallen at all, at least not from male

---

[53]Ute Frevert, *Gefühlspolitik: Friedrich II. als Herr über die Herzen?* (Göttingen: Wallstein, 2012), 53. See also Marco Menin, *Thinking about Tears: Crying and Weeping in Long-Eighteenth-Century France* (Oxford: Oxford University Press, 2022).
[54]Anne Schmidt and Christoph Conrad, eds, *Bodies and Affects in Market Societies* (Tübingen: Mohr Siebeck, 2016).
[55]As to the concept of emotional templating, see Frevert and Pahl, 'Introducing Political Feelings'.

writers. They would, in the meantime, have learned that men were not supposed to weep or cry but to withhold bodily signs of emotions. Such expressions allegedly belonged only to women, children and uneducated people at home and in the European colonies. In contrast, a white, middle-class European man knew what kind of emotions he was supposed to act out and which ones he was expected to hide, suppress, keep to himself. Suppressing emotions, though, could become a habit that ultimately caused those emotions to disappear altogether. As experts on theatre, as well as philosophers and psychologists, had observed since the late eighteenth century, the expression of feelings affected how something was felt, or not.[56] There is a strong connection between, to take up Damasio's or Jerome Kagan's vocabulary, 'feelings' and 'emotions'; the symbolic closely influences the somatic. Feelings that are not symbolically represented would have trouble influencing how people act and behave.

Future prospects

The history of emotions has had a remarkable ascent over the last two or three decades, with centres, book series and journals fostering research and publishing findings. Well received by the larger public, it speaks to the significance of emotions in contemporary culture, be it politically, economically or socially defined. The history of emotions sets out to explain why this is by offering insights into how societies of the past treated emotions (or what were then called affects, passions, drives, appetites and the like). Affect theory, as it has been developed by modern psychology and embraced by literary and media studies, does not seem helpful in this regard. It works with assumptions borrowed from evolutionary biology and reduces culture and learning to marginalia. From a historical point of view, it is more rewarding to study the vocabulary of emotions bound to time and space. Such vocabulary influenced and was influenced by emotional practices that should be analysed for their own sake and in their own grammar, rather than being put under the rather narrow umbrella of late twentieth-century theories that are contested in their own domain.

While encountering widespread enthusiasm among younger scholars, the history of emotions has met with scepticism and resistance from more senior colleagues. The criticism has mostly been directed at three assumptions: one, that emotions motivate how people act – here, critics have judged interests to be more powerful than emotions; two, that emotions are human artefacts

---

[56]Gotthold Ephraim Lessing, *Hamburg Dramaturgy* (New York: Dover Publications, [1767–9] 1962), 13; Charles Darwin, *The Expression of the Emotions in Man and Animals*, 3rd edn (Oxford: Oxford University Press, [1872] 1998); Wilhelm Wundt, 'Ueber den Ausdruck der Gemüthsbewegungen', *Deutsche Rundschau* 11 (1877): 120–33.

that change over time and space – critics have doubted both the substance of the claim and that any evidence could be found to support it; three, that emotions can go beyond individual feelings and acquire a social form and force – critics have deemed this overly speculative. In addition, historians of emotions have been reprimanded for not adding anything new to history in general ('old wine in new bottles') and for lacking a common theoretical foundation.

It is true that grand theory and master narratives do not feature high up on the priorities list of historians who have warmed to the approach. They often employ a patchwork of epistemological concepts such as 'emotives' and 'emotional regimes', 'emotional labour' and 'feeling rules', 'emotional communities', 'affective economies', 'historical economy of emotions', 'emotional styles' and 'emotional practices'.[57] They nevertheless work with shared notions of how emotions function, both in individuals and collectives, and they insist that the concept of interests or – as proposed by behavioural economists – preferences fails to capture the emotional fervour and motivation of why people act the way they did and do.

Putting grand theory and hegemonic narratives aside, historians of emotions have come up with an impressive number of articles, books and overviews that have sketched the field and established its approaches. These texts speak to their intellectual ambitions as well as to the state of methodological reflection and interdisciplinary cooperation.[58] They also offer suggestions and trajectories for future research. Connecting the history of emotions to the history of senses could be one of them; interestingly, 'feeling' was, up to the mid-nineteenth century, exclusively defined as the sense of touch. In this regard, the body and its profound historical transformations should draw ample attention within emotion research. If the human body happens to be the main site of emotions, physical regimes are likely to affect how emotions are felt and enacted. Medical interventions inform those regimes as much as new work habits, sports and structures of mobility do.

---

[57]Reddy, *Navigation*; Arlie Russell Hochschild, *The Managed Heart: Commercialization of Human Feeling*, 20th anniversary edn (Berkeley: University of California Press, 2003); Rosenwein, *Emotional Communities*; Sara Ahmed, 'Affective Economies', *Social Text* 22, no. 2 (2004): 117–39; Frevert, *Emotions in History*; Gammerl, Emotional Styles; Monique Scheer, 'Are Emotions a Kind of Practice (And Is That What Makes Them Have a History)? A Bourdieuian Approach to Understanding Emotion', *History and Theory* 51, no. 2 (2012): 193–220.

[58]Rob Boddice, *The History of Emotions* (Manchester: Manchester University Press, 2018); Matt and Stearns, *Doing Emotions History*; Piroska Nagy and Ute Frevert, 'History of Emotions', in *Debating New Approaches to History*, ed. Marek Tamm and Peter Burke (London: Bloomsbury, 2018), 189–215; Plamper, *History of Emotions*; Barbara H. Rosenwein and Riccardo Cristiani, *What Is the History of Emotions?* (Medford: Polity Press, 2018).

Another question that deserves more attention is what figured as the 'other' of emotions in past societies: was it the absence of feeling,[59] or reason and rationality in Carlyle's or Weber's sense? What does the 'other' of emotion unveil about how emotions were imagined, conceptualized and assessed? Could it be that defending reason or rationality was a particular type of emotional style rather than its counterpart?

More research should be done on how emotions were embodied and embedded in material culture.[60] Studying systematically and historically the impact of institutions (such as families, schools, the military and the state) on how emotions were templated, learned and appropriated appears highly promising and would situate emotions more firmly in the centre of historiography.[61] How emotions served to draw lines between gender, race or age groups in different time periods and regions certainly needs more exploration. Up to now, most research has dealt with European, North American and South Asian countries, with other parts of Asia, Australia, South America and Africa largely left out.[62] Apart from studying each region separately and in its own right, emotional encounters across regional and national borders deserve greater scrutiny.[63] How were emotions communicated across cultures? How were they read and translated, on both sides? What conclusions have been drawn by those who participated in such encounters, on what terms and to what ends? A global history of emotions – which is still far from being implemented – should pay special regard to cross-cultural and cross-regional processes of translation and what came out of them.

As an overall guideline to future research, historians of emotions are well advised, first, to diligently analyse sources that speak about people's feelings either with words, pictures or sounds. They should then position those sources within a wider array of historical references. They should pay attention to the force and function that was attributed to feelings in

---

[59] Rob Boddice, *A History of Feelings* (London: Reaktion Books, 2019), 131–63; Kerstin Maria Pahl, 'De l'insensibilité à l'anesthésie: indifference, indolence, de "défaut de sentiment" au XVIIIe siècle', *Sensibilités. Histoire Critique & Sciences Sociales* 11, no. 1 (2022): 12–25; Xine Yao, *Disaffected: The Cultural Politics of Unfeeling in Nineteenth-Century America* (Durham, NC: Duke University Press, 2021).

[60] Stephanie Downes, Sally Holloway and Sarah Randles, eds, *Feeling Things: Objects and Emotions through History* (Oxford: Oxford University Press, 2018); *Feelings Materialized: Emotions, Bodies, and Things in Germany, 1500–1950*, ed. Derek Hillard, Heikki Lempa and Russell Spinney (New York: Berghahn, 2020), 202–21.

[61] As to the impact of political institutions and how they templated emotions, see Frevert et al., *Feeling Political*.

[62] Margrit Pernau, *Emotions and Modernity in Colonial India: From Balance to Fervor* (New Delhi: Oxford University Press, 2019); Margrit Pernau et al., *Civilizing Emotions: Concepts in Nineteenth Century Asia and Europe* (Oxford: Oxford University Press, 2015); Barclay and Stearns, eds, *Routledge History of Emotions*, part II.

[63] Benno Gammerl, Philipp Nielsen and Margrit Pernau, *Encounters with Emotions: Negotiating Cultural Differences since Early Modernity* (Oxford: Oxford University Press, 2019).

general and in particular; they should be sensitive to how these feelings were judged and commented on. Moving beyond the individual person, they should be open to researching social groups, collectives and institutions and how they utilized and enacted emotions.[64] They can thus provide a complex account of how emotions make history on multiple levels.

What is more difficult to investigate are the changes that emotions go through. How does shame as it was experienced in early modern Europe differ from the shame felt in late modern societies? Did honour feel the same regardless of who felt it: an aristocratic officer in the eighteenth century, a merchant or businessman in the nineteenth, a Viennese lady in 1860 or a Parisian service maid in 1920? How does it relate to the feeling cultivated by male adolescents or immigrant communities of the present? Is the fear that people felt during the cholera epidemic of the late nineteenth century similar to the one that contemporaries experienced during the COVID-19 pandemic of the 2020s? Was the anger expressed by striking workers in the 1920s different from the anger displayed a century later in industrial relations? These are big questions. To find answers, historians have to both meticulously reconstruct and contextualize emotional practices of the past and compare them over time. Historicizing emotions is, ultimately, more demanding and challenging than gauging their impact on people's actions at certain historical events and within historical developments. Everybody knows from experience how much their decisions depend on emotional reckoning. They would be surprised to learn, however, that their emotions differ from how and what former generations felt. Historians should teach them.

---

[64] On a recent attempt to engage with collective emotions, see *Histoire des émotions collectives: Épistémologie, émergences, expériences*, ed. Damien Boquet, Piroska Nagy and Lidia Zanetti Domingues (Paris: Classiques Garnier, 2022).

PART ONE
Emotional Concepts and Practices

CHAPTER TWO

Trust Talk and Trust Work

Much of what goes wrong in the world is currently attributed to a lack of trust, in the economy as much as in politics or in personal relationships. Apparently trust, even more than money, makes the world go round. A lack of trust, meanwhile, creates problems and makes them difficult to solve.

Accordingly, trust talk is ubiquitous. A Google search returns millions of results for *confidence, confiance, confidencia, Vertrauen*. Bankers, business people and politicians constantly demand trust or claim that their services can be trusted. Trust figures as a major factor both in a person's psychological well-being and in the smooth functioning of economic transactions and political communications. The economist and Nobel Prize winner Kenneth Arrow called it a central 'lubricant of a social system'.[1] Any social system, we may ask? From a historical viewpoint, the obsession with trust is neither a recent phenomenon, nor one that pertains to all societies. Rather, it stands out as a central feature of modernity and liberal democracy.

What is trust, and who needs it?

There are multiple definitions of trust, and they vary according to discipline.[2] The philosopher Annette Baier conceives of trust as an emotional attitude that entrusts something of great value to another person's (or institution's) safekeeping. The level of trust rises with the worth of what is entrusted, and the risk of losing it. For Baier it is the moral dimension – the expectation of

---

This chapter includes material published in *The Moral Economy of Trust: Modern Trajectories* (London: German Historical Institute, 2014) and 'Trust as Work', in *Work in a Modern Society: The German Historical Experience in Comparative Perspective*, ed. Jürgen Kocka (New York: Berghahn, 2010), 93–108.
[1] Kenneth J. Arrow, *The Limits of Organization* (New York: Norton & Co., 1974), 23.
[2] Geoffrey Hosking, *Trust: A History* (Oxford: Oxford University Press, 2014), discusses various definitions in ch. 2 (22–49).

goodwill on the part of the trusted – that distinguishes conscious trust from simple reliance or dependence.[3]

A similar distinction is suggested by sociologist Niklas Luhmann, who connects trust to intentional risk-taking and attributes confidence to those who do not consider alternatives. Confidence, in this view, is the positive expectation of future events that cannot be directly influenced by one's own behaviour (like weather, traffic or the Dow Jones). Trust, conversely, presupposes the presence and awareness of risk. It depends on the perception that a person's decisions can have unexpected and unpleasant consequences. Trust allows the person to make decisions anyway, hoping that ill consequences will not ensue. The degree of unpleasantness directly relates to the amount of trust that has to be invested in the transaction.[4]

Luhmann was not the first sociologist to take an interest in the phenomenon of trust and confidence. As early as 1908, Georg Simmel wrote about trust as a psychological mechanism that bridges the gap between knowing and not-knowing. According to Simmel, somebody who knew everything did not need trust; he who was unaware and could not control the consequences of his actions, however, had no choice but to trust. Trust was thus thoroughly linked to the future and closely associated with conditions of uncertainty and risk. Consequently, trust seemed less crucial in 'primitive' societies in which everybody knew one another than in modern, highly differentiated systems whose members see each other as strangers. Sharing this view, Luhmann, who conceptualized trust as a mechanism to reduce complexity, framed it as a functional necessity in modern societies and basically irrelevant in earlier types.[5]

Other social scientists have a different perspective. They agree that modern societies are more complex and interactive than pre-modern ones (people are required to cooperate with more people on more issues). But since modern citizens rely on an ever denser network of social, legal and economic institutions, they can easily do without trust. In contrast, trust is in far greater demand in societies that lack such institutions.[6]

---

[3]Annette C. Baier, *Moral Prejudices: Essays on Ethics* (Cambridge, MA: Harvard University Press, 1994), 98 ff., 132.
[4]Niklas Luhmann, 'Familiarity, Confidence, Trust: Problems and Alternatives', in *Trust: Making and Breaking Cooperative Relations*, ed. Diego Gambetta (Oxford: Basil Blackwell, 1988), 94–107, here 97 ff.
[5]Georg Simmel, *Sociology: Inquiries into the Construction of Social Forms*, trans. and ed. Anthony J. Blasi, Anton K. Jacobs and Mathew Kanjirathinkal, vol. 1 (Leiden: Brill, 2009), 307 ff.; Niklas Luhmann, *Trust and Power* (Chichester: Wiley, 1979). For a discussion of sociological approaches to trust, see Barbara A. Misztal, *Trust in Modern Societies: The Search for the Bases of Social Order* (Cambridge: Polity Press, 1996).
[6]See, above all, Karen S. Cook, ed., *Trust in Society* (New York: Russell Sage Foundation, 2001); Russell Hardin, *Trust and Trustworthiness* (New York: Russell Sage Foundation, 2002).

What do historians say about this? How do they conceptualize and historicize trust? What is their take on functionalist explanations? And what do they think about universalist claims like the one made by psychoanalyst Erik Erikson in 1950? Erikson, like many of his colleagues, defined trust as a general human behavioural trait. Small children, he observed, develop basic trust through interactions with their mother (or primary caregivers).[7] Yet further questions must be asked, such as: do all children develop basic trust? If trust is a feeling acquired through learning and dependent on experiencing reliable care and affection, can we then assume that this feeling is available to each and everyone, regardless of social circumstances and cultural background? Are Erikson's findings globally and historically valid? Is trust always and everywhere generated through the mother–child interaction? What would people living in ancient, medieval or early modern societies think?

Pre-modern settings

First, they would probably frown upon the suggestion that the mother–child dyad forms the foundation of trust behaviours. Most babies and many mothers of these times did not have the chance to experience an intense dyadic relationship due to high rates of infant and maternal mortality. For newborns who survived the first months of their lives, mothers were by no means the only or the most engaged caregivers; the idea of motherly devotion to the child's needs and desires had yet to be invented. The constant availability and reliability of mothers as would-be prerequisites of trust were notions that only entered the human heart and mind in later centuries.

Second, people of earlier times would contest that their societies were as homogeneous, face-to-face and self-contained as contemporary sociologists would have us believe. Besides experiencing structural asymmetries and hierarchies that influenced flows of information and communication, they were familiar with the figure of the stranger: someone who knocks on the door at night asking to be let in. His visit might prove fortunate or unfortunate; no one knew in advance. Fairy tales and proverbs are full of the ambiguity and anxiety those encounters provoked, and so too are religious texts. Tribal, ancient and medieval societies developed rituals of varying sophistication for dealing with strangers: welcoming them or not, excluding or including them, giving and building trust or withholding it.

Third, uncertainty has haunted humans across time and space. Threats to one's well-being were ubiquitous in the past, and people tried different strategies to avoid or cope with them, whether dangers posed by the

---

[7] Erik Erikson, *Childhood and Society*, 2nd rev. edn (New York: Norton & Co., [1950] 1963), 247–51.

environment (like food shortages, epidemics or natural disasters), or risks (defined as self-inflicted uncertainties). Risky behaviour was the domain of kings like the Macedonian Alexander the Great, who led his armies as far as India in the fourth century BCE; it accompanied Marco Polo on his voyage to China in the thirteenth century, and the Fuggers' far-flung trading, which began in the fifteenth century. All these endeavours required trust – in God and in people whose behaviour could never be entirely predicted.

Seeking advice on how to deal with such risks and dangers, many people relied on household texts such as the Holy Bible or the Talmud. Others reached out to magicians and wise women who purported to tell the future. Some consulted highbrow literature by philosophers and poets. Noblemen could turn to educational treatises such as the 'mirrors for princes' that became popular manuals for governance in the late Middle Ages. Merchants drew up notebooks recording the vicissitudes of trading operations and shared best practices and strategies. Such sources form the backbone of what historians can glean about the definitions, functions and conditions of trust in pre-modern times. There is also pictorial evidence, such as the Flemish tapestry given to Charles V for his wedding in 1526. Here, *fiducia* was shown as a virtue subservient to *justitia*. The moral message was obvious: the emperor should practise and gain trust in order to appear and be a just ruler. Trust belonged to the lexicon of love and friendship and was closely tied to *veritas*, or truthfulness. Only those who were sincere and despised cheating and treachery were deemed trustworthy.[8]

But the culture of the court did not exactly lend itself to *veritas* and *fiducia*. In his 1513 treatise *Il Principe*, Niccolò Machiavelli openly declared that appearances were all that mattered. Princes had to be as cunning as foxes in order to rule successfully, but they must simultaneously seem pious, loyal, benevolent and honest.[9] In his German translation of the Bible, Martin Luther warned against trusting others and, above all, against trusting those in power. The only exception was God.[10] A century later, the Spanish Jesuit Baltasar Gracián advised worldly wise men to trust today's friends as if they were tomorrow's enemies.[11]

---

[8]Guy Delmarcel, *Los Honores: Flemish Tapestries for the Emperor Charles V* (Antwerp: Pandora, 2000); Petra Schulte, 'Die Ethik politischer Kommunikation im franko-burgundischen Spätmittelalter', in *Zwischen Pragmatik und Performanz: Dimensionen mittelalterlicher Schriftkultur*, ed. Christoph Dartmann, Thomas Scharff and Christoph Friedrich Weber (Turnhout: Brepols, 2011), 461–89.
[9]Niccolò Machiavelli, *The Prince*, trans. and ed. Peter Bondanella (Oxford: Oxford University Press, 2005), 60–2; Michael Stolleis, 'Löwe und Fuchs: Eine politische Maxime im Frühabsolutismus', in *Staatsrecht – Völkerrecht – Europarecht*, ed. Ingo von Münch (Berlin: De Gruyter, 1981), 151–63.
[10]Dorothea Weltecke, 'Gab es "Vertrauen" im Mittelalter?', in *Vertrauen: Historische Annäherungen*, ed. Ute Frevert (Göttingen: Vandenhoeck & Ruprecht, 2003), 67–89, esp. 81–8.
[11]Baltasar Gracián, *The Pocket Oracle and Art of Prudence* (London: [Span. Orig. 1647] Penguin Books, 2011), 82.

In the same vein, the first German-language encyclopaedia from 1746 shied away from generally recommending trust between mortals. Instead, the author distinguished between substantiated and unsubstantiated modes of trust. The former could be found among people who were not only able but also willing to improve another person's lot and would do so on a regular basis. Yet as human beings were generally volatile, inconsistent and fragile, it was preferable not to trust them. God, in contrast, was strong, steady and benevolent, and therefore the only one who deserved unconditional trust.[12]

Warnings and counsels such as this were commonplace during the pre-modern era. Trust and trustworthiness, although cherished as major virtues, seemed to be in short supply. As human relations lacked stability and consistency, the only safe haven was with God. Those who placed their trust in him did not have to worry about the future, which was out of their control anyway. Existential threats and dangers like famines, wars, epidemics, disease, earthquakes and floods abounded. Since no one could prevent them, trust in God helped people to keep calm, stay composed and have confidence.[13]

Given the fundamental insecurities and uncertainties people faced in those times, this sounds like a good piece of pragmatic advice. Furthermore, it nicely fits the mental map of medieval and early modern European societies, which were profoundly shaped by Christian faith and religion. During the eighteenth century, however, those maps began to change, and Johann Heinrich Zedler's encyclopaedia entry formed part of those changes.

Modern trust

Although the author devoted eleven out of fifteen pages to trust in God, he also mentioned, albeit disapprovingly, modern inclinations to 'trust in other people's help'. Zedler radically dismissed these as flaws and 'weaknesses', attributing them to modernizing tendencies. *Erneuerung* (renewal) and *Erneuerte* (renewed) were contemporary buzzwords favoured by reformist movements in education and theology. Among Pietists and Methodists, everyday piety and common religious practices ranked highly; just as they praised brotherly unity among members of their congregations, they valued trust as a shared bond. Pedagogues likewise started to preach the gospel of trust as a vital component of teacher–student relations.[14] Enlightenment

---

[12]Johann Heinrich Zedler, *Grosses vollständiges Universal-Lexicon aller Wissenschafften und Künste*, vol. 48 (Leipzig: Zedler, 1746), 19–33.
[13]Christian Wolff, *Vernünfftige Gedancken von Gott, der Welt und der Seele des Menschen*, new edn (Halle: Renger, [1720] 1752), 289; Christian Wolff, *Grundsätze des Natur – und Völkerrechts*, 2nd edn (Halle: Renger, [1754] 1769), 107.
[14]Douglas A. Shantz, ed., *A Companion to German Pietism, 1660–1800* (Leiden: Brill, 2015).

thinkers like Christian Wolff confirmed that only rulers who used their power in a well-ordered and benevolent manner deserved their people's 'good' and 'joyful' trust, while others could merely claim obedience and submission.[15] In 1753, French *encyclopédistes* approvingly defined *confiance* as the 'effect of the knowledge and good opinion that we have of the qualities of someone else regarding our attitudes, our needs, our goals, and more generally any given interest'.[16]

Trust, however, was more than an effect of knowledge and opinion. It was a feeling that connected people and positively informed their actions towards one another. As such, trust entered the modern emotional lexicon. New trust words began to appear in everyday speech and were recorded in nineteenth-century dictionaries: *Vertrauensfragen* (trust issues), *Vertrauenslehrer* (trusted teachers), *Vertrauensärzte* (trusted doctors), *Vertrauensämter* (positions of trust), *Vertrauensbeweise* (evidence of trust), *Vertrauensmänner* (trusted colleagues and representatives). Meanwhile, the opposite of trust – distrust or mistrust – was mentioned less often. This did not mean that it no longer existed, however. The old saying *Fide, sed cui, vide* (trust but be careful whom you trust) never lost currency. Still, it was pitted against a profoundly affirmative interpretation of trust that emphasized its advantages, opportunities and gains. Someone trusting was considered amiable, generous, open, frank and sympathetic to their fellow citizens. An openly distrustful person, by contrast, was not somebody people wanted as a friend.

Looking at definitions and explanations of trust as they appeared in nineteenth- and twentieth-century lexicons and dictionaries, one cannot but notice a major change: the reference to God, which had been so prominent in 1746, disappeared completely. While Luther and Zedler had declared God the only reliable recipient of trust, later authors recommended trusting people. This was a decisive departure from older ways of thinking about trust. It also marked the beginning of a new regulative idea or principle, in Kantian terms. According to this idea, societies should be organized so as to enable their members to trust one another. Trust, as Simmel put it around 1900, was the glue that made social integration possible; without it, human interaction and cooperation were bound to fail, and societies would fall apart.[17]

Yet trust did not come naturally. It depended on enabling structures and conditions, and it had to be actively nurtured. Institutions characterized by strong emotional bonds and long-term commitments, like the middle-class

---

[15]Christian Wolff, *Vernünfftige Gedancken von dem gesellschaftlichen Leben der Menschen und insonderheit dem gemeinen Wesen*, 6th edn (Frankfurt: Renger, [1721] 1747), 540.
[16]Denis Diderot and Jean le Rond D'Alembert, *Encyclopédie: Ou dictionnaire raisonné des sciences, des arts et des métiers*, vol. 3 (Paris: Briasson, 1753), 849–50.
[17]Simmel, *Sociology*, 315.

family, seemed to be perfect breeding places; at least they were described as such more than one hundred years before Erikson wrote so positively about the mother–child dyad as the primordial trusting relationship. Nineteenth-century advice manuals increasingly urged mothers to behave lovingly, consistently and trustingly in order to allow their children to build trust in turn. Distrust, they warned, would morally weaken a child, while trust would strengthen their best faculties. By experiencing trust, the child developed self-confidence: a word that also emerged during that period and was closely linked to trust in others. As Friedrich Fröbel, a famous educator and founder of the German kindergarten, claimed in the early 1820s, those others may be kin but could also include strangers and theoretically might encompass all people and even the state.[18]

Alongside family, friendship was classed as another sphere that promoted the learning and practice of trustful relations. Since the late eighteenth century, the new cult of friendship had prepared contemporaries to consider friends highly important for their own emotional well-being and stability. Friends, unlike family, were freely chosen; furthermore, economic or financial duties usually played a reduced role in the relationship. Instead, friends were there to share intimate secrets and relish the perfect harmony of common interests, tastes and feelings. Friendship without trust was unthinkable.

The coalition between friendship and trust was so strong precisely because there was so much at stake: those who trusted a friend made themselves vulnerable to fraud and betrayal. They offered their trust as a generous gift and hoped for – but could not be sure of – reciprocity. Ideally, the trust-giver was also a trust-receiver. Rituals such as gestures, letters, poems and dedications sought to confirm mutual trust and censure the breach of trust as the most detrimental act between friends.[19]

For the very reason that friendship was voluntary and unprotected by other institutions like family, law or markets, it required strong personal commitment and assurances. A famous example is the friendship between Richard Wagner and Friedrich Nietzsche (which also included Wagner's wife, Cosima). For about a decade in the 1870s, the relationship was as close as it could be – Nietzsche later spoke of a 'trust without bounds' (*Vertrauen ohne Grenzen*).[20] But limitless trust had its price: it demanded

---

[18]Gunilla-Friederike Budde, 'Familienvertrauen – Selbstvertrauen – Gesellschaftsvertrauen: Pädagogische Ideale und Praxis im 19. Jahrhundert', in *Vertrauen*, ed. Frevert, 152–84.
[19]Wolfram Mauser, '"Ich lasse den Freund dir als Bürgen": Das Prinzip *Vertrauen* und die Freundschaftsdichtung des 18. Jahrhunderts', in *Das Jahrhundert der Freundschaft: Johann Wilhelm Ludwig Gleim und seine Zeitgenossen*, ed. Ute Pott (Göttingen: Wallstein, 2004), 11–20; Klaus Manger and Ute Pott, eds, *Rituale der Freundschaft* (Heidelberg: Winter, 2007).
[20]Friedrich Nietzsche to Georg Brandes, 10 April 1888, in Friedrich Nietzsche, *Werke in drei Bänden*, vol. 3 (Munich: Hanser, 1956), 1285; Ute Frevert, *Vertrauensfragen: Eine Obsession der Moderne* (Munich: C.H. Beck, 2013), 79–81.

total dedication and loyalty and was constantly put to the test. Nietzsche ultimately failed the test. Insisting on a certain measure of personal freedom, he betrayed Wagner's expectations and proved to be disloyal to master and mistress alike.

Trust, though, was not only to be found and worked on in mutual friendships. It was also present between members of larger social associations that mushroomed during the nineteenth century. Masonic lodges, art and music societies and charitable organizations bloomed, predominantly in urban middle-class milieus. They served many purposes and functioned as vehicles for marriage and business as well as incubators of political involvement and agenda-setting.[21] Their inclusionary power (which was accompanied by an equally strong exclusionary dimension) largely rested on the forging of trusting relations among their members and members' families. Trust nurtured through weekly gatherings and 'active sociability' went far beyond family, kinship and close friends.[22] It might not have been as 'thick', intense and vulnerable as in personal friendships.[23] But it was more than pre-modern societies had to offer.

This does not mean that trust was exclusively a modern phenomenon. Religious congregations as well as members of medieval or early modern guilds undoubtedly formed bonds of trust. Guilds, however, were only available to certain trades, and relied on mandatory membership. Therefore, relations were far more formalized and regulated, and trust was never at the forefront as an affective attitude. A different case can be made for associations that were established on a voluntary basis, like the Vertraute Gesellschaft in Leipzig, founded in 1680. Here, merchants met for 'friendly gatherings' and 'confidential community', in order to share joyful moments and collect money for the less fortunate. At the time, though, such societies were still rare and could by no means compare to the dense network of clubs and associations that emerged during the nineteenth century.[24]

---

[21] Stefan-Ludwig Hoffmann, *Civil Society, 1750–1914* (Basingstoke: Palgrave, 2006); Stefan-Ludwig Hoffmann, *Politics of Sociability: Freemasonry and German Civil Society, 1840–1918* (Ann Arbor: University of Michigan Press, 2007).

[22] Thomas Nipperdey, 'Verein als soziale Struktur in Deutschland im späten 18. und frühen 19. Jahrhundert', in *Thomas Nipperdey, Gesellschaft, Kultur, Theorie: Gesammelte Aufsätze zur neueren Geschichte* (Göttingen: Vandenhoeck & Ruprecht, 1976), 174–205, esp. 185–6.

[23] As to the notion of 'thick' versus 'thin' trust, see Robert D. Putnam, *Bowling Alone: The Collapse and Revival of American Community* (New York: Simon & Schuster, 2000), 134 ff. For Putnam, 'thick' trust not only developed among friends and family but also among members of voluntary associations who met frequently and over a long time. In contrast, 'thin' trust defined a general kind of 'social trust' among people who encountered each other only randomly and anonymously. Putnam assumed that 'thick' trust relations worked as a breeding ground for 'thin' trust. Historical case studies do not support this claim, nor does the existence of organized crime networks like the mafia, where trust among members goes hand in hand with a complete distrust towards other segments of society (Diego Gambetta, 'Mafia: The Price of Distrust', in Gambetta, *Trust*, 158–75).

[24] Herbert Helbig, *Die Vertrauten 1680–1980: Eine Vereinigung Leipziger Kaufleute* (Stuttgart: Hirsemann, 1980), 11–16, quote 11.

Trusting relations proved to be particularly 'thick' among younger people. From the late eighteenth century, male students in university towns would gather in regional clubs that served as a home away from home. Around 1800, these clubs took on a more political character without, however, losing their socially and emotionally inclusive functions. Venturing into unknown social territory, many students appreciated being part of an organized community that offered structure and belonging. It protected newcomers against isolation and loneliness and helped them find their feet among fellow students. By the end of the nineteenth century, the number of fraternities had multiplied, diversifying across a wide social, religious and political spectrum. A deep sense of shared emotions and emotional practices attracted adolescents to the manifold groups and *Bünde*. In the early 1930s, a 19-year-old student who had joined a Catholic youth club talked about trust as the primary bonding principle:

> I firmly trust my comrades in my *Bund* (who are thus called *Bundesbrüder* [brothers, confederates]). I trust them because they loyally try to understand everything that I say and do, and judge me in honesty and fairness. I can completely confide in them, without a third person interfering. They also trust me. Our mutual trust is based on our common goal: to resemble Jesus Christ.[25]

What is clear from this first-hand account is that such trust had a lot in common with trust within personal friendships: it entailed acceptance and understanding, and the sharing of secrets and intimate thoughts, fears, doubts, longings and desires. It was founded on mutual honesty, transparency and fairness. Two elements, though, distinguished it from trust between close friends: first, it was based on a common belief and commitment (in this case, a religious commitment); second, it involved more than two people.

Trust as it formed in youth organizations was thus emotionally strong and intense and yet also extended to each and every member of the organization. This proved to be superbly enticing for young men, who joined the movement in growing numbers. To that effect, the philosopher Herman Schmalenbach described the *Bund*, in 1922, as a new sociological category and 'way of existence' based on emotional needs and experiences.[26] Two years later, his colleague Helmuth Plessner cast a more critical eye on the contemporary craze for community (*Gemeinschaft*). He warned of its radicalness and in-built totalitarianism, and he was sceptical about the emphasis on closeness, intimacy and 'unlimited trust'. Members, he claimed, gave up their sense of

---

[25] Marianne Englert, *Das Vertrauen insbesondere seine Bedeutung für die Erziehung*, PhD thesis Munich 1934, quote 63–4.
[26] Herman Schmalenbach, 'Die soziologische Kategorie des Bundes', *Die Dioskuren* 1 (1922): 35–105, quotes 79.

privacy and got swept up in the experience of a community that no longer allowed for distance, difference and individuality. Plessner explicitly referred here to the communist and fascist movements that were gaining momentum in the 1920s.[27]

Yet 'unlimited trust' as it existed in those community-building organizations was by no means infinite or without restraint. For one, it was accompanied by deep mistrust of people who did not join, either due to voluntary non-compliance or formal exclusion. Moreover, trust among members was always precarious. Commitment to the common creed and cause was constantly questioned and put to the test. Treason and betrayal were par for the course, especially in times of crisis or repression. He who posed as a trustworthy comrade could in fact be a spy or traitor. Communists, for instance, acting under conditions of illegality and persecution, could not afford to be overly trusting. At the same time, they relied on networks of trust. The historian Jürgen Kuczynski, who spent the 1930s and early 1940s working illegally for the German Communist Party, wrote in retrospect:

> Those years turned us into better comrades, into better fighters for progress – but they did not let us be amiable people. We became deeply distrustful in our daily lives, while at the same time putting all our confidence in the great path of humanity, in the future, in youth, in the victory of the good and the beautiful.[28]

The quote highlights the value and esteem that trust enjoyed among modern people. A trustworthy person was held to be 'amiable' and loveable. Still, Kuczynski claimed that the times did not allow him to be *liebenswert* and trusting. That is why he put all his faith in the bright future of socialism, when people would finally be able to lead secure lives and build trusting relationships with each other and with their political leaders. The GDR (where Kuczynski lived as a prominent scholar and political figure) promised to provide those trustworthy relations and repeatedly invoked the mantra of 'indestructible trust' between party, state and citizen. Yet the

---

[27]Helmuth Plessner, *The Limits of Community: A Critique of Social Radicalism*, trans. Andrew Wallace (Amherst: Humanity Books, [Germ. Orig. 1924] 1999), 103.
[28]Jürgen Kuczynski, *Memoiren: Die Erziehung des J.K. zum Kommunisten und Wissenschaftler* (Berlin: Aufbau-Verlag, 1973), 271. Interestingly, Kuczynski's sister Ruth Werner, herself a famous communist spy, was much less self-critical in her autobiography: *Sonjas Rapport* (Berlin: Neues Leben, 1977). As for trust and betrayal in political movements, see Doris Danzer, *Zwischen Vertrauen und Verrat: Deutschsprachige kommunistische Intellektuelle und ihre sozialen Beziehungen (1918–1960)* (Göttingen: Vandenhoeck & Ruprecht, 2012); Daniel Brückenhaus, '"Every Stranger Must Be Suspected": Trust Relationships and the Surveillance of Anti-Colonialists in Early Twentieth-Century Western Europe', *Geschichte und Gesellschaft* 36, no. 4 (2010): 523–66.

party simultaneously preached 'revolutionary vigilance' in order to 'weed out' all enemies and 'agents of imperialism'.[29] The enormous growth of the Stasi apparatus during the 1970s in particular, at a time of East–West rapprochement and peaceful coexistence, cast profound doubt on just how much trust could be expected and granted. It also confirmed Hannah Arendt's observation that communist regimes, very much like fascist states, were based on universal suspicion and mistrust.[30] As recent studies show, trust in such contexts was largely confined to familial relations and absent in the wider social realm.[31]

Trust in the emotional economy of civil society

Those studies invite us to think more systemically about trust as a modern promise and predicament. Why was it that people placed so much trust in trust? How could and did trust become a major regulative idea? Under which conditions did men and women extend trust to others who were not related to them through kinship ties?

Trust, the argument goes, is a vital element in the emotional economy of civil societies. Civil societies, as they took shape in Europe from the late eighteenth century onwards, entirely changed the status of the individual person. Rather than embedding that person in a web of social dependencies – on family, profession, religion and monarch – they envisaged him (and, somewhat later, her) as a free citizen, equal to others in rights and opportunities. Together citizens formed a social and political body that was supposed to be self-governing and sovereign.

A society of equals required institutions that both protected their members' rights and freedoms and facilitated mutual cooperation and communication. It also needed a new economy of passions and inclinations

---

[29]Matthias Judt, ed., *DDR-Geschichte in Dokumenten. Beschlüsse, Berichte, interne Materialien und Alltagszeugnisse*, 2nd edn (Berlin: Links, 1998), 487 (quotes from GDR President Wilhelm Pieck in 1950); Jens Gieseke, 'Whom Did the East Germans Trust? Popular Opinion on Threats of War, Confrontation, and Détente in the German Democratic Republic, 1968–1989', in *Trust, but Verify: The Politics of Uncertainty and the Transformation of the Cold War Order, 1969–1991*, ed. Martin Klimke, Reinhild Kreis and Christian F. Ostermann (Washington: Woodrow Wilson Center Press, 2016), 143–66. See Chapter 14 in this volume.
[30]Hannah Arendt, *The Origins of Totalitarianism* (New York: Schocken Books, 2004), 555–6: 'Mutual suspicion, therefore, permeates all social relationships in totalitarian countries and creates an all-pervasive atmosphere even outside the special purview of the secret police.'
[31]Sarah Davies, '"Us against Them": Social Identity in Soviet Russia, 1934–41', in *Stalinism*, ed. Sheila Fitzpatrick (London: Routledge, 2000), 47–70; Ivana Marková, ed., *Trust and Democratic Transition in Post-Communist Europe* (Oxford: Oxford University Press, 2004); see the special issue on 'Trust and Distrust in the USSR', *Slavonic & East European Review* 91, no. 1 (2013): 1–146; Hosking, *Trust*, ch. 1.

that answered the same purpose. As early as 1728, the Scottish philosopher Francis Hutcheson had sought to define a 'just *Ballance and Oeconomy*, which would constitute the most happy State of each Person, and promote the greatest Good in the whole'. *Oeconomy* here was not restricted to the handling of goods and commodities: it meant, above all, the conduct of individual 'passions and affections' so as to render them compatible and consistent 'with the publick Good'.[32]

Although Hutcheson did not specifically mention trust, it figured prominently in that new emotional economy. It could be viewed as a private as well as a public 'inclination'; it served private ends as much as it encouraged 'services to Offspring, Friends, Communities, Countries'. It built short- and long-term relations, and it enabled exchange and cooperation among people who would otherwise refrain from associating with one another or working together on a common project. Such projects could be of a financial nature, such as trading goods or starting a joint business. They could equally have aims not related to profit, like founding a political party or mobilizing people's support and running for parliament. In all these (and many other) endeavours, trust was essential.

Yet trust could not simply be ordered and claimed. Trust was granted voluntarily, and could be withdrawn *al gusto*. It functioned like a gift generously given (as captured by the German notion *Vertrauen schenken*). At the same time, it made demands and set conditions: A trusted B as long as B gave A reason to trust them and behaved in accordance with A's best interests. As soon as A had reason to doubt this, A could withdraw their trust and put an end to the relationship. The notion of trust as a gift was connected to the feelings of joy and pride experienced by the person who had gained someone's trust. To be recognized and appreciated as trustworthy was considered enviable and beneficial, and was often rewarded with social capital.

Its conditional character distinguished trust from loyalty. Being loyal – to a guild master or a king or queen – was an obligation enshrined in the emotional economy of the *ancien régime*. Theoretically, such loyalty should and could not be broken. Doing so constituted treason and was punished harshly. Trust, in contrast, came with expectations; if they were not met, trust might be withdrawn without further ado. In this sense, unconditional trust was a *contradictio in adiecto*. Seen as a bet on the future, trust had to be based on some amount of previous knowledge and experience.

---

[32]Francis Hutcheson, *An Essay on the Nature and Conduct of the Passions and Affections, with Illustrations on the Moral Sense*, ed. Aaron Garrett (Indianapolis: Liberty Fund, [1728] 2002), 47. Hutcheson's notions resonated in the article on 'Moral Philosophy, or Morals', in *Encyclopaedia Britannica*, 1st edn, vol. 3 (Edinburgh: Bell & Macfarquhar, 1771), 270–309. The author frequently mentioned the 'economy of powers and passions' or the 'just oeconomy of our nature' (274).

Accordingly, Christian Wolff linked trust in a ruler to the quality of his government.

Gaining people's trust went hand in hand with moral obligations and emotional investments. Those who received trust did so because they were considered trustworthy. Trustworthiness entailed far more than being reliable, consistent and calculable. It was not just about keeping and delivering on promises, it was about the promise itself, which was supposed to be generous and aimed at preserving the 'security and well-being' of the trusting person.[33] Definitions of trust usually had moralistic overtones. An equally strong moral judgement was issued against those who betrayed someone's trust. This was condemned as the 'worst character flaw' and a clear sign of 'infamy', since trust called upon the trusted to act with 'deep moral commitment'.[34]

Given the lofty moral status of trust, it becomes clearer why modern civil societies valued it as an essential component of social, economic and political relations and put considerable effort into promoting trust as an educational objective. First, civil societies are, structurally speaking, in a position to both produce and afford trust. They render the ordinary life of citizens far more secure and calculable, primarily by building and strengthening formal institutions. Those institutions make predictable claims and provide reliable services. By stabilizing expectations, they function as prerequisites of generalized social trust. The professionalization of the legal system and the extension of state governance are cases in point. They allow citizens to be more confident about the future and to take risks that are at least partially protected by legal provisions and sanctions. Equality before the law, as well as inclusive institutions such as schools, police, water and energy supplies, healthcare and welfare systems, contribute to an overall sense of security and confidence.

Under these conditions, people can afford to trust their fellow citizens, even if they do not know them personally.[35] Institutions that regulate our behaviour undoubtedly help to narrow Simmel's gap between knowing and not-knowing. Still, they cannot close it completely. Taxi drivers, for instance, need a fair amount of trust when accepting passengers. How do they know that they will get paid rather than assaulted? How do they evaluate and establish their customers' trustworthiness? A recent study of taxi drivers in New York and Belfast revealed interesting differences. While

---

[33]Zedler, *Universal-Lexicon*, vol. 48, 19. Baier's definition likewise emphasizes the moral and emotional features of trust. Baier, *Moral Prejudices*, 88 ff., 132.
[34]*Der Große Herder: Nachschlagewerk für Wissen und Leben*, 4th edn, vol. 12 (Freiburg: Herder, 1935), 283.
[35]Claus Offe, 'How Can We Trust Our Fellow Citizens?', in *Democracy and Trust*, ed. Mark E. Warren (Cambridge: Cambridge University Press, 1999), 42–87.

New Yorkers responded positively to ethnic sameness, drivers from Belfast based their trust on religious grounds.[36] This indicates that trustworthiness is contingent on matters of class, age, gender, sexual orientation, religion, ethnicity and nationality. An Englishwoman on a public bus relayed the story of how she had been cheated by a seemingly trustworthy man. He had impressed her with his manners, his Oxford accent and the way he dressed. All this prompted her to give him the fifty pounds that he had requested and promised to send back immediately. People from other countries might have prioritized other signs of trustworthiness in strangers.

There is thus a lot to be discussed regarding how markers of trustworthiness depend on variable cultural codes and social perceptions. As a general rule, contiguity and resemblance seem to allow for higher degrees of trust. By the same token, they render those we hold distant or different extremely susceptible to distrust. Institutions have an important role to play here. Rather than reducing the need for trust, they facilitate 'thin' social trust and promote it by fostering cooperative relationships. Generalized confidence in institutionally guarded principles and regulations enables trusting relations on a personal level. It helps to transform strangers into fellow citizens and allows the extension of trust to people who are neither kith nor kin. Although this still might be considered risky at times, the risk is hedged; it no longer poses an existential threat. Voluntary associations as they have developed freely and abundantly in modern civil societies – like sports clubs, choirs, professional organizations and NGOs – nurture trust among their members and permit relationships that, under other historical terms, would hardly have been possible.

The second explanation draws on the morality of trust. From the outset, civil societies emphasized the importance of morally sanctioned values and emotions. Seeking a contrast with aristocratic mores and what they deemed to be uncivilized behaviour among the lower classes, men and women of the educated bourgeoisie characterized themselves as honest, sincere and trustworthy. Criticizing the *ancien régime* as corrupt, fraudulent, treacherous and self-serving, they claimed moral supremacy and promised a better world – better not only in terms of economic or political efficacy but also of social fairness and human decency. Along with the promise of freedom and equality, this included forging and invigorating fraternal ties between the citizens of a nation. Trust was inextricably woven into this new moral landscape, both as its foundation and its consequence. Trust defended it against charges of social disintegration, anomy and cold rationality. It secured social cohesion and built communities without infringing on people's free will. Since trust could be conditional and flexible, it offered the possibility of withdrawal and resetting the clock.

---

[36]Diego Gambetta and Heather Hamill, *Streetwise: How Taxi Drivers Establish Their Customers' Trustworthiness* (New York: Russell Sage Foundation, 2005).

Trust and economic transactions

Beginning in the nineteenth century, this logic increasingly pervaded economic relations. Businessmen and professionals had to constantly prove their trustworthiness to clients, partners and creditors alike. Trust was a major means of doing business and ensuring continuous and long-term gains, as the German entrepreneur Robert Bosch confirmed in 1918: 'I'd rather lose money than trust. The inviolability of my promises, the belief in the value of my goods and in my word to me always seemed more valuable than momentary gains.'[37] Bosch thus testified both to the general necessity of trust and to the prerequisites that had to be met in order to earn it. For him, trust was crucial to achieving the kind of economic success he was after: not short-term or fleeting, but sustained and dependable.

Economic trustworthiness was only partly achieved on its own terms, however. The 'value of goods' was not enough to produce it, as Bosch and his colleagues knew all too well. To make customers and partners believe in their 'promises' and 'word', they had to build a reputation supported by other sources as well. When these sources were lacking, as was often the case for the first generation of industrial entrepreneurs, they had to rely on kinship ties (where trust was a given) for financial credit and economic expansion.[38] Many used family members to set up branches in foreign countries, like Werner von Siemens, whose brother Carl ran the Saint Petersburg office. But even in the British case, which is normally seen as the prime example of individualistic entrepreneurship, economic historians have recently stressed the 'collective nature of business diversification'. Active networking in social, cultural and business associations, they argue, boosted trust and trustworthiness among potential partners and investors. This was hard work, requiring time, money and effort, as the Manchester cotton merchant Benjamin Braidley pointed out in his memoir. In 1824, as he was preparing to co-found the Manchester fire insurance office, he spent over thirty-six hours each week 'on matters totally unconnected with my own business', including committee meetings, correspondence, social calls and charitable and educational work. This extended networking helped him to gain a reputation as a respectable, solid and trustworthy person. His

---

[37] Robert Bosch, '"Lieber Geld verlieren als Vertrauen"', *Der Bosch-Zünder: Eine Zeitschrift für alle Angehörigen der Robert Bosch AG und der Bosch-Metallwerk AG* 1, no. 2 (1919): 1.
[38] Jürgen Kocka, 'Entrepreneurs and Managers in German Industrialization', in *The Cambridge Economic History of Europe*, vol. 7, pt. 1, ed. Peter Mathias and Michael M. Postan (Cambridge: Cambridge University Press, 1978), 492–589; Leonore Davidoff and Catherine Hall, *Family Fortunes: Men and Women of the English Middle Class, 1780–1850* (London: Hutchinson, 1987).

partners' trust in him relied on their judgement of his general conduct and his adherence to common values like probity and independence.[39]

Only recently has this conspicuous triangle of reputation, trust and economic cooperation come to the fore in economic theory and history. While neoclassical economists generally paid little attention to non-economic influences and frames of reference, new institutional economics have acknowledged them as crucial factors in economic stability and growth.[40] Trust is increasingly seen as an element inherent in each and every commercial exchange. It greatly reduces the costs of transactions and so is indispensable even in narrowly defined economic terms. Without trust, cooperation between business partners and industrial enterprises would be endlessly complicated, time-consuming and expensive. Trust relations can dispense with contracts and legally administered sanctions, make communication smoother, more informal and more productive. By circumventing the negotiation, litigation and enforcement of formal regulations, trust enables economic cooperation at much lower costs.[41]

Accordingly, economists and economic historians have started to look more closely at the processes and structural conditions that rendered trust possible. They have eagerly taken up the concept of social capital, which could be gained and grown through cooperation and exchange in multiple domains.[42] Choosing to trust another person meant engaging in a relationship that generated more trust, on both sides. In such settings, trust served as a specific form of social capital accumulated through networking within a given set of societal norms and cultural prescriptions. Benjamin Braidley's behaviour is indicative: by investing his time and money in social and cultural activities, by connecting to people in matters not directly related to his economic interests, he presented himself as a trustworthy person to potential business partners. Another prime example of social capital formation is the large number of cooperative societies that sprang up during the nineteenth century. In particular, mutual credit associations that banded together people of limited financial resources relied heavily on reciprocal trust among their members. At the same time, they served to consolidate trust relations by engaging in continuous operations of borrowing and lending money at relatively low interest rates. Assisted

---

[39] Robin Pearson and David Richardson, 'Business Networking in the Industrial Revolution', *Economic History Review* 54, no. 4 (2001): 657–79, quotes 676, 674 (Braidley).
[40] See Chapter 8 in this volume.
[41] Francis Fukuyama, *Trust: The Social Virtues and the Creation of Prosperity* (New York: Simon & Schuster, 1995); Martin Fiedler, 'Vertrauen ist gut, Kontrolle ist teuer: Vertrauen als Schlüsselkategorie wirtschaftlichen Handelns', *Geschichte und Gesellschaft* 27, no. 4 (2001): 576–92; Tanja Ripperger, *Ökonomik des Vertrauens* (Tübingen: Mohr Siebeck, 1998).
[42] On social capital, see James S. Coleman, *Foundations of Social Theory* (Cambridge, MA: Belknap Press of Harvard University Press, 1990); James S. Coleman, 'Systems of Trust', *Angewandte Sozialforschung* 10, no. 3 (1982): 277–99.

by auditors who checked the associations' accountancy, they worked so well that they rivalled newly emerging alternative institutions like savings banks.[43]

Trust thus became a major prerequisite for economic cooperation and it was largely established before cooperation began. It depended on social knowledge acquired through politics of reputation. Simultaneously, cooperation helped to generate, stabilize and increase trust by providing a shared experience of trustworthy behaviour in economic interactions. Empirical case studies have amply proven how trust-based communication between business partners enhances their respective gains and enables efficient, long-term cooperation grounded in continuous learning and adjustment processes. The more cooperation is needed in a capitalist economy with an accelerating division of labour, the more trust is valued and cherished.[44]

Trustful relations are not restricted to economic cooperation between companies and enterprises. They also occur between experts and their clients. Doctor–patient relationships are as dependent on mutual trust as the contact between lawyers and those who seek their counsel. Generally speaking, the growing service sector (including the financial and insurance markets) cannot function without trust and is extremely vulnerable to the perceived danger of losing trust. The same holds true for consumer markets that depend on generating trust and fostering the long-lasting emotional allegiance of customers. Since the 1870s, trade-marking goods has proven to be a successful means of building trust among prospective buyers. The trademark functions as a 'trust mark', suggesting accountability and reliability. By assuring ongoing quality control, it lowers the risk of the transaction for the customer.[45]

---

[43]Timothy W. Guinnane, 'Cooperatives as Information Machines: German Rural Credit Cooperatives, 1883–1914', *Journal of Economic History* 61, no. 2 (2001): 366–89; Carlos G. Vélez-Ibañez, *Bonds of Mutual Trust: The Cultural Systems of Rotating Credit Associations among Urban Mexicans and Chicanos* (New Brunswick: Rutgers University Press, 1983); Frevert, *Vertrauensfragen*, 111–14. For a more general perspective, see Robert D. Putnam, *Making Democracy Work: Civic Traditions in Modern Italy* (Princeton: Princeton University Press, 1983).

[44]Edward H. Lorenz, 'Neither Friends nor Strangers: Informal Networks of Subcontracting in French Industry', in *Trust*, ed. Gambetta, 194–210; Bernard Baudry, 'Trust in Inter-Firm Relations', in *Trust and Economic Learning*, ed. Nathalie Lazaric and Edward Lorenz (Cheltenham: Elgar, 1998), 64–77; Bertrand Moingeon and Amy Edmondson, 'Trust and Organisational Learning', in *Trust and Economic Learning*, ed. Lazaric and Lorenz, 247–65; Martin Fiedler, 'Netzwerke des Vertrauens', in *Großbürger und Unternehmer: Die deutsche Wirtschaftselite im 20. Jahrhundert*, ed. Dieter Ziegler (Göttingen: Vandenhoeck & Ruprecht, 2000), 93–115.

[45]Hartmut Berghoff, 'Die Zähmung des entfesselten Prometheus? Die Generierung von Vertrauenskapital und die Konstruktion des Marktes im Industrialisierungs- und Globalisierungsprozess', in *Wirtschaftsgeschichte als Kulturgeschichte*, ed. Hartmut Berghoff and Jakob Vogel (Frankfurt: Campus, 2004), 143–68, here 160–1.

In addition to principal–agent and customer dynamics, trust also played a role in labour relations, between employers and employed, capitalists and workers. Even though modern industrial production thoroughly changed traditional patterns of work and work relations, many first-generation entrepreneurs tried to hold on to authority structures that emphasized cohesion and loyalty. Alfred Krupp time and again praised the 'old trust' that reigned in his thriving company. From his workers he demanded unconditional allegiance; in return, he promised to care for them in good times and bad.[46] Other factory owners, equally attuned to the merits of trustful relations with those on the shop floor, turned to new codes and practices of trust. During the late nineteenth century, more and more companies introduced factory councils that consisted of elected colleagues or *Vertrauensmänner*. They were supposed to represent workers' interests and negotiate these with the owner or manager. On the employer's invitation, the councils held regular meetings, voicing complaints and suggesting improvements in social and economic matters. This procedure was widely regarded as bringing about 'essential advantages': it fostered 'mutual understanding' between workers and employers and 'surmounted mutual distrust'.[47]

On all levels, trust was seen as a crucial enabler of communication between people whose economic success and well-being increasingly depended on closer cooperation. Open distrust, in turn, was dismissed as disrupting and obstructing cooperation and hampering the efficiency of economic transactions. Modern industrial society invented all kinds of schemes to minimize distrust among principals and agents, consumers and producers, workers and employers. Some of these were highly formalized and regulated, others depended on rather weak modes of assurances and promises. In this sense, trade-marking and other systems of certification served as much as 'guardians of trust' as the gradual introduction of workers' participation in company decision-making processes.[48]

Political trust

In politics, trust is, historically, a new concept. It can be traced back to John Locke, the late-seventeenth-century British liberal philosopher who coined the phrase 'government by trust'. In his view, trust defined the relations between citizens and the parliament that held supreme power, i.e. the power to pass laws. The parliament acted as the trustee of the people, with which

---

[46]Alfred Krupp, *Ein Wort an die Angehörigen meiner gewerblichen Anlagen* (Essen: Krupp, 1877). See Chapter 7 in this volume.
[47]Frevert, *Vertrauensfragen*, quotes 122.
[48]Susan P. Shapiro, 'The Social Control of Impersonal Trust', *American Journal of Sociology* 93, no. 3 (1987): 623–58, quote 635.

it shared not only interests but also, as Edmund Burke put it a century later, feelings and desires.[49] Such trusting relations were essentially absent on the European continent, where monarchs held absolute power and parliament in the British sense was unknown. Instead of trust, Continentals spoke of loyalty and fidelity. The absolutist princes commanded their subjects' loyalty and obedience, not their trust.

So what, then, is the difference between trust and fidelity/loyalty? The main distinction concerns issues of fluidity and stability. Fidelity/loyalty, in the medieval sense, characterized relationships that were bound to last. Once sworn, it could not be broken. Doing so was synonymous with treason, which was considered a major crime. In contrast, trust was reversible and could be lost. Although it remained within the traditional lexicon of allegiance, love and reverence, it gradually cast off its passive connotations and acquired a more active character. Talking trust increasingly meant negotiating power relations. Those who offered trust made demands: they stated the conditions under which trust would be granted and threatened to withhold it if those conditions were not met.

Trust thus became part of the new political language of emotions introduced in Continental Europe by the upheaval of the French Revolution. Even in countries that did not follow the French model, it made itself felt. Monarchs disinclined to share the fate of Louis XVI were eager to 'strengthen the bonds of trust between Us and Our people'. Self-confident citizens in turn urged monarchs to trust the people and promised good returns. 'Trust breeds trust': this is how German citizens in the 1830s and 1840s sought to convince kings and magistrates to share their political power and draft a liberal constitution. Authorities could only be trusted when they trusted the people and entrusted them with political rights that allowed their participation in legislative and governmental functions. In 1848, many campaigned for a transparent and 'trusting state' that no longer monopolized power. Secrecy was believed to harm and impede trust, while openness enabled it to flourish.[50]

During these negotiations, trust was presented as a scarce resource, something which had to be built and consolidated by a chain of favourable decisions and careful policy-making. Beneath this message lay an abundance of distrust. Distrust, too, was a new lemma in the emotional lexicon of nineteenth-century politics. Talking about trust as a political demand made it possible to talk about the lack thereof, or, stronger still, the state of distrust. Distrust was defined as the weapon of the powerless or the less powerful – certainly a newly discovered weapon, since it could only be used in a political system that valued trust.

---

[49]John Locke, *The Second Treatise of Government*, ed. Thomas P. Peardon (New York: Liberal Arts Press, 1952), 81 ff.; Edmund Burke, *Works*, vol. 3 (London: Bohn, 1855), 334.
[50]See Frevert, *Vertrauensfragen*, 147–66.

Parliamentary democracy, as it exists now, emerged as a form of politics that greatly depended on the delicate balance between trust and distrust. It started with the constitution as an embodiment of trust – an act of power-sharing that was either forced upon or coaxed out of the previous monopolist. There were at least two echelons of trust: one between government and parliament, the other between parliament and citizens. Both were accompanied by inbuilt mechanisms of distrust. Citizens chose their representatives for a limited amount of time and could withdraw their trust in subsequent elections. Parliament likewise relied on a mixture of trust and distrust. It controlled and supervised governmental actions, and it was free to bring down the government with an explicit vote of distrust.

Modern politics, then, rely heavily on institutionalized mechanisms of trust and distrust. At the same time, these mechanisms tend to devour the intensely emotional nature of trust. This is why people generally find it hard to trust abstract systems. What matters to them are personal 'access points', which Anthony Giddens defines as 'meeting grounds of face-work and faceless commitments'.[51] Rather than placing their trust in governments, parties, courts or welfare bureaucracies, citizens choose to trust (or distrust) the head of government, local or national party leaders or specific judges and clerks whom they could potentially meet face to face.

This poses problems for politics in parliamentary democracies that work within narrow time constraints. As governments and their leaders can change every four or five years (or, as in Italy and, recently, in the UK, far more frequently), trust – which generally requires and privileges a longer chain of communication and interaction – is somewhat difficult to build. Parliamentary democracies also tend to place more importance on political issues and programmes than on political personnel. If trust primarily determines relationships between people, it is not easy to install in modern democracies whose 'access points' are constantly switching.

At first glance, autocratic systems or (semi)constitutional monarchies seem to fare better in this regard. Kings and queens whose reigns lasted several decades, usually entertained robust direct communication with citizens. The more bourgeois or middle class the royal family appeared, the more they inspired popular imagination and invited personal engagement. Hundreds of thousands wished the king or queen happy birthday and sent poems commemorating royal marriages or births. The death of a monarch sent shock waves through the populace, even when – due to old age or poor health – it had been expected. People were interested in personal stories, and newspapers eagerly provided them. This far exceeded the 'star power' of present times. It was more encompassing, more general and more focused. The monarch embodied material and symbolic power, rooted in tradition and political structure. Furthermore, they personified – or pledged to personify – the nation, the fatherland and the community of

---

[51] Anthony Giddens, *The Consequences of Modernity* (Cambridge: Polity Press, 1990), 83.

citizens who, during the nineteenth century, came to recognize the monarch as one of their own: someone amiable and trustworthy.[52]

Interestingly, such allegiances survived the radical rupture that occurred in countries like Germany where the monarchy was forcefully abolished and a republic was established. The letters that citizens addressed to the first German president after the 1918 revolution convey a surprising sense of continuity. This continuity was even more evident when his conservative successor, a former First World War general, took office in 1925. The outpouring of trust was breathtaking. It became stronger still after Adolf Hitler, a truly charismatic figure, was made chancellor in 1933 and president in 1934. The great majority of letters he received were unsolicited and without material purpose. Very few people wrote to request a favour – although many asked for a signed photograph (and received it). Most letter-writers just took pleasure in initiating a personal connection and assuring the Führer of their boundless love and trust.

What had been lost in this communication, however, was the conditional character of trust that had been so dominant in the transformative period of constitutional politics. In comparison, the autocratic rhetoric of trust was more akin to older concepts of loyalty and fidelity. Moreover, it bore a close link to obedience; 'follow the Führer's commands' was a familiar slogan that apparently found ready acceptance. At least this is what the letters articulated in an almost identical language of personal dedication and soaring expectations. The Führer had made many promises, and people trusted him to keep them. Openly withdrawing their trust and changing sides would prove impossible. Denunciations were ubiquitous and often resulted in severe, potentially life-threatening sanctions.

At the same time, National Socialist propaganda did its very best to proclaim and kindle trust between the Führer and his people. Trust talk abounded, in political speeches as well as in the renaming of institutions. What had been called the 'factory council' during the Weimar Republic now figured as a 'council of trust'. Trust and fidelity became the core concepts of industrial relations, connecting 'leaders' and 'followers' in a supposedly harmonious symbiosis. Distrust, conflict and struggle were outlawed, but only among those who were racially and politically aligned. In fact, the emphasis on trust within the national community contrasted sharply with the amount of distrust stoked against those who did not belong: foreigners, Jews, communists and socialist 'internationalists'.[53]

Totalitarian dictatorships thus completely distorted the emotional economy of trust. Although they hijacked the term in order to benefit from its reputation, they stripped it of its fundamental meaning and core components: voluntariness, conditionality and reciprocity. Citizens and

---

[52]See Chapter 12 in this volume.
[53]See Chapter 13 in this volume.

workers no longer had a choice: they had to trust. Yet they were not trusted in return. By effectively reducing trust to pre-modern notions of unconditional fidelity, National Socialism negatively confirmed trust's connection with modern notions of freedom and individual choice. It also underscored how pervasive and attractive those semantics had become; autocratic regimes were eager to adopt them even as they worked to thoroughly undermine them.[54]

Current developments and dilemmas

Subversion did not stop in 1945 or 1989. In the last three decades or so, trust talk has proliferated against the background of what philosopher Onora O'Neill has diagnosed as a growing culture of suspicion.[55] Talking and writing endlessly about trust (or its lack) clearly evokes and nurtures the spectre of distrust. Each and every conflict is now framed and presented as a crisis of trust. Banks, in particular, find reasons to court their clients' trust, and have come to evaluate it as a major economic asset. Trust Management institutes are sprouting, and so are trust surveys. On the political level, the Euro crisis was framed as a crisis of trust between EU countries, while the NSA's spying on European stateswomen, politicians and citizens has been compared to a breach of trust among close friends.

What do we make of this from a history of emotions perspective? First, we can observe a remarkable shift of meaning. Trust, as it was defined during the late eighteenth and early nineteenth centuries, has undergone profound semantic changes. Once restricted to close personal relations among family and friends, neighbours and colleagues, it is now attached to all kinds of remote transactions and services in economics and politics. Considering the ongoing moral underpinnings of trust as something utterly valuable and intrinsically positive, we can detect a subtle moralization of social, economic and political relations among allegedly trustworthy partners. Still, the 'thick' and emotionally 'hot' interpersonal quality of trust is mostly absent from those relations. They work instead on rather 'thin' expectations of reliability and accountability. The social proliferation and delimitation of trust thus goes together with the emptying-out of content, or, to put it more precisely, with a shift from altruistic care and concern to calculable behaviour and strategic planning.

Second, this shift poses questions as to how, why and under which circumstances it occurred. Who were and are the agents of change, and

---

[54]For communist and post-communist Poland, see Piotr Sztompka, 'Trust and Emerging Democracy: Lessons from Poland', *International Sociology* 11, no. 1 (1996): 37–62.
[55]Onora O'Neill, *A Question of Trust* (Cambridge: Cambridge University Press, 2002). See also Geoffrey Hosking, *Trust: Money, Markets and Society* (London: Seagull Books, 2010), 6–9.

what is on their agenda? Emotions never come naturally or automatically, nor does their status simply reflect or react to developments in other social domains. In the case of trust, we can see deliberate and intentional semantic politics at work. When, during the latter half of the eighteenth century, progressive reformers dethroned God as the sole bearer of trust and emphatically encouraged people to trust others, they were promoting a new kind of society that valued horizontal rather than vertical and hierarchical relations. When citizens in the 1830s and 1840s turned trust upside down and presented themselves as both trusting and trustworthy, they challenged traditional political authority and demanded a seat at the table.

So what is at stake in contemporary society when banks and other businesses adopt the language of trust and aggressively market themselves as trustworthy instead of, say, reliable or accountable? Why do politicians who talk about domestic and international political relations use and usurp notions of personal friendship, trust included? The purpose seems obvious: they all want to buy into the emotional economy of trust and benefit from its moral zeal. Talking trust means acknowledging humanity and its basic needs, conveying a shared sense of vulnerability and mutual dependency, and promising fairness, generosity and empathy. These are concepts and values that have had a growing influence since the latter half of the twentieth century, as processes of global connectivity and interaction proliferate. They also have a role to play in the ongoing transformations that are turning Western economies into service industries. The not-so-new figure of the citizen–consumer is increasingly wooed by those industries, and the language of trust comes in handy during the courtship: it promises transparency as well as control, and it evokes neoliberal notions of accountability that seemingly aim at empowering those who hold others accountable.

There is a dilemma, though. Those who market trust as a winsome commodity run the risk of depleting it of its moral and emotional substance.[56] Without that substance, trust is no more than an empty shell. It loses its promise and appeal, and boils down to mere calculativeness. This is how present-day economists think of trust.[57] Historians know that the semantics of trust are far richer and connect to a wide array of social practices. They emerged as crucial elements of a modern emotional economy that, in Francis Hutcheson's terms, facilitated personal well-being and promoted the common good.

---

[56]Jakob Tanner, '"Die Währung der Finanzmärkte ist Vertrauen": Nachhaltigkeit und Hinterhältigkeit eines mentalen Phänomens in historischer Perspektive', in *Was ist Vertrauen?*, ed. Jörg Baberowski (Frankfurt: Campus, 2014), 73–100.
[57]As a critique, see Oliver E. Williamson, 'Calculativeness, Trust and Economic Organization', *Journal of Law & Economics* 36, no. 1, pt. 2 (1993): 453–86.

CHAPTER THREE

Practising Honour: Social, Gender and Legal Perspectives

When, in 1728, Francis Hutcheson envisaged an emotional economy that balanced 'passions and affections' and served both the interests of the individual and the common good, he placed honour front and centre. Humans, he wrote, possessed a 'natural Love of Honour' and, in its pursuit, sought to distinguish themselves 'by some *singular Ability*, or by some Circumstance, which, however trifling in its own Nature, yet had some honourable Ideas commonly joined to it, such as *Magnificence, Generosity*, or the like'. Honour figured as a 'desire' or 'sense' that nurtured other passions like ambition, pride or shame.[1]

The Scottish philosopher was living in a world brimming with honour. Honour had a firm footing among merchants and artisans as well as among noblemen and the upper middle classes. In each strata and circumstance, it was strictly codified and observed. What counted as honourable conduct was established by rules and values shared by all members of a social group. Dishonourable behaviour was met with sharp sanctions, even exclusion.

Honour thus served a crucial purpose. It worked, as sociologist Georg Simmel put it in 1908, as an instrument of social self-preservation, stabilizing a group by ensuring its internal cohesion and external prestige. In performing this task, honour was translated from a corporate norm into a

---

[1] Francis Hutcheson, *An Essay on the Nature and Conduct of the Passions and Affections, with Illustrations on the Moral Sense*, ed. Aaron Garrett (Indianapolis: Liberty Fund, [1728] 2002), 21–2, 55–6.

personal action, from a 'social duty' into 'personal salvation' and well-being. Though it was in fact regulated by strong social expectations, individuals usually accepted and internalized these as their 'most inward, deepest, the most personal self-interests'.[2]

For Simmel's contemporary Max Weber, honour belonged to a pre-modern world that was stratified into estates or status groups (*Stände*) rather than classes as defined by the market. Status honour stood 'in sharp opposition to the pretensions of sheer property' that determined an individual's class position. Instead, the honour of status was based on a 'specific conduct of life' that favoured 'distance and exclusiveness' and rested on a 'distinctive traditional ethic reinforced by education'. That ethic, as Weber observed with regard to the medieval nobility, 'made personal relations central to the conduct of life and impressed every individual with the obligations of a status honour that was jointly held and thus a unifying bond for the status group as a whole'. According to the sociologist, the medieval tradition had proved influential among the European upper classes ever since. Both in the United Kingdom and on the Continent, the contemporary 'ideal of manliness' and *Lebensführung* clearly demonstrated that 'feudal knighthood', with its strong sense of 'personal honour' and chivalry, still served as the dominant 'center of orientation'.[3]

Is honour an emotion?

Neither Simmel nor Weber had referred to emotions when they analysed honour and its functions. Similarly, in his seminal study on Kabyle society, Pierre Bourdieu perceived honour as a form of 'social capital' and as a system of 'dispositions' that produced and structured social practices.[4] Evidently, Hutcheson's perspective on honour as a private passion, desire and sense had been altogether lost or overlooked, along with claims by other eighteenth-century authors about honour being 'rooted in the heart' (the undisputed site of feelings and emotions).[5] In fact, phenomenological accounts of honour as 'physiologically felt' persisted until the early twentieth century and included

---

[2] Georg Simmel, *Sociology: Inquiries into the Construction of Social Forms*, trans. and ed. Anthony J. Blasi, Anton K. Jacobs and Mathew Kanjirathinkal, vol. 1 (Leiden: Brill, 2009), 387–9, 476–80, quotes 479.
[3] Max Weber, *Economy and Society: An Outline of Interpretive Sociology*, ed. Günther Roth and Claus Wittich, vol. 2 (Berkeley, CA: University of California Press, 1978), 932–7, 1068–9. While the translation speaks of 'styles of life', I have used 'conduct of life' as it comes closer to the original *Lebensführung*.
[4] Pierre Bourdieu, *Outline of a Theory of Practice*, trans. Richard Nice (Cambridge: Cambridge University Press, 1977).
[5] A., 'Betrachtung über das Duelliren', *Neue Mannigfaltigkeiten* 1 (1774): 765–8, here 765.

bodily manifestations, which contemporary psychologists considered as emotions proper.[6] Lexical entries, meanwhile, associated honour with violent urges, drives and desires, testifying to its properties as a feeling, or even a passion.[7] As late as the 1940s, in an attempt to make sense of recent French history, historian Lucien Febvre spoke of honour as a long-standing 'sentiment' and 'mot-force' that was still alive 'in our hearts'.[8]

What do we gain, then, by identifying honour, in line with historical accounts and self-descriptions, as a sentiment, an emotion, a passion? And what do we lose by distancing ourselves from long- and well-established sociological concepts and approaches?

First, by no means does taking some distance amount to a complete denial or refutation. What sociologists (and anthropologists) have written about the social operation and function of honour remains valid and noteworthy.[9] Simmel's point about honour as a 'social duty' that is internalized, subjectively appropriated and publicly endorsed is important and has to be kept in mind. Paying attention to the ways in which this internalization actually works, however, brings us closer to people's motivations and actions. We may understand more fully why someone behaved in a certain manner and what they intended by justifying their actions (or lack thereof) as honour-driven. Perceiving honour as an emotion gives credit to processes of identification and subjectivization often overlooked by social scientists. To incorporate them into our analysis is to assign agency to people, rather than viewing them solely as performing specific scripts, templates and roles.

When, for instance, nineteenth-century men explained the urge to defend their honour by referring to personal feelings and ideals of selfhood, they touched an emotional chord that cannot be easily factored into structural–functionalist analyses. Of course, they were acting as members of a social class and were shaped by their environment. But they were doing far more

---

[6] Rudolf Czernin, *Die Duellfrage* (Vienna: Gerolds Sohn, 1904), 3; William James, 'What Is an Emotion?' in *What Is an Emotion? Classic and Contemporary Readings*, ed. Robert C. Solomon, 2nd edn (New York: Oxford University Press, 2003), 66–76.

[7] Johann Georg Krünitz, *Ökonomisch-technologische Encyklopädie, oder allgemeines System der Staats-, Stadt-, Haus- und Landwirthschaft und der Kunstgeschichte*, vol. 75 (Berlin: Pauli, 1798), 92; ibid., vol. 188 (1846), 3.

[8] Lucien Febvre, *'Honneur et patrie': Une enquête sur le sentiment d'honneur et l'attachement à la patrie* (Paris: Perrin, 1996), 30–1. 'Honour' and 'fatherland' were rallying cries for both the Vichy regime and Charles de Gaulle's Free France movement.

[9] For anthropologists' work on, in particular, Mediterranean honour, see, e.g., John Kennedy Campbell, *Honour, Family and Patronage: A Study of Institutions and Moral Values in a Greek Mountain Community* (Oxford: Clarendon Press, 1964); Jean G. Peristiany, ed., *Honour and Shame: The Values of Mediterranean Society* (Chicago: University of Chicago Press, 1966); Julien Pitt-Rivers, *The Fate of Shechem: Or the Politics of Sex* (Cambridge: Cambridge University Press, 1977); David D. Gilmore, ed., *Honor and Shame and the Unity of the Mediterranean* (Washington: American Anthropological Association, No. 22, 1987).

than merely fulfilling their 'duty' and conforming to class rules: they regarded honour as their most private possession, their innermost sentiment, and went to great pains to include it in their profound sense of personal integrity and dignity. Disregarding or denying this emotional aspect would do an injustice to men like Max Weber who felt strongly about his own honour (as well as the honour of his feminist wife, Marianne).[10]

Reclaiming honour as an emotion certainly does not sever its ties to social norms and obligations. Emotions are more than spontaneous, subjective states; as relational practices, they form an integral part of social interactions that usually occur in well-defined settings and environments. A person might experience an emotion as an inner feeling accompanied by physiological changes. And yet, the state of feeling is itself highly contextualized and conditioned. People are generally quite good at distinguishing between feelings that resemble one another in terms of their physical manifestations. Shedding tears of sadness feels different from shedding tears of joy. We constantly relate our inner feelings to the outer world in a search for cause or referents, and thus evaluate them in a specific context. This kind of cognitive work cannot be separated from how emotions do what they do in real life. Both operations are closely linked and influence one another. Naming an emotion as such undoubtedly adds to the experience of feeling it. Denying or suppressing an emotion, on the other hand, dims its physiological presence, as Friedrich Nietzsche noted in the 1880s when he connected the linguistic or gestural manifestations of passion to the actual feeling. Stifling or holding in emotional language and gestures, he found, eventually stifled the passion itself.[11]

How emotions are felt and displayed is, above all, a social convention and artefact, not simply an expression of personal whims or allegedly authentic urges. Words bear meaning, and so do gestures and body language. From the earliest days of childhood, people learn them, just as they learn how to feel what under which circumstances.[12] The history of emotions is thus not about people's apparently spontaneous and clandestine affects, but about their socially framed and culturally embedded feelings and passions.[13] In this way and as a result, the history of emotions is (also) about honour.

---

[10] Ute Frevert, *Men of Honour: A Social and Cultural History of the Duel* (Cambridge: Polity Press, 1995), 4, 182: Joachim Radkau, *Max Weber: Die Leidenschaft des Denkens* (Munich: Hanser, 2005), 71–2, 633–7.
[11] Friedrich Nietzsche, *The Gay Science*, ed. Bernard Williams, trans. Josefine Nauckhoff (Cambridge: Cambridge University Press, 2001), 60.
[12] Ute Frevert et al., *Learning How to Feel: Children's Literature and Emotional Socialization, 1870–1970* (Oxford: Oxford University Press, 2014).
[13] See Chapter 1 in this volume.

Social and gender differences

Historians agree with Weber that early modern European societies were politically, socially and culturally structured as honour societies. Honour operated as a central category of social inclusion and exclusion. Each estate possessed its own honour, which was regulated and safeguarded from within. Urban merchants and artisans drafted specific honour codes for themselves, as did the landed gentry and the emerging class of civil servants. Guilds that governed economic (and much of political) life in European cities until around 1800 had clear ideas and rules about honourable behaviour and established harsh sanctions for those who violated them. A merchant who committed fraud would lose his honour and, along with it, his credit. A craftsman who married a woman deemed dishonourable would be made a social outcast, and prevented from pursuing his trade among fellow guildsmen. A nobleman who cheated at cards or did not pay back his gambling debt would ruin his own reputation.[14]

Although each estate bore honour, it was not equally distributed or valued. The honour of the aristocracy carried more weight than the honour of merchants or craftsmen. This reflected the social hierarchy of early modern societies: while the aristocracy was closest to the king as the centre (in Continental Europe, the monopolist) of power, other estates were more distant and thus possessed less honour. The gradation of honour was legally enshrined. In Prussia's *Allgemeines Landrecht* or General Law, issued in 1794, the aristocracy figured as the *Ehrenstand* (estate of honour) par excellence. Its honour was considered so important that any libel must be severely punished. Consequently, the law imposed harsh penalties on anyone who insulted or humiliated a nobleman. Among members of the bourgeoisie, insults only weighed half as much and were treated accordingly. Peasants and artisans could expect even more leniency when hurling insults among themselves. According to lawmakers, their sense of honour and related sensibilities were less developed than that of noblemen, military officers and high-ranking civil servants.[15]

It was not until the French Revolution – and, in Prussia, until 1848 – that the social hierarchy of honour was seriously questioned and ultimately abolished. Yet social differences survived formal legal equality. The

---

[14]Ronald G. Asch, '"Honour in All Parts of Europe Will Be Ever Like Itself": Ehre, adlige Standeskultur und Staatsbildung in England und Frankreich im späten 16. und im 17. Jahrhundert', in *Staatsbildung als kultureller Prozess*, ed. Ronald G. Asch and Dagmar Freist (Cologne: Böhlau, 2005), 353–79; Klaus Schreiner and Gerd Schwerhoff, eds, *Verletzte Ehre: Ehrkonflikte in Gesellschaften des Mittelalters und der Frühen Neuzeit* (Cologne: Böhlau, 1995); Sibylle Backmann, ed., *Ehrkonzepte in der Frühen Neuzeit: Identitäten und Abgrenzungen* (Berlin: Akademie-Verlag, 1998).
[15]Hans Hattenhauer, ed., *Allgemeines Landrecht für die Preußischen Staaten von 1794* (Neuwied: Luchterhand, 1996), §§ 607–36.

aristocracy, the wealthy bourgeoisie and the educated middle classes all preserved (or acquired) rules of honourable conduct that were not shared by lower strata. Even if the newly institutionalized civic form of honour pertained to all citizens, class still structured feelings and practices of honour.

Honour was not just socially diverse and unequal. Within each class or estate, there were substantial gender differences too. Women's honour was categorically and substantially different from men's, even though the difference was never legally codified. Rather, it was common knowledge and convention that women were not just appraised according to the general standards set by their social status and line of descent, but also had to comply with norms and regulations connected to their gender identity. These norms were particularly strict for members of the ascending bourgeoisie. While noblemen and noblewomen had long been notorious for having rather loose sexual morals, the concept of sexual purity and chastity carried extraordinary weight among the middle classes.[16] The daughters of teachers, professionals, entrepreneurs and merchants were raised to behave decently and modestly. 'Familiarizing' with the other sex was monitored and frowned upon to ensure that 'reserve, modesty and shamefacedness' were maintained, while blushing and lowering the eyes were applauded as appropriate gestures of genuine feminine shame.[17] Women's honour was thus intimately linked to the feeling and expression of shame, even in the absence of actual reasons to be ashamed.

As was typical for the nineteenth century, nature was used to justify the gendered notion of honour. Nature had supposedly based the 'complete moral existence of women on modesty and chastity, while men's morality depends on courage and strength'. A 'fallen woman' was judged as bereft of honour as a man too faint-hearted to fight in a duel.[18] Carl Welcker, a progressive liberal professor and politician, echoed this in 1838 when he wrote: 'A woman whose shamefacedness and chastity is being violated, and a man who displays unmanly cowardice both lose honour and respect'.[19] Six decades later, the Prussian general Albert von Boguslawski revived those 'natural' links when he defined 'physical and moral courage' as the essence of male honour and 'purity of body and soul' as the basis for female honour.[20]

---

[16]See, for further explanation, Ute Frevert, *'Mann und Weib, und Weib und Mann': Geschlechter-Differenzen in der Moderne* (Munich: C.H. Beck, 1995), 202–12.
[17]Joachim Heinrich Campe, ed., *Wörterbuch der Deutschen Sprache*, vol. 5 (Braunschweig: Schulbuchhandlung, 1811), 390.
[18]Friedrich August Ferdinand von Greveniz, *Unterricht zur Kenntniß der vorzüglichsten und wichtigsten Abweichungen der gesetzlichen Vorschriften des Code Napoleon von den in den neuerlich abgetretenen preußischen Provinzen sowohl den deutschen, als polnischen, bisher gültig gewesenen* (Leipzig: Gräff, 1808), 66, 90.
[19]Carl Welcker, 'Geschlechtsverhältnisse', in *Staats-Lexikon*, ed. Carl von Rotteck and Carl Welcker, vol. 6 (Altona: Hammerich, 1838), 629–65, here 641.
[20]Albert von Boguslawski, *Die Ehre und das Duell* (Berlin: Schall & Grund, 1897), 2.

Honour and violence

Such definitions hint at the interrelation of male honour and physical prowess. This connection has been demonstrated in many historical contexts, and it also appeared in nineteenth-century classifications. Being a coward was above all synonymous with shying away from conflicts that demanded a public display of personal steadfastness. Avoiding a fight nearly always raised doubts about a man's courage and vigour. Male youth cultures provided (and continue to provide) perfect opportunities to observe in detail the intimate relationship between bodily engagement and social recognition.

Conflicts among adolescents and young men generally erupted over personal slights. Slights (or what were perceived as such) could occur in multiple forms: as a lack of attention or ritualized respect, as a verbal assault on someone's self-image or social rank/status or as a physical attack that violated a person's corporal integrity. Insulting a man in public meant humiliating him in front of his (imagined) peers. While slights that happened behind closed doors could be ignored, negotiated or apologized away, insults slung in public demanded a formal reaction. If this reaction failed to materialize, the offended party had to bear the consequences: he was, more often than not, sanctioned by his peers, who might look down on him or even exclude him from the group. As a general rule, men were supposed to stand their ground and defend themselves against any attacks that called their personal and social integrity into question. While former generations called this integrity 'honour', contemporary youth cultures know it as 'respect'.[21]

Violence in various shapes was part and parcel of male honour codes. Slights could take the form of violent physical assaults which had to be paid back in the other's own coin; failing to actively respond to a slap or a beating was practically inconceivable. Violence had to be met with violence. Further, a violent reaction reaffirmed the offended man's physical strength, determination and moral courage. Choosing to refrain from violence would raise serious doubts about his willingness and ability to defend his right to be treated respectfully and honourably. Honour thus provided a language that helped to make sense of, and confront, conflicts of self-affirmation.

---

[21]On the ritualized honour codes in contemporary youth cultures in Western and non-Western societies, see William Labov, *Language in the Inner City: Studies in the Black English Vernacular* (Philadelphia: University of Pennsylvania Press, 1972), ch. 8 ('Rules for Ritual Insults'); Roger D. Abrahams, 'Black Talking on the Streets', in *Explorations in the Ethnography of Speaking*, ed. Richard Bauman and Joel Sherzer (London: Cambridge University Press, 1974), 240–62; Alan Dundes, Jerry W. Leach and Bora Özkök, 'The Strategy of Turkish Boys' Verbal Dueling Rhymes', *Journal of American Folklore* 83, no. 329 (1970): 325–49; Hermann Tertilt, *Turkish Power Boys: Ethnographie einer Jugendbande* (Frankfurt: Suhrkamp, 1996); Ahmet Toprak and Aladin El-Mafaalani, 'Eine Frage der Männlichkeit: Duelle bei muslimischen Jugendlichen in Deutschland', in *Das Duell: Ehrenkämpfe vom Mittelalter bis zur Moderne*, ed. Ulrike Ludwig, Barbara Krug-Richter and Gerd Schwerhoff (Konstanz: UVK, 2012), 49–59.

How this played out in different historical contexts has been the subject of sustained research in recent years. Historians, sociologists and anthropologists have produced a wealth of knowledge about male youth cultures and how they have dealt with questions of honour and violence. In early modern Europe, three groups stood out as prime actors in this contested field: aristocrats, students and journeymen. Each group made specific honour claims: whereas noblemen felt entitled to the highest honour available in a monarchically governed society, students (who often came from noble families) saw their university years as a rite of passage with special rules of conduct, as well as special liberties and duties. Journeymen found themselves in a similar state of transition, which they explored through various means of asserting themselves and clashing with one another (and with competitors, like students or soldiers). Time and again, young peasants or rural labourers also challenged one another, as well as adjoining groups, to fights and brawls.[22]

Early modern legislation and court cases provide ample evidence as to the frequency of such encounters. In 1660, Hamburg's municipal government strongly condemned the surge of so-called duels among 'common people' who acted 'ad exemplum' of superior ranks. Urban artisans, journeymen and peddlers offended one another and engaged in deadly fights, just like noblemen. Concerned local authorities were determined to stop the proliferation of violence among commoners. Even though they had no power to do anything about lower-class men fighting with fists or sticks, they eventually succeeded in prohibiting the use of lethal weapons like swords and, later, pistols.

State interventions among the nobility were limited, however. The right to bear arms could not be revoked, as it was linked to the nobility's traditional role as the ultimate defender of the state's 'external grandeur' and 'internal condition', to quote the Prussian General Law of 1794. That estate had to be treated with deference and respect. Although its political autonomy had long since been lost to absolutist power, its social autonomy was to be preserved. Even if the princely state did not forgo its right to ban and punish private killings among citizens, it proceeded with caution whenever

---

[22]Scott K. Taylor, *Honor and Violence in Golden Age Spain* (New Haven: Yale University Press, 2008); Maren Lorenz, *Das Rad der Gewalt: Militär und Zivilbevölkerung in Norddeutschland nach dem Dreißigjährigen Krieg (1650–1700)* (Cologne: Böhlau, 2007), esp. chs 2 and 4; Marian Füssel, 'Devianz als Norm? Studentische Gewalt und akademische Freiheit in Köln im 17. und 18. Jahrhundert', *Westfälische Forschungen* 54 (2004): 145–66; Stefan Brüdermann, *Göttinger Studenten und akademische Gerichtsbarkeit im 18. Jahrhundert* (Göttingen: Vandenhoeck & Ruprecht, 1990), esp. 169–213; Barbara Krug-Richter, '"Ein stund erennenn unnd im ein schlacht lieffern": Anmerkungen zum Duell in der studentischen Kultur', in *Duell*, ed. Ludwig et al., 275–87; Katharina Simon-Muscheid, 'Gewalt und Ehre im spätmittelalterlichen Handwerk am Beispiel Basels', *Zeitschrift für historische Forschung* 18, no. 1 (1991): 1–31; Andreas Meier, 'Handwerkerduelle im frühneuzeitlichen Kursachsen als (außer)gewöhnliche Gewaltrituale', in *Duell*, ed. Ludwig et al., 289–99.

noblemen were involved. Notwithstanding the fact that duels – defined as deadly fights of honour among aristocrats – were legally banned, duellists could expect leniency. As long as no one was killed, the authorities turned a blind eye. Should the outcome be fatal, the surviving party was given a mild sentence and pardoned soon after.[23]

Fighting for honour: the modern duel

These practices prevailed throughout the long nineteenth century. Even though the law was rewritten and adapted to the new principle of legal equality, it retained a special privilege for so-called 'crimes of honour'. This reflected both the respect that matters of honour enjoyed among lawmakers and the political influence of those social strata whose honour was at stake. For members of the aristocracy and military officers, honour continued to be of major importance; it was a deeply felt commitment. They passionately defended the duel as a crucial means of safeguarding their honour and upholding decent behaviour. They also pointed to the civilizing efforts they themselves had undertaken to extricate the duel from its somewhat murky traditions and customs.

This was a significant point. While early modern duels had often involved crude and unmitigated violence, the modern duel, as it developed in Europe from the late eighteenth century on, discarded its former brutishness.[24] It was now defined and framed by rules of conduct which were carefully monitored by third parties. These rules had to be established and agreed upon by both participants in advance. This meant that duels would not take place directly after a slight; arranging them required a few days. The time that elapsed in the interim had the effect of abating emotions and allowing disciplined, restrained behaviour on the duelling site. Furthermore, the

---

[23]Frevert, *Men of Honour*, ch. 2.
[24]Although this chapter primarily uses German sources to examine the duel as an affair of honour, the underlying patterns are similar throughout Europe, from Spain to Russia, the United Kingdom to Italy. See, for further reference, Pascal Brioist, Hervé Drévillon and Pierre Serna, *Croiser le fer: Violence et culture de l'épée dans la France moderne (XVIe–XVIIIe siècle)* (Paris: Champ Vallon, 2002); Jennifer A. Low, *Manhood and the Duel: Masculinity in Early Modern Drama and Culture* (New York: Palgrave Macmillan, 2003); Irina Reyfman, *Ritualized Violence Russian Style: The Duel in Russian Culture and Literature* (Stanford: Stanford University Press, 1999); Uwe Israel and Gherardo Ortalli, eds, *Il duello fra medioevo ed età moderna* (Rome: Viella, 2009); Steven C. Hughes, *Politics of the Sword: Dueling, Honor, and Masculinity in Modern Italy* (Columbus: Ohio State University Press, 2007); Markku Peltonen, *The Duel in Early Modern England: Civility, Politeness and Honour* (Cambridge: Cambridge University Press, 2003); Robert B. Shoemaker, 'The Taming of the Duel: Masculinity, Honour, and Ritual Violence in London, 1660–1800', *Historical Journal* 45, no. 3 (2002): 525–45; James Kelly, *'That Damn'd Thing Called Honour': Duelling in Ireland, 1570–1860* (Cork: Cork University Press, 1995); Taylor, *Honor*.

presence of witnesses (seconds) guaranteed that a duel would not get out of hand and become uncontrollably violent.

Violence was thus tamed in the modern, rule-abiding duel, with the consensus of all participants. Nobody was officially forced to issue or accept a challenge (although there were, especially in the military, group expectations to do so under particular circumstances). If one decided to fight a duel, he consented to the conditions that had been negotiated by friends and seconds. Both participants knew and followed the rules because they guaranteed equal treatment in terms of weapons, chances and risks. Nobody was unduly privileged, and nobody could be taken by surprise. This distinguished the duel from the infamous *rencontres* that were amply documented throughout the early modern period. Moreover, it differentiated it from premeditated murder or homicide, which was structured as a one-sided act of violence against which the other party could not defend themselves.

The civilization of the duel into a tamed and consented-to exercise of violence was precisely what ensured its continuation throughout the nineteenth and early twentieth centuries. By refining its procedures and attuning them to principles of equality and personal autonomy, it gained acceptance even among men who otherwise would have cast a critical eye on anything that stemmed from traditional noble society. Accordingly, liberals praised the duel as the 'brightest side of our modern culture', one which both reflected 'moral freedom' and served as a 'powerful bulwark against despotism and the disgraceful reign of materialism and vulgarity'.[25]

Just as early liberals applauded the principle of 'moral freedom' that they saw institutionalized in the contemporary practice of duelling, they cherished the principle of equality that rested on shared qualifications and merits. Once the duel was extended to the aspiring middle classes and no longer monopolized by noblemen, it could act as a cultural and social bridge between old and new elites. Instead of distinguishing aristocrats, it became a mechanism of social integration and cohesion.

Starting in the late eighteenth century, claims to 'popularize the duel in all classes' (effectively meaning the educated ones) abounded in literary as well as in legal genres. In 1819, the writer Ludwig Robert published a 'bourgeois tragedy' in which he strongly criticized the nobility's pretence to a special honour that should not be shared with anybody else. In Robert's play, the young author Weiß, son of a clergyman, reprimands a noble officer who makes advances to his young sister without serious intentions. The officer slaps Weiß in the face, whereupon Weiß proffers a challenge. Not surprisingly, the officer refuses to duel because he does not consider Weiß an equal opponent. Weiß then shoots him and considers himself 'a martyr of

---

[25] Carl Welcker, 'Infamie, Ehre, Ehrenstrafen', in *Staats-Lexikon*, ed. Rotteck and Welcker, vol. 7 (1847), 377–404.

honour': an honour that has been denied to him but that belongs, as he sees it, to all people regardless of social class or family origin.[26]

The true story behind the play further illustrates the duel's social demarcations. In 1811 in Berlin, the young Jewish landowner and librarian Moritz Itzig wrote a letter to Achim von Arnim, the Romantic Christian author, who had behaved impolitely when attending a salon hosted by Itzig's aunt Sara Levy. Itzig felt his aunt's honour had been insulted and demanded Arnim 'answer for his behaviour'. When Arnim responded with 'sarcastic derision', Itzig issued a challenge. Arnim wrote back rejecting the duel and enclosing a list of signatures from his aristocratic friends, all of whom agreed that a nobleman could not be forced to duel with a Jew. Itzig's swift reaction arrived in a third letter: if Arnim 'refused the sword' in such an 'ignoble and cowardly' manner, he was to expect 'the blow of the club'. Arnim did not take the threat seriously, but Itzig did. One evening, he attacked Arnim in public, calling him a 'dishonourable coward'. Under normal circumstances, both the physical and verbal slight would have done the trick, forcing Arnim to challenge Itzig to the duel that the latter so passionately desired. But Arnim once again refused, and instead took the matter to the courts.[27]

This incident can be read as a clear case of antisemitism (which it undoubtedly was). It can also be seen as proof of noble pretensions against non-nobles. Arnim and his friends were trying desperately, but in vain, to preserve the duel exclusively for the nobility. Middle-class men were gradually warming to the practice, to which they had been introduced while studying at university. This was how Moritz Itzig became familiar with duelling, like thousands of sons of teachers, clergymen, doctors and businessmen who earned academic degrees. Students cultivated noble passions like duelling as part of their social identity. As the student body was increasingly dominated by young men from educated middle-class families, the habit survived and was incorporated as an important practice in academic culture. Aside from the military (whose officers around 1800 were exclusively of noble descent), universities thus figured as the main 'schools' of duelling and were responsible for its rapid 'embourgeoisement' during the nineteenth century.[28]

Universities offered a meeting place for young men and initiated them into a lifestyle substantially different from the one they had known at home. Joining a student association allowed them to find a new 'family' that helped them to adjust to the challenges and insecurities of academic life. An effective way to feel secure and settled was to subscribe to the corporate code of

---

[26]Ludwig Robert, *Die Macht der Verhältnisse: Ein Trauerspiel* (Stuttgart: Cotta, 1819). The play was first staged in 1815.
[27]Deborah Hertz, *Jewish High Society in Old Regime Berlin* (New Haven: Yale University Press, 1988), 258–9; Deborah Hertz, 'Dueling for Emancipation: Jewish Masculinity in the Era of Napoleon', in *Jüdische Welten: Juden in Deutschland vom 18. Jahrhundert bis in die Gegenwart*, ed. Marion Kaplan and Beate Meyer (Göttingen: Wallstein, 2005), 69–85.
[28]Frevert, *Men of Honour*, chs 3 and 4.

honour that those associations had drafted. The young man who embraced the code as his own felt both sheltered and adept. He was protected by academic culture, and at the same time he was exposed to the many threats generated by it. As members of elite clubs, regional societies and liberal fraternities, students were advised to be sensitive to slights and insults. Once they occurred, they had to be answered resolutely: by seeking redress and 'satisfaction'. Duels were accordingly arranged on a daily basis, much to the dismay of university authorities, who feared for peace and social order.

Yet, many professors had themselves participated in duelling as students and remembered it as a positive experience. Duels were supposed to cultivate strong male characters who would not shy away from moral, political or physical danger. For future academics who would spend their lives reading, writing and debating, such an education was particularly crucial. After all, civil society depended on 'the whole man' who was capable of connecting heart and mind, body and soul.[29] To quote Thomas Mann's hero from *The Magic Mountain*, the liberal philosopher Settembrini:

> Whoever is unable to offer his person, his arm, his blood, in the service of the ideal, is unworthy of it; however intellectualized, it is the duty of a man to remain a man.[30]

Honour and masculinity

By the time Settembrini and Naphta negotiated their duel (over a disagreement on a 'matter of abstractions'), they were no longer young men insecure about their identities or status. Indeed, most duels that came to the attention of authorities during the nineteenth and early twentieth centuries were fought by adults who earned their livelihoods as civil servants, doctors, merchants, entrepreneurs or attorneys. There was no generational need for them to prove their manly courage, steadfastness and strength. Nevertheless, they found it important to stand tall as men of honour. Mann's quote provides a crucial hint as to why: in order to 'remain a man'. Being and remaining a man in those days and social circles obviously meant displaying exactly the kind of masculine character traits that young men had to acquire when they came of age. These traits were never taken for granted; they had to be put to the test time and time again. What had been learned during adolescence had to be practised during adulthood, albeit in a more refined and restrained

---

[29]See, with a slightly different focus, Martina Kessel, 'The "Whole Man": The Longing for a Masculine World in Nineteenth-Century Germany', *Gender & History* 15, no 1. (2003): 1–31.
[30]Thomas Mann, *The Magic Mountain*, trans. Helen Tracy Lowe-Porter (London: Penguin, 1960), 699. First published in 1924, the novel's setting encompassed the late nineteenth century up until the First World War.

manner. While young men were taught to take any slight to their honour seriously, older men could and should be more forgiving. People who were known for being short-tempered and quick to challenge others were not coveted by civil or civilized society. When men in their thirties and forties demanded satisfaction from other men in the form of a duel, they had to give robust justification as to why such violence was necessary.

Among those reasons, three figured most prominently and convincingly. One was provided by the 41-year-old liberal politician Georg von Vincke when he confronted conservative Prussian diplomat Otto von Bismarck (who would later become the Prussian and German chancellor) in 1852. Vincke challenged the 37-year-old Bismarck because the latter had publicly criticized him for making statements that lacked the 'usual discretion a gentleman should observe'. Vincke took this personally, considering it an offensive slur. Casting doubt on his gentlemanly education and virtues – good manners, honesty and sincerity – was synonymous with questioning his honour. A duel was therefore necessary in order to reaffirm it.[31]

When Ferdinand Lassalle, the 39-year-old Jewish lawyer and founder of Germany's first social-democratic party, challenged the father of his beloved Helene von Dönniges in 1864, he was driven by a different motive. Helene's father had made it very clear that Ferdinand was not the son-in-law he desired, being neither an aristocrat nor a Christian. Lassalle interpreted this as a major insult that he was determined to wash away with blood. The duel to which Wilhelm von Dönniges consented would establish their basic social equality. Unfortunately for Lassalle (and for the future development of the German labour movement), this equality was to be paid for with his own blood.[32]

While Vincke's case highlights honour as a matter of social upbringing and personal virtue, Lassalle's story concerns honour as a contested bridge between social elites and different religions. The duel that Adolf von Bennigsen fought in 1902 reveals a third logic that drew widespread public recognition and appraisal. The 41-year-old head of the district authority of Springe (close to Hanover) had learned of rumours that his 30-year-old spouse Elisabeth was entertaining intimate relations with the 27-year-old tenant of their domain, Oswald Falkenhagen. Falkenhagen had been a neighbour and close family friend; his breach of trust was, therefore, a particularly grave betrayal. Bennigsen challenged him to a duel that left the deceived husband mortally wounded. He passed away a day later, whereupon Falkenhagen

---

[31] *Fürst Bismarcks Briefe an seine Braut und Gattin*, ed. Herbert Bismarck (Stuttgart: Cotta, 1906), 328.
[32] Ina Britschgi-Schimmer, ed., *Lassalles letzte Tage* (Berlin: Juncker, 1925). Although he accepted the challenge, the 50-year-old Bavarian diplomat Wilhelm von Dönniges asked his future son-in-law, the Romanian aristocrat Janko von Racowicza, to step in and fight the duel in his place.

was sentenced to six years in prison – quite an extraordinary punishment in a juridical context that tended to treat duellists mildly.[33]

The kind of honour at stake here was thoroughly and vigorously discussed in public discourse. Even men who officially denounced duelling and joined associations that campaigned against it generally allowed for exceptions in cases like Bennigsen's. Although few duels in fact stemmed from such cases, they dominated people's imaginations. Almost archetypically, they brought to the fore a widely held belief in 'decent' nineteenth-century society: that male honour depended on controlling a wife's (or daughter's, or sister's) sexuality. If this failed, the controller's honour was lost at the hands of the man who had approached a woman in an inappropriate manner. There was only one way to regain honour: by challenging the perpetrator to a duel.

Affairs of honour, as duels were usually called, were affairs among men only. They were explicitly about male honour, not about female honour – even though some people argued that men fought on behalf of women and out of chivalry. Adolf von Bennigsen did not confront his wife after learning of her infidelity. He challenged her lover instead. The adulterer was thought to be the one responsible: he had betrayed Bennigsen's trust and friendship by seducing his wife. Elisabeth was not considered the main culprit (although she had to bear the consequences too: following her husband's death, she was separated from her five children and forced to leave the family home). According to public opinion, she was a 'fallen woman' who had lost her honour and brought shame upon herself by being unfaithful to her husband. His honour, though, was impaired not by what she had done to him but by her lover's audacity in intruding into what the Prussian minister of war called, in 1914, 'the peace of his home'. As the minister's colleague in the Department of Justice had argued previously, adultery not only humiliated a husband but also challenged his masculinity and ability to fight for his honour.[34]

Crimes of honour, crimes of passion

A minister of justice openly legitimizing duels that the law considered criminal acts might have posed a problem. Indeed, there were contemporary critics who saw it this way. At the same time, the law and legal practice were not without ambiguity. When a duellist appeared in court – which happened rarely, and only in lethal cases – the judge usually recognized attenuating circumstances and issued a mild sentence (which was further reduced by the monarch's pardon). The law and its practitioners (who, due to their social status and academic education, belonged to those very strata who could give satisfaction for an offence against honour) understood intimately

---

[33]Frevert, *Mann und Weib*, 180–1.
[34]Ibid., 214.

the duellist's motives and condoned them. They stated repeatedly that a death in a duel was nothing like murder or manslaughter. Even if duels were technically outlawed, they should not be confused with acts of homicide or, for that matter, other 'crimes of passion', as they were conveniently called.

Phenomenologically, the argument was correct. The duel, as the archetypical crime of honour in European societies, fundamentally differed from crimes of passion committed by men who felt deceived and humiliated by a woman and lashed out against her (and her lover). Duels were equal fights between two men who sought to safeguard their honour. It was not revenge that drove them to seek redress by exchanging blows or shots. Nor did the outcome matter; wounding or killing the opponent was not what the duel was ultimately about. As much as violence proved a man's determination to defend his honour with his own life, physical harm was neither the *movens* nor the final goal. Duels rarely ended fatally – and were not supposed to.[35]

Crimes of passion, in contrast, were meant to inflict wounds, pain and, more often than not, death. They usually occurred between sexual partners and/or spouses, and they were all about men's rage and frustration at women's failure to comply with expectations of fidelity, respect and love. When legal codifications referred to 'affects' or 'passions' as motives for criminal action, they were describing one situation in particular: a husband finding his wife in bed with another man and, in a fit of fury and jealousy, killing the man and/or the wife on the spot. Out of his rational mind and overcome with passion, the cuckolded husband resorted to violence in an act of revenge and punishment.[36]

In this vein, the French Penal Code of 1810 found wilful homicide 'excusable' in the case of adultery: 'Murder committed upon the wife as well as upon her accomplice, at the moment when the husband shall have caught them in the fact, in the house where the husband and wife dwell, is excusable.' In such cases, the death penalty 'shall be reduced to an imprisonment, of from one year to five years'.[37] This echoed ancient Roman law. Under the auspices of absolute paternal power, a Roman father could kill his daughter's violator and the daughter herself without being punished for his actions. It was chiefly a question of property: a daughter belonged to her father's household, and her abuser was perceived as a thief who had broken in and stolen her virginity. The same logic applied to the husband of an adulterous wife, though not to the wife of an adulterous husband.

---

[35]Frevert, *Men of Honour*, 150–71.
[36]Adrian Howe, *Sex, Violence and Crime: Foucault and the 'Man' Question* (New York: Routledge-Cavendish, 2008); Cynthia Lee, *Murder and the Reasonable Man: Passion and Fear in the Criminal Courtroom* (New York: New York University Press, 2003).
[37]*French Penal Code of 1810*, https://www.napoleon-series.org/research/government/france/penalcode/c_penalcode3b.html (accessed 28 October 2022); Patricia Mainardi, *Husbands, Wives, and Lovers: Marriage and its Discontents in Nineteenth-Century France* (New Haven: Yale University Press, 2003), 24.

When French legislators considered a wife's infidelity a valid excuse for killing her and/or the lover, they revived the Roman tradition without, however, letting the death go unpunished. It was still called a crime, albeit one committed under extenuating circumstances. Just what those circumstances might be, and whether they were driven by notions of honour or by undiluted passion, was not elaborated any further.

English law was more explicit. Faced with the question of whether a perpetrator had had no or only limited control over his actions, courts attempted to establish the subjective degree of his rage. Since the eighteenth century, rage was increasingly qualified and quantified by introducing the concept of the 'reasonable man' and measuring the adequacy of a provocation. As case law taught, insulting words or the sight of an unfaithful fiancée were not sufficient to provoke manslaughter. Physical assault and witnessing adultery were, however, as confirmed in 1707: 'Jealousy is the rage of man and adultery is the highest invasion of property.'[38]

One and a half centuries later, that line was repeatedly quoted by Daniel Sickles's lawyers during the trial against their client. Sickles, a New York congressman, had shot and killed District Attorney Philip Barton Key after learning of the latter's ongoing affair with his wife. Lawyer James Brady convinced the jury to acquit Sickles by arguing that he had only 'yielded to an instinct which the Almighty has implanted in every animal or creature that crawls the earth'. No man who found before him 'in full view, the adulterer of his wife', could be asked to be 'cool and collected'; 'jealousy will be the rage of that man, and he will not spare in the day of vengeance'.[39]

Sickles had killed Key shortly after learning of his wife's infidelity. It could thus be argued that he had acted 'in the heat of passion', which granted him leniency. This became known as an 'unwritten law' in US jurisprudence. Francis Wharton, one of the country's leading legal commentators, explained in 1855 that 'a man smarting under a sense of dishonor' (by finding 'another in the act of adultery with his wife') and killing the adulterer 'in the first transport of passion' was guilty only of manslaughter and 'entitled to the lowest degree of punishment'. Dishonouring acts such as adultery were thus considered 'grievous' provocations to which a husband might 'instinctively' react in a passionate and vengeful way.[40]

---

[38]Susan S.M. Edwards, 'Anger and Fear as Justifiable Preludes for Loss of Self-Control', *Journal of Criminal Law* 74, no. 3 (2010): 223–41, here 230; Joshua Dressler, 'Rethinking Heat of Passion: A Defense in Search of a Rationale', *Journal of Criminal Law and Criminology* 73, no. 2 (1982): 421–70, here 426–8. The following elaboration on Anglo-Saxon legal practices draws on my article 'Honour and/or as Passion: Historical Trajectories of Legal Defenses', *Rechtsgeschichte/Legal History* 22 (2014): 245–55.

[39]Dawn Keetley, 'From Anger to Jealousy: Explaining Domestic Homicide in Antebellum America', *Journal of Social History* 42, no. 2 (2008): 269–97, here 285.

[40]Francis Wharton, *A Treatise on the Law of Homicide in the United States* (Philadelphia: Kay, 1855), 33, 177.

'Honour defences' of this sort usually found a favourable reception. Juries, composed of 'average laymen', were sympathetic to the claim made in 1907 that 'every man who has a family' knew exactly which feelings would be aroused by an adulterous wife and the man who 'invades the sanctity' of his home. To the 'legalistic mind', however, as a 1934 article in the *Yale Law Journal* claimed, the recognition of honour motives condoned extra-legal justice and 'encourages a general disregard for all law'.[41]

The rift between public opinion and 'all law' became particularly obvious in 'honour killings' (as the *Journal* called them) that occurred after 'the first transport of passion'. On 25 June 1906, at 11 p.m., 35-year-old Harry Kendall Thaw, son and heir of a Pittsburgh coal and railway baron, shot and killed Stanford White, a well-known New York architect, in the rooftop theatre of Madison Square Garden. In his case, the heat-of-passion defence did not apply. Instead, Thaw's lawyer tried to present the murder as a crime of honour. His client's honour, he argued, had been insulted when he learned about the architect's disdainful treatment of the woman who would later become Thaw's wife. In his closing statement, the defence lawyer somewhat ironically claimed that Thaw had been motivated by a

> species of insanity which, if you desire to give it a name, I will ask you to label it *dementia Americana*. It is that species of insanity which makes every home sacred. It is that species of insanity which makes a man believe that the honour of his wife is sacred; it is that species of insanity which makes him believe that whoever invades the sanctity of that home, whoever brings pollution upon that daughter, whoever stains the virtue of that wife, has forfeited the protection of human laws and must look to the eternal justice and mercy of God.[42]

The lawyer's plea was noteworthy for two reasons: first, by translating the legal concept of insanity into the language of honour he described the killing as an act of chivalry. Second, he deliberately blurred the distinction between adultery ('staining the virtue of a wife') and treating a single, unmarried woman with disrespect. Both tactics extended the notion of male honour to encompass moral concerns that went beyond narrow property rights ('invading the sanctity of the home').

In legal terms, the defence held no water. The jury, although generally sympathetic to honour defences, was hung. What stood in the way of granting Thaw a mild sentence was the length of time between finding out about his wife's liaison and carrying out the attack on White. Experts

---

[41] 'Recognition of the Honor Defense under the Insanity Plea', *Yale Law Journal* 43, no. 5 (1934): 809–14, here 814; Martha Merrill Umphrey, 'The Dialogics of Legal Meaning: Spectacular Trials, the Unwritten Law, and Narratives of Criminal Responsibility', *Law & Society Review* 33, no. 2 (1999): 393–423, here 417.

[42] *New York Times*, 10 April 1907; Umphrey, 'Dialogics', 417.

framed this as a 'cooling period', which allowed 'immediate passion' to be succeeded by 'sober reflection'. 'However great the provocation may have been', homicide committed after a 'cooling time' was murder and would be punished accordingly.[43]

But did slandered honour know 'cooling periods'? Was the insult perceived and felt with decreased intensity after a day or two had passed? This was the question that Thaw's lawyer had shrewdly asked and answered in the negative. It was also one of the questions that continued to haunt 'legalistic minds' when, time and again, they tried to make criminal justice less 'inchoate' and 'distorted'.[44] Criticism was voiced not only by psychologists and psychiatrists, whose expertise was increasingly sought from the late eighteenth century onwards.[45] In the 1970s, feminists launched a major attack on the discriminatory bias of the heat-of-passion doctrine. In their view, it privileged male behavioural patterns while putting women at a disadvantage: battered wives, who after a long period of suffering killed their abusive husbands, could not make use of the doctrine's extenuating circumstances.[46]

This criticism notwithstanding, the heat-of-passion doctrine is still recognized in the US.[47] In Britain, it was limited to explicitly exclude what, for a long time, had been its major justification: adultery. In 2000, Leonard Hoffmann, Lord of Appeal in Ordinary and Life Peer of the House of Lords, opined that 'male possessiveness and jealousy should not today be an acceptable reason for loss of self-control leading to homicide, whether inflicted on the woman herself or on her new lover'. In 2003, the Law Commission followed his recommendation, and the 2009 Coroners and Justice Act ruled out sexual infidelity as a qualifying trigger.[48]

A similar development had unfolded in West Germany some thirty years earlier. Since the 1970s, courts had become increasingly reluctant to classify adultery as a grave insult that could produce a fit of fury and justify

---

[43]'Recognition', 810; Wharton, *Treatise*, 179.

[44]'Recognition', 810, 813; Dressler, 'Rethinking'.

[45]Ernst Ferdinand Klein, *Grundsätze des gemeinen deutschen peinlichen Rechts nebst Bemerkung der preussischen Gesetze* (Halle: Hemmerde & Schwetschke, 1799), 28; C.A. Diez, 'Ueber die praktische Anwendung der psychologischen Untersuchungen über die Zurechnungsfähigkeit bei Verbrechen', *Archiv für Psychologie, für Ärzte und Juristen* 1, no. 1 (1834): 30–73; Johannes B. Friedreich, *Systematisches Handbuch der gerichtlichen Psychologie für Medicinalbeamte, Richter und Vertheidiger* (Leipzig: Wigand, 1835); Recognition, 814.

[46]Melissa Spatz, 'A "Lesser Crime": A Comparative Study of Legal Defenses for Men Who Kill Their Wives', *Columbia Journal of Law and Social Problems* 24, no. 4 (1991): 597–638; Edwards, Anger.

[47]Reid Griffith Fontaine, 'The Wrongfulness of Wrongly Interpreting Wrongfulness: Provocation, Interpretational Bias, and Heat of Passion Homicide', *New Criminal Law Review* 12, no. 1 (2009): 69–92, here 72.

[48]Edwards, Anger, 230; Kate Fitz-Gibbon, 'Replacing Provocation in England and Wales: Examining the Partial Defence of Loss of Control', *Journal of Law and Society* 40, no. 2 (2013): 280–305.

homicide.⁴⁹ In part, they reacted, as in the US, to feminist criticism of the highly gendered model of spontaneous affect. Changing attitudes towards marriage and gender equality in society at large also influenced the law and legal practice.

In the 1840s, in total alignment with contemporary opinion, Prussian lawyers had boldly stated that a wife's infidelity was far more harmful to the family than a husband's and should therefore be punished more harshly.⁵⁰ Implicitly, they also excused a husband whose rage over his wife's adultery had driven him to kill the other man (and the wife). Prussian and, after 1871, German law accepted 'just' (*gerecht*) affect as an extenuating circumstance in cases of homicide. If a person killed someone after having been unjustifiably (*ohne eigene Schuld*) provoked into a rage by the other's 'abuse' or 'grave insult', he would be sentenced mildly: instead of receiving a life sentence, he would escape with just two years in prison. While the law did not specify what constituted abuse or grave insult, legal commentaries explained that it included emotional as well as physical abuse. They also clarified that adultery figured 'notably' among the former as 'deeply hurting' the husband's 'sense of honour'.⁵¹

Fury as 'just affect' could thus be aroused by a man feeling that his honour had been attacked and violated. In this vein, a crime of passion was ultimately linked to an issue of honour. Still, this was not set in stone and it was ultimately contested by liberal opinion. In 1902, a regional appeal court denied that adultery alone could be considered an offence against the husband. Although it destroyed the fiduciary relationship between husband and wife, this was not sufficient to qualify the act as a personal insult. Only if the other man had treated the husband with disrespect and contempt could the latter feel offended – and sue him in private claims rather than getting physical.⁵²

---

⁴⁹Silvia Tellenbach, 'Rechtsvergleichende Zusammenfassung', in *Die Rolle der Ehre im Strafrecht*, ed. Silvia Tellenbach (Berlin: Duncker & Humblot, 2008), 723–808, here 787. A commentary from the 1960s still listed adultery as a prominent (in fact, the only) example of insult: Eduard Kohlrausch and Richard Lange, *Strafgesetzbuch mit Erläuterungen und Nebengesetzen*, 43rd edn (Berlin: De Gruyter, 1961), 480. Anette Grünewald, *Das vorsätzliche Tötungsdelikt* (Tübingen: Mohr Siebeck, 2010), 243, quotes the 1962 draft of a revision of the Penal Code that explicitly mentioned adultery as an extenuating circumstance and referred to 'frequent' cases that it deemed 'tragic'. For criticism, see ibid., 340–1.
⁵⁰Werner Schubert, ed., *Gesetzrevision (1825–1848)*, sec. 1, vol. 5 (Vaduz: Topos, 1994), 135.
⁵¹Georg Beseler, *Kommentar über das Strafgesetzbuch für die Preußischen Staaten und das Einführungsgesetz vom 14. April 1851* (Leipzig: Weidmann, 1851), 351–2; Hans Rüdorff, *Strafgesetzbuch für das Deutsche Reich*, 3rd edn (Berlin: Guttentag, 1881), 499; Ludwig Ebermayer, Adolf Lobe and Werner Rosenberg, *Reichs-Strafgesetzbuch mit besonderer Berücksichtigung der Rechtsprechung des Reichsgerichts*, 3rd edn (Berlin: De Gruyter, 1925), 638.
⁵²*Archiv für Strafrecht und Strafprozeß* 49 (1903): 324–5. Signs of disrespect and contempt were found when an adulterer had repeatedly and for a long time met the wife in her husband's house or apartment. Such behaviour was considered contemptuous of the husband's 'personality' and his rights as the head of family and household. See, for a similar opinion, ibid., 63 (1917): 469–70. The personal offence was even starker when husband and adulterer had been old friends (*Sächsisches Archiv für Rechtspflege* 8 (1913): 449).

The ruling was in perfect harmony with liberal legal theory that strongly disapproved of collective notions of honour. As early as 1901, Germany's Supreme Court had declared that honour as a legally protected good was only due an individual person, not a family.[53] After 1933, this opinion attracted severe criticism. In 1936, the Supreme Court (which had since been purged of its liberal and Jewish members) took an altogether different stance. It restated the notion of family honour which, upon closer inspection, was identical to that of the husband who, as head of the family, felt directly targeted by any attack that violated the honour of his wife or other family members. As Minister of Justice Franz Gürtner emphasized, the National Socialist sense of justice not only held honour to be the most precious property of the German people, but also believed in the honour of communities and corporations. The honour of individuals ranked far lower.[54]

Similar notions prevailed in fascist Italy. While the 1889 liberal Zanardelli Code did not explicitly mention slighted honour as an extenuating circumstance in homicides in which the perpetrator had caught his wife in the act of adultery (*in flagrante adulterio*), the Rocco Code of 1931 openly acknowledged and vastly expanded the applicability of the 'causa di honore'. The relevant article, 587, read:

> Whoever discovers unlawful sexual relations on the part of their spouse, daughter or sister and in the fit of fury occasioned by the offence to their or their family's honour causes their death, shall be punished with a prison term from three to seven years. Whoever, under the same circumstances, causes the death of the paramour of their spouse, daughter or sister shall be subjected to the same punishment.[55]

The article thus spoke assertively of a 'family honour' that could only be violated by female family members and had to be protected by husbands, fathers and brothers.

---

[53] *Archiv für Strafrecht und Strafprozeß* 48 (1901): 441 (in one case, parents had argued that their 'family honour' had been insulted by someone claiming that their daughter had given birth to an illegitimate child); see also ibid., 57 (1910): 209; *Juristische Wochenschrift* 41 (1912): 934.

[54] *Entscheidungen des Reichsgerichts in Strafsachen* 70 (1936): 94–100: 'Anyone who infringes on a woman's honour – even with her consent and thus not subject to prosecution – injures the honour of her husband. This opinion is rooted in the German notion of family' (97–8); Franz Gürtner, ed., *Das kommende deutsche Strafrecht: Besonderer Teil: Bericht über die Arbeit der amtlichen Strafrechtskommission*, 2nd edn (Berlin: Vahlen, 1936), 400, 411–12, 419, 97–8; ibid., 1st edn (1935), 286. Otto Schwarz, *Strafgesetzbuch mit allen wichtigen Nebengesetzen und Verordnungen*, 3rd edn (Munich: C.H. Beck, 1935), 317, called adultery a 'harsh personal offence' against the husband.

[55] Maria Gabriella Bettiga-Boukerbout, '"Crimes of Honour" in the Italian Penal Code', in '*Honour*': *Crimes, Paradigms and Violence against Women*, ed. Lynn Welchman and Sara Hossain (London: Zed Books, 2005), 230–44, here 234–5; Luigi Franchi, *Codice penale e di procedura penale*, 3rd edn (Milan: Hoepli, 1908), art. 377.

As late as 1972, the Cassation Court called the honour defence 'anachronistic'. A decade earlier, the film *Divorce Italian Style* (1961) had highlighted, in the absence of legal divorce, a potentially convenient method for getting rid of an unwanted wife. Finally, in 1981, Article 587 was repealed and the honour clause dropped. Sexual infidelity, though, continued to be seen as a serious provocation and 'unjust act' that could lead to an act of homicide 'in a fit of fury'.[56]

Browsing European legal history for references to passions and emotions, it is striking how closely intertwined heat-of-passion defences and honour-related arguments were. Very often, if not always, passion and fury were seen as the result of attacks on honour. Up until recently, legal codes and commentaries used the case of adultery – defined as a grave offence against a husband's honour – to shed light on how passions could overwhelm a man and prompt him to kill. Everyone, including judges, juries and the public, seemed to agree that even 'reasonable men', as they were called in British Common Law, might lose their temper and self-control under such circumstances. Legally, the killing was still considered a crime; culturally and socially, however, it was justifiable and 'excusable'. In places with a strong tradition of clan and family power, such as southern Italy, a cuckolded husband who failed to attack his opponent would have been socially ostracized as a coward, unworthy of his status as head of the family.

What to make of present-day honour killings?

Considering the intimate connection but also the differences between crimes of passion and crimes of honour, we might wonder about the place of contemporary 'crimes of honour' or 'honour killings', as they have been termed since the late 1980s. In such cases, a male family member kills a female relative in order to restore what they refer to as 'family honour'. That honour can purportedly be violated by the woman transgressing the boundaries of what is perceived as appropriate behaviour, which mainly concerns sexual and moral standards. Honour killings of this sort have been carried out in migrant communities all over Europe: in families of Turkish (in Germany), Somali or Indonesian (in the Netherlands), North African (in France) or Pakistani (in Britain) origin, predominantly Muslim. The numbers have been low. Even though some incidences may have gone unreported, honour killings do not qualify as a daily occurrence.[57]

---

[56]Bettiga-Boukerbout, Crimes, 236–7, 243; Ivo Caraccioli, 'Causa di onore', in *Digesto delle discipline penalistiche*, vol. 2 (Turin: Utet, 1988), 116–19.

[57]Carina Agel, *(Ehren-)Mord in Deutschland* (Lengerich: Pabst, 2013); Dietrich Oberwittler and Julia Kasselt, *Ehrenmorde in Deutschland 1996–2005* (Cologne: Luchterhand, 2011); Katherine Pratt Ewing, *Stolen Honor: Stigmatizing Muslim Men in Berlin* (Stanford: Stanford University Press, 2008); Clementine van Eck, *Purified by Blood: Honour Killings amongst Turks in the Netherlands* (Amsterdam: Amsterdam University Press, 2003).

Yet they have made headlines, and caused public imagination to run wild. Whenever a new case became known, it was portrayed not as what it was – a rare and socially complex case of traditional patriarchal morality and power – but as the epitome of 'Muslim culture'.[58] What tended to be forgotten was that non-Muslim cultures had embraced similar feelings about family honour until very recently and that European legal codes long sympathized with, or at least reserved some understanding for, men who killed women (as well as men) out of passion.

Where, exactly, do the honour killings of today sit between crimes of passion and crimes of honour? At first glance, they seem to have a lot in common with crimes of passion. In both instances, men attack women without giving them the opportunity to protect themselves or retaliate. Violence is at the heart of the act and serves to punish and annihilate. This distinguishes honour killings from earlier crimes of honour, i.e. duels that were fought between two men on equal terms. Those fights were not meant as punishment or revenge, but rather testified to a passionately held sense of male pride and self-worth.

Still, there are also commonalities between the honour crimes of yesterday and today, particularly with regard to the gendered dimension of honour. Honour and shame meant – and mean – completely different things to men and women. While male honour was closely associated with courage and steadfastness, female honour depended on sexual restraint, purity and decency. A 'fallen woman' who had given herself to a man that was not her husband was condemned as dishonourable. General opinion held that she had brought shame not only on herself but also on her husband, or on her father or brother should she be unmarried. Male honour largely depended on managing to control a wife's (or daughter's, or sister's) sexuality.

The actions that brought dishonour thus clearly differed between men and women. While wives, daughters or sisters dishonoured themselves by engaging in illegitimate sexual conduct, husbands, fathers or brothers were dishonoured by the men who had engaged in inappropriate relationships with 'their' women. These men humiliated the legal and legitimate guardians of female sexuality and challenged their masculine prowess. Such assaults demanded a forceful reaction. During the long nineteenth century, polite society in many European countries considered it a *point d'honneur* to call

---

[58]See, for a valid critique, Lila Abu-Lughod, 'Seductions of the "Honor Crime"', *Differences* 22, no. 1 (2011): 17–63. The argument that honour killings represent traditional patriarchal morality rests on the observation that those who kill are usually first-generation immigrants who find it hard to adjust and accept that women – their daughters, wives, sisters – hold different ideas from their own. The cultural clash experienced by those families leads to a heightened sense of insecurity and rigidity when it comes to values, habits and customs. Honour killings might thus be more frequent in diaspora cultures than 'at home'. But even 'home' is changing, as witnessed in Turkey or Pakistan, where women are increasingly challenging and renegotiating traditional notions of honour and chastity.

the offender out and challenge him to a duel. Though forbidden by law, it was regarded as honourable conduct both because of its 'noble' motives and the way it was practised: with emotional restraint, in cold blood, on equal terms.

But even if violence was not 'civilized' and controlled, and instead followed the spontaneous 'affect' of rage, jealousy and humiliation, it was condoned by Western law, which viewed the 'affect' as justified by the assault on male or family honour. When taken to court, men who had murdered their adulterous wives and/or competitors 'in a fit of fury' could count on understanding and compassion.[59] Nevertheless, the law insisted on the immediacy of emotional stress. Only when an act of homicide had been committed in the heat of passion did it deserve lenient treatment.

This distinguishes crimes of passion from contemporary honour killings that are generally not of a spontaneous and passionate nature. 'Affect' is not involved when brothers, fathers or husbands contemplate the most suitable perpetrator and method to kill the deviant sister, daughter or wife. In this sense, honour killings resemble premeditated murder, which generally receives far harsher legal sentences than crimes of passion.

Still, they do not necessarily share the provision of a base motive that catalyses the act. Perpetrators commonly invoke the duty of upholding the family's honour, which they allege has been sullied by the woman's inappropriate conduct. In their view, her failure to comply with community mores and rules brings shame on all members of the family. They are held responsible for this failure and consequently suffer from their peers' contempt and derision. In order to cast off the shame and restore the family's social status, they kill the woman in a planned and deliberate manner that strengthens the family's ultimate control and power.[60]

Although the concept of family honour, with its inbuilt bias towards male supremacy, appears alien to contemporary Western culture and therefore engenders collective indignation, it has played a prominent role in European social practices and legal traditions. Rape, for instance, has long been interpreted as an attack on and a violation of 'family honour'.[61] It took

---

[59] Katharina Linka, *Mord und Totschlag (§§ 211–213 StGB): Reformdiskussion und Gesetzgebung seit 1870* (Berlin: BWV, 2008), 139; Edward Berenson, *The Trial of Madame Caillaux* (Berkeley: University of California Press, 1992), 28.

[60] It should be mentioned, though, that men are also sometimes victims of honour killings. A recent survey in Germany identified 78 cases (1996–2005) with 109 victims, 47 of whom were male (43 per cent). Among the perpetrators, almost all were male (113 out of 122). See Oberwittler and Kasselt, *Ehrenmorde*.

[61] Regarding international law, see the Brussels Declaration of 1874, Article 38 (not ratified), and the Peace Conferences at the Hague 1899 and 1907, Article 46 of the Conventions concerning the laws and customs of war on land mentioned that 'family honor' had to be protected. James Brown Scott, ed., *The Hague Conventions and Declarations of 1899 and 1907* (New York: Oxford University Press, 1915), 123.

many decades of feminist struggle for it to finally be redefined as a violation of a person's autonomy, integrity and right to sexual self-determination.[62]

A common conviction unites those who considered rape a violation of family honour and those who perpetrated honour killings. In both cases, family honour was assumed to be injured by a woman compromising her sexual integrity – either actively or passively, voluntarily or involuntarily, by mutual consent or by force. Such reasoning was (and is) based on the perception of a person (typically but not exclusively a female person) as part of a larger group that offers her status and protection. If the person is attacked, the entire group feels attacked and assumes responsibility. If the person violates the written and unwritten group rules, the group takes action and punishes the transgression.

The close-knit relationship between person and group was a cornerstone of honour cultures as they prevailed in Europe until the early twentieth century and continue to prevail in other parts of the world. As Georg Simmel observed around 1900, honour is the connective tissue of the small circles that stand between the individual and society. As those circles multiplied and diversified throughout the twentieth century, they lost their exclusive grip on individuals. Since each and every member of (late) modern society belongs to a variety of social groups and institutions (family, religious congregations, voluntary associations and the like), they have to constantly juggle and choose between different values, behavioural codes and emotional styles. This involves maintaining some distance and refusing to become fully immersed in one group or institution at the expense of all others. In accordance with such long-term developments, in 1970 sociologist Peter Berger declared the notions of honour and chastity (closely intertwined where family honour was concerned) remnants of the past – a past that was relevant only to military officers and 'ethnic grandmothers' who still followed a single hegemonic code.[63]

Remembering this part of the European past is by no means akin to condoning honour killings in the present or advocating leniency in how they are socially and legally dealt with. Acknowledging concepts of family honour that defy a woman's right to live her own life is clearly at odds with how modern Western societies are normatively and legally structured. Establishing those standards has been a lengthy and laborious process, strewn with controversy and struggle. Discrimination against women has long been inherent in Western legal systems. Just as the honour defence worked to consolidate male dominance and power, the heat-of-passion argument privileged male acts of violence over women. Honour, as a private passion and collective emotional practice, has, for centuries, undergirded

---

[62]Joanna Bourke, *Rape: A History from 1860 to the Present* (London: Virago, 2008).
[63]Peter Berger, 'On the Obsolescence of the Concept of Honor', *European Journal of Sociology* 11, no. 2 (1970): 339–47.

a regime of social and gender inequalities that have encouraged violence and upheld rigid codes of conduct for both men and women. Softening those codes, alleviating gender differences, outlawing violent behaviour and liberalizing the law have all led to the dampening of what former generations described as the passion for honour rooted in people's hearts and felt in their bodies. Deconstructing and de-prioritizing honour has also meant lowering the heavy emotional burden that women and men alike had to bear during its reign.

CHAPTER FOUR

Honour and Shame in International Relations

The passion for honour not only governed people's sentiments and behaviour towards one another, it also figured in the communications and interactions between states. Honour played a prominent role in international relations from the early modern period onwards, fuelling conflict and helping to solve it. War and peace were often framed as questions of honour; accordingly, defeat was seen as a humiliation and accompanied by feelings of shame.

How did honour (and, concomitantly, shame) enter the regime and language of intergovernmental affairs? By looking at international law, we can trace the historical process that transformed princely honour into state honour into national honour. The First World War, in particular, reflects the influence of honour on a major European conflict that enlisted governments and citizens alike. In its aftermath, and especially in countries that had suffered defeat or for whom peace was a bitter pill to swallow, right-wing movements successfully whipped up support by promising to restore honour and vanquish humiliation. New wars followed.

State honour

Heinrich von Treitschke, an eminent professor of history in Berlin and a member of parliament, frequently commented on politics and current affairs. Famous for his engaging teaching style, in the 1880s and early 1890s his lectures on politics mainly focused on the state as the bearer of sovereign

---

This chapter partly draws on material published in 'Emotions in Times of War: Private and Public, Individual and Collective', in *Total War: An Emotional History*, ed. Claire Langhamer, Lucy Noakes and Claudia Siebrecht (Oxford: Oxford University Press, 2020), 21–39.

power. Treitschke's state was, in a Hegelian sense, imbued with moral meaning and possessed a highly developed and 'excitable' sense of honour. Honour was equivalent to power; it had to shine bright and 'stand proudly, for all the world to see, and it cannot allow even the symbols of it to be contested'. Such contestation was immediately identified as an insult 'to the honour of a State' and 'casts doubt upon the nature of the State'. Therefore,

> if the flag is insulted, the State must claim reparation; should this not be forthcoming, war must follow, however small the occasion may seem; for the State has never any choice but to maintain the respect in which it is held among its fellows.[1]

Treitschke was not the first scholar to link honour, power and the state in this way. Nor was he alone in perceiving the state as a living being rather than an abstract institution. As early as the seventeenth century, Gottfried Wilhelm Leibniz had imagined the state as a *persona civilis*, with a will of its own. Thomas Hobbes conceived of the state or 'common-wealth' as *persona civitatis*, the 'person of the state'. Samuel Pufendorf described it as *persona moralis* – a concept popularized in the widely influential treatise *Le Droit des gens*, written by the Swiss jurist Emer de Vattel in 1758. The English edition, published two years later, addressed the state as a distinct 'moral person' and 'body politic'. Nineteenth-century writers likewise saw the state as a 'collective person' with a proper soul, or a 'living organism' imbued with will and power.[2]

They were continuing a long tradition of personifying the state that drew on the pre-eminence of kings and emperors in medieval Europe. Distinguishing the ruler from the state turned out to be a difficult process which suffered serious setbacks during the early modern period. While state and sovereign tended to merge under absolutism, enlightened rulers like the Prussian King Friedrich II described themselves as 'first servant to the state'. In 1788, the philosopher Christian Garve addressed the prince as master of 'the entire state body'. His task was, Garve suggested, to govern the state well and to support the 'well-being' of his subjects. A sovereign should not hesitate to immediately 'avenge insults' to his honour, since the regard 'which other nations should have towards yours' depended on 'the esteem you personally enjoy'.[3]

---

[1] Heinrich von Treitschke, *Politics*, vol. 2 (London: Constable & Co., 1916), 595.
[2] Quentin Skinner, 'A Genealogy of the Modern State', *Proceedings of the British Academy* 162 (2009): 325–70; Ulrich Häfelin, *Die Rechtspersönlichkeit des Staates*, vol. 1 (Tübingen: Mohr, 1959), on Leibniz (42), Carl von Rotteck (71) and Robert von Mohl (76); Albrecht Koschorke et al., *Der fiktive Staat: Konstruktionen des politischen Körpers in der Geschichte Europas* (Frankfurt: Mohr, 2007), 110–11, 319–82.
[3] Christian Garve, *Abhandlung über die Verbindung der Moral mit der Politik* (Breslau: Korn, 1788), 143–4, 150.

Appraising such insults one hundred years later, Treitschke explicitly mentioned symbolic acts like disrespecting the national flag. He might also have alluded to the multiple instances of contravening the protocol of politeness that regulated honourable conduct at court. Written down in thick volumes of 'ceremonial science', these regulations detailed all kinds of transgressions, which, when they occurred, could be interpreted either as careless breaches of protocol or as deliberate insults to the sovereign.[4] International law as it had first been drafted in the seventeenth century sought to provide recourse to solve such conflicts, and framed honour in a way that rendered it internationally communicable and practicable.

In his 1758 book, Vattel explicitly advised states to be on the alert for potential insults to their honour: 'Every nation, every sovereign, ought to maintain their dignity by causing due respect to be paid to them; and, especially, they ought not to suffer that dignity to be impaired.' If the prince's dignity was impaired, he 'has a right to demand, even by force of arms, the reparation of an insult'. Choosing to accept, overlook or excuse insults would be taken as a sign of weakness or cowardice. In contrast, the quest for 'a complete satisfaction' of the incident testified to the sovereign's power and status.

What exactly was meant by 'satisfaction' and 'reparation'? Vattel mentioned several instruments that could amend or atone for insults: material restitution, compensation, the other side's acknowledgement of blame and symbolic gestures of recognition and estimation. The latter he reserved 'for such injuries as cannot be repaired'.[5]

Subsequent iterations of international law differentiated more clearly between the right to 'reparation' and the right to 'satisfaction'. Reparations were understood as financial compensation for material damages; satisfaction was a possible remedy in cases in which moral or political slights were levelled against the state.[6] It was repeatedly emphasized that

---

[4]Julius Bernhard von Rohr, *Einleitung zur Ceremoniel-Wissenschafft der großen Herren* (Berlin: Rüdiger, 1733); Miloš Vec, *Zeremonialwissenschaft im Fürstenstaat: Studien zur juristischen und politischen Theorie absolutistischer Herrschaftsrepräsentation* (Frankfurt: Klostermann, 1998).

[5]Emer de Vattel, *Le Droit des gens, ou principes de la loi naturelle, appliqués à la conduit & aux affaires des nations & des souverains*, new edn, vol. 1 (Neufchatel: Société Typographique, 1773), 178, 452–3; Emer de Vattel, *The Law of Nations: Or, Principles of the Law of Nature, Applied to the Conduct and Affairs of Nations and Sovereigns: From the New Edition by Joseph Chitty* (Philadelphia: Johnson, 1852), 153–4, 274. See also Rohr, *Einleitung*, 413, who stated that the prince who did not receive 'satisfaction' for an insult to his honour might as well start a war.

[6]Franciszek Przetacznik, *Protection of Officials of Foreign States According to International Law* (The Hague: Nijhoff, 1983), 217–26. Borzu Sabahi, *Compensation and Restitution in Investor-State Arbitration* (Oxford: Oxford University Press, 2011), 7–42, traces the sources of the international doctrine of state responsibility and reparation for material restitution and compensation only, not for moral satisfaction in cases such as 'an insult to the dignity of the state, eg. its flag' (12).

such slights were on principle more destructive and dangerous than material losses or damages. Johann Caspar Bluntschli, professor of international law at Heidelberg University, underscored in 1868 that insults were categorically different to other violations of international law for which compensation could be claimed. Yet if a state 'injures the honour of another state, or disregards its dignity', the principle of 'satisfaction and atonement' prevailed. Bluntschli explicitly referred in this context to 'the *ideal* character of the slighted right to honour' and to the 'deeper sentiment of the state's *insulted political consciousness*'. This sentiment justified the appetite for appropriate satisfaction. The jurist (one of the founders of the *Institut de Droit International* in 1873) added, however, that the satisfaction must not involve anything 'immoral'. A 'humiliation incompatible with the continuation and dignity of an independent state' was, he assured his audience, completely unacceptable.[7]

Notions of honourable satisfaction persist to this day. Contemporary international law continues to arbitrate material and immaterial slights, violations and injuries between states and it holds states accountable and liable for damages. Since 1949, an International Law Commission has been working on behalf of the United Nations to penalize states for internationally wrongful acts. In 2001, the commission finally submitted draft articles, which the UN General Assembly adopted in the same year (Resolution 56/83) and recommended to governments for their consideration. Articles 33 to 37 defined the concrete consequences that would arise from breaches of international law. Measures of restitution, compensation and satisfaction were subsumed under the generic term 'reparation'. While restitution and compensation chiefly covered financial recompense, satisfaction involved the responsible state acknowledging the damage it had caused, expressing regret or even formally apologizing. Under no circumstances, however, was satisfaction to take a form that was 'humiliating' for the party concerned – just as Bluntschli had argued in 1868.[8]

International law accordingly regarded states as actors that could be insulted, degraded, injured, humiliated, and that themselves insulted, degraded, injured and humiliated. This notion persisted into the twenty-first century. Although the concept of honour no longer appeared in the 2001 documents, its semantics and pragmatics were omnipresent in the term 'satisfaction'. This originated from a Europe-wide lexicon of honour consulted in the modern era not only by states and princes but also by individual citizens, typically men from aristocratic and bourgeois circles.

---

[7]Johann Caspar Bluntschli, *Das moderne Völkerrecht der civilisirten Staten* (Nördlingen: C.H. Beck, 1868), 260, 263. See also Bertrand Badie, *Humiliation in International Relations: A Pathology of Contemporary International Systems* (Oxford: Hart Publishing, 2017).
[8]International Law Commission, *Draft Articles on Responsibility of States for Internationally Wrongful Acts*, 11/2001, supp. no. 10 (A/56/10), ch. IV.E.1, https://www.refworld.org/docid/3ddb8f804.html (accessed 14 November 2022).

The lexicon gave them precise instructions for how to act and feel if they wanted to maintain a proper conduct of life. Since honour was of central importance to this conduct, everything revolved around the question of how to preserve and protect it. Special attention was paid to dealing with honour offences and those who had committed them. The offending party owed full satisfaction to the offended, and essentially had two options: an apology or a duel waged with deadly weapons.[9]

That the honour of men and the honour of the state were fundamentally related was common knowledge. Contemporaries in the nineteenth and early twentieth centuries spoke matter-of-factly of the state as a male being: as to the conservative and widely read ethnologist Wilhelm Heinrich Riehl in 1855, it was clearly of the 'male sex' and possessed 'a purely *masculine* essence'.[10] For the liberal Bluntschli, too, the state was 'unquestionably a male entity', which is why the 'conventional custom of all peoples' regarded it as 'the task and concern of men'.[11] After male citizen–soldiers had secured the founding of the German Empire in 1871, this was not a notion that would be questioned anytime soon. 'It is self-evident', Treitschke told his students in Berlin, that 'all governmental functions belong to the manly sphere'. To further emphasize his point, the professor noted 'the purely physical part of government, which must be backed by armed men. Now armed men do not like taking their orders from a woman'.[12]

Such arguments were voiced on all sides of the political spectrum. Treitschke's national liberal views were echoed in a popular encyclopaedia whose middle-class readers received, in 1894, the clear message: 'To the man the state, to the woman the family!' For the conservative writer Max Lorenz, politics

> is at any rate the domain of men, because the essence of the state and its actual and innermost task is not the greatest possible happiness of the greatest possible number, but the *outward development of power* and the wrangling of nations with one another in the struggle for existence. Political questions are in truth and ultimately questions of power and the very existence of states and the life of its peoples culminate in war. *That is why the state's legislation must show, even in times of peace, a masculine spirit.*[13]

---

[9]See Chapter 3 in this volume.
[10]Wilhelm Heinrich Riehl, *Die Familie*, 3rd edn (Stuttgart: Cotta, 1861), 6, 13.
[11]*Deutsches Staats-Wörterbuch*, ed. Johann Caspar Bluntschli and Karl Brater, vol. 11 (Stuttgart: Expedition des Staats-Wörterbuchs, 1870), 130. See also Johann Caspar Bluntschli, *Allgemeines Statsrecht*, 4th edn, vol. 1 (Munich: Cotta, 1868), 196–200.
[12]Treitschke, *Politics*, vol. 1 (1916), 252.
[13]*Meyers Konversations-Lexikon*, 5th edn, vol. 6 (Leipzig: Bibliographisches Institut, 1894), 822; Max Lorenz, *Das Deutschland der Gegenwart* (Berlin: Wedekind, 1906), 43–4 (original emphasis).

Insisting on the gendered character of the state and its authority was not uniquely German. The same argument was used to reject demands for women's suffrage across Europe. At the same time, the notion of a masculine state, as represented by the triad of honour, power and war, was potent beyond the domestic political arena. Under no circumstances should a state allow its honour to be attacked and violated but instead it must defend it with arms, just as duellists did into the early twentieth century.

National honour

Such obligations did not diminish during the modern era – on the contrary. Even though the fight over pre-eminence in ceremonial matters had been settled and the equality of European states established in the early nineteenth century, honour continued to be a bone of contention. When state honour was transferred to the nation, conflicts between states were increasingly characterized as struggles for national honour.

After 1789, the nation – understood as a community of equal (male) citizens – gradually became a powerful political actor. Rather than the prerogative of elites, politics evolved into an activity open to all citizens. Mass participation in political deliberations and decision-making changed the very notion of the state, which morphed into an organization of and for all. Accordingly, the mantle of state honour was boldly taken up by the national community. Citizens began to personally identify with the honour of their country and to interpret any (perceived) attack on that honour as an attack on their own.

What might seem at first glance a democratizing process soon turned out to be highly problematic. In the age of fervent nationalism, arguments about national honour were exceptionally acerbic. Fuelled by the press and nationalist associations, citizens quickly adopted the language of insult and satisfaction when it came to international affairs, thereby encouraging their governments to deploy honour arguments with vigour. States that tended to view 'illegal violations of their honour as justified grounds for war' could now do so with the full support of people at home.[14]

German citizens, for instance, were spoon-fed the decision to go to war with France in 1870. This proved an easy task, since Napoleon III declared war first. The French emperor, whose authoritarian reign was supported by and depended on plebiscite, promised his nation a *satisfaction éclatante* for the insults that France had supposedly been suffering at Prussian hands. Political communications since 1866 had been rich with references to 'humiliation', 'degradation' and insulted national honour. Fearing a

---

[14]Carl Welcker, 'Injurie', in *Das Staats-Lexikon*, ed. Carl von Rotteck and Carl Welcker, 2nd edn, vol. 7 (Altona: Hammerich, 1847), 404–22, here 409.

loss of prestige in Europe and among his own people, Napoleon and his government pushed for war. In their efforts, they found a congenial partner in the Prussian prime minister Otto von Bismarck. His carefully crafted Ems Dispatch, which exposed French ambassador Vincent Benedetti's impertinent behaviour towards King Wilhelm I, was viewed by Paris as an affront to France's national honour. For his part, Wilhelm was aggravated that Benedetti had the cheek to demand a 'letter of apology' from him, as this reviled 'my personal [honour] and the honour of the nation'.[15]

All of these insults and rebuttals were exchanged in public; the citizens of each nation were bombarded with updates and actively engaged in the drama. Governments forwarded their missives directly to the national press, though journalists stoked the aggression all on their own. Even socialist papers ran inflammatory articles covering supposed attacks on national honour and urging politicians to act firmly. 'National feeling and national honour' had become, in Bismarck's words, 'powers of great moral force', and public opinion a major political player. Accordingly, no politician wanted to 'compromise' himself and risk falling foul of it.[16]

Each side portrayed itself as victim, and everyone felt – or pretended to feel – that they had been humiliated and insulted without themselves having humiliated or insulted anyone. At most, countries framed their actions as revenge for past humiliations. Wilhelm Camphausen's watercolour *Vengeance* was a case in point. The painter, who had been hired to accompany the Prussian army to France, contrasted two scenes of surrender, 'Tilsit 1807' and 'Sedan 1870'. In 1807, Queen Luise of Prussia had in vain asked Napoleon I for a lenient peace agreement; sixty-three years later, the emperor's nephew appeared before Luise's son, Wilhelm, to surrender his sword. Both were moments of humiliation, and the painting explicitly suggested that the latter was an act of vengeance for the former which thereby restored Prussia's and Germany's honour.[17]

---

[15]Michael Jeismann, *Das Vaterland der Feinde: Studien zum nationalen Feindbegriff und Selbstverständnis in Deutschland und Frankreich 1792–1918* (Stuttgart: Klett-Cotta, 1992), 174–85; Birgit Aschmann, 'Ehre – das verletzte Gefühl als Grund für den Krieg: Der Kriegsausbruch 1870', in *Gefühl und Kalkül: Der Einfluss von Emotionen auf die Politik des 19. und 20. Jahrhunderts*, ed. Birgit Aschmann (Stuttgart: Steiner, 2005), 151–74; Birgit Aschmann, *Preußens Ruhm und Deutschlands Ehre: Zum nationalen Ehrdiskurs im Vorfeld der preußisch-französischen Kriege des 19. Jahrhunderts* (Munich: Oldenbourg, 2013), 367–465, quote 454. More general: Barry O'Neill, *Honor, Symbols, and War* (Ann Arbor: University of Michigan Press, 1999), 139–63.

[16]Aschmann, *Preußens Ruhm*, quotes 357, 359, 397.

[17]The painting belonged to Wilhelm I's private collection. On the surrender of the sword in 1870 see Verena Steller, *Diplomatie von Angesicht zu Angesicht: Diplomatische Handlungsformen in den deutsch-französischen Beziehungen 1870–1919* (Paderborn: Schöningh, 2011), 34–7. On French sentiments of revenge after 1871 see Wolfgang Schivelbusch, *The Culture of Defeat: On National Trauma, Mourning, and Recovery*, trans. Jefferson Chase (London: Granta Books, 2003), ch. 3.

Anton von Werner's famous painting *Proclamation of the German Empire*, in its multiple versions and countless reproductions, had a similar function. It drew attention to the murals in the Hall of Mirrors at the Palace of Versailles that celebrated the victories and triumphs of Louis XIV, including the annexation of Alsace as a French province. Thanks to the recent victory over France, the province would be rightfully 'returned' to Germany. As a military chaplain explained in a sermon on the occasion, the proclamation had thus 'repented the shame that was once heaved upon our German people from this place and from this royal throne'.[18]

Shame and disgrace: these were the counterparts to honour which were frequently evoked in the nineteenth century. The Third French Republic, which followed Napoleon III's Second Empire, likewise subscribed to this rhetoric. For the scholar Ernest Renan, Bismarck's triumph was France's downfall. 'A weakened and humiliated France', he wrote in 1870, 'would be incapable of survival. The loss of Alsace and Lorraine would mean the end of France.'[19] Yet the experience of humiliation and weakness was precisely what ignited the forces of resistance, thanks to a vigorous propaganda campaign. Victor Hugo was not alone in calling on France in March 1871 to wage hateful revenge in order to restore the fatherland's glory and honour and to win back the lost provinces. In the future,

> France will have only one thought: [...] to raise her children, to nourish with holy anger these little ones who will then grow up and be great; to forge cannons and form citizens, to create an army that shall be made from and represent the people.[20]

Schools in particular took their patriotic duties seriously. The famous textbook of the Third Republic, of which 6 million copies were distributed in 1900, followed two brothers, aged 14 and 7, on their way from German-annexed Lorraine to *la vieille France*. They were fulfilling the last wish of their father, who had died in 1871 from a war wound: to remain French at all costs. At Notre-Dame, they prayed for 'la grandeur de la France'; near Orléans, they rebuilt a farm destroyed in the war. According to the (female) author of the book, which was first published in 1877, the diligence, sense of duty and love of country felt by its children was what made France prosperous so soon after the damages of wartime. The wound of the lost provinces continued to bleed, however, and the map tracing André's and

---

[18] Theodor Toeche-Mittler, 'Die Kaiserproklamation in Versailles am 18. Januar 1871', *Beihefte zum Militär-Wochenblatt* (1896): 1–106, here 21; Thomas W. Gaethgens, *Anton von Werner: Die Proklamierung des Deutschen Kaiserreiches: Ein Historienbild im Wandel preußischer Politik* (Frankfurt: Fischer, 1990).
[19] Schivelbusch, *Culture of Defeat*, quote 110.
[20] *Œuvres Complètes de Victor Hugo: Actes et Paroles III* (Paris: Hetzel, 1884), 95–104, quote 102 (translation author's own).

Julien's journey still showed Alsace and Lorraine as parts of France (albeit with dashed borderlines).[21]

Even the 'convinced materialist' Jean-Paul Sartre, who was born in 1905, could not escape the 'epic idealism' of that powerful narrative. Raised by his grandfather – who taught German and generously expressed his sympathy for 'nice, good-natured Germans' – he was nevertheless 'marked', as he wrote in the 1963 autobiographical work *Les mots*, as a 'grandchild of defeat'. Throughout his life he would make amends 'for an insult I have not endured, a shame I have not suffered, and the loss of two provinces which have been given back to us long since'.[22]

First World War: honour and dishonour

The giving back did not happen until 1918, after Germany's defeat in the First World War. Four years earlier, each warring party had stressed that they had no choice but to take up arms in the name of honour.[23] The manifesto of the Austrian emperor, issued on 28 July 1914, justified the war against Serbia 'in Protection of the Honour of My Monarchy'. When the Russian ambassador in Vienna announced his country's military mobilization on 29 July, he observed that Russia's honour as a major power had been slighted, whereupon the nation had to take the necessary steps. This allegation was refuted by the German emperor, who assured the tsar in a telegram that 'nobody is threatening the honour or power of Russia'. Tsar Nicholas was not convinced. His imperial manifesto of 2 August asserted that 'We must also safeguard the honour, dignity, and integrity of Russia and her position among the Great Powers'.

For his part, on 5 August, Wilhelm II explained that he was 'forced to draw the sword in order to ward off an unjustified attack and fight for our national honour'. A day later, he issued a proclamation to the German

---

[21]G. Bruno [i.e. Augustine Fouillée], *Le Tour de la France par deux enfants* (Paris: Belin, 1877). See Jacques Ozouf and Mona Ozouf, *La République des instituteurs* (Paris: Seuil, 1992), 134–44; See Jacques Ozouf and Mona Ozouf, 'Le Tour de la France par deux enfants: The Little Red Book of the Republic', in *Realms of Memory: The Construction of the French Past*, ed. Pierre Nora, trans. Arthur Goldhammer, vol. 2 (New York: Colombia University Press, 1997), 125–48.

[22]Jean-Paul Sartre, *Words*, trans. Irene Clephane (London: Hamish, 1965), 81.

[23]Ute Frevert, 'Honor, Gender, and Power: The Politics of Satisfaction in Pre-War Europe', in *An Improbable War: The Outbreak of World War I and European Political Culture before 1914*, ed. Holger Afflerbach and David Stevenson (New York: Berghahn, 2007), 233–55; Paul Robinson, *Military Honour and the Conduct of War* (London: Routledge, 2006), 138–63. Avner Offer, 'Going to War in 1914: A Matter of Honor?', *Politics and Society* 23, no. 2 (1995): 213–41, distinguishes between the passion-led 'short term consideration of honour' and the 'prudential, longer term preference for survival'. Survival, however, usually depended on the maintenance of state sovereignty of which honour was seen as an integral and non-negotiable part.

people, in which he argued that Germany's 'power and honour' would be ruined if the nation allowed its friend and major ally, the Habsburg Empire, to suffer 'humiliation'. On the very same day, British Prime Minister Herbert Asquith told the Commons:

> We are fighting in the first place to fulfill a solemn international obligation which, if it had been entered into between private persons in the ordinary concerns of life, would have been regarded as an obligation not only of law but of honour, which no self-respecting man could possibly have repudiated.[24]

These words and related imagery were quickly printed by newspapers and on posters, postcards and brochures that circulated widely. They also found their way into lyrics and poems. Among the war sonnets that brought 26-year-old Rupert Brooke to the attention of the First Lord of Admiralty, Winston Churchill, and gained him an appointment as temporary sub-lieutenant in the Royal Naval Volunteer Reserve, was 'The Dead':

> Honour has come back, as a king, to earth/And paid his subjects with a royal wage;/And nobleness walks in our ways again;/And we have come into our heritage.[25]

As if he did not quite trust this reappearance of honour, British Foreign Secretary Sir Edward Grey continuously referred to 'our respect and good name and reputation before the world'.[26] Using honour as a synonym for prestige and reputation was nothing new; sociologist Max Weber had done the same in his theoretical texts, thus modernizing a concept that to him seemed somewhat alien in a world supposedly governed by the rational assessment of prosaic interest. For Weber, the anachronism of honour stemmed primarily from its roots in a society composed of estates rather than market classes, and from its emotional thrust. Still, this thrust was by no means lost on Weber. When, in his wartime speeches, he repeatedly referred to honour as a given fact, he knew from personal experience what he was discussing.[27]

---

[24] *The Times*, 30 July 1914, 7; 4 August 1914, 3; Imanuel Geiss, ed., *July 1914: The Outbreak of the First World War: Selected Documents* (London: Batsford, 1967), 280, 324; Ernst Johann, ed., *Innenansicht eines Krieges: Deutsche Dokumente 1914–1918* (Munich: dtv, 1973), 24; Michael Brock, 'Britain Enters the War', in *The Coming of the First World War*, ed. Robert J.W. Evans and Hartmut Pogge von Strandmann (Oxford: Clarendon Press, 1988), 145–78, quote 177.
[25] Rupert Brooke, *1914 and other Poems* (London: Sidgwick & Jackson, 1915), 13.
[26] Viscount Grey of Fallodon, *Twenty-Five Years 1892–1916*, vol. 3 (London: Hodder & Stoughton, 1935), 316.
[27] Max Weber, *Economy and Society: An Outline of Interpretive Sociology*, ed. Guenther Roth and Claus Wittich, vol. 2 (Berkeley: University of California Press, 1978), 932–7, 1068–9. For Weber's sensitivity to the *point d'honneur*, see Ute Frevert, *Men of Honour: The Social and Cultural History of the Duel* (Cambridge: Polity Press, 1995), 182; for his wartime speeches, see Max Weber, *Zur Politik im Weltkrieg: Schriften und Reden 1914–1918* (Tübingen: Mohr, 1988), esp. 40, 77.

Even members of the British Labour Party, who questioned the government's argument about honour compelling the country to go to war, did not dismiss honour in general as a valid and legitimate motive to take up arms. 'If', Ramsay MacDonald proclaimed in the House of Commons on 3 August, 'the nation's honour is in danger, we would be with him' ('him' being Foreign Secretary Grey, who had defended the decision to enter the war on exactly those grounds).[28] David Lloyd George from the Liberal Party, then chancellor of the exchequer and later prime minister, stood by the decision, yet not without conceding

> that whenever a nation has been engaged in any war she has always invoked the sacred name of honour. Many a crime has been committed in its name; there are some crimes being committed now. But, all the same, national honour is a reality, and any nation that disregards it is doomed.[29]

Attesting to honour's 'reality' both confirmed and reacted to the opinion of the public, who readily took the bait and framed the conflict as an *affaire d'honneur*. When he alluded to the 1839 treaty that bound Britain (as well as Prussia and other European nations) to safeguard Belgium's neutrality and independence, Asquith went further, explicitly comparing it to a private obligation 'in the ordinary concerns of life'. By deliberately linking national honour and personal honour, he drew on the underlying culture of promises made and kept, of remaining faithful to one's commitments, of forcefully rejecting signs of disrespect – even at the risk of losing life and limb.

Honour culture as it prevailed in most parts of Europe placed a huge burden on the individual man. It put him in a position of utmost insecurity as he felt vulnerable to insults and transgressions morning, noon and night. On the other hand, the honour code offered a means of mediation and control that enabled men to deal with conflicts without disgrace. Though some insults (like adultery, or a slap in the face) could not be mediated away, there were many others that could. Inbuilt procedures allowed tempers to cool and dissuaded men from engaging in further aggression. They also summoned the intervention of third parties. Seconds had to be nominated to solve the conflict in a non-violent fashion, by clearing up misunderstandings or inviting and facilitating apologies. If their attempts failed, the resulting duel was fought according to strict rules that guaranteed an equality of chances and risks and set limits on the violence enacted. Most duels ended without a drop of blood being spilled. And they ended, moreover, if we believe those duellists who reported on their feelings during and after the event, in perfect harmony. The fight had not only done justice to the moral order that governed upper-class men's behaviour, it had also restored balance

---

[28]*The Times*, 4 August 1914, 6–7.
[29]David Lloyd George, *Honour and Dishonour: A Speech* (London: Methuen, 1914), 2.

between the two opponents. Each one had saved face, shown courage and determination and acted in accordance with his principles. Furthermore, the duellists had accepted each other as equals, despite and beyond their initial conflict. The duel was regarded as an act of mutual respect: it was based on a notion of equality, in terms of means and social status, and it sought to rebuild that respect in cases where it had been dented or doubted.[30]

It was no coincidence, then, that contemporaries, among them the Prussian officer Carl von Clausewitz, conceived of wars as 'extended duels'.[31] Wars clearly differed from classic *affaires d'honneur* in the number of participants and in the intended outcome; unlike duels, they were about victory, defeat and, since Napoleon's time, annihilation.[32] Yet they still retained elements of chivalry and honourable conduct. As they were fought between Europeans, basic rules of respect and recognition were thought to prevail (in contrast to wars with non-Europeans).[33] This is at least how German students imagined the war when they voluntarily enlisted in 1914: as if they were embarking 'on *Mensur*' and fighting a students' duel in the part brazen, part chivalric tradition of the academic youth culture. Students from Cambridge entered the war with similar notions, happily trading the cricket ground for the field of honour.[34]

The wider public, meanwhile, revelled in the sight of modern knights who could wage war even in the skies – one to one, eye to eye, as perfectly mannered gentlemen.[35] Down on the ground, Ernst Jünger, a young German officer deployed on the Western Front, recorded in his diary how, despite increasingly unbearable conditions and abundant violence, soldiers recognized and admired bravery whenever and wherever they found it,

---

[30]Frevert, *Men of Honour*, 150–71. See Chapter 3 in this volume.
[31]Carl von Clausewitz, *On War*, trans. J.J. Graham, vol. 1 (London: Kegan Paul, Trench, Trübner & Co., 1908), 1. See the references in Frevert, *Men of Honour*, 151–2, as well as Ernst Jünger, *The Storm of Steel: From the Diary of a German Storm-Troop Officer on the Western Front* (New York: Fertig, 1975), 62, 233.
[32]Jehuda L. Wallach, *The Dogma of the Battle of Annihilation: The Theories of Clausewitz and Schlieffen and Their Impact on the German Conduct of Two World Wars* (Westport: Greenwood Press, 1986).
[33]As to colonial wars, see Dieter Langewiesche, '"Savage War" as "People's War": Nineteenth-Century African Wars, European Perceptions, and the Future of Warfare', *Journal of Modern History* 94, no. 3 (2022): 537–63; Dieter Langewiesche, *Der gewaltsame Lehrer: Europas Kriege in der Moderne* (Munich: C.H. Beck, 2019), 341–400.
[34]Philipp Witkop, ed., *Kriegsbriefe gefallener Studenten* (Munich: Müller, 1928), 11; Sonja Levsen, *Elite, Männlichkeit und Krieg: Tübinger und Cambridger Studenten 1900–1929* (Göttingen: Vandenhoeck & Ruprecht, 2006), 123 ff., Sonja Levsen, 'Constructing Elite Identities: University Students, Military Masculinity and the Consequences of the Great War in Britain and Germany', *Past & Present* no. 198 (2008): 147–83.
[35]John H. Morrow Jr., *The Great War in the Air: Military Aviation from 1909 to 1921* (Washington: Smithsonian, 1993); Florian Schnürer, '"But in Death He Has Found Victory": The Funeral Ceremonies for the "Knights of the Sky" during the Great War as Transnational Media Events', *European Review of History/Revue européenne d'histoire* 15 (2008): 643–58; Stefanie Schüler-Springorum, *Krieg und Fliegen: Die Legion Condor im Spanischen Bürgerkrieg* (Paderborn: Schöningh, 2010), ch. 2.

including among their enemies. From time to time, they negotiated periods of truce in order to recover dead and wounded comrades, and they used ceasefires over Christmas or Easter to fraternize with enemy soldiers.[36] As early as August 1914, social-democratic newspapers had reminded their readers, many of them already on active duty, to remain 'humane' on the battlefield and not forget that they were fighting 'class comrades' on the enemy side. They advised them to exercise caution when reading exaggerated press reports about *franctireurs* or horrible cases of mutilation. They also warned against believing Allied propaganda that told equally exaggerated stories about German soldiers violating women and bayonetting children. What mattered most 'for us proletarians' was to 'show chivalry' and to resist all manner of brutish, hateful, cruel or mean behaviour.[37]

Chivalry and gender

Chivalrous and honourable conduct especially referred to armed men's behaviour towards unarmed persons, among them, most conspicuously, women. In this vein, 46-year-old Berlin artist Käthe Kollwitz, whose two sons served in the German army, wrote approvingly in her diary about chivalric soldiers protecting or saving unarmed civilians, women and children.

> Heavenly sounds, sweet weeping sounds of peace when I read of French soldiers sparing or even helping wounded Germans, of German soldiers marking houses in Franc-tireur villages: 'Spare! Here lives an old woman who has been kind to me' or 'Spare! Here lives a woman who has just given birth'.[38]

War propaganda from all sides played heavily on notions of chivalry – denying it to the enemy, reclaiming it for one's own army. After Germany invaded Belgium, people in France and Britain were inundated with images of female bodies that had been raped and mutilated by brutish German

---

[36]Jünger, *Storm of Steel*, 23, 51–2, 84–5, 122–3, 261; Ernst Jünger, *Kriegstagebuch 1914–1918*, ed. Helmuth Kiesel (Stuttgart: Klett-Cotta, 2010), 51, 55, 60, 65–6, 97, 220–1. As to informal ceasefires and moments of fraternization, see Benjamin Ziemann, *Front und Heimat: Ländliche Kriegserfahrungen im südlichen Bayern 1914–1923* (Essen: Klartext,1997), 97–106; Malcolm Brown and Shirley Seaton, *Christmas Truce* (London: Cooper, 1984); Modris Eksteins, *Rites of Spring: The Great War and the Birth of the Modern Age* (Boston: Houghton Mifflin, 1989), ch. 3; Aribert Reimann, *Der große Krieg der Sprachen: Untersuchungen zur historischen Semantik in Deutschland und England zur Zeit des Ersten Weltkriegs* (Essen: Klartext, 2000), 185 ff.; Anne Lipp, *Meinungslenkung im Krieg: Kriegserfahrungen deutscher Soldaten und ihre Deutung 1914–1918* (Göttingen: Vandenhoeck & Ruprecht, 2003), 185 ff.
[37]'Unsere Feinde' [our enemies], *Vorwärts*, 23 August 1914.
[38]Käthe Kollwitz, *Die Tagebücher*, ed. Jutta Bohnke-Kollwitz (Berlin: Siedler, 1989), 158 (diary entry of 27 August 1914).

soldiers. The 'rape of Belgium' and German warfare against civilians, cities and cultural treasures like the Louvain library were met with outrage. British newspapers published drawings like 'The March of the Huns' and the sarcastically titled 'Triumph of "Culture"' which depicted German soldiers slaying women and children.[39] French propaganda issued a series of graphics that showed German soldiers violating French women and raiding their homes. *Les Boches* appeared as despicable animals sending up an abominable and disgusting stench.[40] American posters urging citizens to sign up for 'liberty loans' likewise used the image of savage German soldiers laying their greedy hands on young girls and mothers.[41]

In Germany, schoolteachers wrote poems urging men to go to war in order to protect children, women and the 'pure bodies of your virgins' who would otherwise be violated by Russians and Frenchmen.[42] In a 1915 address, the professor Philipp Witkop inversely subscribed to such images, recommending to educators a song that bluntly sexualized the fall of Liège. 'Jungfer Lüttich' had initially been courted by Germany, but chose another lover (France). In the end, however, she lustfully fell for the German invader, who took her by force. According to Witkop, the song was an excellent example of contemporary war lyrics and should be sung in every classroom.[43] His colleague Max Weber also referred to Belgium's 'rape' and 'castration', although more symbolically and in a critical tone.[44]

As Weber knew only too well, rape and castration had different targets. Rape affronted female honour, and, through the concept of family honour, sullied male honour as well. Castration deprived men of their masculinity altogether. This was reflected in Allied war propaganda's call to male citizens and citizen–soldiers to defy the stereotype of passivity and impotence.

---

[39] *The Times*, 29 August 1914, 9; *Punch*, 26 August 1914. See Michael L. Sanders and Philip M. Taylor, *British Propaganda during the First World War, 1914–18* (London: Macmillan, 1982); Reimann, *Krieg*, 168 ff.; Martin Schramm, *Das Deutschlandbild in der britischen Presse 1912–1919* (Berlin: Akademie-Verlag, 2007).

[40] Rainer Rother, ed., *Die letzten Tage der Menschheit: Bilder des Ersten Weltkrieges* (Berlin: Ars Nicolai, 1994), 468–71 ('Les atrocités allemandes'); Juliette Courmont, *L'odeur de l'ennemi: L'imaginaire olfactif en 1914–1918* (Paris: Colin, 2010); *Der Erste Weltkrieg in der internationalen Karikatur*, ed. Eberhard Demm (Hannover: Fackelträger Verlag, 1988), 62–5; Ruth Harris, 'The "Child of the Barbarian": Rape, Race and Nationalism in France during the First World War', *Past & Present* no. 141 (1993): 170–206; Nicoletta F. Gullace, 'Sexual Violence and Family Honor: British Propaganda and International Law during the First World War', *American Historical Review* 102 (1997): 714–47; Reimann, *Krieg*, 173 ff. Cf. John Horne and Alan Kramer, *German Atrocities, 1914: A History of Denial* (New Haven: Yale University Press, 2001).

[41] *Les Affiches de la Grande Guerre*, ed. Véronique Harel (Péronne: Historial de la Grande Guerre, 1998), 45.

[42] Hermann Stehr, 'Der Krieg bricht los', *Die neue Rundschau* 25 (1914): 1185–7. Käthe Kollwitz read this poem to her son Hans in September 1914, without further comment (Kollwitz, *Tagebücher*, 161).

[43] Philipp Witkop, 'Der deutsche Unterricht', in *Der Weltkrieg im Unterricht* (Gotha: Perthes, 1915), 53–67.

[44] Weber, *Politik im Weltkrieg*, 18, 21–2, 70.

By caricaturing the enemy as inept, indulgent and drunk, German media questioned his masculine prowess and honour.[45] In return, French and Belgian citizens were encouraged to actively protect the honour of their wives, sisters and daughters, which was synonymous with defending their own honour as husbands, brothers and fathers, as well as the honour of the nation. Quite explicitly, male honour and national honour were seen as synonymous. To shield women's sexual integrity was part and parcel of men's duty and their claim to honour. Since the nation, too, had to be defended and kept pure and safe, it was a man's job to go forth and fight the aggressor and thereby uphold national honour.

Notions of chivalry also echoed in the language of international relations in the summer of 1914. For Russia, protecting 'little Serbia' from the Habsburg menace was a matter of honour. British politicians framed the decision to go to war as an act of saving a small country overrun by German military might. When Lloyd George addressed a large audience at Queen's Hall, London, on 19 September 1914, he called it 'an honourable obligation' to safeguard Belgium's liberty and integrity. If Britain had not come to Belgium's rescue, 'our shame would have rung down the everlasting ages'. It was not just a matter of upholding treaties, Lloyd George insisted. It was also the nation's moral duty to help a small, weak country which was being 'treated brutally' by its mightier neighbour. In short: it was an act of chivalry (the politician was sure to mention the slaughtered 'women and children' who had to be avenged).[46]

For France, which had also signed the 1839 treaty, it was not so much a matter of protecting Belgium, but rather of shielding its own territory and, as a veritable *point d'honneur*, of reclaiming Alsace-Lorraine. The 1870 failure to maintain its territorial integrity had severely 'shamed' the French nation, and the 'lost provinces' had been mourned ever since. Vivid gendered images were used to illustrate Alsace-Lorraine's suffering under German rule. The provinces were depicted as young girls in traditional dress desperately waiting to be rescued and returned to the motherland. Occupation and annexation were seen as a violation of their honour and a threat to the honour of mother France and her sons. In 1914, those sons eventually took up arms as *soldats–citoyens* to liberate the land from Germany's masculine presence.[47]

They had been prepared and trained for this purpose from early on, at school as well as during their years of compulsory military service. General

---

[45]Demm, *Weltkrieg*, 65, 68, 71; Reimann, *Krieg*, 177 ff.
[46]Lloyd George, *Honour and Dishonour*, 1, 5, 7, 10. Lloyd George also alluded to German 'insults against British courage' and promised that Britain would prove those insults (among them, that Brits were unheroic, timorous and craven) wrong on 'the battlefields of France and Germany'.
[47]Ouriel Reshef, *Guerre, mythes et caricature: Au berceau d'une mentalité française* (Paris: Presses de la Fondation Nationale des Sciences Politiques, 1984), ch. 1; Michael Burns, 'Families and Fatherlands: The Lost Provinces and the Case of Captain Dreyfus', in *Nationhood and Nationalism in France: From Boulangism to the Great War, 1889–1918*, ed. Robert Tombs (London: HarperCollins, 1991), 50–62; Edward Berenson, *The Trial of Madame Caillaux* (Berkeley: University of California Press, 1992), 114–17.

conscription taught young men the fundamentals of patriotism, comradeship and honour. Continental armies thus served as comprehensive 'schools of manliness'.[48] British citizens were spared this kind of education prior to 1916. Yet military manliness nevertheless sparked adolescent imaginations. Although the definition of a gentleman was remarkably civil, it held tight to notions of chivalry, bravery and steadfastness. The heroes worshipped in juvenile literature and the national press who embodied those virtues, such as Henry Havelock or T.E. Lawrence, were more often than not engaged in military campaigns and colonial escapades.[49] Many British boys and youngsters felt compelled to follow in these footsteps and tested their mettle in boy-scout brigades and volunteer associations, just as their French and German contemporaries did in *bataillons scolaires* or the Jungdeutschland Bund.[50]

Shame and shaming

For those who shied away from the swell of patriotism and military service in 1914, the public had nothing but contempt. Propaganda posters showed women (and children) reminding men of their duties and questioning their sense of bravery. In Britain, women handed out white feathers to men who failed to voluntarily enlist before 1916.[51] Young men without uniform were seen as cowards evading their most solemn task: protecting the honour of the fatherland and with it the honour of its women.

---

[48]Ute Frevert, *A Nation in Barracks: Modern Germany, Military Conscription and Civil Society* (Oxford: Berg, 2004); Christa Hämmerle, *Ganze Männer? Gesellschaft, Geschlecht und Allgemeine Wehrpflicht in Österreich-Ungarn (1868–1914)* (Frankfurt: Campus, 2022); Alan Forrest, *The Soldiers of the French Revolution* (Durham, NC: Duke University Press, 1990); Jakob Vogel, *Nationen im Gleichschritt: Der Kult der 'Nation in Waffen' in Deutschland und Frankreich 1871–1914* (Göttingen: Vandenhoeck & Ruprecht, 1997).

[49]Graham Dawson, *Soldier Heroes: British Adventure, Empire and the Imagining of Masculinities* (London: Routledge, 1994); Heather Streets, *Martial Races: The Military, Race and Masculinity in British Imperial Culture, 1857–1914* (London: Palgrave, 2005).

[50]Christoph Jahr, 'British Prussianism – Überlegungen zu einem europäischen Militarismus im 19. und frühen 20. Jahrhundert', in *Militarismus in Deutschland 1871 bis 1945*, ed. Wolfram Wette (Münster: LIT, 1999), 293–309; Levsen, *Elite*; Christian Jansen, ed., *Der Bürger als Soldat: Die Militarisierung europäischer Gesellschaften im langen 19. Jahrhundert* (Essen: Klartext, 2004); Vogel, *Nationen*; Markus Ingenlath, *Mentale Aufrüstung: Militarisierungstendenzen in Frankreich und Deutschland vor dem Ersten Weltkrieg* (Frankfurt: Campus, 1998); Klaus Saul, 'Der Kampf um die Jugend zwischen Volksschule und Kaserne', *Militärgeschichtliche Mitteilungen 9* (1971): 97–143; Jürgen Reulecke, 'The Battle for the Young: Mobilising Young People in Wilhelmine Germany', in *Generations in Conflict: Youth Revolt and Generation Formation in Germany, 1770–1968*, ed. Mark Roseman (Cambridge: Cambridge University Press, 1995), 92–105.

[51]Nicoletta Gullace, 'White Feathers and Wounded Men: Female Patriotism and the Memory of the Great War', *Journal of British Studies* 16 (1997): 178–206; Will Ellsworth-Jones, *We Will Not Fight: The Untold Story of the First World War's Conscientious Objectors* (London: Aurum, 2007), 49 ff.; Sharon Crozier-De Rosa, *Shame and the Anti-Feminist Backlash: Britain, Ireland and Australia, 1890–1920* (New York: Routledge, 2018), 172 ff.

By publicly shaming them, women made men acknowledge and adhere to traditional gender roles and characteristics. For their part, men complained about women's lack of empathy. In 1917, the Austro-Hungarian officer Andreas Latzko anonymously published an account of war at the Isonzo front, where he had served in the Imperial and Royal Army until the previous year. One of the protagonists talked about the 'great disillusionment' they felt during the war – not due to the war itself, but because of women's behaviour: instead of maternally protecting their sons and passionately defending their fiancés and husbands, they smiled, threw roses and waved their handkerchiefs as the men departed. 'They sent us – *sent* us! Because every one of them would have been ashamed to stand there without a hero.' To meet this expectation, men enlisted, became heroes and returned with medals that raised their value on the sexual marketplace: 'His girl will like him better, and the other girls will run after him, and he can use his medal to hook other men's women away from under their noses.'[52]

Men's belief that women would 'rescue' them from the horrors of war was based on their perception of women's role as devoted mothers and loving wives. That perspective overlooked what was truly at stake: the gendered division of honour and shame. Honour made different demands on men and women. Being a man of honour could carry multiple meanings, depending on class, profession and situation. Still, it always boiled down to displaying courage and determination. Lacking the nerve to stand up for one's own concerns and commitments meant being unmanly and effeminate. For men, being called a coward incurred shame and humiliation. For women, shamefacedness was considered a genuine virtue. Behaving in a shameful and indecent way caused women to lose their honour and allowed others to treat them disrespectfully. Once lost, a woman could do nothing to restore her honour; she relied on her father, brother, fiancé or husband to act in her place. This was sold as a chivalrous gesture: the strong man stepping in for his weak woman. A woman's honour therefore largely depended on her male guardian's willingness to protect her. If he lacked that courage and failed to come to her rescue, such behaviour was inevitably perceived as utterly dishonourable, shameful and unchivalrous.

Shame, however, was not reserved solely for so-called cowards, shirkers, traitors and deserters.[53] It also befell those soldiers who had suffered the fate of falling into enemy hands. Already in the early days of the war, Germany had captured thousands of prisoners, who were interned in camps and

---

[52] Andreas Latzko, *Men in War* (New York: Boni & Liveright, 1918), 40–5. Latzko's book was quickly translated into nineteen languages, but it was banned in all of the warring countries. After his authorship became known, he was demoted by the Austrian army's Supreme Command.
[53] On the treatment of deserters (or, even worse, defectors), see Christoph Jahr, *Gewöhnliche Soldaten: Desertion und Deserteure im deutschen und britischen Heer 1914–1918* (Göttingen: Vandenhoeck & Ruprecht, 1998), 177 ff.

labour battalions on German territory. Other countries followed suit, and by the end of 1918 around 6.6 million soldiers had been taken prisoner.[54] The way that POWs were dealt with offers a particularly candid insight into questions of honour and shame as they were negotiated during the Great War. In late August 1914, Käthe Kollwitz was 'very moved to read that French soldiers who have been taken prisoners of war cover their faces in shame'.[55] What did those men feel ashamed of, exactly?

In 1899 and 1907, the Hague Conventions had explicitly removed POWs from the theatre of war, exempting them from the usual rules of enmity. It was commonly understood that they should not be treated as enemies or criminals, but 'with humanity'. During the First World War, this obligation was met rather differently. Each government ostentatiously praised themselves for displaying kindness, dignity and benevolence towards POWs, while accusing the enemy of denying their own soldiers the same generous and honourable treatment. As a German family journal bluntly put it in 1916:

> Daily, troupes of prisoners are being marched through the streets of Berlin, but nobody ever spit into their faces or graphically cut their throats – a pleasure that Parisians, men and women, continuously indulge in when they are shown a few Germans. Since POWs have become everyday occurrences, even curious people no longer stare at them as if they were something special.[56]

That initial act of staring had in fact been widely reported on. Whenever POWs approached, large crowds would gather in order to catch a glimpse or sneer at them.[57] Kollwitz witnessed such gatherings in September 1914 as Russian, Belgian and French soldiers arrived by train. 'The French look reduced. Many small and miserable men.' She kept her distance from the new arrivals: 'All in all, this mass of captured enemies is depressing. It reminds me somewhat of Hagenbeck.'[58] Hagenbeck was a popular zoo in Hamburg that not only presented exotic animals in natural environments,

---

[54] Richard B. Speed III, *Prisoners, Diplomats, and the Great War: A Study in the Diplomacy of Captivity* (New York: Praeger, 1990), 195.
[55] Kollwitz, *Tagebücher*, 158.
[56] Uta Hinz, *Gefangen im Großen Krieg: Kriegsgefangenschaft in Deutschland 1914–1921* (Essen: Klartext, 2006), quote 188; Panikos Panayi, *Prisoners of Britain: German Civilian and Combatant Internees during the First World War* (Manchester: Manchester University Press, 2012), 231–2; Heather Jones, *Violence against Prisoners of War in the First World War: Britain, France, and Germany, 1914–1920* (Cambridge: Cambridge University Press, 2011), ch. 1; Brian K. Feltman, *The Stigma of Surrender: German Prisoners, British Captors, and Manhood in the Great War and Beyond* (Chapel Hill, NC: University of North Carolina Press, 2015).
[57] Panayi, *Prisoners*, 62, 64; Jones, *Violence*, 38–9.
[58] Kollwitz, *Tagebücher*, 165. In 1870, French POWs in German camps complained about civilian visits, stating that they felt as if they were in a 'menagerie': Katja Mitze, '"Seit der Babylonischen Gefangenschaft hat die Welt nichts derart erlebt": Französische Kriegsgefangene und Franctireurs im Deutsch-Französischen Krieg 1870/71', in *In der Hand des Feindes*, ed. Rüdiger Overmans (Cologne: Böhlau, 1999), 235–54, here 248.

but also exhibited people from far-away places, including Inuit, Samoans and Nubians. The latter typically drew a great number of curious spectators, though some contemporaries were appalled by this derogatory act of exposure.[59]

While Kollwitz clearly did not enjoy seeing POWs (or, for that matter, 'exotic' races) on public display, others did. Women, in particular, were criticized for showing 'unpatriotic' curiosity whenever French or Belgian soldiers were marched through the streets of their city or village. This was said to dishonour both the women who violated norms of female decency and shamefulness and the prisoners who, in becoming a spectacle, were humiliated.

Generally, staring was considered impolite and tactless, and children learned early on not to do it. But normal standards of behaviour did not always apply. Given the circumstances of captivity, staring at POWs became a downright insult. Those who stared were in a position of power, one they made no attempt to conceal. The captured were powerless and thus had to endure being stared at. Hiding one's face, as Kollwitz had recounted, was a way of skirting the stares, but it could not prevent the shame.

In some sense, these men were reliving the experiences of those who had once been displayed for committing petty crimes. Medieval societies had invented the institution of the pillory for people who had offended collective morality. Being put in the stocks or a pillory erected in the marketplace or at a crossroads was a method of public shaming. Offenders were exposed to stares and comments and were often treated harshly by those who passed by or deliberately joined the crowd to watch and jeer. As a legal device, the pillory was abolished in the 1830s. Semantically, though, it has lived on into the present, a sign of its long-lasting effect on people's imaginations and sensibilities.[60]

Being marched through foreign streets and squares, still wearing their uniforms but without their rifles (widely and fondly referred to as the infantry soldier's 'bride'[61]) forced men to confront the loss of power and control over their own lives. They were now squarely in the hands and at the mercy of the enemy. Although international law protected them and obliged

---

[59]See, for Hagenbeck and other human exhibitions, Sierra A. Bruckner, 'Spectacles of (Human) Nature: Commercial Ethnography between Leisure, Learning, and *Schaulust*', in *Worldly Provincialism: German Anthropology in the Age of Empire*, ed. H. Glenn Penny and Matti Bunzl (Ann Arbor: University of Michigan Press, 2003), 127–55; Anne Dreesbach, *Gezähmte Wilde: Die Zurschaustellung 'exotischer' Menschen in Deutschland 1870–1940* (Frankfurt: Campus, 2005).
[60]Frank Rexroth, *Deviance and Power in Late Medieval London*, trans. Pamela E. Selwyn (Cambridge: Cambridge University Press, 2007); Liliane D'Artagnan, 'Le Rituel punitif du pilori au Moyen Âge', *Francia* 44 (2017): 99–121. See Chapter 5 in this volume.
[61]This is how Käthe Kollwitz described the rifle after watching her son be sworn into his regiment (*Tagebücher*, 158). She was following a long tradition of military language and customs, see Frevert, *Nation in Barracks*, 77–8, 115 ff., 181 ff.

the enemy government to treat them honourably, they were made to feel their impotence keenly. Bystanders spat in their faces, tried to beat them up and hurled insults at them; the press published caricatures and illustrations ridiculing them or depicting them as ruthless perpetrators of atrocious war crimes. Those who came from non-European countries or colonies met with openly racist prejudice and particular contempt.[62]

POWs could thus not help but notice that they had failed in their duty to defend home, hearth and fatherland. Their efforts had been insufficient and they experienced blame and shame as a result.[63] In the face of expectations of manly strength, courage and determination, defeat and captivity were understood and felt as clear signs of emasculation and dishonour.

Defeat as dishonour? The demise of honour culture

And what about those soldiers who dutifully fought until the very last for their nation's honour but were defeated anyway? By the autumn of 1918, Germany was facing precisely this predicament. Defeat came as a shock; the Supreme Army Command had not prepared the public in advance. Their reactions varied greatly. On 22 October, well-known poet and writer Richard Dehmel appealed to young men who would rather die than suffer a 'disgraceful peace'. Their sense of honour, he believed, would spur them to sacrifice themselves in defence of 'our nation's honour and human dignity'. He himself set a heroic example: although he was already in his mid-fifties and had been severely wounded in 1916, he enlisted to fight on the front lines once more.

Eight days later, Käthe Kollwitz published a response to Dehmel in the same social-democratic newspaper. She fervently rejected his call to arms and passionately criticized his argument about personal and national honour. Remembering her own sons' enthusiasm and spirit of sacrifice in the autumn of 1914, she firmly declared that those days were over. Four years of war and millions of dead men had taught different lessons about honour, shame and sacrifice. What was important now was building a future, and the future needed youth. Acknowledging defeat and accepting unfavourable conditions of peacemaking should not stand in the way: 'We did not see Russia as infamous when she agreed to the incredibly harsh conditions

---

[62]Jones, *Violence*, 79 ff.; Hinz, *Gefangen*, 163 ff.; Uta Hinz, '"Die deutschen "Barbaren" sind doch die besseren Menschen": Kriegsgefangenschaft und gefangene "Feinde" in der Darstellung der deutschen Publizistik 1914–1918', in *Hand des Feindes*, ed. Overmans, 339–61.

[63]Annette Becker, 'Paradoxien in der Situation der Kriegsgefangenen 1914–1918', in *Kriegsgefangene im Europa des Ersten Weltkriegs*, ed. Jochen Oltmer (Paderborn: Schöningh, 2006), 24–31, esp. 25.

of Brest-Litowsk [set by the German government] only because she felt compelled to save the remaining strength for domestic reconstruction.' Likewise, Germany should not feel dishonoured if the Allied Powers decided to dictate peace rather than negotiate it under law. Rather, Kollwitz wrote, the nation should be proudly aware that its honour was unblemished, just as the honour of an individual who deferred to 'overwhelmingly strong forces' remained intact.[64]

In Kollwitz's view, as in that of many others, the armistice – which was finally concluded on 11 November 1918 – did not impinge on German national honour. Defeat had not come from a lack of courage or determination, but rather from a blatant asymmetry of resources, both human and material, on the battlefield.

The asymmetry persisted after the guns fell quiet. Rather than rebalancing European power structures and rebuilding respect between winners and losers, as the Congress of Vienna had done after the Napoleonic wars in 1814 and 1815, the victors chose to follow the path traced in Paris in 1871 and Brest-Litowsk in 1918 (and, it must be noted, in the imperial wars that had been fought in China and other places beyond Europe): they unilaterally determined the conditions for peace and treated the losers with condescension and dismissiveness. Honour culture as it rested on the notion of equality and mutual recognition was discarded. Overlooking its potential for mediating conflicts and enabling future cooperation, policymakers deliberately abandoned it in favour of a system that confirmed the power of the victor and the powerlessness of the conquered.

This system was on full display during the signing ceremony that took place in Versailles, in June 1919, in the very Hall of Mirrors where the German Empire had been proclaimed after France's defeat in 1871. It was no coincidence that French Prime Minister Georges Clemenceau chose this location. The atmosphere at the ceremony was icy and hostile. The two German delegates – Social Democrat Hermann Müller and Johannes Bell of the Catholic Centre Party – were led in, permitted to sign the treaty and escorted away again. At the hotel, Müller, who had until then tried to contain himself, collapsed in a cold sweat. On the same evening, after the 'worst hour of my life', he travelled back to Berlin.[65]

Others were not pleased with the ceremony either. Edward House, an advisor to US President Woodrow Wilson, found it reminiscent of a Roman triumphal procession in which 'the conqueror dragged the conquered at his chariot wheels'. He deplored that the signing lacked any 'element of chivalry' and that it 'was elaborately staged and made as humiliating to the

---

[64]Kollwitz, *Tagebücher*, 839–41. Dehmel's appeal was published in *Vorwärts* on 22 October 1918, Kollwitz's reply on 30 October. The controversy was widely commented on and reprinted in *Vossische Zeitung* on 30 October 1918.
[65]Margaret MacMillan, *Paris 1919: Six Months that Changed the World* (New York: Random House, 2003), 27, 474 ff.

enemy as it well could be'. British diplomat Harold Nicolson empathized with the German ministers, who, as members of the new post-revolutionary government, had had no part in the martial politics of the German Empire.[66]

In Germany, the Treaty of Versailles was seen as deeply humiliating, and politicians of all parties strove to distance themselves from it.[67] The War Guilt Clause, which forced Germany to accept complete responsibility, and the harsh reparations the country had to pay made Germans feel dishonoured. Naval officer Adolf von Trotha – whose father had been killed in the Franco-Prussian War in 1870 – joined the chorus in condemning the treaty's 'disgraceful paragraphs' in June 1919, deeming them 'incompatible with the honour of the navy and the fatherland'.[68] Socialist and liberal parties also rejected the treaty as an ignoble peace but, in view of the threatened sanctions, saw no option but to sign it. Consequently, the far-right denounced them as dishonourable traitors and murdered in broad daylight those they considered 'fulfilment politicians'.

The military occupation of the Rhineland, another of the treaty's terms, was seen as particularly demeaning, above all the stationing of French units that included soldiers from Africa. In 1920, the entire Weimar National Assembly, with the exception of the far-left, voted for a resolution declaring this an 'indelible dishonour' for Germany and a 'horrifying danger' for German women and children. Social Democratic President Friedrich Ebert called 'on the world' to acknowledge the 'provocative offence against the laws of civilization' that 'coloured troops of the lowest culture are stationed to watch over a people of such high spiritual and economic significance as the Rhinelanders'. In the same vein, a leaflet condemned the 'outrageous humiliation and rape of a highly cultured white race by a still half-barbaric coloured' one.[69]

---

[66] Edward House, *The Intimate Papers of Colonel House*, ed. Charles Seymour, vol. 4 (London: Benn, 1926–8), 502; Harold Nicolson, *Peacemaking 1919* (New York: Grosset & Dunlap, [1933] 1965), 366–71.

[67] As to the Austrian case, see Ute Frevert, '"There was opportunity for emotion": Gefühlspolitik in St. Germain', in Österreichische Akademie der Wissenschaften, *Akademie im Dialog 16: 100 Jahre Vertrag von Saint Germain* (Vienna: ÖAW, 2019), 43–9.

[68] Adolf von Trotha, *Volkstum und Staatsführung: Briefe und Aufzeichnungen aus den Jahren 1915–1920* (Berlin: Grossdeutsche Verlagsanstalt, 1928), 167.

[69] Friedrich Ebert, *Schriften, Aufzeichnungen, Reden*, vol. 2 (Dresden: Reissner, 1926), 290; Michael Wildt, *Hitler's Volksgemeinschaft and the Dynamics of Racial Exclusion: Violence against Jews in Provincial Germany, 1919–1939* (New York: Berghahn, 2012), 166; Iris Wigger, *The 'Black Horror' on the Rhine: Intersections of Race, Nation, Gender and Class in 1920s Germany* (London: Palgrave Macmillan, 2017), 164, 5; Sandra Maß, 'The "Volkskörper" in Fear: Gender, Race and Sexuality in the Weimar Republic', in *New Dangerous Liaisons: Discourses on Europe and Love in the Twentieth Century*, ed. Luisa Passerini, Liliana Ellena and Alexander C.T. Geppert (New York: Berghahn, 2010), 233–50, esp. 235–9; Peter Collar, *The Propaganda War in the Rhineland: Weimar Germany, Race and Occupation after World War I* (London: I.B. Tauris, 2013), 94–129.

Again, national honour and male/female honour were closely intertwined. In mentioning 'humiliation and rape', the leaflet hinted at the (sometimes forced, sometimes consensual) relationships between soldiers from French colonies and German women. Under the auspices of racism, such relationships – and their offspring – were deemed utterly despicable, and not only by Germans. In an article for the *Sunday Times*, a Conservative MP who had served as a British officer in the war and toured the occupied territories in 1921 stated that he was not opposed to humiliating Germany, but that he was fiercely against allowing black people to rule over whites. This, he argued, was 'searing the soul of Germany and building up in her heart a desire some day to punish indignity with greater indignity'. He predicted that this would surely lead to another war.[70]

Right-wingers and National Socialists hurried to fulfil this prophecy. After 1933, Hitler tenaciously sought revisions to the Treaty of Versailles. In 1936, he justified the military 'liberation' of the Rhineland as a struggle for 'equality' that would restore 'national honour and freedom'. At the Nuremberg 'Party Congress of Honour' he declared that the honour-loving German people had 'come to the close of a most dishonorable chapter in its history'.[71] Four years later, he made sure that the French defeat was particularly ignoble, insisting on holding armistice negotiations at the site where France had 'humiliated' Germany on 11 November 1918. He had the train car in which the French, British and Germans had signed the armistice removed from the museum and returned to its historical location. On 22 June 1940, the second armistice was signed in Compiègne. According to Minister of Propaganda Joseph Goebbels, the ceremony was not meant as 'a demonstrative humiliation'; supposedly, neither 'hate' nor 'revenge' played a role. 'But', he wrote, 'the ignominy of 1918 is now over. One feels born again.' The train car was then brought to Berlin and exhibited in the centre of the city.[72]

Honour was also at stake for the French. Head of state Philippe Pétain and the foreign minister Paul Baudouin objected to armistice conditions that would compromise France's honour. At the same time, Pétain, a marshal and First World War hero who was ready to capitulate, denied British Prime Minister Winston Churchill the right to act as judge of '*l'honneur français*'. In a radio address, he confirmed that 'our flag remains unblemished'.[73] Meanwhile, Charles de Gaulle, under-secretary of state for national defence and war, sided with Churchill, who wanted to continue the war against

---

[70]Edward A. Bagley, 'The Black Watch on the Rhine', *The Sunday Times*, 23 October 1921.
[71]Max Domarus, ed., *Hitler: Speeches and Proclamations 1932–1945*, vol. 2 (Wauconda: Bolchazy-Carducci, 1992), 765, 778 (Speech in the Reichstag, 7 March 1936); 827–8.
[72]*Die Tagebücher von Joseph Goebbels*, ed. Elke Fröhlich, part I, vol. 4 (Munich: Saur, 1987), 212–13. On 1 July 1940 Goebbels himself visited Compiègne, 'place of shame and site of national resurrection' (224).
[73]*Le Matin*, 19 June 1940, 1; 24 June 1940, 1.

Germany. In exile in London, de Gaulle accused the Pétain government of having forgotten the nation's honour and abandoning the country to servitude. *France Libre* radio broadcasts, transmitted by the BBC, aired under the motto '*Honneur et Patrie*', a slogan which also adorned the movement's posters.[74]

Pétain making the motto his own prompted historian Lucien Febvre, in 1945, to trace the history and interpretive power of the terms 'honour' and 'fatherland'.[75] For him, both were '*mots-force*' that conveyed strong feelings, laden with history. Even in the middle of the twentieth century, the sentiment of honour was still alive in French hearts. It was expressed, Febvre wrote, in a '*sensibilité*' that resisted all diminutions and degradations of the person and cultivated 'a great sense of the beauty of his life'. This sense could become 'a most ardent passion' and result in a commitment to immediately parry every attack, every 'defilement'.[76]

Honour, humiliation and apology after 1945

It is questionable whether this ardent passion for honour really survived the Second World War unscathed. The process of European integration played a crucial role in de-dramatizing and disarming feelings of national honour, at least among the countries involved. In Germany, the inflated and manipulative use of honour under National Socialism helped to bury the concept altogether.

In other parts of the world, though, honour and humiliation have remained *mots-force* and often serve strategic political goals. Whenever the Chinese government alludes to the 'century of humiliation' – starting in 1839 with the first Anglo-Chinese War and ending with the communist revolution in 1949 – it is assuring its citizens that those days are definitively behind them, thanks to the foresight and steadfastness of the Communist Party.[77] The

---

[74]See Charles de Gaulle's 'Appeal of 18 June 1940' (in French): https://www.dhm.de/lemo/bestand/objekt/aufruf-de-gaulles-1940.html (accessed 14 November 2022); Julian Jackson, *France: The Dark Years 1940–1944* (Oxford: Oxford University Press, 2001), 43; Luc Capdevila, 'The Quest for Masculinity in a Defeated France, 1940–1945', *Contemporary European History* 10, no. 3 (2001): 423–45.
[75]See Pétain's speech of 28 November 1942 (Jean-Claude Barbas, 'L'Idée de patrie et de nation dans les discours de Philippe Pétain', *Guerres Mondiales et Conflits Contemporains* 177 (1995): 3–61, here 35).
[76]Lucien Febvre, '*Honneur et patrie*': *Une enquête sur le sentiment d'honneur et l'attachement à la patrie* (Paris: Perrin, 1996), 30–1, 54, 67–8.
[77]Adcock Alison Kaufman, 'The "Century of Humiliation", Then and Now: Chinese Perceptions of the International Order', *Pacific Focus* 25, no. 1 (2010): 1–33; William A. Callahan, *China: The Pessoptimist Nation* (Oxford: Oxford University Press, 2010), 31–125; Zheng Wang, *Never Forget National Humiliation: Historical Memory in Chinese Politics and Foreign Relations* (New York: Columbia University Press, 2012).

leitmotif of never being humiliated again legitimizes an assertive posturing that emphasizes one's own power and strength. Something similar can be observed in the many Arab states that celebrate a 'culture of humiliation', or in Russia, where the long-term president Vladimir Putin has carefully and purposefully cultivated a 'humiliation syndrome' in his dealings with the West.[78] Considering the 1991 demise of the Soviet Union the greatest geopolitical catastrophe of the twentieth century, he justified his war on Ukraine in 2022 as a defence of Russia's historical glory and prowess.

Even when the Soviet Union was still intact and powerful, its leaders were preoccupied with matters of recognition, appreciation and explicit deference.[79] The fear of being 'humiliated' and 'degraded' by the Americans ran deep, especially for Nikita Khrushchev. Though he presented himself assertively in his dealings with politicians and journalists from the US, he stubbornly insisted on signs of mutual respect. In 1960, incensed by the presence of US spy planes in Soviet airspace, which he called a 'deliberate violation of the Soviet Union', he demanded that President Dwight Eisenhower apologize, put a stop to the flights and punish those responsible. In this instance, he was acting in line with international law which in such cases provided for appropriate satisfaction. For the Soviet leader, however, there was more at stake: he wanted to see Eisenhower crawl 'on his knees' to satisfy the 'righteous anger of the government and the entire population of the Soviet Union at the impudence of the American government'. Eisenhower, for his part, refused 'to crawl on my knees to Khrushchev' and declined to issue an apology.[80] Khrushchev also levelled the charge of 'humiliating our state' against Eisenhower's successor, John F. Kennedy, in 1961. Kennedy, however, was no more cooperative than Eisenhower.[81]

US administrations did not generally gloss over issues of honour and humiliation either. When the Vietnam War ended with the withdrawal of American forces, President Richard Nixon defended the 1973 Paris Agreement as a 'peace with honor'.[82] Six years later, Iranian students occupied the American embassy in Tehran to force the extradition of the Shah, who

---

[78]Dominique Moïsi, *The Geopolitics of Emotion: How Cultures of Fear, Humiliation, and Hope Are Reshaping the World* (New York: Doubleday, 2009), ch. 3; Lilia Shevtsova, 'Humiliation as a Tool of Blackmail', *The American Interest*, 2 June 2015, https://www.the-american-interest.com/2015/06/02/humiliation-as-a-tool-of-blackmail/ (accessed 14 November 2022).
[79]Michael Donelan, *Honor in Foreign Policy: A History and Discussion* (New York: Palgrave Macmillan, 2007), 169–70.
[80]Susanne Schattenberg, 'Die Angst vor Erniedrigung: Die U-2-Krise und das Ende der Entspannung', in *Angst im Kalten Krieg*, ed. Bernd Greiner, Christian Th. Müller and Dierk Walter (Hamburg: Hamburger Edition, 2009), 220–51; Peter Lyon, *Eisenhower: Portrait of the Hero* (Boston: Little, Brown & Company, 1974), quote 811.
[81]Gerhard Wettig, ed., *Chruschtschows Westpolitik 1955–1964*, vol. 3 (Munich: Oldenbourg, 2011), 242, 249, 258.
[82]https://watergate.info/1973/01/23/nixon-peace-with-honor-broadcast.html (accessed 14 November 2022).

had fled to the US after the Islamic Revolution. The American government considered the occupation an attack on national honour and sought to counter what it perceived as an intolerable international humiliation with a military rescue mission – which failed spectacularly.[83]

In comparison, supposedly disrespectful treatment of American presidents on the part of their foreign hosts looked trifling. Nevertheless, they were attentively registered by public opinion and protocol offices alike. In 2016, when Barack Obama was forced to unceremoniously disembark onto the tarmac via an alternative staircase rather than receiving a red-carpet welcome upon his landing in Hangzhou, China, the US media interpreted this as a deliberate slight.[84]

Reporters and journalists also watched very closely to see whether the president himself adhered to the standards of honourable behaviour. Bill Clinton, who received the Japanese emperor at the White House in 1994, incurred the wrath of the conservative press for his obsequious body language – apparently he had bowed far too low. Fifteen years later, Obama was rebuked for virtually kowtowing to Tenno Akihito. His bowing to Saudi King Abdullah was also thought too submissive; he was accused of degrading the might of the United States and damaging its honour.[85] In 2010, the perceived humiliations reached a tipping point: the right-wing conservative Tea Party movement called for a march on Washington under the slogan 'Restore Honor'. From the marchers' point of view, the president's conduct – constantly apologizing for everything the nation had ever done and thus robbing them of their pride and self-respect – violated the country's honour.[86]

Clearly, then, honour can still ignite, mobilize and direct national passions. As an emotion, it is no longer the exclusive property of the highest

---

[83] *Akten zur Auswärtigen Politik der Bundesrepublik Deutschland 1980*, vol. 1 (Munich: De Gruyter, 2011), 499; Zbigniew Brzezinski, *Power and Principle: Memoirs of the National Security Adviser 1977–1981* (New York: Farrar, Straus & Giroux, 1983), 492–3.

[84] Mark Landler, 'Confrontations Flare as Obama's Traveling Party Reaches China', *New York Times*, 3 September 2016, https://www.nytimes.com/2016/09/04/world/asia/obama-xi-staff-shouting-match.html; Mark Landler and Jane Perlez, 'Obama Plays Down Confrontation with China over His Plane's Stairs', *New York Times*, 5 September 2016, https://www.nytimes.com/2016/09/05/world/asia/china-obama-group-of-20-summit-airport-arrival.html (both accessed 14 November 2022).

[85] Douglas Jehl, 'The President's Inclination: No, It Wasn't a Bow-Bow', *New York Times*, 19 June 1994, https://www.nytimes.com/1994/06/19/weekinreview/the-world-the-president-s-inclination-no-it-wasn-t-a-bow-bow.html; 'Obama Draws Fire for Bow to Japanese Emperor', *Fox News*, 24 December 2015, https://www.foxnews.com/politics/obama-draws-fire-for-bow-to-japanese-emperor; 'Barack Takes a Bow', *Washington Times*, 7 April 2009, https://www.washingtontimes.com/news/2009/apr/07/barack-takes-a-bow/ (all accessed 14 November 2022).

[86] Jen Chung, 'Beck at DC Rally: "America Today Begins to Turn Back to God"', *Gothamist*, 29 August 2010, https://gothamist.com/news/beck-at-dc-rally-america-today-begins-to-turn-back-to-god (accessed 14 November 2022).

representatives of the state, as it was at the beginning of the modern era. Since the nineteenth century it has been claimed by citizens who identify with their state and nation. Legitimized and protected by international law, an injured sense of honour demands satisfaction. However, there was and is a consensus that it must not take on humiliating forms. What is perceived as humiliating is, of course, a matter of opinion. The view changes with the power dynamics. Those who have power and feel superior to others usually refuse to apologize for alleged violations of honour, yet they demand apologies from the less powerful, as the treatment of China by imperial states in the nineteenth century demonstrates.[87]

Apologizing continues to be a political hot potato nationally and internationally. In 1970, Willy Brandt's genuflection in Warsaw in front of the Jewish Ghetto monument unleashed a bitter debate in West Germany. Almost half of those surveyed considered the chancellor's gesture of humility 'excessive', and some called it 'undignified', comparing it to Heinrich IV's walk to Canossa. A kneeling head of state obviously did not fit the image of upright, assertive and honour-conscious statehood any more than the social democrat Carlo Schmid who felt ashamed of German crimes in the Second World War and, in 1958, publicly called them a 'German disgrace'; he, too, was accused of having violated 'national dignity'.[88]

Fifty years later, Brandt's gesture figures as an archetypical case of new 'moral politics'. Since the 1990s, such politics ushered in the 'age of apologies' in international relations.[89] Assuming responsibility and admitting guilt for past crimes and misdemeanours was no longer seen as a sign of weakness or yielding, but as an expression of political maturity and strength. Behind this historic shift lay the socio-cultural transformation of democratic societies that began in the 1960s. A culture of honour fed by images of warring masculinity, as it had been shaped in the long nineteenth century, finally succumbed to the forces of liberalization, among them feminism, which no longer privileged models of male identity based on aggressive self-assertion at any price. This transformation contributed to establishing other models of conduct on the international stage as well.

---

[87] See Ute Frevert, *The Politics of Humiliation: A Modern History* (Oxford: Oxford University Press, 2020), 162 ff.
[88] On Brandt as well as on Schmid, see Frevert, *Politics*, 192–7.
[89] O'Neill, *Honor*, 177–92; Melissa Nobles, *The Politics of Official Apologies* (Cambridge: Cambridge University Press, 2008); Michael R. Marrus, 'Official Apologies and the Quest for Historical Justice', *Journal of Human Rights* 6, no. 1 (2007): 75–105; Alexis Dudden, 'Is History a Human Right? Japan and Korea's Troubles with the Past', in *The Human Rights Revolution: An International History*, ed. Akira Iriye, Petra Goedde and William I. Hitchcock (New York: Oxford University Press, 2012), 311–26.

Those models, to be sure, are not uncontested and still meet with significant resistance from right-wing, conservative and populist camps as well as from authoritarian regimes. For them, honour and shame continue to work as emotion claims and *mots-force* that can be appealed to and used to mobilize people. Even here, though, the 'excitable sense of honour' has lost much of the intensity that Heinrich von Treitschke and Emer de Vattel had in mind.

CHAPTER FIVE

Shame and Shaming in Modern History

In social and political practice, shame has been conceptualized as the complete opposite of honour in terms of how it is felt and how the feeling is expressed. A person or a state that inhabits honour in the sense outlined in Chapters 3 and 4 carries themselves proudly, erectly, eyes bright and looking forward. Those who are experiencing shame, meanwhile, cast their eyes down, try to hide, do not wish to be seen. They project an aura of failure, defeat and an utter lack of self-confidence.

And yet, shame directly correlates with honour. Questioning or infringing on the honour of a person or a state is seen as an act of shaming. In pragmatic terms, honour can be demonstrated by a 'keen sensitivity to the experience of humiliation and shaming', as William Miller put it and as the history of duelling testifies.[1] Being treated dishonourably is often followed by an intense feeling of shame, which can sometimes be masked or discharged by counter-aggression. Lashing out at one's opponent is one way to get over shame.[2] If this is not possible, resentment is another option. Shame can also be accepted and endured, depending on the respective conditions of power and powerlessness. There are instances in which accepting shame actually serves to restore and regain honour lost.

Shame has been a crucial emotion in both private and public matters and in many ways it still is. It plays an important role in most, if not all, societies,

---

[1] William Ian Miller, *Humiliation and Other Essays on Honor, Social Discomfort, and Violence* (Ithaca, NY: Cornell University Press, 1993), 84.
[2] Thomas J. Scheff and Suzanne M. Retzinger, *Emotions and Violence: Shame and Rage in Destructive Conflicts* (Lexington: Lexington Books, 1991).

and performs vital social as well as political functions.³ This chapter will focus on the modern history of shame as a publicly produced emotion by examining shaming practices, predominantly in Western Europe, with a glimpse at the United States and China. How and why have such practices been enacted? Who criticized them, for what reasons? And how have shame and shaming fared in the recent past and in the present?

Psychological, sociological and historical inquiries

Until now, it has mainly been philosophers and psychologists who have tackled the subject of shame. They view it as a self-conscious response to the perception of failing to meet expectations, our own and those of others. The feeling of shame relates to us in our relationships with people who observe and assess us and whose acceptance is important to us. Those we despise cannot make us feel ashamed. Similarly, if we have not internalized the norms and behavioural conventions that we have violated, we will not necessarily feel ashamed of our transgressions. Shame, therefore, emotionally binds individuals to a group or a society; it is a profoundly social emotion, one which forces people to face themselves and both emphasizes and reduces their self-consciousness or *Ichbewusstsein*.⁴

But shame also arises when a person has not done anything wrong or inappropriate for which they must be held to account. Psychoanalyst Léon Wurmser, who was born and grew up in Switzerland, recalled the sense of shame he felt in the 1930s:

> When I was about seven I was dismayed to learn from other children that I was unacceptable because I belonged to another 'race'. Even

---

³The older distinction between shame cultures and guilt cultures, as suggested, for example, by Ruth Benedict in her study on Japan, *The Chrysanthemum and the Sword: Patterns of Japanese Culture* (Boston: Houghton Mifflin, 1946), has since been dismissed as overly simplistic: Takie Sugiyama Lebra, 'The Social Mechanism of Guilt and Shame: The Japanese Case', *Anthropological Quarterly* 44, no. 4 (1971): 241–55; Scheff and Retzinger, *Emotions and Violence*, 5–6; June Price Tangney, 'The Self-Conscious Emotions: Shame, Guilt, Embarrassment and Pride', in *Handbook of Cognition and Emotion*, ed. Tim Dalgleish and Mick J. Power (Chichester: Wiley, 1999), 541–68.

⁴Donald L. Nathanson, ed., *The Many Faces of Shame* (New York: Guilford Press, 1987); Tangney, Self-Conscious Emotions; Gabriele Taylor, *Pride, Shame, and Guilt: Emotions of Self-Assessment* (Oxford: Clarendon Press, 1985), 53–84, with a special emphasis on audience and self-consciousness. As to the distinction between guilt and shame, see Bernard Williams, *Shame and Necessity* (Berkeley: University of California Press, 2008), 89–94, 219–22. On how shame affects *Ichbewusstsein*, see Georg Simmel, *Zur Psychologie der Scham*, in Simmel, *Schriften zur Soziologie*, ed. Heinz-Jürgen Dahme and Otthein Rammstedt (Frankfurt: Suhrkamp, [1901] 1983), 140–50.

though my family had lived in that little town for three generations, we still were treated as foreigners and intruders. For years my feeling of being an inferior, derided outcast was incessantly deepened by German propaganda from across the border only a few miles away, heaping shame and contempt on all I was and knew.[5]

Wurmser's feeling of shame was linked to the contempt that non-Jewish Swiss children showed him. They scorned him not because he had behaved in an offensive manner, rather, their contempt was related to what he was: a Jew. For philosopher Martha Nussbaum, shame 'pertains to the whole self, rather than to a specific act of the self'. It 'focuses on defect or imperfection, and thus on some aspect of the very being of the person who feels it'.[6] This manifests in the physiology of shame. A person who feels ashamed blushes, bows their head and avoids eye contact, trying to make themselves small and inconspicuous. The unpleasant feeling grips the whole body, from head to toe. According to psychologists, the negative experience implodes and destroys the self, at least temporarily.[7]

The language of psychologists attests to the period of its creation in the late twentieth century. During the therapeutic turn of the 1960s and 1970s, the self was the centre of all attention and care.[8] A little later, with the rise of neoliberalism, came the obsessive optimization of the self. The self is clearly a historically variable construction, bound to time and space as well as to social categories. It is by no means an eternal or universal truth.[9]

What does this mean with regard to history? Can contemporary notions of shame and the shameful self be easily transposed back to earlier times? Does self-consciousness or *Ichbewusstsein*, of which sociologist Georg Simmel wrote in 1901, refer to the same self defined by American psychologists eighty or ninety years later? Are the feelings that accompany this consciousness the same today? Did the corporeality of shame remain constant over decades and centuries?

Such questions are at the heart of the history of emotions. They also mark the distance between historians and psychologists or neuroscientists. The latter assume that feelings – as physical sensations and cognitive perceptions – are ahistorical, inscribed in the human mind and body through evolution

---

[5]Léon Wurmser, *The Mask of Shame* (Baltimore: Johns Hopkins University Press, 1981), 2–3.
[6]Martha C. Nussbaum, *Hiding from Humanity: Disgust, Shame, and the Law* (Princeton: Princeton University Press, 2004), 184, 207.
[7]Helen Block Lewis, 'Shame and the Narcissistic Personality', in *Many Faces*, ed. Nathanson, 93–132, here 95.
[8]Nikolas Rose, *Inventing Our Selves: Psychology, Power, and Personhood* (Cambridge: Cambridge University Press, 1996).
[9]Eva Illouz, *Saving the Modern Soul: Therapy, Emotions and the Culture of Self-Help* (Berkeley: University of California Press, 2008); Elizabeth Lunbeck, *The Americanization of Narcissism* (Cambridge, MA: Harvard University Press, 2014).

and biology. The definition of shame and how it feels does not seem to them to be subject to any historical change whatsoever, even in varying contexts. Many psychologists claim that shame is biologically patterned; Silvan Tomkins calls it an 'innate auxiliary affect'.[10] Others, however, note that the earliest age children feel shame is eighteen months. This indicates that shame is acquired and learned in close connection with the processes of separation and individualization that are associated with the formation of self-consciousness.[11] Ethnographic research shows that such processes are highly variable across different cultures. Consequently, shame comes with different temporalities, targets, causes and effects. It may well be felt differently, in its intensity and in its feedback loops.

Historians, unlike scholars in literary and cultural studies or philosophy, find it difficult to fruitfully engage with the concept of 'innate affect' – which is, needless to say, impossible to put to the historical test. They do better with the notion of social learning. The plasticity of the brain, as emphasized by neuroscientists, likewise appeals. The assumption that human brains interact with their environment and adapt to its challenges and rewards opens the door to contemplate historical change. The same holds true for the human body. As historical research has proven, bodies as well as the concept of a body have undergone multiple changes, triggered by shifts in religious, social and economic epistemologies and practices. Modern medicine, hygiene, health and sports, but also work and fashion, have greatly influenced and shaped the ways in which people perceive and treat their bodies. If the body is subject to wide-ranging interventions and alterations, why would feelings, which are almost always expressed through the body, remain and feel the same?

There is an additional bridge to the historicization of feelings. Every feeling clearly contains an element of judgement; situations and actors are assessed against the backdrop of one's own experiences and memories, but also against social norms and conventions. This process does not have to be overly time-consuming; it often happens in a nanosecond and without the person even realizing it. Yet it is crucial for allocating a feeling its place and intensity, for ascribing or denying it meaning. To be sure, judgement is by no means impervious to historical change. As far as shame is concerned, it heavily depends on which standards of decent and acceptable behaviour a society or a social group upholds, and how strongly people have internalized those standards.

Seen from a social science perspective, then, shame works to reinforce such standards. It ensures that people behave appropriately and conform

---

[10]Silvan S. Tomkins, *Affect – Imagery – Consciousness*, vol. 2: *The Negative Affects* (New York: Springer, 1963), 123.
[11]Donald L. Nathanson, 'A Timetable for Shame', in *Many Faces*, ed. Nathanson, 1–63, suggests that shame does not appear until eighteen months (7), while Tangney, Self-Conscious Emotions, 542, sees it develop in children older than two years.

to the norms of the group or society to which they belong. Failure to do so incurs shame and a loss of status. This extrinsically demands and ensures conformity.[12] Without shame or embarrassment, it has been argued, decency and the implementation of norms can hardly be guaranteed.

The argument is not only to be found with Plato and Thomas Aquinas.[13] It was also supported by authors from the late eighteenth century who praised 'modesty' as a necessary instrument for maintaining 'order in the state'.[14] In the 1930s, sociologist Norbert Elias analysed how, starting with the nobility, standards of modesty and shame became stricter and were incorporated into social conduct during the early modern period. People increasingly learnt how to control their affects for fear of losing acceptance and esteem. Self-constraint replaced external compulsion; shame rendered violence superfluous.[15]

In cases where self-constraint was not sufficient, however, harsh punishment followed. Social groups used it to actively shame members who failed to meet collective expectations. Authorities were – and sometimes still are – just as fond of imposing shame sanctions on offenders. To this very day, lower courts in the US sentence people to public exposure and shame for minor transgressions. One well-known case is that of Shena Hardin from Cleveland, Ohio. In 2012, she was made to stand at the corner of a busy intersection holding a sign that read: 'Only an idiot would drive on the sidewalk to avoid a school bus.'[16] This was exactly what Hardin had done, numerous times. Consequently, her licence was suspended, and she had to pay a fine. But the judge's aim was not to just discipline and punish Hardin. Exposing her to public scorn would, it was hoped, make her remorseful and change her future behaviour. Criminologist John Braithwaite calls this 'reintegrative shaming'. Its goal is not to stigmatize or seek revenge. On the contrary, shaming practices are meant to reintegrate perpetrators into decent society through a process of confrontation and publicity.[17]

---

[12]Thomas J. Scheff, 'Shame and Conformity: The Deference-Emotion System', *American Sociological Review* 53, no. 3 (1988): 395–401; Sighard Neckel, 'Sociology of Shame', in *Shame and Social Work: Theory, Reflexivity and Practice*, ed. Liz Frost et al. (Bristol: Bristol University Press, 2020), 39–54.
[13]For a philosophical tour d'horizon, see Christoph Demmerling and Hilge Landweer, *Philosophie der Gefühle* (Stuttgart: Metzler, 2007), 219–37.
[14]Leonhard Meister, 'Ueber die Schamhaftigkeit', in Meister, *Fliegende Blätter größtentheils historischen und politischen Innhalts* (Basel: Flick, 1783), 112–39.
[15]Norbert Elias, *The Civilizing Process: Sociogenetic and Psychogenetic Investigations* (Malden: Blackwell, [Germ. Orig. 1939] 2010).
[16]https://www.cbsnews.com/news/shena-hardin-update-ohio-woman-who-drove-on-sidewalk-around-school-bus-completes-her-punishment-of-holding-idiot-sign/ (accessed 14 December 2022).
[17]John Braithwaite, *Crime, Shame, and Reintegration* (Cambridge: Cambridge University Press, 1989). In order to achieve the goal of reintegration, however, shaming must be done, as Braithwaite insists, in a 'respectful' way and refrain 'from rejecting the wrongdoer as a person' (Foreword to Scheff and Retzinger, *Emotions and Violence*, xii).

Similar practices persist in contemporary China, where they are administered strategically and on a far broader scale. In December 2021, four men accused of smuggling people across China's borders during the COVID-19 pandemic were paraded through the streets of Jungxi city by police, carrying placards with their names. The spectacle was thought to encourage compliance with state rules.[18] It is regularly used for criminals, who have to appear in public, face their fellow citizens and kneel down in a gesture of excessive deference.[19] Even those found guilty of minor offences like jaywalking bear the weight of public shaming. In 2017, the city of Jinan, the capital of Shandong province, installed facial recognition equipment that took snapshots of pedestrians crossing roads at red lights. Within twenty minutes, public screens displayed the offender's photograph and personal information. Police informed the offender's employers or residential committees.[20]

Such state-mandated shaming sanctions find little support in Europe. Even in the US, there is no lack of opposition. Many hold the state responsible for protecting the dignity of every human being, including criminals. In their view, public shaming deliberately violates this dignity.[21] In a similar vein, the Israeli philosopher Avishai Margalit has advocated a 'decent society' in which no one is degraded and humiliated or violated in his or her self-esteem.[22] This clearly turns the relationship between decency and shame on its head. While liberals like Margalit or Nussbaum focus on individuals and their human dignity, the opposing camp, whether Plato or the communitarians of today, emphasizes the state or society and its needs instead.

Shame sanctions versus human dignity

The controversy can be traced back to the late eighteenth and early nineteenth century. The first matter of dispute was the pillory, the public exposure of people who had violated binding norms and regulations. Historically, the pillory existed in two versions: in a figurative sense as a form of reprimand organized by a local community, and in the literal sense as a tool of punishment used by legal authorities.

---

[18]https://www.bbc.com/news/world-asia-china-59818971 (accessed 14 December 2022).
[19]http://www.chinatoday.com/law/law_enforce_pictures/henan_zhoukou_xiangcheng_handle_criminals.htm (accessed 14 December 2022).
[20]https://www.chinadaily.com.cn/regional/2017-06/21/content_30284411.htm (accessed 14 December 2022).
[21]Nussbaum, *Hiding*, 223 ff., against Dan M. Kahan, 'What Do Alternative Sanctions Mean?', *University of Chicago Law Review* 63, no. 2 (1996): 591–653, and Amitai Etzioni, 'Back to the Pillory?', *The American Scholar* 68, no. 3 (1999): 43–50.
[22]Avishai Margalit, *The Decent Society* (Cambridge, MA: Harvard University Press, 1998), 1, 41, 44.

Research on the early modern period has unearthed a wealth of information on collective shaming practices, the aim of which was to publicly punish and ridicule those who had acted against customary rules of conduct. In the notorious English skimmington ride, wives who had beaten their husbands (sometimes together with the battered men) were forced to sit backwards on a donkey and paraded through town to the mockery and laughter of their neighbours. French charivaris or 'rough music' often targeted older men who had married very young women.[23] Such shaming rituals were found all over Europe. Their function was to defend the local moral economy against violations, whether by women who fell pregnant out of wedlock or members of the magistrate whose decisions clashed with people's sense of justice.[24]

More often than not, though, local authorities and ordinary village or townspeople collaborated on infractions of public morality. In 1721 in rural Scotland, Jenny Forsyth was accused of fornication and, at the behest of church officials and community leaders, was supposed to be 'branked'. Several women from the parish gathered outside Mrs Forsyth's house, singing loudly and banging pots and pans before dragging her out and fitting the brank, an iron helmet, over her head. They then paraded her through the village until she swore to behave decently in the eyes of God. Such collective rituals of public shaming persisted in Scotland until 1858, as did similar practices in other parts of Britain and on the Continent.[25]

In contrast to these communal practices, the actual pillory was an official instrument of punishment. In 1703, London authorities ordered the writer Daniel Defoe to stand in the pillory. The year before, he had published, anonymously, a satirical pamphlet that offended not only the Anglican Church but also secular institutions. Defoe was brought to court and sentenced to a hefty fine and prison time. Additionally, he was pilloried for three consecutive days.[26]

---

[23]David Nash and Anne-Marie Kilday, *Cultures of Shame: Exploring Crime and Morality in Britain, 1600–1900* (Basingstoke: Palgrave, 2010); Edward P. Thompson, 'Rough Music', in Thompson, *Customs in Common* (London: Penguin, 1991), 467–538; Natalie Zemon Davis, *Society and Culture in Early Modern France* (Stanford: Stanford University Press, 1975), 152 ff.; Martin Ingram, 'Shame Punishments, Penance and Charivari in Early Modern England', in *Shame between Punishment and Penance: The Social Usages of Shame in the Middle Ages and Early Modern Times*, ed. Bénédicte Sère and Jörg Wettlaufer (Florence: Sismel, 2013), 285–308.
[24]On the concept of moral economy, see Edward P. Thompson, 'The Moral Economy of the English Crowd in the Eighteenth Century', *Past & Present* no. 50 (1971): 76–136; *Moral Economies*, ed. Ute Frevert (Göttingen: Vandenhoeck & Ruprecht, 2019).
[25]Nash and Kilday, *Cultures*, 32–46; Richard J. Evans, *Tales from the German Underworld: Crime and Punishment in the Nineteenth Century* (New Haven: Yale University Press, 1998), 98–101.
[26]*The Earlier Life and the Chief Works of Daniel Defoe*, ed. Henry Morley (London: Routledge, 1889), 219–56; John Robert Moore, *Defoe in the Pillory and Other Studies* (New York: Octagon, [1939] 1973), ch. 1.

As a general rule, public exposure was embarrassing for those who had to endure it. Being subjected to the comments and interventions of spectators and passers-by was no fun. The public ridiculed and insulted the pilloried, hurling rotten eggs or excrement at them. Such behaviour played into the hands of the authorities that used the pillory as a deterrent, but it also worked to ensure social cohesion. It discouraged those who might be contemplating a similar transgression, while asserting and strengthening the moral economy of those who were witnessing the transgressor being punished and who were asked to endorse the official course of action.

Such endorsement, however, could no longer automatically be expected by the eighteenth century. 'Excesses' happened in both directions, and sometimes the public turned against authorities, as with Defoe. His many friends and supporters managed to shift the mood by distributing copies of the incriminating pamphlet and a poem that Defoe had written especially for the occasion: the *Hymn to the Pillory*. Onlookers merrily drank to Defoe's health and decorated the pillory with flowers.[27]

Other times, public shaming turned into a spectacle of violence and retaliation, as in the case of two Londoners charged with homosexuality in 1780. Having to stand in the pillory, they were seriously injured when people threw stones at them. In the House of Commons, Edmund Burke sharply criticized this transformation of the pillory from an 'instrument of reproach and shame' to an 'instrument of death and murder'.[28] Others used such violent incidents to cast doubt on the institution of public shaming altogether:

> If it is the object of the law that the punishment of the guilty should operate beneficially upon the feelings of the spectators, what shall we say of that mode, which, instead of impressing awe on the rabble by its solemnity, invites them to brutalize themselves, by taking up the task of the executioner, and pelting, stoning, and sometimes murdering a wretch, who has neither the means of flight nor resistance![29]

---

[27]Nash and Kilday, *Cultures*, 81–5. A similar incident happened in 1758 when the political satirist John Shebbeare had to stand in the pillory for libel at Charing Cross, London. He was cheered by the crowd that had been invited by printed leaflets to come and applaud him (*The Edinburgh Annual Register for 1815* 8 (1817): 29).
[28]*The Speeches of the Right Honorable Edmund Burke in the House of Commons and in Westminster Hall*, vol. 2 (London: Longman et al., 1816), 156–9; Peter Bartlett, 'Sodomites in the Pillory in Eighteenth-Century London', *Social and Legal Studies* 6, no. 4 (1997): 553–72.
[29]*The Edinburgh Annual Register for 1815* 8 (1817): 30–1.

In order to avoid brutalization, judicial authorities increasingly refrained from imposing public shame sanctions.[30] But there were also more mundane motives at play. In Salzburg, Austria, judges stopped sentencing craftsmen to the shameful exposure of the pillory because the guilds would subsequently expel them for it. This clashed with the magistrate's interest in maintaining undisturbed economic activity rather than reflecting concern for out-of-work families without the financial means to support themselves. Such interests were shared by Prussian King Friedrich II who, in 1756, warned the courts against declaring criminals infamous. The judgement would render the delinquent a 'useless member of society', unable to earn his or her keep in an honest way after having served the sentence.[31]

The pillory was regarded as degrading an official punishment as beating, which was meted out in public up until the mid-nineteenth century. The degradation affected not just the punished person but also their relatives. In 1760, a woman in London was publicly flogged for theft. Her son, a master mason, pleaded for mercy for his mother, not for her sake but for his own: 'Publickly Wipt itt being Shuch a Grate Scandell to Me in My Business & Wood Go Nere to Be My Ruing'.[32]

How the mason's mother felt about the 'scandal' is not known. Was she ashamed of the punishment, did she resent it being carried out in public for all to see? How would she have expressed her feelings? Sources from the late eighteenth century suggest that people who were pilloried or whipped were by no means indifferent to or detached from their punishment. They feared being spit at and cast out. Those who could afford it would rather pay a fine, even if it meant selling their last cow. 'Ordinary people', who represented the vast majority of the accused and punished, apparently had too much 'honour in their bodies' to tolerate public exposure and the ensuing shame

---

[30] James A. Sharpe, 'The Decline of Public Punishment in England, Sixteenth to Nineteenth Centuries: Law, Public Opinion, and Modernity', in *Strafzweck und Strafform zwischen religiöser und weltlicher Wertevermittlung*, ed. Rainer Schulze et al. (Münster: Rhema, 2008), 73–87; Greg T. Smith, 'Civilized People Don't Want to See That Kind of Thing: The Decline of Public Physical Punishment in London, 1760–1840', in *Qualities of Mercy: Justice, Punishment, and Discretion*, ed. Carolyn Strange (Vancouver: University of British Columbia Press, 1996), 21–51; Robert Shoemaker, 'Streets of Shame? The Crowd and Public Punishments in London, 1700–1820', in *Penal Practice and Culture, 1500–1900: Punishing the English*, ed. Simon Devereaux and Paul Griffiths (Basingstoke: Palgrave, 2004), 232–57.

[31] Gerhard Ammerer, '"Durch Strafen [...] zu neuen Lastern gereizt": Schandstrafe, Brandmarkung und Landesverweisung', in *Arme und ihre Lebensperspektiven in der Frühen Neuzeit*, ed. Sebastian Schmidt (Frankfurt: Lang, 2007), 311–39, here 317; 'Rescript, an das Criminal-Collegium, wegen Erkänntniß auf die Strafe der Infamie (July 19, 1756)', in *Novum Corpus Constitutionum Prussico-Brandenburgensium*, vol. 2 (Berlin: Akademie der Wissenschaften), no. 64, 115–16.

[32] Smith, 'Civilized People', quote 38. For similar developments in colonial North America, see Peter N. Stearns, *Shame: A Brief History* (Urbana: University of Illinois Press, 2017), 43–8.

and loss of honour. They considered it an 'insult' that also affected 'close relatives'.[33]

Yet not every shaming sanction was effective or achieved its goal. Whether it actually triggered shame depended on whether the transgressor accepted its logic and morals. This was more likely when the audience regarded the shaming as fair and deserved. Further, it was contingent on the purpose that the punishment served. If its aim was to act as a deterrent, then it hardly mattered whether the delinquent was ashamed or not. In fact, many public floggings were followed by the person's expulsion from their town or village. In these cases, social reintegration and improvement were clearly not the point. If they were, however, as was increasingly the case from the late eighteenth century, the transgressor's own feelings became more important.

It was with regard to those feelings that around 1800 a crucial transformation took place. When the philosopher Johann Adam Bergk translated Cesare Beccaria's *Crimes and Punishments* into German in 1798 and extensively commented on the text, he stated that shame sanctions were completely 'inappropriate' as they did not improve the person but instead stripped them of dignity and respect.[34] Bergk's idea of human dignity directly derived from Immanuel Kant's moral philosophy. According to Kant's famous definition, dignity was a 'holy' asset of humanity, an 'inner worth' without 'price' or 'equivalent'.[35]

> Humanity itself is a dignity; for a human being cannot be used merely as a means by any human being [...] but must always be used at the same time as an end. It is just in this that his dignity (personality) consists, by which he raises himself above all other beings in the world that are not human beings and yet can be used, and so over all *things*.[36]

By way of conclusion, Kant added that every human being thus had 'a legitimate claim to respect from his fellow human beings and is *in turn* bound to respect every other'.

Such respect was clearly absent from actual practices of public shaming, both in their official configuration and in their popular support. This was

---

[33]Michael Frank, *Dörfliche Gesellschaft und Kriminalität: Das Fallbeispiel Lippe 1650–800* (Paderborn: Schöningh, 1995), quotes 198 (from a 1778 case).
[34]Johann Adam Bergk, ed., *Des Marchese Beccaria's Abhandlung über Verbrechen und Strafen*, part 1 (Leipzig: Beygang, 1798), 197.
[35]Immanuel Kant, *Groundwork of the Metaphysics of Morals*, ed. and trans. Mary Gregor and Jens Timmermann, rev. edn (Cambridge: Cambridge University Press, 2012), 46.
[36]Immanuel Kant, *The Metaphysics of Morals*, ed. Lara Denia, trans. Mary Gregor, rev. edn (Cambridge: Cambridge University Press, 2017), this and the following quote 225. See Oliver Jensen, *Kant on Human Dignity* (Berlin: De Gruyter, 2011); Rachel Bayefsky, 'Dignity, Honour, and Human Rights: Kant's Perspective', *Political Theory* 41, no. 6 (2013): 809–37; Stephen Darwall, 'Kant on Respect, Dignity, and the Duty of Respect', in Darwall, *Honor, History, and Relationship* (Oxford: Oxford University Press, 2014), ch. 11.

increasingly criticized by people like Bergk, but also by high-ranking political figures. In 1794, for instance, the Prussian Grand Chancellor Johann Heinrich von Carmer wrote that public shaming was 'a chief obstacle to any refinement of morality'. Consequently, he advised provincial authorities to use such penalties 'with great care and as rarely as possible'.[37] Carmer, Bergk and many others were applying a rhetoric of moral and social progress that would benefit state and civil society alike. At the same time, they were tapping into a new discourse on human dignity. This marked a fundamental shift in perspective: away from the state and society, towards the individual person and protecting them from degradation.

From the early nineteenth century onwards, contemporaries who spoke out against shame sanctions expressed the idea of human dignity more and more frequently. As a Prussian legal report stated in 1818, 'human dignity has to be respected, even that of the guilty, the criminal'. Any punishment that 'destroys honour, and degrades man to the level of an animal' – like corporal punishment – should be dismissed.[38] Similarly, the French Penal Code of 1791 no longer permitted public beatings as a penalty, but it still ordered that those sentenced to hard labour be publicly exposed. In 1832, the *exposition publique* was annulled for non-life sentences and abolished completely in 1848, as it was thought to diminish human dignity and impede the rehabilitation of offenders.[39] One year later, the revolutionary Frankfurt Constitution declared the pillory, branding and state-mandated corporal punishment null and void across Germany. Although the constitution never entered into force, its spirit permeated the new codes of criminal law: the Prussian Code of 1851 made no mention of the pillory or branding.

The return of public shaming

Yet, the story of deliberate public shaming was not over. Admittedly, the state and criminal law essentially refrained from imposing publicly humiliating punishments.[40] Liberalism as it had developed in European

---

[37]*Ergänzungen und Erläuterungen des Preußischen Criminal-Rechts durch Gesetzgebung und Wissenschaft*, ed. Heinrich Gräff et al., sect. 1, part 2 (Breslau: Aderholz, 1838), quote 337.
[38]Ernst Landsberg, *Die Gutachten der Rheinischen Immediat-Justiz-Kommission und der Kampf um die rheinische Rechts- und Gerichtsverfassung 1814–1819* (Bonn: Hansteins, 1914), quote 47.
[39]Ute Frevert, *The Politics of Humiliation: A Modern History* (Oxford: Oxford University Press, 2020), 29–31; James Q. Whitman, *Harsh Justice: Criminal Punishment and the Widening Divide between America and Europe* (New York: Oxford University Press, 2003), 113–28.
[40]As Michel Foucault's classic study showed, shaming and humiliation only moved indoors. The prison (or workhouse) removed convicts from public sight while subjecting them to all-encompassing observation and control. At the same time, it excluded the public from taking part in the performance and ceremony of administering justice and enacting power (Michel Foucault, *Discipline and Punish: The Birth of the Prison* (New York: Pantheon Books, 1977)).

politics generally prided itself on a higher regard for individual honour and dignity (which were often used synonymously, even though they carried different meanings). Authoritarian states, in contrast, quickly dismantled such concerns. Replacing them with strong notions of community, they actively endorsed feelings of class or racial belonging and enacted harsh measures of exclusion to target those they felt did not or should not belong.

Under National Socialism, the authorities valued so-called shaming processions that put on public display those who had allegedly violated the newly installed racial norms. Mostly, this pertained to non-Jewish women who had had affairs with Jewish men (but not the reverse!) or, during the war, with forced labourers or POWs from occupied countries. Nazis also used this sanction against their political opponents. Predominantly, though, they lashed out at 'German–Aryan' women who had supposedly disgraced their own sexual honour as well as the honour of the national community.[41] Concerns for human dignity were bluntly ignored, not just by Nazi thugs but also by respected legal scholars who dismissed them as remnants of a weak and sentimental past.[42]

Public shaming continued after the war, in liberated countries like France and Norway as well as in newly occupied countries like Germany and Austria. Citizens, male and female alike, took revenge on women whom they accused of 'horizontal collaboration' with the enemy. Again, male collaborators were spared the spectacle of being led through the streets and shorn as objects of public derision, contempt and *Schadenfreude*.[43] Similar practices occurred in Northern Ireland during the 1970s, when Catholic women dating British soldiers risked being tarred and feathered.[44]

In some ways, those events bore a resemblance to the early modern culture of reproach and reprimand. Manifestations of that culture, whether 'rough music' or the skimmington ride, had been instigated by members of the local community who acted on behalf of, and in accordance with, a situated moral economy. Such manifestations had not ceased with the advent of the modern era; they continued in various forms and disguises. In 1826, Bristol shipbuilders shamed a fellow worker for scabbing by tying him to a mast and dragging him around town. In rural Bavaria in the nineteenth century, citizens (predominantly male) – peasants, craftsmen, labourers – gathered

---

[41] See Chapter 4 in this volume.
[42] Frevert, *Politics*, 54–65.
[43] Fabrice Virgili, *Shorn Women: Gender in Punishment in Liberation France* (Oxford: Berg, 2002); Anette Warring, 'Intimate and Sexual Relations', in *Surviving Hitler and Mussolini: Daily Life in Occupied Europe*, ed. Robert Gildea, Olivier Wieviorka and Anette Warring (Oxford: Berg, 2006), 88–128; Benjamin Frommer, 'Denouncers and Fraternizers: Gender, Collaboration, and Retribution in Bohemia and Moravia during World War II and After', in *Gender and War in Twentieth-Century Eastern Europe*, ed. Nancy M. Wingfield and Maria Bucur (Bloomington: Indiana University Press, 2006), 111–32.
[44] *New York Times*, 11 November 1971, 1, 17; Patrick Carville, 'Ulster Girl, 19, Tarred by Crowd', *Chicago Tribune*, 11 November 1971, sect. 2, 17.

to blame and shame those who had behaved indecently and violated local customs. They would go to the culprit's house at night, read defamatory poems aloud and make hellish noises in the charivari tradition. In the 1920s, German miners put up shaming posts to publicize the names of strikebreakers. As late as the 1970s, Italian workers used 'rough music' to shame their bosses and supervisors. And in 2020, at the beginning of the COVID-19 pandemic, a 'public shaming frenzy' spread both offline and online, with people naming, shaming and blaming those who did not comply with official rules of social distancing.[45]

What distinguished those actions from similar practices during Nazi rule was that the latter enjoyed the tacit or outspoken consent and permission of the state. Whereas the popular culture of shaming was eventually curtailed by authorities seeking to safeguard the modern state's monopoly on violence and legal sanction, the fascist regime strategically drew on traditional customs and conventions in order to further a politics of exclusion and stigmatization. It only withdrew its support once the local population turned against public exposure and shame processions.

Under state socialism, shaming practices likewise occurred because the regime wanted and sometimes ordered them done. Public exposure was a powerful means of sanctioning behaviour viewed as incompatible with socialist values and norms. Displaying the names of students or workers who did not perform well on banners in school or factory halls invited publicly voiced disdain, criticism and *Schadenfreude*. It made the deviators feel that they existed outside of the collective body and had been marked as such. At the same time, shaming was meant to help the shamed person regain social acceptance by repenting and improving their conduct. The goal was, as in former times, threefold: deterring followers, stabilizing the community and reintegrating the offender. In general, socialist education, as harsh and dogmatic as it could be, was ultimately not about exclusion.

What it clearly did intend, though, and where National Socialism and GDR socialism overlapped, was to strengthen the collective at the expense of the individual. In this vein, East Germany's regime established a system of popular justice (modelled on the Soviet Union) that operated mainly in factories but also in neighbourhoods and peasants' cooperatives. Citizens who had misbehaved (by beating their wives, showing up for work drunk,

---

[45]Martin Gorsky, 'James Tuckfield's "Ride": Combination and Social Drama in Early Nineteenth-Century Bristol', *Social History* 19, no. 3 (1994): 319–38; Wilhelm Kaltenstadler, *Das Haberfeldtreiben* (Munich: Unverhau, 1999); Klaus-Michael Mallmann and Horst Steffens, *Lohn der Mühen: Geschichte der Bergarbeiter an der Saar* (Munich: C.H. Beck, 1989), 158, 168; Ilaria Favretto, 'Rough Music and Factory Protest in Post-1945 Italy', *Past & Present* no. 228 (2015): 207–47; Stephen Banks, *Informal Justice in England and Wales 1760–1914: The Courts of Popular Opinion* (Woodbridge: Boydell & Brewer, 2014); https://www.theguardian.com/science/2020/apr/04/pandemic-shaming-is-it-helping-us-keep-our-distance (accessed 14 December 2022).

or committing slander) were tried in front of and by their peers, in so-called conflict or dispute commissions. This reportedly caused them enormous shame and embarrassment.[46]

In countries that favoured more liberal-minded approaches, such officially instigated policies of popular justice were considered inconsistent with notions of individual dignity and personal honour. Yet the state did not fully or successfully prevent citizens – especially and increasingly acting through the media – from shaming others, be they public figures or ordinary people. Even though there were laws in place that sanctioned insults, libel, defamation and slander, shaming or even humiliating practices often skirted the grasp of legal action. Tabloid journalism proved to be particularly savvy in this regard. Exposing a person's alleged misdemeanour and whipping up scandal around his or her transgression became tremendously popular during the twentieth century. Famous targets guaranteed higher sales and impact, as in 1919, when the newly elected German president, Social Democrat Friedrich Ebert, was deliberately ridiculed by an illustrated journal. On the day Ebert took his oath on the republican constitution, the cover showed him and another left-wing politician in bathing trunks on a beach, a photo that had already been circulating among right-wingers who sought to delegitimize the new republic of Weimar. Putting it on the front page of a widely read journal was as much an affront to the democratic state – the first ever on German territory – as it was a violation of contemporary standards of public decency.[47]

Defamatory tactics gathered momentum after 1933, when media directly served the interests of the National Socialist state. Yet they also continued during the second half of the twentieth century and into the present. In 2015, the tabloid *BILD* (which sells 1.7 million copies daily and boasts a huge online readership) published what they called a modern pillory: they printed the names, headshots and comments of people who had posted racist messages online. This was in step with voices which have recently recommended public shaming as a 'nonviolent form of resistance' against people who violate relevant social rules. Exposing tax evaders, for instance, has been promulgated as a convenient and effective tool to both defend the norm of tax compliance and improve people's behaviour, in the classic tradition of shame sanctions.[48]

That tradition has gained many new followers in the last decade. Inducing 'flight shame' is the tactic of a social movement that seeks to discourage leisure and business habits detrimental to the environment.[49]

---

[46]Frevert, *Politics*, 52 ff.; Paul Betts, 'Property, Peace, and Honour: Neighbourhood Justice in Communist Berlin', *Past & Present* no. 201 (2008): 215–54.
[47]https://museenkoeln.de/portal/bild-der-woche.aspx?bdw=2000_06 (accessed 14 December 2022).
[48]Jennifer Jacquet, *Is Shame Necessary? New Uses for an Old Tool* (New York: Pantheon Books, 2015).
[49]https://www.theguardian.com/commentisfree/2020/jan/17/the-guardian-view-on-flight-shaming-face-it-life-must-change (accessed 14 December 2022).

Food- or meat-shaming targets those who produce or consume livestock, especially cattle, which emit a large amount of greenhouse gas and thus contribute significantly to the warming of the earth. Some even encourage shaming (potential) parents as a way of prompting them to think about their individual carbon footprint and reduce the number of children they have.

In such cases, shaming is done in the name of a good and moral cause, like saving the planet or reminding the rich of their obligations towards the rest of society. It tries to avoid stigmatization, which harms and humiliates a person's dignity. Yet, the boundaries between shaming and humiliation are highly porous, even more so when moral issues are at stake. Public shaming frequently satisfies the needs of those who take the moral high ground and feel entitled to degrade others whom they consider morally inferior. The righteous claim to superiority is equivalent to the claim to power that is demonstrated through practices of humiliating others, whether individuals or groups.

Through the internet, shaming and humiliation have acquired a new dimension and quality. Some argue that digital technologies have had a democratizing effect by wresting the power to shame away 'from opinion leaders and the state' and putting it 'in the hands of citizens'.[50] Others object, pointing to the negative consequences that online shaming has for both the shamed and the shaming.[51] As long as platforms for shaming 'fat people' or 'sluts' proliferate, the internet's democratic capacities are not beyond doubt. Online shaming can cause immense harm, as it spreads quickly and extensively and expands the site of direct confrontation between the shaming and the shamed person beyond its usual spatial, temporal and social limits. Particularly for teenagers, such amplification has at times proven life-threatening.

The shame paradox

Interestingly, the return, persistence or even increase of public shaming among citizens both coincides and collides with growing demands for respect and recognition. Since the end of the Second World War those demands have been on the rise, most strikingly in the 1960s and 1970s, and they go hand in hand with a rebuke of shame and shaming.

That rebuke was not limited to criticizing the state and its legal system for shaming perpetrators, as liberal citizens and legal practitioners had started doing around 1800. It also targeted social institutions like the family, church, school and welfare systems. Schools in particular had long functioned as laboratories of shame. Wayward students who disobeyed their

---

[50]Jacquet, *Shame*, 18.
[51]Jon Ronson, *So You've Been Publicly Shamed* (London: Picador, 2015).

teachers were punished in degrading ways: they were forced to stand in the corner with their backs to their classmates; they had to wear a donkey's cap that made them look ridiculous; they received public floggings and numerous other unpleasant punishments that were meant to debase them in the eyes of their fellow students. Many generations of schoolteachers and pedagogues spoke in favour of such disciplinary practices. They vehemently dismissed the argument that the honour and dignity of young children and adolescents might be seriously harmed and violated, believing instead in the benefits of shaming as the ultimate means of habituating young people to social rules and conventions.[52]

This changed only gradually. Since around 1900, an increasing number of experts had warned against mistreating students and children (at home too, where parental conduct often mirrored practices at school). Yet it took several generations for the criticism to be heard and heeded. Until the 1970s, teachers in West Germany considered it their right to physically punish unruly children aged 10 and under. In British state schools, corporal punishment was formally abolished in 1986; in private schools it was not until 1998 that such treatment was banned.[53]

Two decades later, in 2016, the BBC published a letter written by Northern Irish primary school teachers to their students, urging them not to be too disappointed if their grades were lower than they had hoped. Surely, everyone had done their best and worked hard. In any event, test scores did not say anything about who you were as a person or your attitude, which was all that counted. The letter quickly went viral and garnered the school much praise. It neatly demonstrated the cultural shifts that had heralded a radical transformation of the student–teacher relationship. While teachers in the 1950s and 1960s used to embarrass weaker students in front of the entire class by reading out their grades, such shaming now seems wholly inappropriate – the quest for mutual respect and recognition has gained the upper hand.[54]

This reflects major changes in Western societies that can be summed up as democratization and liberalization. Democratization meant not only equal access to political power or broader participation in civic spaces, but also challenging authority and disputing social hierarchies. If authority and hierarchies were to continue, they needed sound, convincing arguments. Questioning authority included critiquing the means by which it was upheld and protected: through physical and psychological violence, whether inflicted by state officials, teachers or parents.

---

[52]Frevert, *Politics*, 79 ff.
[53]Stephen Cretney, 'Children, Cruelty, and Corporal Punishment in Twentieth-Century England: The Legal Framework', in *Childhood and Violence in the Western Tradition*, ed. Laurence Brockliss and Heather Montgomery (Oxford: Oxbow Books, 2010), 151–8.
[54]https://www.bbc.com/news/uk-northern-ireland-35449405 (accessed 14 December 2022).

Liberalization (which occurred alongside pluralization, the acceptance of different lifestyles, tastes and values) required paying attention to the rights and desires of the individual instead of imposing a one-size-fits-all set of social regulations and normative claims. It also meant constructing society from the bottom up, not from the top down. The taste for community dwindled, or at least weakened. Liberalizing tendencies could be observed at all levels: in state legislation and legal reforms as much as in dress codes, romantic relations or union membership.

Liberalization increased the demand for respect for individuals, and it also changed what respect actually meant. Up until the 1960s, respect – translated as deference, tact and decency – had been advocated as a grease to make society function. It had ensured social hierarchies were maintained, because a person who commanded respect was always someone of greater social status or age. Respect, as deference, travelled upwards, not downwards. Respect, as tactful conduct, also signalled deliberate distance and thereby, as German philosopher Helmuth Plessner wrote in 1924, protected the dignity of the individual person. It served as a counterweight to the contemporary tendency to drown dignity and individuality in warm 'brotherhood in the community'. It was not intimacy, Plessner claimed, but tactful detachment that modern society needed in order to safeguard civilized interaction.[55]

The new version of respect that gained ground in the final decades of the twentieth century implied something completely different. It was about neither deference nor tact. Instead, it focused on people's desire for acceptance and esteem, which had to be fully acknowledged and actively addressed. Respect was regarded as a means of meeting a person's claim to social recognition, rather than as a tool for guaranteeing civilized behaviour. Both Plessner's concept of distancing and the older tradition of paying deference to superiors or elders disappeared from view.

For its part, the demand for personal recognition enjoyed considerable growth due to ongoing processes of individualization. As collective institutions like the church, voluntary associations, parties and unions lost their cohesive force and as social bonds weakened, individuals were forced to redefine their proper place, status and worth. This process was reflected in the use of words and concepts. Instead of claiming 'honour' and subscribing to a notion of belonging to a distinct social group or profession, people increasingly referred to their 'dignity' as human beings. The shift clearly corresponded to the equalizing trends of democratic societies that dismissed

---

[55]Helmuth Plessner, *The Limits of Community: A Critique of Social Radicalism*, trans. Andrew Wallace (Amherst: Humanity Books, [Germ. Orig. 1924] 1999), 70. In 1966, Theodor W. Adorno made a similar point in a radio talk on 'Education after Auschwitz'. Against the background of Nazism, he warned against the 'blind identification with the collective' that eliminated the autonomy and self-determination of the individual; Theodor W. Adorno, 'Education after Auschwitz', in Adorno, *Critical Models: Interventions and Catchwords*, trans. Henry W. Pickford (New York: Columbia University Press, 1998), 191–204, quote 197.

and delegitimized hierarchical systems of social honour. As dignity pertained to all people, regardless of social class, ethnic origin, gender, age, religion and the like, it served as a great unifier.

At the same time, it changed perceptions and expectations. The quest to be treated in a dignified manner came with an ever more sensitive apprehension of potential transgressions and encroachments. It also came with new language. Humiliation became a watchword that both described individual perceptions and stated a serious accusation. Feeling humiliated had far stronger ethical implications than feeling hurt, insulted, offended or slandered. Humiliation was thought to target the person at her very core, her dignity. It degraded and debased her, brought her to her knees and kept her there. Humiliation stigmatized, and did so intentionally and enduringly. While shaming, in theory, had a reintegrative purpose and effect, humiliation was all about exclusion and, perhaps, annihilation.

Purpose and effect, though, mattered less and less to the people subject to such measures. Acts of shaming, like having a student stand in the corner of the classroom, were increasingly felt and labelled as outright humiliations. In 2015, a woman in southern Germany drafted a petition to abolish the annual sports competitions for schoolchildren aged 8 to 19. Her young son had returned home with tears in his eyes because he had scored badly. For him and many others, the mother claimed, the event caused a 'feeling of being humiliated in front of their peer group'.[56] When British Prime Minister Gordon Brown encouraged competitive sports in schools after the Olympic Games in 2008, he received a similar reaction.[57] Many East Germans likewise report feelings of humiliation when they narrate their post-unification experiences in the 1990s.[58]

Framing these experiences as humiliating (rather than as insulting, embarrassing or unpleasant) might be a strategy of dramatization and scandalization. But the new language also reflects and supports new expectations, interpretations and feelings that mirror the importance now placed on basic equality and mindfulness: each person should be protected and respected in their human dignity. At the same time, the assurance of equal rights and the promise of fair living conditions in a democratic society permit and even foster diversity, differentiation and pluralization. When social belonging and identities are no longer traditionally defined

---

[56] https://www.news4teachers.de/2015/06/bundesjugendspiele-eine-oeffentliche-demuetigung-petition-zur-abschaffung-ist-angelaufen/ (accessed 14 December 2022).

[57] Naomi Alderman, 'Imagine if We Taught Math like PE – A Competition, with Public Humiliation if You Got a Sum Wrong', *The Guardian*, 25 September 2008: https://www.theguardian.com/commentisfree/2008/sep/25/youngpeople.youthjustice (accessed 14 December 2022).

[58] Ute Frevert, 'Das Narrativ der Demütigung und die Gefühle der Ostdeutschen', in *Das umstrittene Erbe von 1989: Zur Gegenwart eines Gesellschaftszusammenbruchs*, ed. Alexander Leistner and Monika Wohlrab-Sahr (Vienna: Böhlau, 2022), 257–78.

or set in stone, the door opens to a dynamic world of competing claims and offers. New standards of social worth and status are perpetually being negotiated, practised and contested. They might not be hegemonic any longer or appeal to every member of society. Yet they are no less effective when it comes to ensuring conformity among peer groups, especially for young people. Whoever fails to comply with these standards – regarding, most often, body weight, physical appearance, emotional styles and sexual behaviour – is bound to suffer contempt, derision, bullying and debasement.

Such debasement feels particularly painful and humiliating in a culture that privileges extensive explorations of individuality, singularity and uniqueness.[59] Through constant comparison, these searches often end in what psychologists have diagnosed as narcissism. Since the 1960s, the trend towards self-centredness and excessive self-love has been identified (and criticized) time and again.[60] Starting in the United States, it was connected to post-war demographic and social changes. Smaller families and the round-the-clock presence of a loving mother and housewife who devoted her entire energies to the well-being of her children increased the chances that all attention would be given to the one (or two) and only, from infancy through to middle age. The culture of therapy further strengthened the new generation's obsession with themselves.

Many observers related this development to what they perceived as the demise of shame. Devaluing shame in the wake of individualistic and anti-authoritarian movements paved the way, they argued, for a narcissistic 'preoccupation with exposure'.[61] Narcissism or 'the state of loving or admiring oneself' defended the self 'against the hatred of the self in shame', as Helen Block Lewis summed up the clinical findings in the field of psychotherapy.[62] Warding off shame and humiliation thus allowed narcissism to thrive.

But there is a flipside. Just as narcissism might protect a person against the negative emotion of shame, it emphasizes the person's inherent vulnerability and insecurity. Being preoccupied with one's self renders one highly susceptible to processes of social shaming. Societies that breed narcissism predispose people towards feeling attacked. Taking oneself overly seriously, being wholly absorbed and enraptured by one's own personality, makes a person an easy target for those who wish to empower themselves by degrading others. A project launched by the Californian government in 1987 to 'promote self-esteem' exemplified both trends: on the one hand, it

---

[59] Andreas Reckwitz, *The Society of Singularities* (Cambridge: Polity Press, 2020).
[60] Philip Rieff, *The Triumph of the Therapeutic: Uses of Faith after Freud* (New York: Harper & Row, 1966); Christopher Lasch, *The Culture of Narcissism: American Life in an Age of Diminishing Expectations* (New York: Norton & Co., 1978).
[61] Nathanson, 'Timetable', 5.
[62] Lewis, 'Shame', 95–6; Henry Lowenfeld, 'Notes on Shamelessness', *The Psychoanalytic Quarterly* 45, no. 1 (1976): 62–72.

highlighted the general perception that self-esteem was under threat; on the other, it tapped into people's growing obsession with who they are and how to improve their status in society.[63]

We can see on a daily basis how this obsession plays out and in turn invites all kinds of shaming practices. Hundreds of thousands stand in line for TV casting shows, like *Pop Idol* or *Next Top Model*, which regularly expose young candidates to public ridicule. The candidates are aware of this but choose to take the risk anyway because the possibilities – publicity, money, a career in fashion or entertainment – override the potential for humiliation. Similarly, members of fraternities and sororities in the US accept utterly debasing hazing rituals for the chance to be initiated into a community of brothers or sisters.[64] Quite obviously, there are occasions and reasons to endure humiliation and forgo the claim to being acknowledged, respected and protected in one's human dignity. On other occasions and for other reasons, the claim has been imperiously stated. It can, and has been, used to shelter a person from being besieged by bullies who seek to take advantage of his or her weakness and vulnerability in order to prove and fortify their own power and status. But it can – and does – also work to thwart criticism and hamper self-reflection.

Here, the circle closes, and the paradox remains: the more modern liberal-democratic societies support citizens in asserting their self-esteem and being sensitive to all kinds of shaming (which is increasingly framed as humiliation), the more they enhance people's vulnerability to such infringements and render them painful. The need to counter the pain and restabilize the self in turn feeds narcissism and the omnipotent feeling of social entitlement – which breeds resentment and competition, and invites more shaming.

Shame now and then

There was a moment in the 1970s when Western societies seemed to be moving towards shamelessness. At least this is what concerned citizens observed and warned against. Shame and shaming were indeed denounced as repressive by the feminist movement, the gay rights movement and sexual reformers, all of whom considered shame an obstacle to individual liberation and group emancipation.[65] Shame, as they saw it, was a means of ensuring social conformity that kept being defined by those who held power and

---

[63]Lunbeck, *Americanization*, 110; Christopher Lasch, 'For Shame', *The New Republic*, 10 August 1992, 29–34, for a critical view.
[64]Frevert, *Politics*, 111 ff.
[65]Kate Millett, 'The Shame is Over', *Ms.* (January 1975): 26–9; Sally R. Munt, *Queer Attachments: The Cultural Politics of Shame* (Aldershot: Ashgate, 2007); *Gay Shame*, ed. David M. Halperin and Valerie Traub (Chicago: University of Chicago Press, 2009).

were not prepared to let it go. Shame thus worked against those in favour of questioning conformity and breaking the rules as a means of liberating and democratizing society. Traditionally, breaking rules had induced shaming, both by the state (if those rules were legally enshrined) and by community agents (for rules that had emerged from social conventions).

In modern societies, shaming and humiliation have found less and less social acclaim, at least rhetorically. Still, social practices have not always lived up to the standard of dignity and respect. Women, in particular, have long been made to bear blame and shame. Although second-wave feminists declared shame was 'over', their demand did not succeed. Women continue to be abused and assaulted and, out of shame and embarrassment, often shy away from naming the perpetrators. Shame for women has many faces: first, they have for a long time been taught to feel shame about their sex and gender as inferior and flawed. Second, they have, for an equally long time, suffered from an obsession with female 'purity' and modesty, especially regarding bodily and sexual conduct. Third, they have been taught to attribute men's assaults to their own comportment. Being raped or molested was, so they were told, due to how they behaved; as long as they complied with standards of decency and modesty, girls and women had nothing to fear. It was therefore women's fault if they were treated shamefully, and they should not complain but feel ashamed of their shortcomings.[66] Starting in 2017, the Me Too movement courageously broke this cycle of shame by criticizing gender prejudices and biases, by publicizing male transgressions and showing how humiliating they have been for the women concerned.

Under the hashtag #MeToo, the campaign undoubtedly benefited from the prevalence of social media, which allowed it to go viral. In this case, new digital technologies drew mass attention to demeaning practices that almost always took place behind closed doors. Enabling women to speak out about their feelings has helped to liberate them from the shame and humiliation they had been made to endure. In other cases, though, the internet does exactly the opposite: it provides a forum for shaming and humiliating others. Exposing those whose values or behaviour do not match one's own has become a popular pastime. Some activists use it for political purposes, claiming it as a convenient weapon with which the powerless can bring down the powerful. In more mundane contexts, it is combined with a culture of narcissism that adds to its destructive potential.

Still, shame has undoubtedly lost its centrality. Modern liberal democracies have enabled and witnessed a pluralization of lifestyles, tastes and opportunities for self-fashioning. They no longer facilitate central institutions that authoritatively set rules to be followed by all and shame those who misbehave. Unlike in the past, neither church nor state have the

---

[66]Ute Frevert, 'Die Macht der Scham', in *Geschlechterverwirrungen*, ed. Barbara Rendtorff, Claudia Mahs and Anne-Dorothee Warmuth (Frankfurt: Campus, 2020), 179–86.

power to shame citizens in front of a generalized public. As that public has diversified into many smaller publics, they define their own standards of appropriateness. Shame and shaming thus retreat to ever narrower circles. This does not make them less painful, but it does give individuals the possibility to pick and choose where they want to belong. If, say, a tax-evader does not accept the value of tax compliance, he or she cannot be shamed by those who do. They can easily find a new social home with people of their kind. Within that group, though, they might encounter other rules that have to be followed.

Shame has thus by no means left the modern world. But it has changed its face, forms and intensity. It has waived its homogenizing function, as there are no central agencies left that might shame their members into social conformity. Escaping shame has become easier because individuals can move between different social groups and switch whenever they feel unable or unwilling to abide by a group's code of conduct. Shaming practices have a shorter range and work on a smaller scale. And yet, new digital technologies enable them to extend their reach and disproportionately enlarge their audience, encouraging ever more people to join the online shaming chorus.

How do those who undergo shaming feel about it? Historical evidence suggests that the sensitivity to shame has grown considerably. Clearly, people never enjoyed standing in the pillory or being mockingly paraded through the streets. Whether they indeed felt shame, however, is up for debate and depended on how they fared within the given community. Feeling shame was not in fact necessary for people to experience the full weight of being publicly shamed. The public did not care how and what the shamed person felt. This began to change during the nineteenth century. Just as modern societies emphasized individual agency and responsibility at the expense of traditional social affiliations, they invested in what Georg Simmel in 1901 called *Ichbewusstsein*: a consciousness of one's individual worth and singularity. Cultivating a strong sense of self usually comes with a heightened sensitivity to what is perceived as harming or debasing that consciousness. Shame – about failing to meet one's own or external expectations – then hits with full force and is increasingly framed as humiliating. This, among other factors, attests to the historicity of shame – a historicity that applies not only to the shifting causes and occasions of shame or to different types of shaming agents and publics, but also to the feeling of shame itself.

CHAPTER SIX

Historicizing Empathy

Empathy has had a stellar career in recent years. Numerous books tout it as the key to a better world and a kinder society.[1] It has become as popular with politicians as it is with educators, psychologists and physicians. Career bibles and management training schemes instruct us on how to empathize with others, to put ourselves in their shoes. An empathy museum, inaugurated in 2015, hosts temporary art installations and the weekly podcast *A Mile in My Shoes*, which invites listeners to tune in to stories of other people's lives.[2] Apparently, empathy even extends to non-humans: in 2016, Audi presented the concept of the empathic vehicle with its slogan *My Audi cares for me*.[3] Other car companies followed their lead.

How can we explain this infatuation with empathy? What makes empathy so attractive and irresistible? How is it defined, and what practices are seen as empathic? Who is supposed to have empathy, and for whom or what? And, most importantly, is empathy a new emotion? Did people before the twenty-first century not know it or feel it? Did they have other, related emotions that made more sense to them? What was the difference?

This chapter partly draws on my article: 'Empathy in the Theater of Horror, or Civilizing the Human Heart', in *Empathy and Its Limits*, ed. Aleida Assmann and Ines Detmers (Basingstoke: Palgrave Macmillan, 2016), 79–99.

[1] Frans de Waal, *The Age of Empathy: Nature's Lessons for a Kinder Society* (New York: Crown, 2008); Jeremy Rifkin, *The Empathic Civilization: The Race to Global Consciousness in a World in Crisis* (New York: Wiley, 2010); Roman Krznaric, *Empathy: Why It Matters and How to Get It* (London: Rider Books, 2014).

[2] https://www.empathymuseum.com/ (accessed 16 December 2022).

[3] https://www.audi-mediacenter.com/en/audi-at-the-ces-2016-5294/audi-fit-driver-5300 (accessed 16 December 2022).

Einfühlung, sympathy, empathy

In Germany, the term *Empathie* only entered the popular Brockhaus encyclopaedia in 1968, where it was described as 'the ability to put oneself in another's position'.[4] Previously, people had used the action verbs *einfühlen* and *mitfühlen* to denote that ability. Both words went back to the late eighteenth and early nineteenth centuries and occupied a prominent place within philosophy, the arts and humanist discourses. Referring to mimetic processes of emotional identification and appropriation, they were mostly applied to relations with human beings and with nature. *Einfühlung* became an even more potent concept after German philosopher Theodor Lipps declared it, in 1900, to be the one and only source of aesthetic pleasure and enjoyment.[5] Thanks to Lipps and his foreign audience, *Einfühlung* travelled abroad. Ultimately, however, its English equivalent *empathy*, which started circulating in the early twentieth century, came out on top, and *Empathie* has become the most common usage in German-speaking contexts.

Mitfühlen was the other verb that described the act of projecting oneself into the experience of another person or animal. While *Einfühlung* and, initially, empathy mainly related to aesthetic experience, *Mitgefühl* (as a noun) encompassed wider social spheres. Feeling *with* someone else, sharing their feelings, was a virtue held in high esteem during the age of sensibility. When Ludwig Gotthard Kosegarten translated Adam Smith's 1759 treatise *Theory of Moral Sentiments* into German in 1791, he chose *Mitgefühl* for Smith's 'fellow-feeling' or 'sympathy'.[6] For Smith, who built on the work of Francis Hutcheson and David Hume, fellow-feeling was made possible through an act of imagination or projection. By imagining, people put themselves in another person's situation:

> we enter as it were into his body, and become in some measure the same person with him, and thence form some ideas of his sensations, and even feel something which, though weaker in degree, is not altogether unlike them.

Such fellow-feeling or 'sympathy' encompassed all kinds of circumstances and relevant emotions. It did not stop, Smith emphasized, at sorrowful

---

[4]*Brockhaus Enzyklopädie*, 17th edn, vol. 5 (Wiesbaden: Brockhaus, 1968), 496.
[5]Theodor Lipps, 'Ästhetische Einfühlung', *Zeitschrift für Psychologie und Physiologie der Sinnesorgane* 22 (1900): 415–50. See Christiane Montag et al., 'Theodor Lipps and the Concept of Empathy', *American Journal of Psychiatry* 165, no. 10 (2008): 1261–76; Robin Curtis, 'An Introduction to Einfühlung', *Art in Translation* 6, no. 4 (2014): 353–76; Susan Lanzoni, *Empathy: A History* (New Haven: Yale University Press, 2018), 21–45.
[6]*Adam Smiths Theorie der sittlichen Gefühle*, trans. Ludwig Gotthard Kosegarten (Leipzig: Gräffsche Buchhandlung, 1791), 14.

emotions, but included pleasant feelings as well. Interestingly, the author used an example from the theatre to argue his point.

> Our joy for the deliverance of those heroes of tragedy or romance who interest us, is as sincere as our grief for their distress, and our fellow-feeling with their misery is not more real than that with their happiness. We enter into their gratitude towards those faithful friends who did not desert them in their difficulties; and we heartily go along with their resentment against those perfidious traitors who injured, abandoned, or deceived them.[7]

Beyond stressing the great variety of feelings that could be imagined and fellow-felt, Smith also pointed out that, according to his observations, everybody was capable of sympathizing with the emotions of others. Sympathy, he stated, was a general human faculty. It was neither confined to people of higher birth or education nor derived from 'self-interested consideration'. As both pleasure and pain 'are always felt so instantaneously', they were bound to reside in and stem from the inherently social character of human beings. That character nicely balanced out man's selfishness or 'self-love' and tempered its potentially destructive outcomes.[8]

It was not by accident that Adam Smith, who several years later would draft capitalism's bible, viewed 'sympathy' or 'fellow-feeling' as crucial and necessary for harmonious human interactions. As Smith famously wrote, capitalism depended on the butcher, the brewer and the baker's regard for their own self-interest or self-love. By securing proper advantages for themselves, they produced the 'wealth of nations'. At the same time, they were embedded in a moral economy that emphasized mutual obligations, social commitment and benevolence.[9] Rooted in religious prescriptions and traditional provisions, that moral economy no longer suited the modern times; one compatible with capitalist modes of production and exchange had to be created. This was where 'sympathy' came in, defined as a 'natural'

---

[7]Adam Smith, *The Theory of Moral Sentiments* (Amherst: Prometheus, 2000), 4–5; Francis Hutcheson, *An Essay on the Nature and Conduct of the Passions and Affections, with Illustrations on the Moral Sense*, ed. Aaron Garrett (Indianapolis: Liberty Fund, [1728] 2002), 56; David Hume, *A Treatise of Human Nature*, ed. Ernest C. Mossner (Harmondsworth: Penguin Books, [1739] 1985), 367 ff., 417–18; Michael L. Frazer, *The Enlightenment of Sympathy: Justice and the Moral Sentiments in the Eighteenth Century and Today* (Oxford: Oxford University Press, 2010), chs 1–4.
[8]Smith, *Theory*, 10, 1.
[9]See, as a classic, Edward P. Thompson, 'The Moral Economy of the English Crowd in the Eighteenth Century', *Past & Present* no. 50 (1971): 76–136. For the concept of moral economy and its applications, see Ute Frevert, 'Moral Economies, Present and Past: Social Practices and Intellectual Controversies', in *Moral Economies*, ed. Ute Frevert (Göttingen: Vandenhoeck & Ruprecht, 2019), 13–43.

affection of humans, a universal faculty to feel what others felt and act accordingly in cases of suffering or harm.

On the Continent, Jean-Jacques Rousseau likewise considered *pitié* one of two principles that guided the 'operations of the human soul', the other being concern for one's own 'preservation and welfare'. *Pitié* both accompanied and restrained man's self-interest and allowed humans to coexist peacefully and pleasantly.[10] In Germany, the playwright Gotthold Ephraim Lessing praised the ultimate moral value of *Mitleid*. Inspired by the Aristotelian tradition and recalling Smith's analogy between the theatre and real life, Lessing wanted tragedies to evoke pity in the audience and thus tease out their very best human faculties.[11]

Philosophers, writers and poets broadly converged in their shared interest in sympathy. Although Rousseau and Lessing tended to define it more narrowly as pity, fellow-feeling was conceived as genuinely object-neutral overall. When Lessing drafted his theory of dramaturgy in the late 1760s, he attended, just as Smith had done in 1759, to a wide range of emotions that actors were taught to feel and express, and that could, if performed well, be experienced by the audience in turn.[12] Be it joy or fear, shame or disgust: people were by nature capable of imagining and feeling whatever others felt. For practical reasons, however, their attention was focused on those 'passions' that were connected with misfortune and suffering and that, in Smith's words, 'more strongly require the healing consolation of sympathy'.[13] What was needed for both the person who suffered and the one who sympathized was not *Mit-Freude*, fellow-joy, but *Mit-Leiden*: pity, compassion, *pitié*.

Many of those who participated in this debate took great care to point out the natural and thus universal character of sympathy. But there were other points of view as well. As the English moralist Samuel Johnson remarked in 1763, 'pity is not natural to man'. Children and 'savages', he found, 'are always cruel'. Pity, in contrast, was 'acquired and improved by the cultivation of reason'.[14] Reason here evoked the notion of a civilized

---

[10]Jean-Jacques Rousseau, 'Discourse on the Origin and Foundations of Inequality among Mankind', in Jean-Jacques Rousseau, *The Social Contract and the First and Second Discourses*, ed. Susan Dunn (New Haven: Yale University Press, [French Orig. 1755] 2002), 84.

[11]Gotthold Ephraim Lessing, Moses Mendelssohn and Friedrich Nicolai, *Briefwechsel über das Trauerspiel*, ed. Jochen Schulte-Sasse (Munich: Winkler, [1756/57] 1972), 55. See Hans-Jürgen Schings, *Der mitleidigste Mensch ist der beste Mensch: Poetik des Mitleids von Lessing bis Büchner* (Munich: C.H. Beck, 1988), ch. 3.

[12]Natalya Baldyga, 'Corporeal Eloquence and Sensate Cognition: G.E. Lessing, Acting Theory, and Properly Feeling Bodies in Eighteenth-Century Germany', *Theatre Survey* 58, no. 2 (2017): 162–85.

[13]Smith, *Theory*, 13.

[14]*The Life of Samuel Johnson, LL.D.*, by James Boswell, new edn, vol. 1 (London: Murray, [1791] 1831), 451.

society that expected its members to place pity at the top of the list of their emotional concerns and moral virtues.

Pity, of course, was hardly new. Pitying those who fared badly had long been a staple of Christian education, dating back to the Passion of Christ, which urgently asked every devotee for compassion and fellow-feeling. Yet compassion had since undergone a significant change: instead of merely identifying with the person who was suffering pain, modern compassion hoped to alleviate pain. Older notions of accepting pain as an unavoidable attendant of suffering were succeeded by fresh opinions that pain denigrated the individual's agency and dignity.[15] In civil societies as they were envisaged by contemporaries of the eighteenth century, pain was not something to be tolerated, nor was it hailed as a means of transcending the realm of material existence, as martyrs did. People no longer thought it was the entry ticket to an afterlife free from suffering, chastisement, humiliation and disempowerment. Rather, pain figured as an infringement on human integrity that was by no means confined to the body. Pain and misery also resided in poor living conditions that prevented people from fully realizing their potential. Furthermore, pain could be inflicted on others by treating them with contempt, haughtiness or indifference. Those who suffered such treatment and lived in such conditions deserved sympathy, pity and, above all, active compassion.

Yet pity and compassion had a downside, one lucidly illuminated by Moses Mendelssohn, a central figure of the German Enlightenment. He critically engaged with Rousseau's arguments on nature, civil society and *pitié* in his 1756 translation of the French philosopher's *Discours* on human inequality. In Mendelssohn's view, pity always carried a touch of condescension because he who pitied another person usually thought of himself as being in a superior or better-off position. Pity thus imposed a hierarchical relationship and structural asymmetry between those who offered it and those who received it. Such asymmetry was familiar to Mendelssohn, who lived as a tolerated Jew in Prussia. In his experience, pity and compassion merely left him at the hands of well-meaning people who nevertheless looked down on him. Their benevolence reminded him of his own inferior status.[16]

In addition to being hierarchical and potentially condescending, pity and compassion were generally difficult to exchange between people with little in common. Even Hume and Smith, who believed sympathy was a naturally given human faculty, acknowledged gradations and variations. The crucial issue here was what Hume named 'resemblance' and what Lessing called 'from

---

[15]Javier Moscoso, *Pain: A Cultural History* (Basingstoke: Palgrave, 2012); Rob Boddice, ed., *Pain and Emotion in Modern History* (Basingstoke: Palgrave, 2014); Joanna Bourke, *The Story of Pain: From Prayer to Painkillers* (Oxford: Oxford University Press, 2014).
[16]Moses Mendelssohn, 'Sendschreiben an den Herrn Magister Lessing in Leipzig', in Jean-Jacques Rousseau, *Abhandlung von dem Ursprung der Ungleichheit unter den Menschen*, ed. Ursula Goldenbaum (Weimar: Böhlau, 2000), 235–50.

the same grain'. Resemblance facilitated sympathy, which in turn fostered social integration and moral consensus. Resemblance was closely linked to contiguity. 'The sentiments of others', Hume reminded his readers, 'have little influence when far remov'd from us.'[17] Removal could occur in various ways: through spatial distance as much as religious, racial, social, gender, generational or sexual differences. The greater the remove, the more difficult it was to regard the other as a neighbour and provide them, following a religious tradition or a secular principle, with love, understanding and practical aid.

The sentiments of others could also be removed in moral terms. Did someone who was punished for a crime deserve sympathy? Did his suffering (at the hands of the state and its legal system or police) arouse pity? To put it more generally, did all kinds of suffering, caused by all kinds of factors, elicit or merit compassion?

This question was hotly debated around 1800. General opinion held that only those who could not be blamed for their own suffering were worthy of sympathy and compassion. Innocence and guiltlessness were viewed as prerequisites for pity. Some, though, advocated extending sympathy even to people whose suffering was self-inflicted:

> We state that those who bear the blame due to their own foolishness or vice do not only deserve pity. Rather, they deserve it more than those who are unhappy through no fault of their own. A true human being loves all human beings – which means that he is a true philanthropist. The person next door does not stop being human even if he or she acted in a misguided and vicious way. He or she thus deserves to be loved and, consequently, pitied by other humane people.[18]

Such a radical quest for human sympathy and compassion was clearly at odds with mainstream attitudes and sensibilities. Most people at the time renounced those who had violated moral norms. Alcoholics or gambling addicts who had lost their fortunes were not entitled to pity; those who had committed crimes and purposefully harmed others garnered even less sympathy. What they deserved was punishment, more often than not of a severe and harsh kind.

Pity shown and withheld

Indeed, communities in the eighteenth century were used to extreme forms of punishment. Torture was part and parcel of police practice, serving as a means of both eliciting confessions and punishing offenders. Legal codes and

---

[17] Hume, *Treatise*, 369.
[18] Johann Georg Krünitz, *Oekonomisch-technologische Encyklopädie, oder allgemeines System der Staats- Stadt- Haus- und Landwirthschaft*, vol. 75 (Berlin: Pauli, 1798), 349–50.

traditions proclaimed the death penalty, often carried out in monstrously cruel ways, for capital crimes such as murder, theft or counterfeiting money. As a general rule, executions took place in public and were attended by large crowds.

Apart from exacting vengeance, harsh penalties aimed to deter potential offenders, who were to imagine their own fate when seeing the convict's execution. Public executions also helped authorities to assert their power and reinforce their monopoly on violence. All this was plainly stated and communicated to the audience, as in the case of Johanna Höhn, who had committed infanticide in 1783. During the open ceremony that preceded her execution in the city of Weimar, the hangman announced that he would administer the death sentence 'in order to strengthen – rather than weaken – the legal powers of the governing prince and to set a warning example for others'.[19]

Even if the principle of deterrence was not as effective as it was thought to be, publicity bore a highly symbolic meaning. As civic peace and moral order had been deliberately broken by the offender, the restoration of that peace had to take place before the general public. The audience was there to observe, ideally, a sincere confession and an apology. This given, the criminal was granted a 'good death' at the hands of a professional executioner. Those who watched the execution witnessed a solemn act of redress, cast in a deeply religious aura.[20]

In such ideal cases, pity prevailed. Writing in the 1780s, the Swiss educational reformer Johann Heinrich Pestalozzi reminded readers of the 'old days' when fathers and mothers called in children and servants as soon as they heard the death bell tolling from the site of an execution. 'Often accompanied by warm tears', they prayed together and warned each other against committing the kinds of crimes that would lead to such an 'unhappy ending'. At the site itself, those present shared a 'quiet and solemn meditation'. As the moment of death approached, people 'bared their heads, clasped their hands, and prayed for the unhappy one'. Most bystanders 'were visibly moved' by what they saw.[21]

Pestalozzi's account might be overly idealized, as he was using these images of former times to criticize contemporary attitudes. Still, historical evidence tends to confirm the pedagogue's testimony, at least in certain

---

[19]W. Daniel Wilson, 'The "Halsgericht" for the Execution of Johanna Höhn in Weimar, 28 November 1783', *German Life and Letters* 61, no. 1 (2008): 33–45, here 42.

[20]Esther Cohen, *The Crossroads of Justice: Law and Culture in Late Medieval France* (Leiden: Brill, 1993), 207; Richard van Dülmen, *Theatre of Horror: Crime and Punishment in Early Modern Germany* (Cambridge: Polity Press, 1990); Pieter Spierenburg, *The Spectacle of Suffering: Executions and the Evolution of Repression: From a Preindustrial Metropolis to the European Experience* (Cambridge: Cambridge University Press, 1984), 59–64.

[21]Johann Heinrich Pestalozzi, 'Lienhard und Gertrud: Ein Buch für das Volk', in *Pestalozzi's Sämmtliche Werke*, vol. 2 (Stuttgart: Cotta, 1819), 19–20.

circumstances. When, in 1617, a few thousand spectators gathered in the city of Nuremberg to witness justice done, they got everything they wanted: the 'poor sinner' who had been sentenced to death for counterfeiting gold and silver coins proved to be full of remorse. On his way to the execution site, he wept and asked for the public's pardon. After arriving at the gallows he made another public confession, pleaded for divine forgiveness, dropped to his knees and recited the Lord's Prayer. While being burned at the stake he repeatedly shouted that he commended his spirit into the Lord's hands. His attitude and behaviour earned him the pity of his chaplain, if not of the spectators, who were evidently satisfied with the outcome.[22]

Through such dramas of cathartic repentance, the condemned person could evoke sympathetic identification with his or her plight. Rather than being ostracized and expelled from the community, by dying a good Christian death he or she was reintegrated into it. Watching the condemned suffer might remind onlookers of Christ's passion and of their own sinfulness and vulnerability. The convict's pain signalled expiation, purgation and salvation, thereby proving them worthy of being welcomed back into the Christian collective. Thus, pain was not condemned as a cruel and inhumane infliction, but was instead thought to possess an inherent spiritual and soteriological efficacy.[23]

Dissatisfaction arose whenever justice failed to be administered in an orderly way, or when a condemned criminal did not meet the public's expectations. Convicts who acted arrogantly or insolently or in what was considered an un-Christian manner faced derogatory jeers and had objects thrown at them from the crowd.[24] Such reactions increasingly drew criticism from reformers like Pestalozzi and many others. It is not clear if people really comported themselves more rudely or violently at public executions as time went by. What did change, however, was how such comportment was viewed and judged. More and more people took offence to and spoke out against the lack of tact, sentiment and decency that they witnessed among those who came to see justice served.

---

[22]Joel F. Harrington, *The Faithful Executioner: Life and Death, Honor and Shame in the Turbulent Sixteenth Century* (New York: Picador, 2013), xiii–xv.
[23]Mitchell B. Merback, *The Thief, the Cross and the Wheel: Pain and the Spectacle of Punishment in Medieval and Renaissance Europe* (Chicago: University of Chicago Press, 1999), 19–20, 126–58; Samuel Y. Edgerton Jr., *Pictures and Punishment: Art and Criminal Prosecution during the Florentine Renaissance* (Ithaca, NY: Cornell University Press, 1985), ch. 5 ('Pictures of Redemption'); Jan Frans van Dijkhuizen, *Pain and Compassion in Early Modern English Literature and Culture* (Cambridge: Brewer, 2012), 248.
[24]Harrington, *Executioner*, 80–3, 87; for later periods see V.A.C. Gatrell, *The Hanging Tree: Execution and the English People 1770–1868* (Oxford: Oxford University Press, 1994), 69–70.

In 1688, the French moralist and writer Jean de La Bruyère strongly criticized his contemporaries for their 'vain, malicious, and inhuman curiosity' towards the 'ignominious' spectacle of public executions:

> They run to see the unfortunates; they line up in haste or they place themselves in windows to observe the demeanor and the countenance of a man who is condemned and who knows that he will die.[25]

Twelve years earlier, the execution of Marie-Madeleine-Marguerite d'Aubray, Marquise de Brinvilliers, had been watched by *tout* Paris. Madame de Sévigné, who was herself present, noted that people were in 'commotion' (*ému*), their attention 'fixed'.[26]

This was confirmed by Brinvilliers's confessor, who accompanied her on her route to the execution. He observed a 'continual murmur' and people who were 'begging God for mercy on her behalf & were pitying her misfortune'. Such conduct was in full accordance with traditional expectations about sympathetic identification with the condemned and their reintegration into the community. But the priest witnessed other attitudes as well: 'A greater number insulted her and heaped curses upon her.' Instead of showing compassion, they indulged in feelings of revenge, contempt and hatred.[27]

Madame de Sévigné herself was torn between different emotional responses. She was curious to see the prominent murderess, and waited on the bridge to Notre-Dame Cathedral where the convicted woman was brought for '*l'amende honorable*'. Finally catching sight of her made her 'shudder'. Shudder from what? Did she feel pity, or awe? Was she seized by disgust, or revulsion? Madame de Sévigné did not say. Yet she frequently attended public executions and recorded them in minute detail and at great length. The lively tone of her letters suggested excitement and curiosity rather than abhorrence or hesitation.

Nevertheless, Madame de Sévigné was one of the most outspoken *femmes sensibles* of her time. In aristocratic circles, *sensibilité*, the ability to feel deeply and sincerely, had become progressively more fashionable during the second half of the seventeenth century, with men and women competing to appear the most *sensible*. They presented themselves as being profoundly affected by what they observed, and as harbouring intense feelings of love, sympathy and fear (among many others).[28] Sévigné's letters to her daughter were full of tenderness, sentiment and tears, and she proudly defended her

---

[25]Paul Friedland, *Seeing Justice Done: The Age of Spectacular Capital Punishment in France* (Oxford: Oxford University Press, 2012), quote 149.
[26]*The Letters of Madame de Sévigné to her Daughter and Friends*, ed. Mrs Hale (Boston: Roberts, 1878), 156 (17 July 1676).
[27]Friedland, *Seeing*, 146–8.
[28]Frank Baasner, *Der Begriff 'sensibilité' im 18. Jahrhundert: Aufstieg und Niedergang eines Ideals* (Heidelberg: Winter, 1988).

expressive sensibility against older notions of stoic control and calmness. That sensibility, however, did not prevent her from eagerly watching scenes of cruelty and human suffering in the theatre of horror. Nor did it prompt her to feel sympathy with those who suffered.

A hundred years later, sensibilities had grown and expanded again. Sympathy was on many people's minds, from the doctors who reconceptualized the sensitive body and the communicative role of the nervous system, to the philosophers who praised sympathy and pity as foundations of civil society and cooperation, to the playwrights and poets who explored the sympathetic effects of tragedy and sentimental novels. What Lynn Hunt has called 'imagined empathy' made headlines and captured people's hearts and minds in the late eighteenth century.[29] Sentimentalism or *Empfindsamkeit* developed into a craze among the educated middle classes, and inevitably attracted scepticism. Immanuel Kant and numerous others criticized what they perceived as a cheap way of feeling pity: weeping for every suffering creature, whether a human being or a butterfly. What was needed in place of such weak and 'feminine' pity was true compassion, in other words, a 'manly' approach to alleviating pain and changing things for the better.[30] For Kant, feeling and acting were two sides of the same coin. He deemed anyone who merely felt pity for a person without coming to their rescue or actively assisting them morally reprehensible.

What effect did this have on scenes of public cruelty? Analysing people's behaviour without applying a normative judgement, Kant referred to the 'principle of contrast' that he saw at work in human psychology. People's enjoyment, he wrote in 1798, 'increases through comparison with others' pain, while their own pain is diminished through comparison with similar or even greater sufferings of others'. What made such comparison possible was sympathy (*Mitleiden*), fellow-feeling, putting oneself in the other's shoes:

> This is why people run with great desire, as to a theater play, to watch a criminal being taken to the gallows and executed. For the emotions and feelings which are expressed in his face and in his bearings have a sympathetic effect on the spectators and, after the anxiety the spectators suffer through the power of the imagination [...] the emotions and feelings leave the spectators with a mild but nevertheless genuine feeling of relaxation, which makes their subsequent enjoyment of life all the more tangible.[31]

---

[29]Lynn Hunt, *Inventing Human Rights: A History* (New York: Norton & Co., 2007), 32.
[30]Immanuel Kant, *Anthropology from a Pragmatic Point of View*, ed. Robert Louden (Cambridge: Cambridge University Press, [Germ. Orig. 1798] 2006), 132; Frazer, *Enlightenment*, ch. 5; John Mullan, *Sentiment and Sociability: The Language of Feeling in the Eighteenth Century* (Oxford: Oxford University Press, 1988).
[31]Kant, *Anthropology*, 134–5.

This kind of value-neutral sympathy was not on the minds of those who called for more civilized and sensible attitudes and social practices, however. They held that the 'sympathetic effect' of seeing other people suffer should engender other outcomes: instead of feeling relaxed or enjoying a renewed zest for life after leaving the site of suffering, advocates of sensibility ought to feel compassion for the victim and call for more humane treatment of criminals.

Sympathy, pity and compassion were thus at the core of the movement to reform the penal system and ban public displays of cruelty. They also informed the abolitionist movement, which sought to put an end to the slave trade and slavery altogether. Furthermore, they fuelled initiatives to stop cruelty to children and animals, along with many other humanitarian concerns and efforts that gathered steam in the nineteenth and twentieth centuries.[32]

Mixed feelings

But sympathy, pity and compassion did not spring out of nowhere. They needed, as Samuel Johnson knew, to be educated, cultivated and practised. Furthermore, they could and would, occasionally, clash with other emotions and passions – or with their lack.

This is what Pestalozzi observed in the 1780s. 'In our days', he complained, 'human hearts have become much more brutish and indifferent than in former times. People often watch executions as coldly and unaffectedly as they would watch irrational cattle being slaughtered'.[33] In 1785, the Berlin-based writer and publisher Friedrich Nicolai was appalled by the mood of 'greatest indifference' that he found among the crowds watching public executions. Common people were, as he saw it, *'fühllos'*, unfeeling, and exhibited a callous numbness at the sight of cruel punishment. At worst, they might even side with the criminals, especially as popular pamphlets

---

[32]Abigail Green, 'Humanitarianism in Nineteenth-Century Context: Religious, Gendered, National', *Historical Journal* 57, no. 4 (2014): 1157–75; Michael Barnett and Thomas G. Weiss, eds, *Humanitarianism in Question* (Ithaca, NY: Cornell University Press, 2008); *Relief in the Aftermath of War*, ed. Jessica Reinisch (*Journal of Contemporary History* 43, no. 3 (2008): 371–551, Special Issue).
[33]Pestalozzi, 'Lienhard und Gertrud', 20.

and street ballads tended to depict them less as vicious felons and more as martyrs whose sorry fates could not help but touch everyone's hearts.[34]

Nicolai, himself an ardent believer in enlightened mores and opinion, was torn. On the one hand, he warned vehemently against any attempt to turn criminals into popular heroes whose martyrdom made them even more famous. Such '*Zärtlichkeit*' (endearment, tenderness) was misplaced, and it threatened to subvert justice and morality. On the other hand, Nicolai did not consider the condemned amoral monsters. He was eager to point out that 'these miscreants are human beings' whose evil deeds had mainly been caused by 'a lack of education, sustenance and good government'.[35]

Even criminals, then, deserved sympathy and compassion. Rather than being heralded as heroes and resisters, they should be pitied. If pity and sympathy were denied, it reflected badly on those withholding them, who were exposed as uncivilized people. This seemed particularly appalling as far as women were concerned. When the German playwright and theatre director Karl von Holtei recorded his memories of attending a public execution in Breslau around 1810, he remembered most keenly a gentle-looking woman who 'while the wheel moved blow by blow, calmly ate a large slice of buttered bread'. This image stayed with him. Nor could he forget the crowds of 'sensitive' (*sanftfühlend*) women who set off the night before for the 'popular spectacle', their 'tender offspring' and baskets full of food in tow, in order to secure a good view.[36] For Holtei and others like him, feminine gentleness and an indifference to violence and suffering could not be reconciled. Women, most of all, ought to be emotionally affected and show compassion towards a person who was being put to death.

This belief reflected contemporary notions of male versus female 'character'. Women's emotions were generally regarded as gentler and softer than men's, particularly with regard to shame and pity. Women were

---

[34]Friedrich Nicolai, *Beschreibung einer Reise durch Deutschland und die Schweiz, im Jahre 1781*, vol. 6 (Berlin: Nicolai, 1785), 762–3. As to the widely popular street ballads, see Richard J. Evans, *Rituals of Retribution: Capital Punishment in Germany, 1600–1987* (Oxford: Oxford University Press, 1996), ch. 4. Thomas W. Laqueur has argued that 'the natural genre of execution is carnival' and that 'the carnivalesque crowd was the central actor in English executions' ('Crowds, carnival and the state in English executions, 1604–1868', in *The First Modern Society: Essays in English History in Honour of Lawrence Stone*, ed. A.L. Beier, David Cannadine and James M. Rosenheim (Cambridge: Cambridge University Press, 1989), 305–55, quotes 340, 309). But carnival not only affirms power relations, it can also turn those relations upside down. Ever since the medieval period, there had been instances when the crowd turned against authorities during executions. Whether those cases really increased in number and thus became more threatening to the state, as Evans argues, is debatable. At least, there is no convincing evidence that this perception and the fear of a loss of control led to the abolishment of public executions in the second half of the nineteenth century.

[35]Nicolai, *Beschreibung*, 766, 768, 761–2.

[36]Karl von Holtei, *Vierzig Jahre*, vol. 1 (Berlin: Buchhandlung des Berliner Lesecabinets, 1843), 130, 133. See also Evans, *Rituals*, 211 ff.; Gatrell, *Hanging Tree*, 68; Friedland, *Seeing*, 180–3, 190.

thought to be more susceptible to inappropriate behaviour and could thus be easily offended by conduct that men were far less inclined to find shameful. For this reason, in 1830, Prussian authorities forbade public corporal punishment for girls over the age of ten, as such chastisement would hurt women's modesty (*Schamhaftigkeit*).[37] It was considered equally shameful for female spectators at executions to behave in an indecent and offensive manner. If they were being true to their nature, women would either stay away altogether, or feel great pity for the condemned. Remaining seemingly calm and indifferent while munching on a piece of bread certainly did not meet those expectations.

Indeed, middle-class observers increasingly voiced concerns about what they perceived as an absence of agreeable feelings in lower-class people, including women. In 1840, Charles Dickens complained that he 'did not see one token in all the immense crowd of any emotion suitable to the occasion' during a hanging at London's Newgate Prison:

> No sorrow, no salutary terror, no abhorrence, no seriousness, nothing but ribaldry, debauchery, levity, drunkenness and flaunting vice in fifty other shapes.[38]

Alongside terror and abhorrence, Dickens was also missing 'sorrow' and 'seriousness', and not only from Londoners. After attending a beheading in Rome a few years later, the writer recorded the same atmosphere:

> Nobody cared, or was at all affected. There was no manifestation of disgust, or pity, or indignation, or sorrow. My empty pockets were tried, several times, in the crowd immediately below the scaffold, as the corpse was being put into its coffin.[39]

In France, public prosecutor Alexandre de Molènes was equally appalled by the public's reaction to shameful sanctions like the garrote or to brutal scenes of hanging. As he wrote in 1830, their response tread 'pity underfoot', defied shame and 'forgot all sentiments of human dignity'.[40] German authorities likewise accused onlookers of insensitive crudeness

---

[37]Evans, *Underworld*, 117.
[38]Peter Gay, *The Cultivation of Hatred* (New York: Norton & Co., 1993), quote 177.
[39]Charles Dickens, *Pictures from Italy* (Leipzig: Tauchnitz, 1846), 198–9. Dickens mentioned a businesslike atmosphere verging on the superstitious: 'The speculators in the lottery station themselves at favourable points for counting the gouts of blood that spirt out, here or there; and buy that number. It is pretty sure to have a run upon it' (199). On magical beliefs in the healing power of blood (and bones), see Spierenburg, *Spectacle*, 30; Wolfgang Schild, 'Das Blut des Hingerichteten', in *Mythen des Blutes*, ed. Christina von Braun and Christoph Wulf (Frankfurt: Campus, 2007), 126–54.
[40]Alexandre Jacques Denis Gaschon de Molènes, *De l'humanité dans les lois criminelles, et de la jurisprudence* (Paris: Locquin, 1830), 401.

(*'fühllose Rohheit'*) and began attempting to restrict the public's access to execution sites.

By the mid-nineteenth century, criticizing lower-class people for their lack of sorrow, pity and sensitivity had become a common trope among members of the educated classes, who proclaimed their own sentiments infinitely more humane and morally superior. As they saw it, a sensible person could not help but feel pity when violence was enacted against a helpless human being, regardless of who that human being was or what crime they had committed. Those whose hearts had not yet been 'civilized' had to be taught an emotional lesson so that they could feel what they were supposed to when confronted with violent and cruel acts.

Some middle-class observers, however, candidly confessed to having mixed feelings. Writing in 1843, Holtei explicitly reprimanded his younger self for his outward curiosity and inappropriate feelings. As a teenager, he had been invited to inspect the instruments of torture (wheel, rope) before an execution, and had reviewed them 'with a peace of mind and an apathy that shocks me even today', thirty years later. He recalled 'the delirium into which curiosity, horror and disgust plunged me' as he had watched the objects being put to use. Sitting on a friend's shoulders, he had seen the whole thing perfectly, and vividly remembered the erotic attraction that he felt for one of the convicts, a young and beautiful woman who, in her agony, had torn her dress from her shoulders.[41]

While Holtei reflected on his state of mind three decades after the event, the British poet Lord Byron recorded his feelings just a few days after he had witnessed three robbers being guillotined in Rome in 1817:

> The first [beheading] turned me quite hot and thirsty, and made me shake so that I could hardly hold the opera-glass (I was close, but was determined to see, as one should see every thing, once, with attention); the second and third (which shows how dreadfully soon things grow indifferent), I am ashamed to say, had no effect on me as a horror, though I would have saved them if I could.[42]

Of course, he could not, and it does not seem as if this caused Byron any particular sadness or outrage. Instead, what he experienced was a mixture of excitement, curiosity and indifference. Only later when he recorded his feelings did he feel 'ashamed' because he knew he ought to have felt otherwise. In a similar vein, in 1840, 29-year-old William Thackeray reported on an execution that he had attended in London. He wrote openly about the 'brutal curiosity which took me to that brutal sight'. Only 'as the

---

[41] Holtei, *Jahre*, 131.
[42] Baron George Gordon Byron, *The Works of Lord Byron*, vol. 4 (London: Murray, 1832), 29–30 (from a letter to his publisher).

last dreadful act was going on' did he shut his eyes. Later, he felt 'ashamed and degraded' by his 'complacent curiosity' and indifference to the culprit's suffering – feelings that he shared with 'forty thousand persons (say the sheriffs), of all ranks and degrees, – mechanics, gentlemen, pickpockets, members of both houses of parliament, street-walkers, newspaper-writers'.[43]

Thackeray's account, not unlike Byron's or Holtei's, refrained from distinguishing between 'us' and 'them', between the civilized, educated, sensible middle classes and the barbarous, brutal and cruel lower ones. Rather, they saw the same cruelty in themselves, in the shape of curiosity or indifference. They experienced emotions that bluntly contradicted emotional norms such as pity, compassion and empathy with fellow human beings in suffering. They felt, instead, a desire for revenge and, in Thackeray's words, a 'hidden lust after blood'. In speaking out against the death penalty, they thus fought against what they detested in themselves, and for this they did not mind being scorned as 'foolish sentimentalists', obsessed with 'morbid humanity' and 'cheap philanthropy'.[44]

Training empathy

Thackeray, Byron and Holtei's shame and shock regarding their lack of appropriate feelings clearly showed that they had digested the latest lesson on morality, even though they were not able to fully live by it. As Johnson and Kant knew, and as recent neuroscientific experiments confirm, pity, compassion and sympathy – or empathy – do not come naturally, and they have limits. Those limits are established by social prejudices, cultural conventions and political incentives.

In contemporary liberal-democratic societies, fairness is highly valued. Not surprisingly, affective neuroscience research has discovered that people tend not to empathize with others who have acted unfairly and are painfully punished as a result. It is not just that the part of the brain responsible for the processing of empathy remains inactive in such cases; researchers actually observed activity in another area that processes rewards, satisfaction and revenge. Unfair players, the study concluded, do not deserve empathy when punished.[45]

Laboratory experiments that have investigated the relationship between empathy and group affiliation have shown similar results. When pain was inflicted on a member of a particular group, here a football club,

---

[43]William M. Thackeray, 'Going to See a Man Hanged', *Fraser's Magazine for Town and Country* 22, no. 128 (1840): 150–8. On the general fascination with executions 'regardless of social standing', see Gatrell, *Hanging Tree*, 242–58.

[44]Thackeray, 'Going', 157.

[45]Tania Singer et al., 'Empathic Neural Responses Are Modulated by the Perceived Fairness of Others', *Nature* 439 (2006): 466–9.

members of the same club not only empathized with the pain, but were willing to undergo it themselves in order to help the sufferer. Conversely, when members of the opposing club were mistreated, the familiar reward signal blinked in the observers' brains.[46]

Neuroscientists also found out that women reacted differently from men. When unfair players were being punished, women could and did empathize with their pain, rather than rejoicing or feeling gratified by their suffering.[47] Again, these findings are consistent with what women have been taught about themselves and their role in society. History, to be sure, has seen numerous women who were just as pitiless as men. Neither Elizabeth I nor the Russian empress Catherine the Great harboured tender feelings towards their enemies or adversaries. Kriemhild, the Burgundian king's daughter from the Middle High German *Nibelungenlied*, took gruesome revenge at Etzel's court on those who had murdered her husband, Siegfried. And Medea, the figure from Greek mythology, killed her own children and her rival in order to wound her unfaithful husband, Jason.

According to modern gender ideology, however, these women were extreme deviations from the norm. The female mind was generally considered soft and mellow. Women, as the philosopher Arthur Schopenhauer saw it in 1840, suffered from weak faculties of reason but widely surpassed men when it came to the virtues of human kindness and compassion.[48] For the educator Friedrich Wilhelm Foerster, women possessed the 'finer forces of the soul' which designated them for the 'protection of the weak', as he wrote in 1917. As such, it was their responsibility to foster a 'social culture' that would overcome selfishness and practice 'care for the lives of others'.[49] Consequently, women seemed particularly at home in nursing and social work, professions claimed by the first women's movement, which believed feminine empathy to be a resource for solving problems and pacifying social conflicts both private and public.[50]

Still to this very day, women are thought to have a special talent for engaging with others. Their capacity for empathic care, in the view of feminist psychologist Carol Gilligan, predestines them to be trailblazers of an ethics of which modern societies are desperately in need. As mothers, teachers, doctors, nurses and lawyers, women shape this ethics of care and compassion for the betterment of their fellow human beings. Men,

---

[46]Grit Hein et al., 'Neural Responses to the Suffering of Ingroup and Outgroup Members' Suffering Predict Individual Differences in Costly Helping', *Neuron* 68, no. 1 (2010): 149–60.
[47]Singer et al., 'Empathic Neural Responses'.
[48]Arthur Schopenhauer, 'Preisschrift über die Grundlage der Moral', in Schopenhauer, *Zürcher Ausgabe*, vol. 6 (Zürich: Diogenes, 1977), 254–5.
[49]Friedrich Wilhelm Foerster, *Lebensführung* (Berlin: Reimer, 1917), 39, 261.
[50]Iris Schröder, *Arbeiten für eine bessere Welt: Frauenbewegung und Sozialreform 1890–1914* (Frankfurt: Campus, 2001).

in contrast, orient themselves more towards the arbitration of justice, as neuroscientific experiments on pain and reward perceptions confirm.[51]

Whether such dispositions are inherent in female and male nature is questionable, though, even if this has been asserted, time and time again, for over two hundred years. Most people seem not to have trusted the claim, investing significant energy in an education that instilled in girls and boys the emotions, attitudes and behaviours they supposedly innately possessed. Empathy, sympathy and compassion were practised and cultivated in families, schools and, later, at work. Girls and young women found role models in their mothers, aunts and teachers, but also in literature for children and adolescents.[52]

Indeed, literature served as a major educational tool for children and adults alike, and often intentionally so. A case in point was Victor Hugo's short 1829 novel *Le dernier jour d'un condamné*, which was about a man who had been sentenced to death and was facing the guillotine the very next day.[53] The novel was meant to elicit sympathy for the culprit and his pain, and thus rally support for Hugo's struggle against what he perceived as cruel acts of state justice. The text was frenetically applauded by readers all over the world, and as a plea to abolish capital punishment it worked well. Twenty-year-old Émile Zola, who read it in 1860, admired its 'shattering' effect:

> A thrill of terror takes hold of you from the first line: you undergo all the anguish of the miserable creature, you climb onto the scaffold with him ... He [Hugo] has taken the shortest route, to address your hearts, your nerves, to make your hair stand on end, to move you to pity, to mix in you the fear with the pity.[54]

How did the text accomplish this? First of all, it does not tell the reader anything about the convict's evil deeds. There is no victim besides the man waiting to be taken to the guillotine. The reader knows, of course, that a criminal act took place, but she is spared the details (and is thus prevented from feeling empathy towards the original victim). Second, the culprit is presented as a man with feelings; Hugo describes his anguish,

---

[51]Carol Gilligan, *In a Different Voice: Psychological Theory and Women's Development* (Cambridge, MA: Harvard University Press, 2003); Carol Gilligan, 'Looking Back to Look Forward: Revisiting in a Different Voice', *Classics@ 9* (2011): http://nrs.harvard.edu/urn–3:hul.ebook:CHS_Classicsat (accessed 16 December 2022).

[52]Ute Frevert et al., *Learning How to Feel: Children's Literature and Emotional Socialization, 1870–1970* (Oxford: Oxford University Press, 2014).

[53]Victor Hugo, *The Last Day of a Condemned*, trans. George W.M. Reynolds (London: George Henderson, 1840).

[54]Émile Zola, *Correspondance*, vol. 1: 1858–1867, ed. B.H. Bakker (Montréal: Presses de l'Université de Montréal, 1978), 231 (Letter to Jean–Baptistin Baille, August/September 1860).

his fear, his desolation as his young daughter pays him a last visit without even recognizing him as her father. Writing about his feelings makes him seem like a human being, not a monstrous criminal. Third, the culprit is astonishingly articulate about his inner state, thoughts and impressions. He speaks the language of an educated and sensitive man, and that language can be immediately understood by the reader, who feels themselves equally educated and sensitive. A communicative bond thus forms between him and his audience, enhancing their proximity.

Another method of training empathy was suggested, nearly two centuries later, by neuroscientist Tania Singer. From 2013 to 2016, she conducted the ReSource Project, a longitudinal study of about 300 men and women who undertook nine months of mental exercises. Meditation practices, Singer found, helped participants to feel more compassionate and empathic by increasing the volume of grey matter in their brain networks. The change was demonstrated by measuring altruistic behaviours like donating money or displaying trust and generosity. Affective training, Singer summed up, 'is the best way to increase compassion'.[55]

Since the dawn of the twenty-first century, many institutions and associations have started to take compassion training seriously. In 2008, Stanford University's Department of Neurosurgery established a 'Center for Compassion and Altruism Research and Education'. In addition to conducting scientific research, the centre offers various online courses. One promises 'the embodied experience of becoming a compassion change agent' to people who hope to 'integrate compassionate action into their occupations, professions, communities, as well as into their personal development'. It is aimed particularly at 'educators, facilitators, consultants, physicians, nurses, coaches and leaders of all kinds'. The other, shorter 'Cultivating the Heart' course teaches 'the skills of (self)compassion, (self)awareness, reflection, meditation and more' and seeks to 'train and incline the mind towards a more compassionate, resilient, and authentic life'.[56]

Such programmes can, in fact, be traced back to the mid-twentieth century. In 1950, the president of the American Sociological Association, Leonard Cottrell, urged his colleagues in the social sciences to study empathy. 'Empathic ability', he told them, would play a crucial role in 'our long struggle ahead for a democratic world community'. As democracies relied on 'maximum participation' and 'experienced consensus', it was vital

---

[55] https://taniasinger.de/the-resource-project/ (accessed 16 December 2022); Marisa Przyrembel, Pascale Vrticka, Veronila Engert and Tania Singer, 'Loving-Kindness Meditation – A Queen of Hearts?', *Journal of Consciousness Studies* 26, no. 7–8 (2019): 95–129; Fynn-Mathis Trautwein, Philipp Kanske, Anne Böckler-Raettig and Tania Singer, 'Differential Benefits of Mental Training Types for Attention, Compassion, and Theory of Mind', *Cognition* 194 (2020): https://doi.org/10.1016/j.cognition.2019.104039.

[56] ccare.stanford.edu/education/applied-compassion-training/; http://ccare.stanford.edu/education/cultivating-the-heart/ (both accessed 16 December 2022).

that people learned to adopt other perspectives and read their fellow citizens. Intellectual leaders like Kenneth Clark, a professor of psychology and a civil rights activist, applauded empathy for its ability to bridge the social distance between people of colour and white Americans. Only a 'universal increase in empathy' – defined as 'the capacity of an individual to feel into the needs, the aspirations, the frustrations, the joys, the sorrows, the anxieties, the hurt, indeed, the hunger of others as if they were his own' – would topple racism and 'save us', he stated in 1979. This increase should be primed and facilitated by new educational tactics that sought to dial down competition and focus on similarities rather than differences. Instead of nurturing 'chauvinistic empathy' with those alike in 'color, religion, nationality, sex and status', Clark declared that the world (and the US, in particular) needed a universal empathy that embraced all human beings.[57]

Comparing Cottrell and Clark's ideas to what the current Stanford programme promises, however, reveals some stark differences. Stanford's courses deliberately focus on the needs and well-being of the individual:

> There is a correlation between compassion and personal well-being. Research suggests that as we become more aware of 'being' with ourselves in a compassionate way, we gradually begin to recognize and experience a more fully integrated sense of connection with our deeper core values and intentions.

Consequently, compassion, awareness and care are directed first and foremost at one's own self: 'We learn how to connect to ourselves first and drop from our head into our heart.' Although the second step is supposed to incorporate 'real-world settings', those are confined to coaching, communication, facilitation and leadership. Compassion here converges with 'mindfulness' and 'resiliency', and bears little to no trace of proactivity. In sum, the programme perfectly suits the notion of empathy as, in Michel Foucault's terms, a 'technology of the self' rather than, as in Clark's time, a 'technology of the social'.

Limits to empathy

As a technology of the self, empathy by no means transcends power; rather, it is itself a site of power. Lessing's maxim, 'the most compassionate person is the best person', has long since acquired a highly competitive edge: those who display more empathy (or, for that matter, mindfulness or wokeness) are morally and socially superior to others. Empathy also pairs neatly with power whenever and wherever business interests are concerned, as in

---

[57]Lanzoni, *Empathy*, quotes 175, 248–9.

training courses for HR or sales staff. Again, such developments date back to the 1950s, when empathy was sold as a way to improve industrial relations and advertise goods and services. Manuals and consultants recommended that bosses use empathy in order to penetrate their employees' psyches and thereby enhance performance.[58] Daniel Goleman and others who have made a fortune teaching empathy to managers since the mid-1990s have simply reinvented the wheel.[59]

Empathy clearly serves and has served multiple functions. Not all of them are compatible with moralistic claims about empathic civilizations. In practical use, similar to pity and compassion, empathy is asymmetrically structured. It often affirms people's own sense of self more than it helps others. Empathy has its limits, set by spatial distance as much as religious, racial, social, gender or age differences. Even if humans are capable of feeling empathy, they are not always prepared or willing to do so. Social, cultural, economic and moral hierarchies construct high barriers to both fellow-feeling and proactive conduct.

Whether current programmes to enhance empathy and compassion can work to lower these barriers remains an open question. Their focus on the self makes one doubtful. At the same time, such initiatives mirror a growing concern with and awareness of the need for empathy. Recalling the late eighteenth century, many people share and indulge in a new sensibility that is marketed as a tool to improve the world and, above all, themselves. But they rarely reflect on empathy's downsides and biases, which tend to be hidden behind a rhetoric of equality and mutuality.

Such rhetoric is in fact more recent, and it responds to contemporary sensibilities. Middle-class men and women in the nineteenth century used different language when they turned compassionately towards the lower classes. In 1848, the young doctor Rudolf Virchow visited Upper Silesia in order to make first-hand enquiries about the devastating typhus epidemic. He found appalling poverty and desperation, including 'uncleanliness and indolence', laziness and alcoholism. This culture of 'moral and physical sunkenness' made 'such a repulsive impression' on him that he felt 'more moved to disgust than pity'.[60] Similar feelings were reported by the economist Minna Wettstein-Adelt, who spent several months in 1893 working in a weaving mill. Just like Virchow, she experienced a sense of 'unspeakable disgust' at her co-workers' 'moral squalidness and crudeness'.[61] Disgust, in these and many other cases, clearly hindered or blocked empathy. If it left any room for pity, it was of a condescending kind. Virchow, himself

---

[58]Ibid., 181–7, 208–10. See Chapter 7 in this volume.
[59]See, for example, 'Getting Better at Empathy, with Daniel Goleman': https://coachingforleaders.com/podcast/391/ (accessed 16 December 2022).
[60]Rudolf Virchow, *Mitteilungen über die in Oberschlesien herrschende Typhus-Epidemie* (Darmstadt: WBG, [1848] 1968), 65, 67, 220.
[61]Schröder, *Arbeiten*, quote 44.

an outspoken liberal, saw medical doctors as custodians of the poor who, due to their physical, mental and moral weakness, could not be relied on to help themselves. The more that people like him professed to see crudeness, brutality and savagery at the bottom rung of society, the less likely they were to practise the sensitive sympathy that they valued in themselves and towards others like them.

Interactions with non-Europeans formed and followed a similar pattern. As colonizers, Europeans typically purported to be shocked by the violence and ruthlessness they found among men and women in Africa and Asia. But instead of bringing the 'European culture' of compassion to the colonized, they quickly adapted themselves to what they termed 'local customs', under the pretext that 'the natives' were used to violence and would not understand anything else.[62] Empathy, when it occurred at all, apparently did so only in Europe and only among Europeans.

Yet there, too, empathy was in no way anti-hierarchical. Rather, it suited the self-image of civilized, educated, considerate citizens, who positioned themselves as proud bearers of their culture. Empathy developed into a social status symbol and criterion for social differentiation. Middle-class ladies had to prove their good manners and intentions by compassionately attending to the 'protection of the weak', organizing charity bazaars, collecting donations for the 'modest poor' or making house visits to the ill and old. Demonstrating a sympathetic heart denoted a person's elevated social position as well as her sense of duty and virtue, which was presented as a shining example to others, worthy of gratitude and emulation.

The question of precisely who deserved these offerings of compassionate virtue and charity was constantly disputed, but 'innocence', preferably that of small children and animals, remained an important rationale for their allocation. New boundaries were drawn by nationalist and racist movements that gained momentum in the late nineteenth century. They reformulated Hume's argument about resemblance as enabling and facilitating sympathy in biological terms and contested such resemblance in groups that they considered culturally or racially inferior. The more alien those groups were posited to be, the more drastically the capacity for empathy shrank. A regime like National Socialism, which denied other nations and races alikeness or equal status, reserved sympathy exclusively for those who belonged to their own ethnic community.

If those who did not belong or had been excluded from that community suffered hardship and misery, they could not count on pity or compassion.

---

[62]Frank Dikötter, '"A Paradise for Rascals": Colonialism, Punishment and the Prison in Hong Kong (1841–1898)', *Crime, History & Societies* 8, no. 1 (2004): 49–63; Daniel Brückenhaus, 'Ralph's Compassion', in Frevert et al., *Learning*, 74–93; Margrit Pernau, 'Civility and Barbarism: Emotions as Criteria of Difference', in Ute Frevert et al., *Emotional Lexicons: Continuity and Change in the Vocabulary of Feeling 1700–2000* (Oxford: Oxford University Press, 2014), 230–59.

People chose to look the other way in order to remain unaffected.[63] 'Personal sympathy', according to a local newspaper in 1937, must be silenced – and completely so – when it came to 'the healthy people's community' getting rid of homosexual 'criminals'. Four years later, Hans Frank, governor-general of occupied Poland, issued the guideline: 'Basically our sympathy lies with the German people alone and with no other in the world.'[64]

Not everyone adhered to this guideline. As the farmer Heinrich List recorded in 1942, he 'felt sorry' for the son of a Jewish business partner and thus decided to hide him. His compassion earned him denunciation; he was murdered in Dachau concentration camp. His was not the only such case.[65] Mass observations conducted by police and security organizations frequently documented 'compassionate considerations' and general sentiments of pity towards Jews. Social proximity mattered: even those who approved of the regime's antisemitic actions and viewed Jews as 'alien elements' showed some reluctance to apply this judgement to their neighbours and acquaintances. When police reserves who participated in mass shootings in Poland in 1942 talked to Jewish victims and discovered that they were Germans from Hamburg or Bremen, the men resolved to stop participating in the executions, and asked for a different assignment.[66]

The darkest chapter of German history confers one more lesson about 'fellow-feeling': the men who tortured prisoners in the basements of police and security headquarters, and in many other places in Germany and the occupied countries, were not callous monsters, on the contrary. Though some of them may have been psychopaths with little disposition to empathy, most were aware of what their victims felt. Empathy let them know exactly where and when torture elicited the highest pain response. They also used their empathic abilities to uncover the victims' mental sensitivities and traumas, which helped them to exert calculated pressure.

Empathy versus solidarity

In order to distinguish the faculty of fellow-feeling from actively helping those in need, psychologists and neuroscientists use different words: empathy

---

[63]Peter Fritzsche, 'The Management of Empathy in the Third Reich', in *Empathy*, ed. Assmann and Detmers, 115–27; Aleida Assmann, 'Looking Away in Nazi Germany', in ibid., 128–48.
[64]Alexander Zinn, '*Aus dem Volkskörper entfernt*'? *Homosexuelle Männer im Nationalsozialismus* (Frankfurt: Campus, 2018), quote 463; Martin Broszat et al., *Anatomie des SS-Staates*, vol. 2 (Munich: dtv, 1989), 333–4.
[65]The Righteous among the Nations Database, https://righteous.yadvashem.org/?search=list%20heinrich&searchType=righteous_only&language=en&itemId=4021464&ind=0 (accessed 16 December 2022).
[66]Christopher R. Browning, *Ordinary Men: Reserve Police Battalion 101 and the Final Solution in Poland* (New York: Harper Perennial, 1998), 67.

for the former, compassion or empathic concern for the latter.[67] Empathy is roughly equivalent to what Adam Smith called sympathy or fellow-feeling and what Kant had in mind when he talked about *Mitleiden*: the act of feeling what another person feels, either through imagination or physiological or mental concurrence. It does not have to be accompanied by acts of kindness and compassion, however. Precisely the opposite might occur, depending on the cultural framing of the event. The curiosity and ease felt by bystanders of cruel rituals can, at times, be translated into feelings of self-righteousness, *Schadenfreude*, vengeance and contempt. This happens to this very day in countries such as Iran and China, where death sentences are deliberately carried out as public spectacles. In many European countries, public executions were abolished in the nineteenth century: in Prussia/Germany they stopped in the 1850s, in Britain in 1868.

Empathic concern, kindness and compassion can also be inhibited by fears of and prejudices against those perceived as foreign and potentially dangerous. During the European refugee crisis of 2015, many Germans went out of their way to donate goods, time and care to Syrians and others who had fled war-torn countries. A wave of *Mitgefühl* prompted active aid and was often related, in terms of proximity, to people's memories of flight and expulsion after the Second World War. But there were also citizens who objected to the 'welcome culture' and raised their voices and fists against the so-called 'intruders'. Compassion, as they saw it, should only embrace people of their own kind. Attitudes of ethnic nationalism and racism thus obstructed and inhibited empathy, as they had done during Nazism and before.

On the other hand, major changes have taken place since 1945. European citizens are increasingly willing to do voluntary work for and with others in need of support and assistance. They donate ever greater sums of money, most of which goes towards humanitarian aid and emergency relief; 50 per cent of donations in Germany are earmarked for international projects. Associations like Terre des Hommes (founded in 1959), Amnesty International (1961) and Médecins sans Frontières (1971) receive a tidy sum and are not at risk of running out of funds. What these and many other NGOs have in common is their impartiality and neutrality: instead of taking sides, they focus on helping people regardless of their national, religious or political backgrounds. Present-day humanitarians thus walk in the footsteps of eighteenth- and nineteenth-century advocates of sympathy.

This appears an impressive success story, speaking to a fundamental change in sensibilities and how they are framed. Resemblance, as a prerequisite of fellow-feeling, has come to be interpreted in a far more basic

---

[67]Frederique de Vignemont and Tania Singer, 'The Empathic Brain: How, When and Why', *Trends in Cognitive Sciences* 10 (2006): 435–41; Jean Decety and William Ickes, eds, *The Social Neuroscience of Empathy* (Cambridge, MA: MIT Press, 2009).

and inclusive way.[68] In a globalized world, proximity is less of an issue; at times, 'distant suffering' raises more empathic concern than what happens next door.[69] The media plays a crucial role in channelling our attention and compassion. Images of helpless, desperate people, particularly children, touch hearts far more effectively than lengthy articles about civil war, torrential rain or earthquakes.

When one reconsiders the long and twisted history of compassion, pity, sympathy and related feelings in the European context, contemporary notions of 'empathy' have definitely relegated them to the margins. Held in high esteem by all major religions, pity and compassion were traditionally considered essential for mercy and charity. From the late eighteenth century onwards, secular notions of sympathy and fellow-feeling began to be mentioned and discussed more frequently. This had an impact on how and where such feelings were learnt and cultivated. Pity was usually taught in and through religion, while sympathy and fellow-feeling found their home in the family and, to some degree, in educational institutions and charity work.

At the same time, secular and religious spheres were by no means neatly separated from one another, neither diachronically nor synchronically. Many men and women who passionately campaigned for the abolition of slavery were deeply inspired by their Christian faith and belief in the brotherhood of mankind. That very concept has also been used since the French Revolution to champion secular demands for practical fraternity.

Although it semantically excluded women, 'fraternity' denoted a symmetrical relationship better suited to the political project of modern democracy than pity and compassion, which reflected social hierarchies. An equal footing was also key to the notion of solidarity that rose to prominence in the second half of the nineteenth century. Adopted and furthered by the socialist labour movement, solidarity was an emotion relating to shared fate, shared forms of resistance and shared dreams about the future. It informed what early socialists had called 'the brotherhood of deeds' rather than that of words. The Kantian ideal of manly compassion obviously found some resonance here. Solidarity differed from compassion, however,

---

[68]See, e.g., Kenneth Clark's 1965 definition of 'a pure kind of empathy' that was based on the acceptance of 'the frailties and anxieties and weaknesses that all men share, the common predicament of mankind' (Lanzoni, *Empathy*, quote 240). Clark here echoed Schopenhauer who, in 1840, had declared compassion (*Mitleid*) with 'the weak, the guilty, *indeed all humanity*' to be the foundation of human kindness (*Menschenliebe*) and the basis of morality (Schopenhauer, Preisschrift, 248–9, italics added).

[69]Luc Boltanski, *Distant Suffering: Morality, Media and Politics* (Cambridge: Cambridge University Press, 1999).

in that it explicitly drew on sameness and mutuality. It thus united people of equal standing and entailed mutual assistance through various kinds of cooperative ventures and undertakings.

Moreover, solidarity had a strong international component. As in the *Communist Manifesto*'s 1848 appeal, 'Workers of all countries, unite!', socialist parties and trade unions connected with one another, and they still do.[70] Taking their lead, students in Western Europe and North America pledged 'international solidarity' to Vietnam in the 1960s and early 1970s. Later on, Vietnam was replaced by Chile, Nicaragua and apartheid South Africa. Although those who offered solidarity and those who received it did not necessarily share a fate, activists spoke of a 'shared utopia'. They showed their support by protesting loudly against 'imperialist' US policies, donating money for those who suffered oppression and demonstrating their personal commitment (by, for instance, joining 'coffee brigades' in Nicaragua).[71]

Empathy, however, was not on their minds. As a political emotion, solidarity proved far more powerful and attractive. In contrast to empathy, solidarity fostered a social bond between people who held common values and goals: whenever one was under attack, others stepped forward to offer their assistance. Individuals learnt and practised solidarity mostly in social movements and organizations, whether trade unions and cooperatives or Third World Stores and political campaigns.

A visible shift occurred when those campaigns faded away in the 1990s. Around the same time, claims on and appeals to empathy started to make headlines. Focusing on the individual's capacity for fellow-feeling, they promised two things simultaneously: to improve a person's individual gains and happiness, and to better society through greater sensibility and mindfulness. Both were congruent with what Ève Chiapello and Luc Boltanski called, in 1999, capitalism's new spirit.[72] The warm gospel of empathy answered the criticism levelled at the 'cold' aura of capitalism, which, since the days of Karl Marx and Friedrich Engels, had been accused of stripping both men and women of 'authentic' feelings and autonomous action.[73]

---

[70]Nicolas Delalande, 'Transnational Solidarity in the Making: Labour Strikes, Money Flows, and the First International, 1864–1872', in *'Arise Ye Wretched of the Earth': The First International in a Global Perspective*, ed. Fabrice Bensimon, Quentin Deluermoz and Jeanne Moisand (Leiden: Brill, 2018), 66–88.

[71]Caroline Moine, 'Feeling Political across Borders: International Solidarity Movements, 1820s–1980s', in Ute Frevert et al., *Feeling Political: Emotions and Institutions since 1789* (Cham: Palgrave Macmillan, 2022), 307–39; Frank Bösch, Caroline Moine and Stefanie Senger, eds, *Internationale Solidarität: Globales Engagement in der Bundesrepublik und der DDR* (Göttingen: Wallstein, 2018); Frank Bösch, 'Euphorie, Angst und Enttäuschung: Die bundesdeutsche Solidarität mit dem sandinistischen Nicaragua', in *Emotionen und internationale Beziehungen im Kalten Krieg*, ed. Hélène Miard-Delacroix and Andreas Wirsching (Berlin: De Gruyter Oldenbourg, 2020), 301–21.

[72]Ève Chiapello and Luc Boltanski, *The New Spirit of Capitalism* (London: Verso, 2005).

[73]See Chapter 7 in this volume.

A postscript: following the Russian military attack on Ukraine in February 2022, solidarity has returned and taken a bold political stand. The sending of weapons, medical aid and financial support to the Ukrainian government so that it can defend its country's independence and self-determination has been labelled an act of political solidarity based on common values. Housing and feeding Ukrainians who have fled to neighbouring countries is likewise cast in the language of solidarity, not empathic concern. Evidently, a dramatic political crisis is no time for empathy, with its object-neutral and often self-centred character. Rather, it is a time for active solidarity that sides with the victim facing a powerful aggressor.

PART TWO

Emotional Economies of Capitalism

CHAPTER SEVEN

Capitalist Cold? Bringing Emotions Back In

Empathy – and, for that matter, sympathy and fellow-feeling – entered the philosophical and social repertoire of endorsed emotions at about the same time as industrial capitalism came knocking on Europe's door. Britain, home to the first Industrial Revolution that began around 1760, led the way, developing the mechanized and centralized factory, the use of steam power and a wide range of other technological innovations. These transformations ushered in large-scale demographic and social changes that left their mark on political and cultural dynamics and shaped the emotional economy of individuals, social groups and societies.

If we believe Max Weber, capitalism was a profoundly rational economic system: rigorously focused on efficiency, purposeful, calculating and calculable. Emotions played no apparent role; whenever they did start to crackle, these 'irrational impulses' were mercilessly subsumed under the sweeping processes of rationalization which augured capitalism. Whoever wanted to avoid the 'iron cage' or the 'cool objectivity' of this way of life could find shelter only in art and eroticism or in the spheres of religion that, by preaching mysticism and orgiastic ecstasy, eluded rational 'routinization'.

Feelings, as something supposedly irrational and libidinal, seemed to Weber beyond the purview of capitalism. At best, they eked out an existence on the margins, foreign to and far from the rationalized activity of everyday life. But is this true? Or did Weber overextend his argument? Had he not in fact noted that the modern capitalist economic and social order was 'affectively' founded and that 'unlimited greed for gain', 'purely mundane passions' and 'emotional values' could all be genuine motivations of economic subjects?[1] Did he not, in other contexts, speak of 'affectual reasons' and a 'purely personal inclination' which might completely contradict rational considerations and yet nevertheless prove decisive?[2] And did he himself in 1915 not say: 'Seen from the standpoint that today is widespread and obviously widely justified, it is the emotional contents that alone are primary and ideas are merely their secondary manifestations'?[3]

On closer inspection, even Max Weber could not overlook the power of emotions to shape values and steer behaviour under modern capitalism. He was equally well aware of how capitalism in turn affected the emotional economies of the time. As a leading member of the Verein für Socialpolitik (Association for Social Policy Reform), a policy-oriented academic think tank, he conducted empirical investigations into the 'psychophysics' of industrial labour, which looked at how workers dealt with the emotional challenges of mechanization. In some ways, Weber thus followed in the footsteps of earlier critics of capitalism.

Doux commerce versus capitalist cold

Capitalism, from its very inception, received both a broadly positive and a highly negative spin. Its proponents proclaimed it to be the source of the 'wealth of nations' and peaceful international cooperation, while its critics denounced its exploitative character and predicted conflicts that would eventually bring it down. Karl Marx and Friedrich Engels, who in 1848 drafted the *Communist Manifesto*, accused capitalism of serving the interests of pitiless and egotistical actors. The 'bourgeoisie', they wrote, 'has left remaining no other nexus between man and man than naked self-interest, than callous "cash payment"'. In particular, it 'has torn away from the family its sentimental veil, and has reduced the family relation to a mere money relation'.[4] Furthermore, capitalism deprived workers of 'the last trace of independent activity' and rendered them 'machines pure and simple', as

---

[1] Max Weber, *The Protestant Ethic and the Spirit of Capitalism*, trans. Talcott Parson (New York: Scribner, 1958), 24; Max Weber, '"Churches" and "Sects" in North America: An Ecclesiastical Socio-Political Sketch', trans. Colin Loader, *Sociological Theory* 3, no. 1 (1985): 7–13, quotes 1; Max Weber, 'Religious Rejections of the World and Their Directions', in *From Max Weber: Essays in Sociology*, trans. and ed. Hans Heinrich Gerth and Charles Wright Mills (London: Paul & al., 1946), 323–59, quotes 332, 340.
[2] Max Weber, 'Three Pure Types of Legitimate Rule', in *The Essential Weber: A Reader*, ed. Sam Whimster (London: Routledge, 2004), 133–45, here 145.
[3] Max Weber, 'Introduction to the Economic Ethics of the World Religions', in ibid., 55–80, quote 74.
[4] Karl Marx and Frederick Engels, 'Manifesto of the Communist Party', in Marx and Engels, *Collected Works*, vol. 6 (New York: International Publishers, 1976), 505–47, here 514. See *Capitalist Cold: On Callousness and Other Economic Emotions in Europe and the US, 1840 to Today*, ed. Agnes Arndt and Kerstin Maria Pahl (London: Palgrave, 2024); Eva Illouz, *Cold Intimacies: The Making of Emotional Capitalism* (Cambridge: Polity Press, 2007).

Engels observed in 1844/5.[5] Workers became mere automatons, bound to the robotic rhythm and logic of industrial production, their senses dulled, their ability to take pleasure or pride in their work or experience real joy or satisfaction in their lives diminished.

Marx and Engels deliberately used sentimental language to put capitalism and its chief agent, the entrepreneurial class, on the pillory. They heavily romanticized pre-industrial conditions in order to accuse capitalism of drowning 'the most heavenly ecstasies of religious fervour, of chivalrous enthusiasm, of philistine sentimentalism, in the icy water of egotistical calculation'. With traces of nostalgia, they charged capitalism with being an emotionally and morally destructive force which 'resolved personal worth into exchange value'. Ultimately, though, capitalism would be destroyed by its own contradictions, clearing the way for a communist society that would harmoniously attend to people's actual needs and desires.[6]

Still, even Marx could see that capitalism had a 'GREAT CIVILIZING INFLUENCE'. It enabled 'the development of the productive forces, the extension of the range of needs, the differentiation of production, and the exploitation and exchange of all natural and spiritual powers'.[7] As such, capitalism was a necessary step on the path to communism and served, in Engels's words, as a prerequisite of the 'mighty movement' that would finally secure everyone 'a position worthy of men'.[8]

While the two German radicals could not help but be mightily impressed by the surge in productivity engendered by the new system and by the potential it held for the future, they were less enamoured with capitalism's emotional economy. In this they differed greatly from Adam Smith and others in the eighteenth century who had stressed the positive effect economic development had on people's feelings and behaviour. Advancing the argument of *doux commerce*, such thinkers posited that the expansion of trade led to the civilization of 'mores'. 'As we see every day', Montesquieu stated in 1748, people were becoming gentler, softer and more polished. In 1763, Smith opined that not only was the Netherlands the most commercially active European nation, but the Dutch also 'the most faithfull to their word'.[9] As early as 1704, the French economist Samuel Ricard famously claimed commerce

---

[5]Frederick Engels, 'The Conditions of the Working-Class in England', in Marx and Engels, *Collected Works*, vol. 4 (1975), 233–689, here 307–9.
[6]See Jürgen Kocka, *Capitalism: A Short History* (Princeton: Princeton University Press, 2016), 7–16, for a concise summary of Marx's understanding of capitalism.
[7]Karl Marx, 'Outlines of the Critique of Political Economy (Rough Draft of 1857–8. First Instalment)', in Marx and Engels, *Collected Works*, vol. 28 (New York: International Publishers, 1986), quote 361 (capital letters in the original).
[8]Engels, 'Conditions', 335.
[9]Montesquieu, *The Spirit of the Laws*, ed. Anne M. Cohler, Basia Carolyn Miller and Harold Samuel Stone (Cambridge: Cambridge University Press, 1989), 338; Adam Smith, *Lectures on Jurisprudence*, ed. Ronald L. Meek, David D. Raphael and Peter G. Stein (Oxford: Clarendon Press, 1978), 538. See Emma Rothschild, *Economic Sentiments: Adam Smith, Condorcet, and the Enlightenment* (Cambridge, MA: Harvard University Press, 2001); Lisa Herzog, *Inventing the Market: Smith, Hegel, and Political Theory* (Oxford: Oxford University Press, 2013).

affects the feelings of men so strongly that it makes him who was proud and haughty suddenly turn supple, bending and serviceable [...] Sensing the necessity to be wise and honest in order to succeed, he flees vice, or at least his demeanour exhibits decency and seriousness so as not to arouse any adverse judgement on the part of present and future acquaintances; he would not dare make a spectacle of himself for fear of damaging his credit standing.

Passions, in sum, were 'superseded by interest' as the 'basis and mobilizing force' of commercial activity.[10]

What might have been true for commercial capitalism did not apply to manufacturing, though. Producing goods, which were then traded, in a predictable and reliable manner required different dispositions and demeanours, from factory owners as well as factory workers. In Marx and Engels's view, the former were driven by unbridled greed for profit and engaged in the 'shameless, direct, brutal exploitation' of proletarian workers, who suffered both physical and mental harm as a result.[11] Capitalists' utter lack of empathy and compassion would no doubt render them despicable to any decent person who felt a sense of responsibility towards the weak or helpless.

Such criticism was echoed by conservatives and, from the 1830s, by the workers' and journeymen's associations that had begun to form in greater numbers.[12] Liberal-minded entrepreneurs felt obliged to defend themselves against the critiques. Friedrich Harkort, a pioneering German industrialist, pointed out that people like him brought progress, innovation and prosperity to a region and its inhabitants, at great personal risk. During the revolution of 1848/9, he called on workers to remain good (*brav*), industrious (*fleißig*) and prudent (*verständig*). In return, he promised each 'respectable man' an adequate livelihood and official support.[13]

---

[10]Samuel Ricard, *Traité général du commerce*, rev. edn, vol. 2 (Amsterdam: Harrevelt, [1704] 1781), 463. The translation is Albert O. Hirschman's (*Rival Views of Market Society and Other Recent Essays* (Cambridge, MA: Harvard University Press, 1992), 108), except the last part, which he omitted; here the translation is my own. Hirschman built on Ricard's argument in his classical study *The Passions and the Interests: Political Arguments for Capitalism before Its Triumph* (Princeton: Princeton University Press, 1977). A more recent endorsement of this view is Deirdre McCloskey's *The Bourgeois Virtues: Ethics for an Age of Commerce* (Chicago: Chicago University Press, 2006).
[11]Marx and Engels, 'Manifesto', 514.
[12]Jerry Z. Muller, *The Mind and the Market: Capitalism in Western Thought* (New York: Knopf, 2002).
[13]Friedrich Harkort, *Brief an die Arbeiter* (May 1849): urn:nbn:de:kobv:109-1-5284930; see Christina von Hodenberg, 'Der Fluch des Geldsacks: Der Aufstieg des Industriellen als Herausforderung bürgerlicher Werte', in *Der bürgerliche Wertehimmel: Innenansichten des 19. Jahrhunderts*, ed. Manfred Hettling and Stefan-Ludwig Hoffmann (Göttingen: Vandenhoeck & Ruprecht, 2000), 79–104, esp. 98 ff.

Alongside formal education, helping workers to help themselves was seen as key to improving their lot and turning them into law-abiding citizens. Consequently, liberal businessmen and factory owners, together with their wives and daughters, became increasingly active in various social and educational reform associations. Conservative manufacturers such as Alfred Krupp, meanwhile, chose to follow a paternalistic 'master in the house' policy, establishing support schemes like pension funds and company housing and demanding workers' gratitude, obedience and acquiescence in return. In 1877, Krupp gave an address to his employees that was by turns proud and self-assured, defensive and worried. For many decades, he explained, he had worked unceasingly to build his enterprise from the ground up. Indeed, he had often earned less money, especially in the early years, than his workers, who generally did not have to worry about whether business went well or badly. Furthermore, it was he, not the workers, who had introduced discoveries and innovations. Workers could be replaced, he could not. Krupp then urged his employees to be peaceable and content:

> Enjoy what you have earned. After work, go home to your own folks, to parents, wife and children and think about the household and education. This should be your politics, and you will have a happy time.

Above all, he exhorted them to stay away from socialists who, as Krupp saw it, respected neither property nor 'discipline, shame and decency'.[14]

In some ways, Krupp's uncompromising attitude worked out. He managed to attract and recruit a large and loyal core workforce (who were not easily replaceable), often across successive generations. They developed a strong sense of pride in being 'Kruppians' and identified with the company's international success. On the other hand, the capitalist's battle against revolutionary 'subverters' would prove a lost cause. Membership of trade unions and socialist parties grew steadily, despite warnings that such involvement would result in dismissal and the loss of privileges as a member of the Krupp 'family'.[15] The class struggle did not stop at the factory gates. What Krupp had touted as acts of benevolence and generosity – offering company housing and cheap groceries, building schools and hospitals – were repudiated by some as plain selfishness. The image of the ugly, brutal, cold-hearted and egotistical capitalist prevalent in socialist rhetoric fed and channelled workers' protest. The protest, however, went far beyond individual entrepreneurs of character, who were seen as mere personifications of a larger

---

[14] Alfred Krupp, 'Ein Wort an meine Angehörigen', in Krupp, *Briefe 1826–1887*, ed. Wilhelm Berdrow (Berlin: Hobbing, 1928), 343–8.
[15] Heinz Reif, '"Ein seltener Kreis von Freunden": Arbeitsprozesse und Arbeitserfahrungen bei Krupp 1840–1914', in *Arbeit und Arbeitserfahrung in der Geschichte*, ed. Klaus Tenfelde (Göttingen: Vandenhoeck & Ruprecht, 1986), 51–91; Klaus Tenfelde, ed., *Bilder von Krupp* (Munich: C.H. Beck, 1994).

system that exploited human labour (as the main source of surplus value) and lacked all concern for the common good.

Such criticism also found support in the domains of art and culture. When Gerhart Hauptmann's play *The Weavers* debuted in 1894, it met with spectacular acclaim. The play depicted a revolt of Silesian weavers from 1844 which had attracted widespread attention and commentary in its time, with poets like Heinrich Heine and Louise Aston writing about it, and artist Karl Wilhelm Hübner powerfully rendering it on canvas. Hübner's painting, as Friedrich Engels explained to British friends in 1844, contrasted 'cold-hearted wealth' and 'despairing poverty'. On tour, where it was seen by middle-class audiences in several cities, it 'prepared a good many minds for Social ideas' and 'made a more effectual Socialist agitation than a hundred pamphlets might have done'.[16]

Fifty years later, Hauptmann's play sparked trouble once more. Authorities in Berlin initially banned its public staging because it allegedly threatened social order by inciting negative feelings among 'discontented' spectators. Hauptmann went to court, claiming his 'social drama' was hardly meant as a social-democratic manifesto. It spoke instead to 'the universal human sentiment called pity (*Mitleid*)'. Whatever the author's intentions, the drama was widely perceived as 'dynamite for revolution' and contemporaries either loved or hated it. Yet even those reviewers who found it too tendentious or disagreed with Hauptmann's portrayal of the bourgeoisie as 'hard-hearted suckers' could not resist applauding the poet, 'because he has managed to shake me deep in my soul and grip my heart and mind'.[17] When the Berlin-based artist Käthe Kollwitz attended a private performance in 1893, she was immediately inspired to begin work on a series of prints. She deliberately placed the events of 1844 in a contemporary setting: in her etchings, the weavers wore clothes that resembled those of her time.[18] Kollwitz's pieces soon became tremendously popular; writer Upton Sinclair included some of them in his 1915 anthology *Cry for Justice*.

Joy in work and capitalist production

How did the workers see themselves and their experiences with and under capitalism? Did they feel like robots, bereft of emotional intensity? Affects and passions seemingly had no place in the industrialized factory, where

---

[16]Friedrich Engels, 'Rapid Progress of Communism in Germany', *The New Moral World*, 13 December 1844, 200; Hodenberg, Fluch, 83 ff.
[17]Gerhart Hauptmann, *Die Weber: Dichtung und Wirklichkeit*, ed. Hans Schwab-Felisch, 17th edn (Berlin: Ullstein, [Germ. Orig. 1892] 2017), quotes 96, 204, 245–6. As to pity and compassion, see Chapter 6 in this volume.
[18]Käthe Kollwitz, Cycle 'A Weavers' Revolt, 1893–1897', available online: https://www.kollwitz.de/en/cycle-weavers-revolt-overview (accessed 22 December 2022).

the production of uniform, precisely calculated and predictable work processes that were tightly synchronized and tolerated no interruptions was paramount. The more these processes were mechanized, the less room there was for individual sensitivities, moods and motivations. Many commented on the deadening effect factory work had on workers. It carried over into their domestic and privates lives, causing them to become 'mechanical' and 'machine-like'.[19]

Since the inception of industrialization, doctors had been concerned about the somatic sicknesses factory work could engender; by the end of the nineteenth century, they began to turn their attention to mental troubles as well. In 1906, neurologist Willy Hellpach stated that rapid technological development caused massive 'damages to emotional health'.[20] A short time later, the social researcher Adolf Levenstein surveyed these damages in an expansive questionnaire.[21] He was interested in workers' 'feelings and thoughts', in their 'mental relationship' to paid work and in their 'enjoyment' and interests. His analysis of the more than 5,000 responses revealed significant 'negative emotions' and even feelings of 'disgust' at the monotony of work. 'Joy in work', which, according to Levenstein, prevented the 'atrophy of the personality', was hard to come by in the mechanized workplace.[22]

Instead, people reported anxiety, fatigue and ill humour. An old metal worker who had experienced the transition from cottage industry to factory work summarized it thus:

> When my profession was equipped with machines, with furnaces and compactors, where now 80–100 people labour, you can imagine that having worked 42 years without the noise and suddenly being immersed in it, how this stirs up the nerves of an old man. I sweat the entire day, I become anxious. I often cry like a little child, at night I cannot sleep. I leave on the lights at night in order to sustain my emotional balance. I am not alone in this. Numerous workers have experienced the same suffering.[23]

---

[19] Official government surveys from the mid-1870s that focused on the physical stress of factory work performed by women and children had already noted negative emotional effects as well; see *Ergebnisse der über die Frauen- und Kinder-Arbeit in den Fabriken auf Beschluß des Bundesraths angestellten Erhebungen* (Berlin: Heymann, 1877), 54, 136.
[20] Willy Hellpach, *Technischer Fortschritt und seelische Gesundheit* (Halle: Marhold, 1907).
[21] Adolf Levenstein, *Die Arbeiterfrage* (Berlin: Reinhardt, 1912), 53 (reference to Hellpach). Levenstein was also in contact with Max Weber and was familiar with his investigations into the psychophysics of industrial work.
[22] Ibid., 5, 51.
[23] This and the following quote ibid., 77.

A metal turner who had moved to the city from the countryside two years earlier complained about the immense fatigue he felt working in a factory:

> Not tired like at home, where we worked all day with the scythe or walked behind the plow. Here my limbs are always shaking. And back in the country there was so much laughter after the work was done. Here all you see are disgruntled faces.

Above all, workers were irritated by the 'perpetual monotony', the 'mind-numbing tedium and uniformity' of mechanical labour. It embittered their enjoyment of work and instilled 'hatred' and 'ill humour for the whole environment'. The machine, wrote one weaver, 'has neither heart nor nerves, knows no fatigue, no fear, no pain, no anger [...] I would like to tear out the steel heart that beats so mercilessly and dispassionately'. Many feared that their work would degrade them into machines too, and render them equally passionless. Feeling lively or experiencing any other strong positive emotions happened only in their free time, if at all.[24]

How seriously such fears were taken is evidenced by the Verein für Socialpolitik's own ambitious enquiry into 'worker psychology', which was launched at the beginning of the twentieth century.[25] In particular, the phenomenon of fatigue piqued the researchers' interest, not least because it manifested as a drop in performance.[26] International congresses on hygiene and demography initiated sections on 'fatigue from occupational work', and Emil Kraepelin's experimental investigations into the 'working curve' and what factors influenced it were widely known. Max Weber studied them as carefully as other medical and socio-hygienic research that highlighted the effects of monotonous work on a person's 'emotional state'. His own lectures and articles on the 'psychophysics of industrial labour' did not adopt the dramatizing tone favoured by Levenstein; in Weber's pragmatic view, workers could adapt, provided they were properly compensated in the form of adequate, stable income. Nevertheless, he stressed the urgent need to study the psychological impact of industrial work processes more rigorously and, if possible, not only in the laboratory.[27]

---

[24]Ibid., 16, 46–7. See also Leo Engel, 'Probleme der Arbeiterpsychologie', *Zeitschrift für angewandte Psychologie und psychologische Sammelforschung* 6 (1912): 79–82; Leo Engel, 'Zur Psychologie der Arbeiter und der Arbeit', ibid., 547–61.
[25]Max Weber, *Zur Psychophysik der industriellen Arbeit: Schriften und Reden 1908–1912*, in *Max Weber Gesamtausgabe*, sect. I, vol. 11 (Tübingen: Mohr, 1995), 63 ff. (here the editorial report on 'Erhebungen über Auslese und Anpassung der Arbeiterschaft der geschlossenen Großindustrie').
[26]Anson Rabinbach, *The Human Motor: Energy, Fatigue, and the Origin of Modernity* (Berkeley: University of California Press, 1990); Philipp Sarasin, *Reizbare Maschinen: Eine Geschichte des Körpers 1765–1914* (Frankfurt: Suhrkamp, 2001), 315 ff.
[27]Weber, *Psychophysik*, esp. 238 ff.

It was in this context he pointed to Harvard's Institute for Applied Psychology, which Hugo Münsterberg had taken over from William James in 1897. The institute had grown into a research centre for industrial psychology, for which there was brisk demand in the US. Under the generic term 'psychotechnics', Münsterberg outlined a broad 'science of the practical application of psychology for the sake of cultural tasks'. It encompassed the selection of personnel, career counselling and vocational aptitude tests, as well as research into monotony in the workplace, the very issue that had preoccupied Weber.[28]

Applied psychology thrived in Germany as well, furnishing a prominent place for the study of 'worker psychology' in institutes and journals specifically founded for that purpose.[29] Monotony and fatigue proved to be evergreen issues as the rationalization and scientific management of the workplace took hold.[30] They were considered the greatest obstacles to joy in work, which economists and sociologists recognized as a productivity-enhancing factor vital to national economic development and performance.[31] The efficiency-conscious 1920s therefore put the 'struggle for joy in work' firmly on the political and scientific agenda.[32]

---

[28]Hugo Münsterberg, *Grundzüge der Psychotechnik* (Leipzig: Barth, 1914), 1; Hugo Münsterberg, *Psychologie und Wirtschaftsleben* (Leipzig: Barth, 1912). For the historical context, see Laura L. Koppes, ed., *Historical Perspectives in Industrial and Organizational Psychology* (Mahwah: Erlbaum, 2007); François Vatin, 'Arbeit und Ermüdung: Entstehung und Scheitern der Psychophysiologie der Arbeit', in *Physiologie und industrielle Gesellschaft*, ed. Philipp Sarasin and Jakob Tanner (Frankfurt: Suhrkamp, 1998), 347–68; Joan Campbell, *Joy in Work, German Work: The National Debate, 1800–1945* (Princeton: Princeton University Press, 1989), ch. 5.
[29]*Zeitschrift für angewandte Psychologie und psychologische Sammelforschung*, ed. William Stern and Otto Lipmann, vol. 1 ff., Leipzig 1907 ff. (it emerged out of the institute of the same name, founded in 1906 by Stern and Lipmann); the journal *Praktische Psychologie* (1919–23), published by Walther Moede, and its successor, *Industrielle Psychotechnik* (1924 ff.) both stemmed from the Institute for Industrial Psychotechnics founded in 1919 at the Technische Universität Berlin.
[30]Robert A. Brady, *The Rationalization Movement in German Industry* (Berkeley: University of California Press, 1933); Heidrun Homburg, *Rationalisierung und Industriearbeit: Arbeitsmarkt – Management – Arbeiterschaft im Siemens-Konzern Berlin 1900–1939* (Berlin: Haude & Spener, 1991); Rüdiger Hachtmann, *Industriearbeit im 'Dritten Reich': Untersuchungen zu den Lohn- und Arbeitsbedingungen in Deutschland 1933–1945* (Göttingen: Vandenhoeck & Ruprecht, 1989), 67–89.
[31]Heinrich Herkner, *Die Bedeutung der Arbeitsfreude in Theorie und Praxis der Volkswirtschaft: Vortrag gehalten in der Gehe-Stiftung zu Dresden am 30. September 1905* (Dresden: Zahn & Jaensch, 1905); Campbell, *Joy in Work*, 53 ff.
[32]Hendrik de Man, *Der Kampf um die Arbeitsfreude: Eine Untersuchung auf Grund der Aussagen von 78 Industriearbeitern und Angestellten* (Jena: Diederichs, 1927); Campbell, *Joy in Work*, 178 ff.; Sabine Donauer, *Emotions at Work – Working on Emotions: The Production of Economic Selves in Twentieth-Century Germany*, PhD thesis, Freie Universität Berlin 2013, available online: (http://www.diss.fu-berlin.de/diss/receive/FUDISS_thesis_000000100445).

Those on the left and on the right, business representatives and trade unionists all had very different ideas about how to win this struggle. On the side of business, there was increasing recourse to scientific expertise; 'industrial psychotechnics', it was said in 1929, no longer had to 'fight for economic recognition today'.[33] This recognition was formalized in the German Institute for Technical Vocational Training (DINTA), which was established in 1925 and had its roots in heavy industry. There, engineers, scientists and industrialists searched for practical ways to remedy the 'crisis of joy in work' and to emotionally pacify 'the human being as a production factor'.[34]

Employers valued and supported such approaches greatly; the methods of 'human rationalization' were poorly received by workers and trade unions, however. Already in 1911, the Verein für Socialpolitik had complained that many workers were reacting with distrust and defensiveness to scientific surveys.[35] DINTA's claim to instruct workers in positive emotions earned it a sharp rebuke from socialist organizations.[36] Only when these critics were silenced in 1933 could the work of emotional education begin in earnest. The National Socialist German Labour Front immediately established a 'Beauty of Labour' office to overcome the 'adverse consequences of rationalization'. It was no coincidence that the office was a part of the 'Strength through Joy' organization, whose name succinctly and fittingly summed up the findings of contemporary psychotechnics.[37]

Interestingly, related interventions in the US seemed to generate less resistance. Workers and trade unions were interested and eager to cooperate in such studies. At least that was the perception of scientists who carried out on-site industrial research at the behest of large firms in the 1920s. As in Münsterberg's time, Harvard led the way with its School for Business Administration. Here, the usual suspects were discussed: decrease in performance due to fatigue or daydreaming, absenteeism, high rates of turnover. Unlike economists or industrial engineers, who posited using

---

[33]Margarita Gagg, 'Die soziale Aufgabe der industriellen Psychotechnik', *Industrielle Psychotechnik* 6 (1929): 195.

[34]Mary Nolan, *Visions of Modernity: American Business and the Modernization of Germany* (New York: Oxford University Press, 1994), 179 ff.

[35]Weber, *Psychophysik*, 410.

[36]Andreas Killen, 'Weimar Psychotechnics between Americanism and Fascism', *Osiris* 22, no. 1 (2007): 48–71, here 63; Gagg, Aufgabe, 195. Heinrich Kautz, *Industriepädagogik und Industriepsychologie*, PhD thesis (Cologne: Benziger, 1928), 38, writes about the 'poisonous sphere of mistrust'. In 1933, Brady harshly criticized psychophysics for ultimately prioritizing the maximization of profits (*Rationalization Movement*, 45).

[37]Wiltraut Best, *Die Überwindung nachteiliger Folgen der Rationalisierung durch das Amt Schönheit der Arbeit*, PhD thesis (Großenhain: Weigel, 1935); Karsten Uhl, 'Die Geschlechterordnung der Fabrik: Arbeitswissenschaftliche Entwürfe von Rationalisierung und Humanisierung 1900–1970', *Österreichische Zeitschrift für Geschichtswissenschaften* 21, no. 1 (2010): 93–117 with relevant bibliographical references.

financial bonuses, higher wages or technical adjustments to solve these problems, psychologists stressed the importance of social and emotional factors.[38]

As Harvard Professor of Industrial Research Elton Mayo stated in 1933, there was a tension between 'a merely economic logic of production' and a 'non-logical social code which regulates the relations between persons and their attitudes to one another'. Workers felt misunderstood by their managers and supervisors whose only goal was to reduce costs and enhance efficiency. 'The industrial worker', Mayo discovered,

> does not want to develop a blackboard logic which shall guide his method of life and work. What he wants is more nearly described as, first, a method of living in social relationship with other people and, second, as part of this an economic function for and value to the group.

Even American workers who had been raised in a highly individualistic society were 'not merely individuals; they constitute a group within which individuals have developed routines of relationship to each other, to their superiors, to their work, and to the policies of the company'. The group provided a sense of community, bonding and belonging. If the group's 'social code' was overridden or neglected by managerial decisions, 'a sense of human defeat' arose which resulted in 'exasperation' and withdrawal among individual workers.[39]

This was the conclusion of about 20,000 interviews conducted by Mayo's team at large firms such as the Western Electric Company in Hawthorne near Chicago. Many workers apparently had something 'on their minds' which they wished to confidentially share with a competent and sensitive listener. The mere fact that someone wanted to hear their concerns and took them seriously produced an 'emotional release' of 'great advantage' and helped workers to 'get rid of useless emotional complications'. At the same time, they knew just how important social interaction, collaboration and communication with their fellow workers was. Strengthening, rather than discouraging, such cooperation was vital: this was a key takeaway Mayo communicated to the senior management who had contracted him. Individual absenteeism and high rates of 'emotional labor turnover' were first and foremost the result of an 'emotional blockage', both within the group unit and between workers and their superiors. If this blockage could be released, the motive for social unrest and political action would dissipate and productivity would be secured. Only then would the 'logic of sentiment'

---

[38]Eva Illouz, *Saving the Modern Soul: Therapy, Emotions and the Culture of Self-Help* (Berkeley: University of California Press, 2008), ch. 3.
[39]Elton Mayo, *The Human Problems of an Industrial Civilization* (New York: Viking Press, [1933] 1960), quotes 111, 116–17.

meet the 'logics of cost and efficiency' to the benefit of all; only then would the 'strategy of cooperation' overcome the 'attitude of wariness, suspicion, hostility, and hatred' that had come to reign in industrial relations and beyond.[40]

Mayo used the concept of the 'therapeutic' interview in order to find out more about the individual worker's emotional problems and how they were related to his or her personal history. He also and more importantly went on to conduct an 'equally close study of groups' and how they influenced the attitudes and feelings of individuals. As he saw it,

> modern civilization for approximately two centuries has done nothing to extend and develop human cooperative capacities and, indeed, in the sacred name of the sciences of material development, has unwittingly done much to discourage teamwork and the development of social skill.[41]

To reverse this, a new form of socially competent industrial leadership was needed.

While the companies which poured large sums into research on 'human relations' on the factory floor obviously took great interest in such findings, critics on the left accused social scientists like Mayo of 'adjusting men to machines'. This is how the young college instructor (and future sociology professor) Daniel Bell put it in a 1947 essay. In his view, industrial research of the kind Mayo had initiated 'merely "psychologize[s]"' instead of looking at the 'larger institutional framework of our economic system'. Furthermore, those 'human engineers' were turning a blind eye to '*alternative* (and better, i.e., more human) modes' of industrial production that might 'best stimulate the spontaneity and freedom of the worker'. They thus adopted 'industry's own conception of workers as means to be manipulated or adjusted to impersonal ends'. This helped the process of 'rationalization' endure as social life was increasingly subsumed under the logic of 'greater efficiency'.[42]

In part, Bell's critique echoed what Marx and Engels had written a century earlier about the deeply negative effect capitalism had on the emotional economy of workers, upsetting its balance and clouding human emotion. His interpretation is rather problematic, however, because it invokes a positive counter-image of robust, lively, spontaneous, natural and healthy

---

[40]Elton Mayo, *The Social Problems of an Industrial Civilization* (Andover: Andover Press, 1945), quotes 77, 81, 84, 117, 123; Fritz J. Roethlisberger and William J. Dickson, *Management and the Worker: An Account of a Research Program Conducted by the Western Electric Company, Hawthorne Works, Chicago*, 13th edn (Cambridge, MA: Harvard University Press, [1939] 1964), 563–7 (with definitions of the different logics).
[41]Mayo, *Social Problems*, quotes 78–9, 116.
[42]Daniel Bell, 'Adjusting Men to Machines: Social Scientists Explore the World of the Factory', *Commentary* 4 (1947): 79–88, quotes 86, 80, 87–8. See Nicolas Rose, *Governing the Soul: The Shaping of the Private Self*, 2nd edn (London: Free Association Books, 1999), part 2.

feelings that supposedly characterized rural and proto-industrial societies. Whether this image had any basis in reality is doubtful.

Meanwhile, plenty of accounts testified to the strong emotional ties factory workers developed both to their work and to their co-workers. As historian Thomas Welskopp has shown with regard to the US and German steel and iron industries during the twentieth century, such emotional attachments often formed the basis for peer group solidarity; further, they strengthened workers' quest for autonomy and emboldened their resistance to interference and control from plant management. Workers often took great pride in their skills and achievements. In 1973, a shipper at the Fairless steelworks remembered the old mills as

> being almost like a social activity. The guy that worked there, the job was more or less like his life. You know, he'd go home and have a garden or he'd go home and have a hobby, something like that. But he really felt that when he worked in the mill, when he worked in the open hearth, that he was accomplishing something.[43]

He was equally aware that he functioned as part of a larger working unit and the accomplishment was also a collective one. While members of the group regulated each other, they also forged bonds of belonging, mutual sympathy and caring. That those bonds were not only crucial for specific 'cultures of production' (Welskopp) but also for workers' self-esteem and social lifeworld became all too evident when steelworks were shuttered in the late twentieth century.

Social relations at work seem to have mattered even more to women than to men. In the mid-1950s, about 300 men and women aged 15 to 18 were asked to write down how they felt about their work in factories, offices and domestic service. Interestingly, female respondents complained far less and were more explicit about positive experiences with their colleagues. The following report from a laundry worker was not unusual: 'During the shift we're singing and laughing a lot. When I started on the first day I was feeling very strange, but soon I forgot it due to all the laughter and singing.'[44]

To be sure, laughter and singing could be heard in the pre-industrial workplace too. For iron- and steelworkers, though, who toiled amid hellish noise, such behaviour was virtually impossible. But even they enjoyed moments of camaraderie and playfulness that helped to ward off fatigue

---

[43]Thomas Welskopp, 'Sons of Vulcan: Industrial Relations and Attitudes toward Work among German and American Iron- and Steelworkers in the Twentieth Century', in *Bodies and Affects in Market Societies*, ed. Anne Schmidt and Christoph Conrad (Tübingen: Mohr Siebeck, 2016), 23–39, quote 31.
[44]Peter-Paul Bänziger, 'What Makes People Work: Producing Emotional Attachments to the Workplace in Post-World War II West-German Vocational Schools', in *Bodies and Affects*, ed. Schmidt and Conrad, 41–57, quote 53.

and release tension. As Mayo reminded business administrators in the 1920s and 1930s, group sociality was of utmost importance and greatly affected people's feelings and attitudes towards work, on the job as much as during breaks.

As a particular mode of economic activity, capitalism, rather than subduing emotions, is therefore clearly sustained by them. The extent to which emotions have been observed, measured, manipulated and instrumentalized in the workplace and beyond has increased over the decades and centuries. Different stages of technological development and capital accumulation have ushered in different emotional economies, of which the twentieth century has seen a great variety, with stark distinctions within the industrial sector as well as between manufacturing and the growing service industries.[45]

As early as the 1920s, female sales assistants and secretaries were urged and taught to project optimism, kindness and care. They had to dress neatly and be aesthetically pleasing; one young woman who worked in a shoe shop lost her job because she did not comply with her employer's demand to don frilly underwear. When she sued the shop owner, he argued in court that male customers deserved a good view as they watched the salesgirl moving up and down the ladder to fetch boxes from the upper shelves.[46] Other shops published photos of particularly pretty employees in local newspapers, promising a reward to customers who figured out where they worked. Department stores commonly organized 'courtesy competitions' among their staff, and in 1926 a marketing agency in Berlin held a 'plebiscite' to crown the loveliest salesgirl in store. The message was clear: 'We all prefer to buy where beauty and grace serve us.'[47] More and more companies adopted the motto 'service with a smile', turning it into a trademark of emotional labour predominantly (though not exclusively) performed by women.

It would be short-sighted and misleading to claim that this development was due solely to market requirements. In many ways, such requirements also responded to new social needs and cultural sensibilities which became particularly evident in the 1960s and 1970s. What the sociologist Nikolas Rose called 'the production of the Self' was supported by a therapeutic turn and an array of techniques stressing self-inspection, self-presentation and self-actualization.[48] These techniques relied heavily on an emotional

---

[45]Katie Barclay, 'Capitalism and Consumption', in *The Routledge History of Emotions in the Modern World*, ed. Katie Barclay and Peter N. Stearns (London: Routledge, 2022), 440–59, also looks at finance, credit and debt as capitalist sites of emotion.
[46]Carl Dreyfuß, *Beruf und Ideologie der Angestellten* (Munich: Duncker & Humblot, 1933), 126.
[47]Berlin: *Berliner Wochenspiegel für Leben, Wirtschaft, Verkehr, Ausstellungs- und Messewesen der Reichshauptstadt* no. 50 (1926): 2. See also Arlie Russell Hochschild, *The Managed Heart: Commercialization of Human Feeling* (Berkeley: University of California Press, 1983).
[48]Rose, *Governing*, 103–19; Illouz, *Saving*.

vocabulary and gave rise to the concept of the 'emotional self', which centred emotions as a 'source of self-authenticity, humanity and self-expression'.[49]

Around the same time, the 'new spirit of capitalism' emerged. As Luc Boltanski and Ève Chiapello analysed, it translated crucial character traits of that self into managerial terms, putting a premium on autonomy, flexibility, mobility and network organizational forms.[50] Part of this new spirit is what science journalist Daniel Goleman has, since the 1990s, popularized and marketed as 'emotional intelligence'. In order to enjoy 'new work' and to be good at it, Goleman argues, people need to be emotionally intelligent. With the aid of an 'emotional competence inventory', emotional intelligence can be measured; special training programmes can then eradicate any shortcomings. A lack of emotional competence can lower people's productivity, moreover, it encourages job hopping and fosters high turnover.[51] In contrast to Mayo, who investigated the blue-collar world sixty years earlier, Goleman and his team have focused on white-collar employees and managers, using the fashionable language of the self to teach them how to improve their emotional skills. The researchers' interest was not on group attachment; instead they emphasized individual performance and a person's ability to read (and manipulate) other people's emotions.

This was a major departure from earlier spirits of capitalism, which, fed by different kinds of companies and other forms of accumulation, called on different values and made other promises to workers. Beginning in the 1920s, however, the 'human factor' was increasingly seen as a problem in need of scientific solutions. Investing in the 'psychotechnics' of work and enhancing employees' 'joy in work' became an important management task during the second Industrial Revolution, meant to enhance productivity and decrease tensions with the shop floor. What in the US was called 'emotional release' and in Germany the 'struggle for joy in work' was framed in the UK as an investment in 'happiness'. The National Institute of Industrial Psychology was 'very directly concerned in largely increasing the commodity of "happiness"', as Sir Charles Sherrington, President of the Royal Society, stated in 1923.[52] This commodity was supposed to be available to factory workers, too, thanks to scientific expertise and human relations knowledge.

---

[49]Deborah Lupton, *The Emotional Self: A Sociocultural Exploration* (London: Sage, 1998), 9.
[50]Luc Boltanski and Ève Chiapello, *The New Spirit of Capitalism* (London: Verso, 2005); Rose, *Governing*, 103–19.
[51]Hay Group, McClelland Center for Research and Innovation, *Emotional Competence Inventory (ECI): Technical Manual*, available online: https://www.eiconsortium.org/pdf/ECI_2_0_Technical_Manual_v2.pdf (accessed 22 December 2022); Illouz, *Saving*, ch. 6.
[52]*Journal of Occupational Psychology*, 7 July 1923, 267. On happiness, see Chapter 10 in this volume.

Consumerism and advertising

Those who spoke of happiness as a 'commodity' alluded not only to the sphere of production but also and especially to consumption which likewise underwent a fundamental revaluation and structural change under capitalism. Mass production multiplied the number of goods available for purchase, and made them far cheaper.[53] Still, people had to be trained to become consumers: they first had to feel they needed a good in order to then buy it. 'Need' no longer referred to necessities, but rather to desire, the ardent wish to own certain things.[54]

This desire had to be actively kindled and connected to various emotions. Consumption without emotions was inconceivable – the two went hand in hand. This was true not only of feelings of greed, or the pleasure of buying or the desire to shop, emotions which keep the wheels of the economy turning. It also included feelings of deprivation, a longing for certain goods and commodities, the fear of being disadvantaged and the shame of not being able to afford certain goods or of being left behind.

That consumption, insofar as it goes beyond covering basic needs, can be something extremely pleasurable, fanning both individual drives and economic production, was already obvious to contemporaries in the eighteenth century. Technically speaking, it was the desire for luxury, for that which was not strictly necessary, which made capitalism possible. If everyone had been content with only what they absolutely needed and could produce and exchange locally in a simple commodity economy, there would be no global market, no long-distance trade, no money economy.[55] From its very inception, capitalist economic activity has been based on arousing and satisfying needs and wants beyond the bare minimum.

Since the nineteenth century, the art of advertising, marketing and publicity has existed for this express purpose. Applied psychology also chipped in. After all, it knew best how to draw consumers' attention to a product and to keep them thinking about it. In this regard, an appeal to the senses was important. Goods had to be described in such a way that their utility value could be felt, seen, heard, smelled, tasted.[56] Sales assistants were called upon to 'prompt and increase needs' and sweet-talk customers into

---

[53]Frank Trentmann, *Empire of Things: How We Became a World of Consumers, from the Fifteenth Century to the Twenty-First* (New York: HarperCollins, 2016).
[54]Anne Schmidt, 'From Thrifty Housewives to Shoppers with Needs: On a Capitalist Program of Education', in *Bodies and Affects*, ed. Schmidt and Conrad, 167–87.
[55]Isabel V. Hull, *Sexuality, State, and Civil Society in Germany, 1700–1815* (Ithaca, NY: Cornell University Press, 1996), 159–60; Neil McKendrick, John Brewer and J.H. Plumb, *The Birth of a Consumer Society: The Commercialization of Eighteenth-Century England* (Bloomington: Indiana University Press, 1982).
[56]Frank Bresbrey, *The History and Development of Advertising* (New York: Greenwood Press, [1929] 1968), 441 ff.

buying through 'pleasure-oriented conversation'. Everything came down to stimulating feelings of desire: through suggestive language and visual cues that extolled not only the functionality but also and above all the beauty of the product on offer.[57]

A perfect place to experience the pleasure of shopping was the modern department store, the epitome of a 'capitalist enterprise'. The concept, which originated in London around 1800, flourished during the second half of the nineteenth century. With their abundance of diverse goods, lavish architecture, huge windows and fixed prices, department stores appealed chiefly to middle-class customers (although there were stores for less affluent shoppers as well). In principle, department stores offered free entrance to each and everybody. Customers, one handbook stated in 1899, 'stream in and out of the wide doors in amazement without feeling watched in any way. Goods lie spread out before astonished eyes, and, for the most part, name their price all by themselves.' Nobody was obliged to buy anything. Sales assistants were told to stay in the background and not bother customers who were happily browsing the sales floor without a predetermined intention to make a purchase.[58]

In fact, department stores were among the first companies to create in-house advertising agencies. They came up with the idea of decorating and redecorating display windows, adapted the store's interior design, sent out letters and other printed materials to customers and placed advertisements in newspapers.[59] In addition to promising pleasure and joy, the advertising industry engaged a whole range of emotions to attract buyers' attention and interest. The fear of being unlucky in love was invoked in one 1928 advert for face soap, which warned: 'If you lack the fresh beauty of fine clear skin your happiness can never be sure!' The happiness of the couple also seemed to be endangered, this time by bad breath: 'Certainly this humiliating and repellant condition is a bar to affectionate advances.' Disgust and humiliation were thus assured to anyone who dared spurn the product on offer – a mouthwash. Early advertising for telephones likewise tugged on the heartstrings: long-distance calls would establish intimacy and familiarity with those absent by communicating 'thought, mood, personality' in a direct and unadulterated way.[60]

As early as the 1920s, psychologists and advertisers worked closely together to emotionally influence purchasing decisions. They drew on emotions such as vanity, curiosity, fear and hope, but also on 'the love of the beautiful' and 'parental instinct' to pique consumer interest.[61] As the

---

[57]F. Müller, 'Zur Psychologie des Verkäufers', *Industrielle Psychotechnik* 5 (1928): 363.
[58]Schmidt, 'Thrifty Housewives', 178–9.
[59]On shop windows, see Franck Cochoy, 'On the Marketization of Curiosity: The Shop Window as a "Captation" Device', in *Bodies and Affects*, ed. Schmidt and Conrad, 145–65.
[60]Bresbrey, *History*, appendice, with further examples from the 1920s.
[61]R.T. Bartlett, 'Psychology and Advertising', *Journal of Occupational Psychology*, 8 October 1925, 377; R.T. Bartlett, 'The Emotional Appeal in Advertising', ibid., 2 April 1926, 104 ff.

appeal of images began to be recognized and harnessed, emotional messages became denser and more compelling. Theories about emotional psychology were readily adopted to give goods an emotional aura which increased their sales value. The tenets of behaviourism, a theory based on the principle that people can be conditioned in every respect, enjoyed great popularity. That its founder, John Watson, worked as a psychologist at the American advertising agency J. Walter Thompson spoke volumes.[62] Later, simple stimulus-response models gave way to finer and more subtle techniques of emotive advertising. At times, the emotional argument seemed to work entirely by itself, as with mineral water or perfume that were labelled 'fresh emotion'.

Even emotions which have long had negative connotations have had their turn in the advertising spotlight. Envy is a case in point. As Susan Matt has analysed of the US before the First World War, envy was considered an unpleasant feeling that should either be hidden or prevented altogether. Beginning in the 1920s, in tandem with ever more abundant consumer markets, the view of envy changed. Economists praised spending over saving and even encouraged consumers to buy more than they could afford. Being envious and discontent was, to them, a sign of a person's 'growing moral development' and a 'higher faculty', because it expressed an aspiration to ascend the social ladder. Today, companies choose to name their goods 'Envy' *tout court*, following the advice of sales agencies. A 2009 marketing guide was titled *All You Need is Envy*. It described in detail how companies could ensure, through branding and positional pricing, 'that the people who buy and own your product can be seen by the people who don't'.[63]

Emotions sell, whether envy, happiness, nostalgia or romance. At times, they are packaged in direct, forthright terms, at others they are more subtly arranged and orchestrated. Consumers were (and are) addressed as emotional selves, their hopes, dreams and fears projected onto the goods promoted to them with all the tricks at advertisers' disposal. In this arena, too, capitalism pulled out the stops, creating an advertising industry that, driven by fierce competition, had to constantly come up with new and better ideas. When

---

[62] Alexander Schlug, 'Missionare der globalen Konsumkultur: Corporate Identity und Absatzstrategien amerikanischer Unternehmen in Deutschland im frühen 20. Jahrhundert', in *Politische Kulturgeschichte der Zwischenkriegszeit 1918–1939*, ed. Wolfgang Hardtwig (Göttingen: Vandenhoeck & Ruprecht, 2005), 307–42; Alexander Schlug, 'Das Ende der Hochkultur? Ästhetische Strategien der Werbung 1900–1933', in *Ordnung in der Krise: Zur politischen Kulturgeschichte Deutschlands 1900–1933*, ed. Wolfgang Hardtwig (Munich: Oldenbourg, 2007), 501–30; Rainer Gries, 'Die Geburt des Werbeexperten aus dem Geist der Psychologie', in *Wirtschaftsgeschichte als Kulturgeschichte*, ed. Hartmut Berghoff and Jakob Vogel (Frankfurt: Campus, 2004), 353–75.
[63] 'All You Need Is Envy', 23 December 2009, available online: https://issuu.com/simonsilvester/docs/envy (accessed 22 December 2022); Susan J. Matt, 'From Sin to Economic Stimulant: Envy's Changing Place in American Capitalism', in *Bodies and Affects*, ed. Schmidt and Conrad, 127–44; Susan J. Matt, *Keeping up with the Joneses: Envy in American Consumer Society, 1890–1930* (Philadelphia: University of Pennsylvania Press, 2003).

competition was lacking, so too were creativity and inventiveness, as the state socialist regimes – with their rather dowdy advertisements – amply demonstrated.[64]

Yet the capitalist advertising sector not only appealed to particular feelings in the consumer, it also linked them to products, without which these feelings floated strangely and immaterially in a vacuum. In order to be properly articulated, the argument went, feelings needed material outlets. Sons and daughters could best express their love for their mother, for instance, by gifting her flowers and chocolates once a year on Mother's Day.[65] Love for one's wife, on the other hand, had to be proven with more expensive purchases: in the 1950s, with electrical household appliances ('Bauknecht knows what women want'); half a century later, with diamond rings.[66]

Sociologist Eva Illouz described this development in her 1997 book *Consuming the Romantic Utopia*.[67] In it, she argues that love and consumption have been closely linked since the early twentieth century. The pairing works in both directions: in one, love is associated with particular practices of consumption and is thus commodified. Lovers meet at the cinema, bond over pasta and cocktails, take walks by the ocean in certain clothes and dreamily watch the sunset from Balinese hammocks. In the other direction, Illouz suggests products are themselves 'romanticized' through their linkage, either directly or indirectly, overtly or covertly, with love and intimacy. This not only happens with jewellery and confectionary but even with products such as motor oil or cornflakes. So advertised, feelings become commodities which can be bought.

The extent to which this was actually an invention of the twentieth century would have to be explored more carefully. Did the late eighteenth century not play with love and (unrequited) longing through particular styles of dress? In fact, the 'Werther fever' triggered by Johann Wolfgang Goethe's popular 1774 novel quickly spread throughout Europe, inspiring young men to dress like its protagonist. For their part, young women brandished Cambric handkerchiefs to signal their attachment to the sentimental style. Originally made of white French linen, the handkerchiefs were soon manufactured from power-spun flax and became available to women of lesser means as well.

---

[64]Anne Kaminsky, '"True Advertising Means Promoting a Good Thing through a Good Form": Advertising in the German Democratic Republic', in *Selling Modernity: Advertising in Twentieth-Century Germany*, ed. Pamela E. Swett, S. Jonathan Wiesen and Jonathan R. Zatlin (Durham, NC: Duke University Press, 2007), 262–86.

[65]See Chapter 11 in this volume.

[66]Martina Hessler, '"Do Companies Know What Women Want?": The Introduction of Electrical Domestic Appliances during the Weimar Republic', *Michigan Feminist Studies* 13 (1998/99), available online: https://quod.lib.umich.edu/cgi/t/text/text-idx?cc=mfsfront;c=mfs;c=mfsfront;idno=ark5583.0013.002;g=mfsg;rgn=main;view=text;xc=1.

[67]Eva Illouz, *Consuming the Romantic Utopia: Love and the Cultural Contradictions of Capitalism* (Berkeley: University of California Press, 1997).

Around the same time, abolitionist Josiah Wedgwood's chinaware imagery of a kneeling slave was reproduced on coins and medallions, on ordinary crockery and in needlework. Just as material culture represented feelings of pity and compassion, it also assisted in producing and disseminating them.[68] Here we can clearly see precursors to the development Illouz attributed to the twentieth century. To be fair, modern times certainly did remove the social restraints on some consumer practices. In principle, the material expression of romantic feelings became accessible to everyone, even if gender and class differences were not entirely smoothed out.

In short, capitalism indeed had a huge effect on the emotional economy of individuals, social groups and societies. It did so directly through enormous changes to the production of goods and services as well as to the ways goods were bought and consumed. But capitalism influenced more than modes of production and consumption. It also transformed people's living conditions and social relations. In the wake of industrialization, urbanization saw men and women alike leaving their villages and moving to cities, where they built and encountered very different material, mental and emotional arrangements.[69] Capitalist societies bred altogether new aspirations and ambitions, frustrations and anxieties.

They also established scientific and professional institutions to identify, name, observe, measure and modify those feelings. By targeting and reflecting on emotions and emotional states, expert and lay discourses eventually exerted a rationalizing influence – not in the way, though, that Max Weber had imagined around 1900. Instead of condemning them as 'irrational' or criticizing their interference in purposeful economic activity, psychologists and sociologists as well as entrepreneurs and trade unionists began to recognize emotions as essential elements of capitalism. They were taken seriously, they were studied and explored, and they were, with various instruments and to various ends, worked upon.

---

[68] G.J. Barker-Benfield, *The Culture of Sensibility: Sex and Society in Eighteenth-Century Britain* (Chicago: University of Chicago Press, 1992), 211–14.
[69] Joseph Ben Prestel, *Emotional Cities: Debates on Urban Change in Berlin and Cairo, 1860–1910* (Oxford: Oxford University Press, 2017).

CHAPTER EIGHT

How Does *Homo Oeconomicus* Cope with Emotions?

When Max Weber reflected around 1900 on capitalism's inherent tendency to 'rationalize' economic activities and, in their wake, human relations, he might well have had in mind the notion of *homo oeconomicus*, the 'economic man', heralded by (neo)classical economists. The notion has been enormously influential in economic modelling and theorizing, though it is riddled with serious flaws and shortcomings, chiefly regarding emotions and 'animal spirits'.

This chapter explores how and why economists tended to build their theories on the assumption that human actors are rationally motivated by self-interest, and examines why competing assumptions were neglected and pushed to the margins. Further, it investigates under which conditions and to what extent the concept of *homo oeconomicus* was ultimately challenged and modified by a new generation of economists, psychologists and neuroscientists.

'Pure' economic theory and its muddled alternatives

In 1932, the economist Joseph Schumpeter gave up his professorship at the University of Bonn and moved to Cambridge, Massachusetts, in order to join the faculty at Harvard. One of his reasons for leaving Europe was the search for 'pure' economic theory. In Schumpeter's view, such a theory was

---

This chapter is an abridged and revised version of the article 'Passions, Preferences and Animal Spirits: How Does Homo Oeconomicus Cope With Emotions?', in *Science and Emotions after 1945: A Transatlantic Perpective*, ed. Frank Biess and Daniel M. Gross (Chicago: University of Chicago Press, 2014), 300–17.

neither interested in the 'essence' of economic behaviour nor in its motives, but instead tried to uncover the empirical logic of the economy by gathering positive knowledge.[1] This, he felt, was not what his colleagues in Germany, who sought to reinvent organic concepts or favoured mildly socialist viewpoints, were doing.[2]

Unlike on the Continent, 'pure' theory and analysis had found a comfortable resting place in North America. Since the time of Adam Smith, the classical approach had supported the vision of a liberal market society. Its underlying assumptions, above all the notion of free individuals pursuing happiness (defined as the fulfilment of material desires) unhampered by political constraints or state intervention, seemed to reflect both the history of the United States and its promise to people from all over the world.[3]

Upon his arrival in New England, however, Schumpeter found himself in the midst of a serious economic crisis. The self-regulating forces of market capitalism had failed and the state stepped in and struck a 'new deal' to ensure the country's economic recovery. Yet following this recovery, classical economic theory that tied wealth to the unrestricted mobility of labour and capital on a free market quickly regained its reputation and became the linchpin of ideological competition with the communist bloc after the Second World War. Strengthened by US-funded economic support in Western Europe, it managed to make headway on the Continent as academic fellowships acquainted European students and academics with universities and research institutions in the US. All of these factors combined to set the stage for the triumph of neoclassical theory in post-war non-Communist Europe.[4]

What was largely lost on the journey across the Atlantic was the sense of an economy's historical and political roots, an aspect that had been accentuated by the German Historical School around 1900 and extensively applied in American institutionalism. Initiated by Thorstein Veblen, institutionalism as an approach had a considerable impact on US economists in the 1920s.[5]

---

[1] Joseph A. Schumpeter, *The Nature and Essence of Economic Theory* (New Brunswick: Transaction Publications, 2010), 49–55; Joseph A. Schumpeter, *Aufsätze zur ökonomischen Theorie* (Tübingen: Mohr, 1952), 598–608.
[2] As to the state of economics during the Weimar period, see Roman Köster, *Die Wissenschaft der Außenseiter: Die Krise der Nationalökonomie in der Weimarer Republik* (Göttingen: Vandenhoeck & Ruprecht, 2011).
[3] On happiness, see Chapter 10 in this volume.
[4] For the West German transformation, with special reference to 'indigenous' schools like ordoliberalism, see Jan-Otmar Hesse, *Wirtschaft als Wissenschaft: Die Volkswirtschaftslehre in der frühen Bundesrepublik* (Frankfurt: Campus, 2010) and Alexander Nützenadel, *Stunde der Ökonomen: Wissenschaft, Politik und Expertenkultur in der Bundesrepublik 1949–1974* (Göttingen: Vandenhoeck & Ruprecht, 2005), ch. 1.
[5] Geoffrey M. Hodgson, *How Economics Forgot History: The Problem of Historical Specificity in Social Science* (London: Routledge, 2001); Geoffrey M. Hodgson, *The Evolution of Institutional Economics: Agency, Structure and Darwinism in American Institutionalism* (London: Routledge, 2004), part III.

Gustav Schmoller, head of the German school and an influence of sorts on Veblen, repeatedly stressed that the economy was part and parcel of social and political life. Economic theory should, therefore, consider the relationship between genuinely economic matters – like the division and organization of labour, transactions and mobility, income distribution and prices – and matters of state, law, customs and morality.

According to Schmoller, every economic phenomenon, be it increases in grain prices or wages, consisted of people's 'feelings, motives and actions' and was shaped by 'morals and institutions' with widely diverging causes. In order to account for those institutions, worldviews and attitudes, historical knowledge was needed. The assumption that people were individuals exclusively governed by egotistical interests and selfish preferences constituted a misreading of the complex frames of reference in which human motives and 'drives' were formed and acted upon. Even when it came to acquisitive impulses and the desire to accumulate wealth, substantial differences could be observed within and among various cultures, social milieus and nations.[6]

Schmoller here directly addressed and attacked the underlying propositions of (neo)classical theory, chiefly that of the *homo oeconomicus* who was allegedly driven by what Adam Smith had called 'self-love' and the ensuing attempt to maximize gains. Thinkers from Smith on had deemed such behavioural patterns natural and universal; indeed, they formed the building blocks of economic reasoning.[7]

Even so, Smith and his followers by no means ruled out that human behaviour might be far more complex and informed by many other motives and feelings. Just as Smith, in an earlier treatise on 'moral sentiments', had noted the power of sympathy to foster social cooperation and communication, John Stuart Mill cited 'those laws of human nature' that called forth 'the *affections*, the *conscience*, or feeling of duty, and the love of *approbation*' among human beings. No political economist, Mill claimed, 'was ever so absurd as to suppose that mankind are really thus constituted', that is 'determined, by the necessity of his nature, to prefer a greater portion of wealth to a smaller in all cases'. Economic science, however, had to 'necessarily proceed' in this mode of narrow determinism in order to reach the proper conclusions in its own field. Needless to say, in other fields, different laws applied.[8]

---

[6]Gustav von Schmoller, *Die Volkswirtschaft, die Volkswirtschaftslehre und ihre Methode* (Frankfurt: Klostermann, [1893] 1949) 12, 15–16, 31, 44, 56. See Erik Grimmer-Solem, *The Rise of Historical Economics and Social Reform in Germany 1864–1894* (Oxford: Clarendon Press, 2003), esp. ch. 4.

[7]Mary S. Morgan, 'Economic Man as Model Man: Ideal Types, Idealization and Caricatures', *Journal of the History of Economic Thought* 28, no. 1 (2006): 1–27.

[8]Adam Smith, *The Theory of Moral Sentiments* (Amherst: Prometheus, 2000); John Stuart Mill, 'On the Definition of Political Economy; and on the Method of Investigation Proper to It', in John Stuart Mill, *Essays on Some Unsettled Questions of Political Economy* (London: Parker, 1844), 120–64, quotes 134, 137–9.

Just what was to be gained by this exclusive concern with man 'as a being who desires to possess wealth, and who is capable of judging on the comparative efficacy of means for obtaining that end' was obvious. Only by neglecting other desires and conduct could political economy establish itself as an independent and autonomous field of scientific enquiry. The decision to make 'entire abstraction of every other human passion or motive' was rewarded with a considerable increase in disciplinary acumen and methodological sophistication.[9]

This was not lost on Schmoller and his adherents. And yet, they were reluctant to discard the notion of economics as a profoundly social and cultural science. They cast a critical eye on tendencies towards formalization and mathematization that isolated economics from the wider web of human interaction. Schmoller even went as far as suggesting that economic phenomena should be perceived as deeply psychological: economists had to account for the 'transformation of psychological causes and how they connected to ethnological and class differences'. As a next step, they should study the ways those transformations shaped how people acted in economic relations.[10]

The price to be paid for such a complex account was high. The perception of economics as a deeply historical science meant that it lacked clearly discernible paradigms and the ability to deductively theorize. By engaging with other disciplines in the humanities and social sciences, economics acquired an interdisciplinary character that made identifying its specific disciplinary profile difficult. Furthermore, the approach of the German school proved unable to address the manifest problems that haunted European economies after the First World War.[11] As a result, its intellectual hegemony, which had peaked in the 1890s, waned after the 1920s.

In contrast, it was far easier for classical and neoclassical economists to develop a distinct profile and gain academic recognition by narrowing their field of scientific inquiry and disregarding human behaviour. Even if many German economists continued to criticize their colleagues in the English-speaking world for putting excessive effort into theoretical models that ignored reality, those models proved relatively successful at shedding light on complicated matters like business cycles, prices and economic growth.

---

[9]Mill, 'Definition', 137. See Joseph Persky, 'The Ethology of Homo Economicus', *Journal of Economic Perspectives* 9, no. 2 (1995): 221–31.

[10]Schmoller, *Volkswirtschaft*, 70. Schmoller was familiar with the work of Wilhelm Wundt and quoted him extensively. In a later version of the text, he wrote even more approvingly of the need to apply psychological insights to economic explanations; Gustav von Schmoller, 'Volkswirtschaft, Volkswirtschaftslehre und -methode,' in *Handwörterbuch der Staatswissenschaften*, ed. Johannes Conrad et al., 3rd edn, vol. 8 (Jena: Fischer, 1911), 426–501. For the concept of economics as a social and cultural science and the enduring criticism of mathematical modelling, see Nützenadel, *Stunde*, ch. 1.

[11]Köster, *Wissenschaft*, 31–59, 316–18.

Thanks to its sophisticated quantitative methods, neoclassical theory even attracted scholars who did not share its subscription to the gospel of the free market. British economist John Maynard Keynes, for instance, formed ideas about the relationship between employment, interest and money that radically confronted the classical belief in economic self-regulation and full employment equilibrium. Still, his concepts could be – and were – easily translated into formal mathematical models that suited mainstream methodologies. As early as 1938, economists like John R. Hicks integrated Keynes's assumptions into a general equilibrium model that has guided the analysis of capital and financial markets ever since. Combining Keynes's theory of employment and income with classical theory eventually produced the 'neoclassical synthesis' (Paul Samuelson) which dominated international economic research in the 1950s and 1960s.[12]

Economic man's rational choices

During those first decades following the war, economists became very influential in politics and public life both in the US and in Western Europe. In 1946, the US government set up the Council of Economic Advisors, whose aim was to brief the president on economic policy matters and to supply him with empirical data and material. In West Germany, which emulated the model in 1963, the demand for economic expertise was equally high and the social reputation of experts at its peak. This was due, in part, to the growing importance and complexity of economic policy in post-war capitalist societies. But it also reflected the confidence that economists had in themselves and their discipline to deliver theory-based knowledge about how the economy worked and what the state could do to improve its function in Keynesian or ordo-liberal terms. This self-confidence was directly related to the increasing uniformity of theoretical paradigms on both sides of the Atlantic. The triumph of the neoclassical synthesis and the omnipresence of econometrics and mathematical modelling helped to boost the self-perception of economists as scientists in their own right.

As the field of economics began to gravitate towards methods from the natural sciences and to sever its ties with the humanities and social sciences, the significance of *homo oeconomicus* as a leitmotif grew. Economic modelling suited and strengthened the understanding of human beings as rational actors guided by self-interest. The surge of microeconomics beginning in the 1960s bolstered it further, to the point where it began to encircle non-economic spheres as well. Having children, raising a family, caring for older relatives, voting for a party or joining an association were

---

[12] John R. Hicks, *Value and Capital: An Inquiry into Some Fundamental Principles of Economic Theory*, 2nd edn (Oxford: Clarendon, 1953); Nützenadel, *Stunde*, 60.

now all framed within the paradigm of rational, autonomous and self-interested human decision-making. Rationality was defined as an algorithmic relationship between input and output, means and ends. The more people were able to maximize their benefits while minimizing the individual effort it took to obtain these, the higher the degree of rationality involved in the operation.

Linking the concept of the economic man with rational choice theory turned out to be a successful move. It helped to reinvent economics as a discipline that aspired to a 'general unified theory', claiming that this theory was universally applicable.[13] Were the economic man a given, present at all times and in all spaces, it would be possible to model and predict his actions or non-actions on a global scale. Questioning the assumption of rationality, or suggesting that factors other than self-interest might inform people's actions, clearly curtailed the explanatory power of economics and threatened economists' newly acquired status as makers of and advisors on economic policy.

The notion of *homo oeconomicus* was rendered so powerful not only because of economic theory's predilection for abstraction and generalization but also because the concept reflected the self-image of nineteenth- and twentieth-century capitalist societies. Instead of being haunted by unruly passions and the lust for tyranny, modern people learned to transform their passions into interests and to pursue them in a rational way. The capitalist marketplace taught them what rationality meant: using the most efficient strategy to achieve one's aims. Since this involved other players, the strategy had to take into account their interests as well. Hence, economic communication and transactions were supposed to function both as self-regulatory processes and as building blocks of civil and civilized society.[14]

Even though the optimistic view was by no means universally shared, it increasingly managed to capture people's imagination and self-perception.

---

[13] Richard W. Kopck, Jane Sneddon Little and Geoffrey M.B. Tootell, 'How Humans Behave: Implications for Economics and Economic Policy', *New England Economic Review* (31 March 2004): 3–35, quote 4.

[14] Albert O. Hirschman, *The Passions and the Interests: Political Arguments for Capitalism before Its Triumph* (Princeton: Princeton University Press, 1977); Emma Rothschild, *Economic Sentiments: Adam Smith, Condorcet, and the Enlightenment* (Cambridge, MA: Harvard University Press, 2001). In 1936, these arguments were redeemed by John Maynard Keynes: 'Moreover, dangerous human proclivities can be canalised into comparatively harmless channels by the existence of opportunities for money-making and private wealth, which, if they cannot be satisfied in this way, may find their outlet in cruelty, the reckless pursuit of personal power and authority, and other forms of self-aggrandisement' (*The General Theory of Employment, Interest and Money* (London: Macmillan, [1936] 1960), 374). On the 'birth' of *homo oeconomicus* as an anthropological construct, see Werner Plumpe, 'Die Geburt des "Homo oeconomicus": Historische Überlegungen zur Entstehung und Bedeutung des Handlungsmodells der modernen Wirtschaft', in *Menschen und Märkte: Studien zur historischen Wirtschaftsanthropologie*, ed. Wolfgang Reinhard and Justin Stagl (Vienna: Böhlau, 2007), 319–52.

Acting rationally, making the right decisions, pursuing one's goals in a calculating and calculable fashion became the guideline of modern and modernizing societies. Enshrined in bureaucratic institutions, it turned into a normative concept that men (more than women) had to embrace early on. Escaping it was possible, if at all, only in the spheres of religious mysticism, art and erotic experience, as Weber argued.[15] In economic affairs, the norm of *homo oeconomicus* prevailed. All those who entered the market, whether as producers or consumers, entrepreneurs or workers, were considered rational agents. As Keynes put it in 1937, they desperately wanted to 'behave in a manner which saves our faces as rational, economic men'.[16] Instead of serving, in Schumpeter's terms, as a methodological tool and 'construct', *homo oeconomicus* had become a social concept that actually informed and framed people's preferences and perceptions of themselves.[17]

Animal spirits

As long as the economy developed in a relatively steady and positive manner, the norm was easy to follow. The experience of the 1920s, however, shattered the widely held belief in stable, self-regulating markets and business cycles. Risk, as Keynes pointed out, was a fundamental feature of the economic process. Contrary to what classical theory believed, it was the rule, not the exception. Decision-making thus took place under the assumption that the future was uncertain, unknown and far from calculable. How were people to handle this dilemma? How could they manage to cope with uncertainty and still believe that they were acting rationally?

As Keynes observed, economic players devised 'a variety of techniques' for this purpose. Among them was projective and habitual behaviour that could not be reduced to 'cold calculation' but rather followed the psychology of 'human nature' and yielded to motives of 'satisfaction' and 'temptation'. Entrepreneurs were often 'not really relying on a precise calculation of prospective profit', but 'embark[ing] on business as a way of life' and playing 'a mixed game of skill and chance'. As human beings and market agents, they also responded to what Keynes called 'animal spirits' – short-lived but intense feelings that induced a 'spontaneous optimism' and urged one 'to action rather than inaction'. These helped bypass situations in which excessive reasoning and calculating might lead to inaction. Particularly in times of crisis and under conditions of insufficient information, animal spirits

---

[15]Max Weber, 'Religious Rejections of the World and Their Directions', in *From Max Weber: Essays in Sociology*, trans. and ed. Hans Heinrich Gerth and Charles Wright Mills (London: Paul, 1946), 323–59.
[16]John Maynard Keynes, 'The General Theory of Employment', *The Quarterly Journal of Economics* 51, no. 2 (1937): 209–23, quote 214.
[17]Schumpeter, *Nature and Essence*, 55.

encouraged people to act, and enabled market transactions to continue. Without those vital energies, Keynes wrote, 'enterprise will fade and die'.[18]

It is not entirely clear from where or whom Keynes borrowed his concept of animal spirits. It might have been René Descartes, who, in his 1649 *Les passions de l'âme*, had described them as delicate and mobile blood particles that flow into the brain, then get transmitted to nerves and muscles and consequently set the body in motion. Sentiment, memory, imagination, desires and passions all originate, according to Descartes, from those particles. Or perhaps Keynes took inspiration from Isaac Newton, who had shared Descartes's interest in animal spirits, as had so many others.[19] The notion that sentiments, passions and affects were closely related to what might be translated as the energy of mind and soul (*spiritus animalis*) had been a staple of early modern philosophy. Just how this relation was perceived and judged, however, varied greatly. While some writers and commentators praised strong passions as dynamic and constructive forces, the majority emphasized their negative effect. In their view, men had too many passions and were inordinately reluctant to curb their overwhelming power. It was thought that emotions of any kind, whether short-lived or long-lasting, should be controlled and channelled so as not to interfere with rational thinking and decision-making. Though they could not, and should not, be dismissed and suppressed altogether, they ought to be transformed into mild and benevolent feelings. Similar strategies of transformation were suggested by Sigmund Freud's theory of sublimation, which turned sexual drives into cultural work and with which Keynes was equally well acquainted.[20]

As a general rule, economists held emotions (far more than drives) to be utterly unpredictable and therefore hard to work with. As strong motivators

---

[18] Keynes, 'General Theory', 214–15; Keynes, *General Theory of Employment*, 150, 161–3. See also Hartmut Berghoff, 'Rationalität und Irrationalität auf Finanzmärkten', in *Kapitalismus. Historische Annäherungen*, ed. Gunilla Budde (Göttingen: Vandenhoeck & Ruprecht, 2011), 73–96, here 80–3; Jens Beckert, 'Was tun? Die emotionale Konstruktion von Zuversicht bei Entscheidungen unter Ungewissheit', in *Kluges Entscheiden*, ed. Arno Scherzberg (Tübingen: Mohr Siebeck, 2006), 123–41, esp. 133–5.

[19] For Descartes, see Catherine Newmark, *Passion – Affekt – Gefühl: Philosophische Theorien der Emotionen zwischen Aristoteles und Kant* (Hamburg: Meiner, 2008), ch. 5; for Newton, see Rob Iliffe, '"That Puzleing Problem": Isaac Newton and the Political Physiology of Self', *Medical History* 39, no. 4 (1995): 433–58. Keynes was fascinated by Newton's manuscripts and, in the early 1940s, prepared a lecture to celebrate the tercentenary of his birth: http://www-history.mcs.st-and.ac.uk/Extras/Keynes_Newton.html (accessed 22 December 2022). See also R.C.O. Matthews, 'Animal Spirits', *Proceedings of the British Academy* 70 (1984): 209–29; Roger Koppl, 'Animal Spirits', *Journal of Economic Perspectives* 5, no. 3 (1991): 203–10; Donald Moggridge, 'The Source of Animal Spirits', *Journal of Economic Perspectives* 6, no. 3 (1992): 207–9.

[20] Newmark, 'Passion'; Sidney Ochs, *A History of Nerve Functions: From Animal Spirits to Molecular Mechanisms* (Cambridge: Cambridge University Press, 2004); Ute Frevert et al., *Emotional Lexicons: Continuity and Change in the Vocabulary of Feeling 1700–2000* (Oxford: Oxford University Press, 2014), 18–24.

of people's actions and non-actions, they undoubtedly played a major role in all areas of life; closely linked to value systems and notions of morality, they informed human behaviour, both in the private and the public sphere. But how could they be integrated into theoretical models of economic processes? According to Schmoller and, to a lesser degree, Werner Sombart, psychology was indispensable here.[21] Others, like Schumpeter, discarded the question of motives and actions altogether, arguing that 'pure' economics should not be concerned with human beings and what they wanted or did and for what reason. What mattered was the number of goods that those beings possessed and traded: 'We want to describe the changes, or better, a certain type of changes, as if they would happen automatically, without looking at the people who are responsible for those changes.'[22]

Interestingly, in his own work Schumpeter did not practise what he preached. As someone fascinated by the innovative figure of the entrepreneur (he himself had been raised in an entrepreneurial family), he was keen to explore the conditions under which men recombined the means of production to fuel economic development. Those conditions were largely framed in psychological terms. Rather than calculating utility or satisfying his needs and wishes, the dynamic entrepreneur was, according to Schumpeter, obsessed with 'the dream and the will to found a private kingdom'; he indulged in the 'joy of creating, of getting things done, or simply of exercising one's energy and ingenuity', and he followed 'the will to conquer: the impulse to fight, to prove oneself superior to others, to succeed for the sake, not of the fruits of success, but of success itself'. An entrepreneurial spirit of this sort surpassed the inbuilt logic of the marketplace and could hardly be subsumed under the banner of 'pure economics'.[23]

Those economists who adhered to the pure ideal and worked hard to mould economics into a precise science accordingly kept their distance when it came to spirits, entrepreneurial or otherwise. Keynes's cautious remark about animal spirits helping to sustain the economic process was not well received. Instead, post-war economists redoubled their efforts to model individual behaviour with the help of mathematical algorithms.

---

[21]Schmoller, *Volkswirtschaft*; on Werner Sombart, see his 1913 book on the development and sources of the capitalist spirit: *Der Bourgeois: Zur Geistesgeschichte des modernen Wirtschaftsmenschen* (Reinbek: Rowohlt, 1988), as well as his *Der moderne Kapitalismus*, vol. 3 (Berlin: Duncker & Humblot, 1928), 23–41 on the modern economic leader's drives and energies.
[22]Schumpeter, *Nature*, 54.
[23]Joseph A. Schumpeter, *The Theory of Economic Development*, 8th edn (Cambridge, MA: Harvard University Press, 1968), 93.

Bounded rationality

From the 1970s, however, it became apparent that these individualistic ontologies were seriously flawed. The hypothesis of individual rationality was called into question, and so too was people's endless capability for calculating and making superbly rational choices. Developments within the discipline of psychology helped to cast doubt on the cherished premises of both microeconomics and macroeconomics. Cognitive psychology, which paid attention to processes of mental planning and prefiguration, became increasingly popular, while orthodox behaviourism lost traction. This resulted in a renewed interest in how people interpreted and framed what they saw and encountered. In the wake of the epistemological shift, the concepts of habit and instinct – perfectly compatible with Keynes's animal spirits – were reinstated.[24]

As early as 1947, Herbert Simon (who was awarded the Nobel Prize for economics in 1975) used insights from cognitive psychology to question the assumption that individuals could ever possess complete information about how to best achieve specific goals and select from alternative actions, thereby underlining the limits to rational decision-making. He argued that individuals develop 'working procedures that partially overcome these difficulties'. They act with 'bounded rationality' that prompts them to resort to a strategy of 'satisficing' instead of maximizing ('satisficing' combines 'satisfy' and 'suffice').[25]

The concept of 'bounded rationality' was strengthened when Daniel Kahneman was awarded the Nobel Prize in 2002. Together with Amos Tversky, Kahneman designed psychological experiments that showed how people attempted to form judgements under uncertain conditions and make decisions in the face of risk. Again, the experiments were not about finding optimal decisions in perfect settings, but about modelling real-life choices. Tversky and Kahneman's findings stressed the importance of intuition and instinct and, furthermore, questioned the assumption that agents are only concerned about the value that they themselves receive from their decision. Rather, the researchers concluded that agents also seem to consider the value obtained by others.[26]

---

[24]Hodgson, *Evolution*, 401–3.
[25]Herbert A. Simon, *Administrative Behavior*, 3rd edn (New York: Free Press, 1976), 82; Herbert A. Simon, 'A Behavioral Model of Rational Choice', *Quarterly Journal of Economics* 69, no. 1 (1955): 99–118; Herbert A. Simon, 'Reply: Surrogates for Uncertain Decision Problems', in Simon, *Models of Bounded Rationality*, vol. 1 (Cambridge, MA: MIT Press, 1982), 235–44; Herbert A. Simon, 'Rational Choice and the Structure of the Environment', *Psychological Review* 63, no. 2 (1956): 129–38.
[26]Daniel Kahneman and Amos Tversky, 'Prospect Theory: An Analysis of Decision under Risk', *Econometrica* 47, no. 2 (1979): 263–91; Daniel Kahneman, Paul Slovic and Amos Tversky, eds, *Judgment under Uncertainty: Heuristics and Biases* (New York: Cambridge University Press, 1982). See also Gerd Gigerenzer, *Gut Feelings: The Intelligence of the Unconscious* (London: Viking, 2007), who goes further than Kahneman in considering intuition a wonderfully efficient way of reaching smart and fast decisions.

Kahneman's work forms part of the burgeoning field of behavioural economics, which has been described as a 'revolution in economics'.[27] Instead of exclusively relying on the rational optimizing model, this approach stresses the frames of reference that inform people's actions beyond sheer utility. It also criticizes, and increasingly so, the standard position on self-regarding preferences. Through laboratory and field experiments, behavioural economists have sought to prove that agents care not only about the outcome of economic interactions but also about the process. They value fairness and punish unfair players even when this reduces their own gains. The evidence furnished by such experiments has consequently given rise to the concept of strong reciprocity, defined as 'a predisposition to cooperate with others, and to punish (at personal cost, if necessary) those who violate the norms of cooperation, even when it is implausible to expect that these costs will be recovered at a later date'.[28]

The concept does not, as its authors point out, 'contradict the fundamental ideas of rationality' but rather expands the understanding of what rationality might mean.[29] Even if they do not follow computational rules of rational behaviour, people have reasons for acting as they do. These reasons might exceed some narrowly defined interest in maximizing economic utility, including moral values, aesthetic tastes and/or emotional needs. Desires, 'fears and hopes' (Keynes) and joyful impulses, as well as moral concerns about fairness and justice, inform human conduct to a degree that economists no longer feel inclined – or compelled – to overlook.

This clearly reflects the current interest in emotions as ubiquitous and appreciated facets of social relations and communication. Since the 1990s, most human and social sciences have taken an 'emotional turn' that has influenced theories and practices of management, among others. Emotional intelligence has become the catchword for those who want to boost job satisfaction or handle business operations more efficiently.[30] In short, emotions have been re-evaluated as prime motivators of economic

---

[27]Robert J. Shiller, 'Behavioral Economics and Institutional Innovation', *Southern Economic Journal* 72, no. 2 (2005): 269–83. See also Luigino Bruno and Robert Sugden, 'The Road Not Taken: How Psychology Was Removed from Economics, and How It Might Be Brought Back', *The Economic Journal* 117, no. 516 (2007): 146–73.

[28]Herbert Gintis et al., eds, *Moral Sentiments and Material Interests: The Foundations of Cooperation in Economic Life* (Cambridge, MA: MIT Press, 2005), 8; Joseph Henrich et al., eds, *Foundations of Human Sociality* (Oxford: Oxford University Press, 2004).

[29]Gintis, *Moral Sentiments*, 5. For the trend to reduce reason to a mathematics of rationality, see *How Reason Almost Lost Its Mind: The Strange Career of Cold War Rationality*, ed. Paul Erickson et al. (Chicago: Chicago University Press, 2013), ch. 1.

[30]See Chapters 1 and 7 in this book. The interest in emotions as enhancing (or reducing) productivity goes back to the early twentieth century, when applied psychology invented '*industrielle Psychotechnik*'. See, for example, Hugo Münsterberg, *Psychologie und Wirtschaftsleben* (Leipzig: Barth, 1912), and, for an overview, Laura L. Koppes, ed., *Historical Perspectives in Industrial and Organizational Psychology* (Mahwah: Erlbaum, 2007).

behaviour. At a time when more and more people in modern economies were working in the service and financial sectors, 'economic man' was encouraged to remodel himself as a true 'entrepreneur of his own self'. As such, he (and, increasingly, she) had, and has, to pay close attention to their emotional management and self-fashioning. Emotions have acquired value as a major individual and socioeconomic resource and are now considered objects worthy of scientific analysis and measurement.[31]

The recent surge of emotion studies has also established close ties between emotions and institutionalized modes of conduct and normative frameworks. Instead of regarding them as spontaneous bodily instincts or drives, scholars increasingly conceptualize emotions as intimately linked to mental processes of appraisal and interpretation. Consequently, emotionality is no longer considered the opposite of rationality. Body and mind evidently work together and are anything but radically separate; both are informed by cultural patterns that strongly influence how emotions are felt, experienced and expressed.

Such insights are compatible with the second shift that has happened in economics since the crisis of general equilibrium theory and its failed claim to explain macroeconomics through the rationality of individual agents. This shift has given rise to a renewed interest in institutional arrangements that, as Nobel Laureate Douglass North has argued, provide 'both formal rules and informal norms of behavior'. Institutions mediate between mental models and belief systems and societal and economic structures. They shape and frame cognitive systems of interpretation that include emotional and moral categories. Through institutions, individuals acquire a more homogeneous perception of their environment; they learn to share certain patterns of thought and emotion and they become acquainted with different modes of rationality in different contexts.[32]

New institutional economics – which builds on older traditions developed by Veblen and the German Historical School – thus offers a far more complex and integrated perspective on how economic interactions

---

[31]This has been stressed more by sociologists than economists: see Mabel Berezin, 'Emotions and the Economy', in *The Handbook of Economic Sociology*, ed. Neil J. Smelser and Richard Swedberg, 2nd edn (Princeton: Princeton University Press, 2005), 109–27; Mabel Berezin, 'Exploring Emotions and the Economy: New Contributions from Sociological Theory', *Theory and Society* 38, no. 4 (2009): 335–46; Viviana A. Zelizer, *Economic Lives: How Culture Shapes the Economy* (Princeton: Princeton University Press, 2011). See also Jocelyn Pixley, *Emotions in Finance: Distrust and Uncertainty in Global Markets* (Cambridge: Cambridge University Press, 2004). On the entrepreneurial self, see Ulrich Bröckling, *Das unternehmerische Selbst: Soziologie einer Subjektivierungsform* (Frankfurt: Suhrkamp, 2007).
[32]Douglass C. North, 'Economic Performance through Time', *American Economic Review* 84, no. 3 (1994): 359–68; Hodgson, *Evolution*, ch. 20. For political institutions and how they template emotions, see Ute Frevert et al., *Feeling Political: Emotions and Institutions since 1789* (Cham: Palgrave Macmillan, 2022).

work and how economic performance changes over time.[33] By challenging neoclassical theory's narrow assumption of rationality, it pays attention to the role of 'ideas, ideologies, myths, dogmas, and prejudices' – and, possibly, emotions – in guiding people's preferences, choices and decisions.[34]

Among the ever more frequent attempts to theorize emotions in economics is George Akerlof and Robert Shiller's 2009 book on 'how human psychology drives the economy'. Loosely referring to Keynes's notion of animal spirits, its authors describe emotions as 'thought patterns that animate people's ideas and feelings'. Because those spirits, ideas and emotions constitute 'a restless and inconsistent element in the economy', they are hard to model but they nevertheless must be incorporated into macroeconomic theory. It remains doubtful, however, how and whether this claim can be implemented, given its basic assumptions. Akerlof and Shiller introduce animal spirits as a *catégorie poubelle* in which many different phenomena are grouped together: ideas and feelings, patterns of behaviour, memories and narratives. How these are linked to each other is left unexplored. Furthermore, they are classified not only as 'noneconomic motivations' but also as 'irrational'.[35]

Describing such a wide set of phenomena as irrational reproduces the truncated understanding of rationality that has been criticized as a grand illusion of (neo)classical theory. Further, it defies what recent psychological and neuroscientific research has uncovered: that emotions are deeply and consistently involved in cognitive processes like forming preferences and judgements and attributing value and meaning. Taking those findings into account and connecting them to (old and new) institutional approaches to economics, *homo oeconomicus* will have to be thoroughly reconfigured – as a human being whose self-love and self-interest have limits and whose rationality embraces passions of all kinds.[36]

---

[33]Werner Plumpe, 'Gustav von Schmoller und der Institutionalismus: Zur Bedeutung der Historischen Schule der Nationalökonomie für die moderne Wirtschaftsgeschichtsschreibung', *Geschichte und Gesellschaft* 25, no. 2 (1999): 252–75.

[34]North, 'Economic Performance', 362. Veblen introduced the concept of 'instincts' rather than emotions: Harold Wolozin, 'Thorstein Veblen and Human Emotions: An Unfulfilled Prescience', *Journal of Economic Issues* 39, no. 3 (2005): 727–40.

[35]George A. Akerlof and Robert J. Shiller, *Animal Spirits: How Human Psychology Drives the Economy, and Why It Matters for Global Capitalism* (Princeton: Princeton University Press, 2009), quotes 1, 4.

[36]For a similar conclusion, see Jocelyn Pixley, 'Emotions and Economics', in *Emotions and Sociology*, ed. Jack Barbalet (Oxford: Blackwell, 2002), 69–89, here 83; Jocelyn Pixley, *Emotions in Finance*, esp. 185–9.

CHAPTER NINE

Greed and Avarice: Feelings about Money

This chapter discusses two feelings that are intimately and inherently connected to capitalism and its emotional economy: greed and avarice. The 'greedy capitalist' has long resided in people's imaginations; workers have time and again grumbled about the 'greedy employer' who 'is determined to break our backs' for the sake of 'abnormal profit'.[1] In such accounts, greed is usually paired with avarice: both speak to a lack of generosity and a hard-heartedness towards other people's grievances. Yet, neither greed nor avarice are the monopoly of capitalist entrepreneurs; they have a longer history that needs to be explored.

Greed and avarice are not the only emotions associated with money. History knows many others, such as joy, pride, envy, fear, sadness, rage and anger. Countless children have listened to Ludwig van Beethoven's story (and music) about the 'anger of the lost penny' in his much-cherished *Rondo a Capriccio Opus 129*.[2] If they had heeded its proverbial lesson, 'take care of the pennies, and the pounds will take care of themselves', they would indeed have sympathized with the composer's rage, although they might also have appreciated its humorous side.

Feelings about money are closely related to cultural norms and social conventions that are themselves tied to what money represents. As

---

[1] Daniel Bell, 'Adjusting Men to Machines: Social Scientists Explore the World of the Factory', *Commentary* 4 (1947): 79–88, here 85 (he quotes from a 1946 union paper at the Ford Motor Company).
[2] Heinz von Loesch, '"Die Wut über den verlorenen Groschen": "Gemütlicher Witz" oder Zeichen der "Entfremdung"?', *Bonner Beethoven-Studien* 8 (2009): 77–88.

anthropologists, sociologists and psychologists have amply demonstrated, money is not simply a medium that can be exchanged for goods and services.³ Money can be far more, depending on situation, scale and necessity, intention and attitude. Similarly, people's feelings about money vary according to their upbringing and experiences.

Stories old and new

These feelings have been widely debated and commented on throughout history. Literature and the visual arts, both religious and secular, popular and scientific, have produced powerful and lasting images and narratives on the topic. Typically, these narratives have been couched in a moral language that seeks to instruct on right and wrong, good versus bad behaviour.

Many people who grew up in Western post-war societies are familiar with the iconic figure of Scrooge McDuck, the richest bird in the world and the greatest miser on earth. Losing just one cent sent him into a rage; he could not rest until he found that cent and returned it to his well-stocked safe. Scrooge, like the original character in Charles Dickens's 1843 novella *A Christmas Carol*, was hardly an amiable creature. Dickens described him as 'a squeezing, wrenching, grasping, scraping, clutching, covetous old sinner', his features frozen by the 'cold within him'.⁴ He treated everyone with disdain and felt bereft by the one generous deed he allowed himself each year: giving his clerk a paid day off at Christmas. Although a very rich man, he opted to live frugally and to hoard his wealth. In short, he was utterly despicable. A century later, Carl Banks, who created the anatine cartoon version, turned Ebenezer Scrooge into a caricature, worthy of ridicule but, in certain ways, also of pity.

The anger over a lost penny that the two Scrooges felt stands in sharp contrast to one particular story from the New Testament. Luke 15 tells the parable of the lost coin: a woman who has ten silver coins in her possession loses one. She then lights a lamp, sweeps the house and searches diligently until she finds it. Full of joy, 'she calls together her friends and neighbours, saying, "Rejoice with me, for I have found the drachma which I had lost"'. Perhaps the woman was a poor peasant for whom a drachma was a lot of money, and justifiably worth every effort to retrieve. Perhaps the silver coins carried additional emotional and symbolic value as a wedding gift or family inheritance. The most important thing about the woman's story,

---

³Marcel Mauss, *The Gift: The Form and Reason for Exchange in Archaic Societies* (London: Routledge, [French Orig. 1925] 2002); Georg Simmel, *The Philosophy of Money*, ed. David Frisby (London: Routledge, [Germ. Orig. 1900] 2004); Christoph Deutschmann, ed., *Die gesellschaftliche Macht des Geldes* (Wiesbaden: Westdeutscher Verlag, 2002).
⁴Charles Dickens, 'A Christmas Carol', in Dickens, *Christmas Books* (London: Oxford University Press, 1974), 1–71, here 8.

however, was that she shared her joy with friends and neighbours and invited them to celebrate with her. The celebrations likely cost her more than a drachma, but this was not the point: joy was what mattered, and was the feeling she wanted to share. In this case, money lost and found represented an opportunity to socialize, be merry and rejoice together.[5]

Stories such as this parable suggest a more complex lesson about the emotional economy of money, and they introduce more complex feelings. Nevertheless, most narratives and images do converge on the themes of greed and avarice. We may therefore regard these as the main and fundamental emotions associated with money.

Self-evidently, people may be and are greedy about other things too: children often covet sweets, while adults may occasionally indulge in food or drink. The German vocabulary includes the word *Neugier* (curiosity), which literally translates as 'greed for the new' – a lust for new knowledge that can take the form of gossip, or, more nobly, be the driving force of science.[6] Yet greed is usually associated with money, as the traditional German term *Habgier* indicates. Another word for *Habgier* – literally, the greed for having – is *Habsucht*. Etymologically, *Sucht* derives from *siechen*, to suffer from a disease. In this instance, the disease is a passion that cannot be cured but takes full possession of a person, emotionally overwhelming them.

The same holds true for avarice. Not only are the two Scrooges greedy for money, but they do not want to spend any, either. They thus embody the opposite of generosity and lavishness. To them, squandering is a foreign concept. Avarice determines both how they treat themselves and how they treat others. They want to hoard their coins, and take great pleasure in touching, revering and counting them. Scrooge McDuck even likes to dive into his money – he literally swims in gold.

As the narratives of the Scrooges imply, greed and avarice usually go hand in hand. Common parlance describes the greedy as having 'long pockets and short arms', arms too short to reach into pockets that are likely to be deep and filled with money. Where does this convergence originate? What does it reveal about moral economies and the passions, sentiments and emotions associated with them? How stable were those moral judgements and what, if anything, caused them to change? Finally, how, if at all, were they related to capitalism as it has developed since the early modern period? Did capitalism produce particular feelings about money, or did it inherit and shift them?

---

[5]Joel B. Green, *The Gospel of Luke* (Grand Rapids: Eerdmans, 1997), 576; Linda Maloney, '"Swept under the Rug": Feminist Homiletical Reflections on the Parable of the Lost Coin (Lk. 15.8–9)', in *The Lost Coin: Parables of Women, Work and Wisdom*, ed. Mary Ann Beavis (London: Sheffield Academic Press, 2002), 34–8, esp. 36.
[6]Ute Frevert, *The Power of Emotions: A History of Germany from 1900 to the Present* (Cambridge: Cambridge University Press, 2023), 59–76.

Transformations and redefinitions: from deadly sin to capitalist virtue

Both greed and avarice have a long history that predates the advent of capitalism. Ancient philosophers such as Plato, Aristotle and Cicero discussed them, primarily as negative attributes.[7] In the Christian tradition, *avaritia*, the desire to acquire and retain money, was clearly labelled and condemned as one of the seven deadly sins. According to Alcuin of York, a famous scholar at the Carolingian court, *avaritia* was 'the appetite to amass, have and keep too many riches'. That appetite amounted to 'an insatiable corruption', since *avaritia* could never be satisfied.[8]

Avaritia had a face, nearly always that of an old woman. In medieval illuminated manuscripts and architectural sculpture, *avaritia* snatches money and other valuable items with her claw-like hands; she presses the well-filled moneybag to her breast; otherwise, it hangs around her neck to illustrate how it enslaves her. Her mouth is stuffed with coins that reach as far down as her heart. At times, *operatio*, representing diligence, grabs her by the throat and kills her in order to distribute her riches to the needy.[9]

Such imagery highlights the ambiguous Christian concept of wealth. Wealth was not inherently bad as long as it was accompanied by duties and moral obligations: if individuals possessed more than they needed to lead a good life and support a family, they were expected to share their excess with less fortunate people. Those who held their purse strings tight and did not give generously were condemned as cold-hearted brutes who sinned against the cherished virtues of *misericordia* and benevolence.[10]

This perspective belonged to a mentality that valued reciprocity and balance. Whoever took had to give, the balance had to be even. The notion of a zero-sum game was characteristic of a society based on an agricultural subsistence economy. It came under pressure, however, when other economic activities, such as trade, gained importance. In Christian terms, merchants

---

[7] David Harris Sacks, 'The Greed of Judas: Avarice, Monopoly, and the Moral Economy in England, ca.1350–ca.1600', *Journal of Medieval and Early Modern Studies* 28, no. 2 (1998): 263–307.

[8] Quoted in Bettina Emmerich, *Geiz und Gerechtigkeit: Ökonomisches Denken im frühen Mittelalter* (Wiesbaden: Steiner, 2004), 193–4; Richard Newhauser, *The Early History of Greed: The Sin of Avarice in Early Medieval Thought and Literature* (Cambridge: Cambridge University Press, 2000).

[9] Ulrich Rehm, 'Avarus non implebitur pecunia: Geldgier in Bildern des Mittelalters', in *Geld im Mittelalter*, ed. Klaus Grubmüller and Markus Stock (Darmstadt: WBG, 2005), 135–81; Hannelore Sachs, Ernst Badstübner and Helga Neumann, *Christliche Ikonographie in Stichworten* (Leipzig: Koehler & Amelang, 1973), 334; Fabienne Eggelhöfer, 'Avaritia/Geiz, Habgier', in *Lust und Laster: Die 7 Todsünden von Dürer bis Nauman*, ed. Kunstmuseum Bern and Zentrum Paul Klee (Ostfildern: Hatje Cantz, 2010), 200–4.

[10] See Chapter 6 in this volume.

were regarded with distrust and contempt, while moneylenders who charged interest were disliked most of all. They were seen as the veritable personification of a greed that took pleasure in the most abstract form of economic activity imaginable.

The best-known example can be found in William Shakespeare's play *The Merchant of Venice*. Shakespeare drew a clear moral distinction between Shylock, the avaricious, egotistical, asocial usurer–capitalist *avant la lettre*, and Antonio, the generous, kind, altruistic, risk-taking merchant–capitalist. Not even Shylock's moving speech against antisemitic discrimination ('*If you prick us, do we not bleed?*') spares him the humiliating fate of not only having to renounce his Jewishness but also shutter his business and hand over his wealth to the state and his Christian son-in-law.[11]

By the end of the sixteenth century, when Shakespeare wrote the play, merchants had evidently managed to free themselves from the negative connotations around accruing wealth. Men like Antonio who sent their ships overseas and brought back goods never before seen in Europe were well regarded, as long as they virtuously gave back to the community. They were allowed to be successful and rich but they still had to follow the laws set by the moral and emotional economy of their times. Within that economy, benevolence was favoured over greed, generosity and friendship over avarice. Even money-lending and charging interest could be considered socially acceptable if accompanied by 'noble' practices, as Matthäus Schwarz, accountant to the Augsburg Fugger merchant dynasty in the early sixteenth century, confirmed.[12]

An enormous surge in long-distance trade and commercial activity saw renewed attempts to recalibrate traditional norms and values.[13] Niccolò Machiavelli openly challenged older attitudes that condemned greed and avarice among rulers.[14] Together with other Italian and French thinkers, he wanted to free avarice from its negative overtones and to stress its social utility.[15] In 1549, Sir Thomas Smith, a distinguished English scholar and statesman, suggested that avarice might in fact promote, rather than hinder,

---

[11]David Nirenberg, *Anti-Judaism: The Western Tradition* (New York: Norton & Co., 2013), ch. 8.

[12]Quotes from Matthäus Schwarz, 'Dreierley Buchhaltung 1518', in Karl-Heinz Brodbeck, *Die Herrschaft des Geldes* (Darmstadt: WBG, 2009), 892.

[13]Keith Wrightson, *Earthly Necessities: Economic Lives in Early Modern Britain* (New Haven: Yale University Press, 2000).

[14]Cary J. Nederman, 'Avarice as a Princely Virtue? The Later Medieval Backdrop to Poggio Bracciolini and Machiavelli', in *Mind Matters: Studies of Medieval and Early-Modern History in Honour of Marcia L. Colish*, ed. Cary J. Nederman, Nancy Van Deusen and E. Ann Matter (Turnhout: Brepols, 2009), 255–74.

[15]Quentin Skinner, *The Foundations of Modern Political Thought*, vol. 1 (Cambridge: Cambridge University Press, 1978), 42–3 and *passim*; Nannerl O. Keohane, *Philosophy and the State in France: The Renaissance to the Enlightenment* (Princeton: Princeton University Press, 1980), 158–63.

civil unity. Though he recognized its destructive potential, Smith asserted that, if efficiently regulated by the state, individual avarice could foster social harmony by increasing the economic interdependence of individuals and nations.[16]

This sounds like an earlier version of Bernard Mandeville's famous *Fable of the Bees,* which, in 1714, pointedly argued in favour of private vices that had potential to yield public benefits through the intervention of what Max Weber would later call the 'Protestant ethic' and its influence on the 'spirit of capitalism'.[17] Calvinism, as it developed in sixteenth-century Geneva, did not depart from traditional Christian mores but reinforced them, and introduced some new rules to boot. Usury was forbidden and the interest rate set at 5 per cent. The poor were looked after – but only if they were deserving. Those unwilling to work could not count on private or public support. Consequently, charity in the traditional sense was transformed into an instrument of social and educational policy.

Under the new regime, things also changed for those who were in a position to give or offer support. Constraints on luxury were imposed throughout Europe. The city of Geneva applied some of the strictest measures, banning gambling, betting and dancing for everybody, including the rich and powerful. John Calvin himself had waged a ferocious battle against squandering resources on lavish dinners and wedding parties. The wealthy ought instead to spend their surplus money on acts of *misericordia*, or reinvest it into profitable enterprises. In this way, parsimony and thrift as propagated by Calvinism could yield extra money that would, in turn, be channelled into new commercial endeavours.[18]

Avarice was thus redefined as parsimony and lauded as a major moral and emotional virtue, especially among urban elites.[19] Yet parsimony was not absolute. It was, firstly, a matter of scale, and, secondly, of social standing. Everybody had to observe rules around expenses and decorum, but these varied depending on one's rank and wealth. Noblemen were bound by particular expectations that differed from those placed on members of the middle classes. Those who failed to comply and spent too little were seen as

---

[16] Neal Wood, 'Avarice and Civil Unity: The Contribution of Sir Thomas Smith', *History of Political Thought* 18, no. 1 (1997): 24–42.

[17] 'The Root of evil Avarice, / That damn'd ill-natur'd baneful Vice, / Was Slave to Prodigality, / That Noble Sin; whilst Luxury / Employ'd a Million of the Poor'. Bernard Mandeville, *The Fable of the Bees,* ed. Phillip Harth (Harmondsworth: Penguin, [1714] 1970), 68; Jared Poley, *The Devil's Riches: A Modern History of Greed* (New York: Berghahn, 2016).

[18] Volker Reinhardt, *Mein Geld! Meine Seele! Die größten Geizhälse und ihre Geschichten* (Munich: C.H. Beck, 2009), 161–9, 31–2.

[19] Johann Heinrich Zedler, ed., *Grosses vollständiges Universal-Lexicon aller Wissenschafften und Künste,* vol. 38 (Leipzig: Zedler, 1743), 1222–5, quote 1222, defined parsimony as 'a virtue of the soul describing a man who has earned his money honestly and who avoids all unnecessary spending and saves a portion of the money for the future'.

niggards, unworthy of respect.[20] A wealthy man who scrimped on clothing or food or lost his temper over a penny became the object of ridicule, like Molière's character Harpagnon in the 1668 play *L'Avare*, who considered money his one and only friend, consolation and joy.[21]

Due to the lack of absolute rules regarding monetary dealings, social practices were flexible. Moral and emotional economies as they developed during the early modern period were by no means static and constant. Even golden rules, such as the rule of reciprocity, could be stretched to accommodate emerging opportunities, of which there were plenty for rulers and subjects alike. European expansion that offered new riches and long-distance trade, of the kind undertaken by Shakespeare's Venetian merchant Antonio, was risky but potentially highly profitable. The mercantile state rewarded growth and development, and so did monarchies whose ferocious battle for honour manifested in conspicuous consumption. As Heinrich von Justi, a leading German political economist, observed in 1761, the prodigality of monarchs boosted the 'circulation' of money and enabled the urban middle classes to thrive.[22]

'Circulation', the buzzword of the day, encompassed far more than reciprocity and was not limited to fair or unfair trade between the rich and poor. Modernity demanded that money change hands, thereby doing 'good'. As a result, commerce was increasingly mediated through a powerful business sector, which introduced new dynamics into the traditional order of things. Why should poverty exist when everyone could benefit from the flow of money? As one economics-focused encyclopaedia claimed in 1773, wealthy people who spent their money reasonably provided work and earnings for a great number of artisans, labourers and merchants who would otherwise be forced to rely on charity. It was far better to turn paupers into industrious workers than to leave them in a state of idleness and dependence.[23]

This required a departure from traditional concepts of social order and moral economy. The circulation of money was no longer perceived as a

---

[20] From Middle English *nigard/nygard*, meaning 'miserly'; Paul Münch, 'Parsimonia summum est vectigal – Sparen ist ein ryche gült: Sparsamkeit als Haus-, Frauen- und Bürgertugend', in *Ethische Perspektiven: 'Wandel der Tugenden'*, ed. Hans-Jürg Braun (Zürich: Verlag der Fachvereine, 1989), 169–87.

[21] Molière, *The Miser*, act IV, scene VII ff.

[22] Johann Heinrich Gottlob von Justi, *Die Grundfeste zu der Macht und Glückseeligkeit der Staaten*, vol. 1 (Königsberg: Woltersdorfs Witwe, 1761) also dedicated a chapter to civil virtues. He claimed that it was necessary for citizens of states that traded with others to seek to enlarge their assets by being diligent and skilful, while others might think less highly of hard work. According to Justi, democracies generally valued thrift and equality, while monarchies indulged in luxury, which again benefited commerce and industry (Paul Münch, ed., *Ordnung, Fleiß und Sparsamkeit: Texte und Dokumente zur Entstehung der 'bürgerlichen Tugenden'* (Munich: dtv, 1984), quotes 20–1).

[23] Johann Georg Krünitz, *Oeconomische Encyklopädie*, vol. 2 (Berlin: Pauli, 1773), 786–9 ('Aufwand').

zero-sum game; the hope, rather, was that it would produce economic growth and enhance the 'wealth of nations'. As Adam Smith observed in 1776, 'every man lives by exchanging, or becomes in some measure a merchant'.[24] Under new conditions of commercial and industrial capitalism, such enterprise was not only highly praised but became increasingly widespread. Moreover, it thoroughly transformed people's feelings about money.

Shifting boundaries and educational messages

Distinguishing between the various aspects of avarice, Smith's contemporary Immanuel Kant considered self-directed avarice the gravest neglect of duty. 'Greedy avarice' (*habsüchtiger Geiz*) per se did not pose a problem, however. Nor was the German philosopher troubled by 'miserly avarice', the lack of benevolence a niggardly person showed towards others (*karger Geiz*). However, he did think it morally objectionable to live below one's means. Parsimony was better suited to slaves than to the owners of goods that brought happiness and well-being.[25] Writing in the 1790s at Prussia's eastern border, Kant had not yet conceived of an expansive economy that would recalibrate notions of greed and avarice. Nevertheless, his views on one's obligation towards one's own needs formed part of a new individualistic mindset that was intimately connected to the modern capitalist economic system. Focusing on the opportunities and duties of the individual was not synonymous with preaching selfishness at the expense of others. Yet it did mean emphasizing self-interest, self-love and self-mastery.

This influenced opinions on money-related feelings. On the one hand, people were becoming less likely to regard greed and avarice as overwhelming passions that disempowered and enslaved human beings by clouding their judgement. Even if they were still considered anthropological constants, inherent in human nature, greed and avarice were now viewed in a more positive light. Passions could deprive a person of their reasonable will under certain circumstances, but they could also prompt them to do great things. Greed was thus progressively framed as congruent with society's need for economic growth and improvement.

---

[24]Adam Smith, *The Wealth of Nations* (London: Dent, [1776] 1960), 20. A century later, Friedrich Nietzsche wrote: 'In former times, trading for money was frowned upon by the genuine aristocracy, even if such trade was necessary. Trade was accepted as a necessary evil; now it has become the ruling power at the heart of modern humankind, the most sought-after activity' (Brodbeck, *Herrschaft*, quote 935).
[25]Immanuel Kant, *The Metaphysics of Morals*, ed. Lara Denia, trans. Mary Gregor, rev. edn (Cambridge: Cambridge University Press, [Germ. Orig. 1797] 2017, 198–9. While *habsüchtiger Geiz* by far surpassed the greedy person's needs, *karger Geiz* neglected 'one's duties of love to others' (*Liebespflichten gegen Andere*). Self-directed (*gegen sich selbst*) avarice meant neglecting one's own needs.

Individual greed, the argument went, could be beneficial if efficiently harnessed and embedded in an emotional economy that took care of the poor and the less fortunate. Once held to be the mother of all vice, the passion to acquire and possess money was now deemed more moderate, easier to tame and less threatening than others. Compared to the desire for money, lust for power or sex appeared far more dangerous and despicable. While the latter drives could get completely out of hand, the former was able to be transformed into a 'calm passion', pursued with proper deliberation and channelled with foresight into economic activity, as David Hume claimed. Under such circumstances, greed proved to be tremendously useful and conducive to society's well-being.[26] It became, in Albert Hirschman's words, a 'privileged passion' that successfully adopted the mask of the rational entrepreneur or banker in the new capitalist system.

At the same time, morally instructive weeklies propagated a thrifty attitude towards money as the cornerstone of a proper middle-class lifestyle. Moral philosophy and sentimental novels preached the gospel of sympathy, compassion and *Schenkfreude*, the joy of giving.[27] How could self-interest and opportunity-seeking coexist with sympathy, benevolence and thrift-based generosity?

First, the boundaries between thrift and avarice had to be newly drawn. While thrift and parsimony were ennobled as the 'typical virtues of the middle classes', avarice was flatly condemned.[28] To the Enlightenment author Adolph Freiherr von Knigge, who published an influential treatise about good manners and tactful behaviour in 1788, avarice constituted 'one of the meanest and most disgraceful passions'. A miser could never be virtuous, Knigge reasoned, since he knew not 'nobler sensations: friendship, pity and benevolence are shut out of his heart if they be not productive of gain'.[29] Second, compassion had to be reframed in order to align with the new (fervently anti-aristocratic) appreciation for work. People began to perceive work not as penance, but as a positive means of self-fulfilment, self-cultivation and self-improvement.[30] The virtues of sympathy and

---

[26]Albert O. Hirschman, *The Passions and the Interests: Political Arguments for Capitalism before Its Triumph* (Princeton: Princeton University Press, 1977); see also Christoph Fleischmann, *Gewinn in alle Ewigkeit: Kapitalismus als Religion* (Zürich: Rotpunktverlag, 2010); Rudi Verburg, 'The Rise of Greed in Early Economic Thought: From Deadly Sin to Social Benefit', *Journal of the History of Economic Thought* 34, no. 4 (2012): 515–39.
[27]Lothar Bornscheuer, 'Zur Geltung des "Mythos Geld" im religiösen, ökonomischen und poetischen Diskurs', in *Mythos im Text*, ed. Rolf Grimminger and Iris Hermann (Bielefeld: Aisthesis, 1998), 55–105, here 74.
[28]Carl Friedrich Bahrdt, *Handbuch der Moral für den Bürgerstand* (1789), quoted in Münch, Parsimonia, 180.
[29]*Practical Philosophy of Social Life: The Art of Conversing with Men after the German of Baron Knigge*, by P. Will, vol. 1 (London: Cadell & Davies, 1794), 110.
[30]Münch, *Ordnung*, 35–6; Jürgen Kocka, 'Work as a Problem in European History', in *Work in a Modern Society: The German Historical Experience in Comparative Perspective*, ed. Jürgen Kocka (New York: Berghahn, 2010), 1–15; Keith Thomas ed., *The Oxford Book of Work* (Oxford: Oxford University Press, 1999).

benevolence were supposed to ensure that such work was available to those who had been deprived of it for social or personal reasons.

In this vein, capitalist entrepreneurs and factory owners in the modern period set out to present themselves as the benefactors of mankind, providing employment to workers and assisting their nation-states to become rich and powerful. They – and their wives – made sure to engage in charitable endeavours in order to appease the sensitivities of those who viewed the triumph of money critically.[31] Together, they would have treated Molière's Harpagnon, who enjoyed a return to the stage in the nineteenth century, with disbelief and contempt. Accruing wealth and hating spending seemed thoroughly out of place in a society dominated by capitalist modes of production and consumption. What had been condemned as a sinful vice for many centuries was now considered an illness or pathological addiction. Modern psychologists explored its underlying causes and identified a fear of losing control and power, a fear of losing independence and a fear of letting go as the chief factors. Sigmund Freud, meanwhile, attributed avarice to the failure to overcome the anal phase of infant development.[32]

While psychologists and psychoanalysts busied themselves with diagnosis or attempts to cure the disease, pedagogues urged mothers to teach their children early how to handle money by saving and spending prudently, without developing an obsession. Thriftiness and parsimony were considered important educational achievements for boys and girls alike. A person who saved money learnt 'how to moderate and control his wishes' and thus 'prevailed over his passions'. Instead of instantly satisfying his desires, he had the ability to postpone immediate gratification for a higher purpose. The higher purpose, however, was not the hoarding of money or the acquiring of possessions, but saving. Saving had noble objectives: providing for the family and educating and cultivating the next generation, thereby producing useful and honourable members of society. Money was thus not 'an end in itself', but a means to achieve good for all concerned.[33]

---

[31]Christina von Hodenberg, 'Der Fluch des Geldsacks: Der Aufstieg des Industriellen als Herausforderung bürgerlicher Werte', in *Der bürgerliche Wertehimmel*, ed. Manfred Hettling and Stefan-Ludwig Hoffmann (Göttingen: Vandenhoeck & Ruprecht, 2000), 79–104; Ute Frevert, *Kapitalismus, Märkte und Moral* (Vienna: Residenz, 2019). As to the ambivalence towards money, which was considered to be both the basis of social well-being and the cause of pathological greed, see Wolf Lepenies, 'Finanzkrisen in der Menschlichen Komödie', in *Kapitalismus. Historische Annäherungen*, ed. Gunilla Budde (Göttingen: Vandenhoeck & Ruprecht, 2011), 17–33, drawing on Honoré de Balzac's 1837 novel *Grandeur et décadence de César Birotteau*.
[32]Sigmund Freud, 'Character and Anal Erotism', in *The Standard Edition of the Complete Psychological Work of Sigmund Freud*, ed. James Strachney, vol. 9 (London: Hogarth Press, [Germ. Orig. 1908] 1995), 167–76.
[33]Sandra Maß, 'Mäßigung der Leidenschaften: Kinder und monetäre Lebensführung im 19. Jahrhundert', in *Das schöne Selbst*, ed. Jens Elberfeld and Marcus Otto (Bielefeld: Transcript, 2009), 55–81, quotes 74, 77; Sandra Maß, *Kinderstube des Kapitals? Monetäre Erziehung im 18. und 19. Jahrhundert* (Berlin: De Gruyter, 2018), ch. 4.

For their part, doctors warned that no child was born avaricious or greedy. If, later in life, a child grew up to be a miser or was overcome by rapacious desires, it was obviously the fault of the mother who had taught him or her such reproachable habits.[34] This sent a clear message: passions, good or bad, were not inherent, but acquired, nurtured and cultivated. They were a prospect, not a pre-ordained or inescapable fate. If a person became overwhelmed by a passion such as greed or avarice, it was due to negative environmental influences. Education – at home, at school and in church – was supposed to counteract such influences, to strengthen a person's capacity and willingness to either resist or constrain self-consuming passions until they were compatible with society's emotional economy. Greed was thus transformed into an entrepreneurial spirit that sought to reconcile individual ambition, creativity, innovation and the common interest. Avarice, too, had to be reconfigured into a prudent saving habit that enabled future or long-term activities and served both the individual and society at large.

The modern gospel of tamed and changed passions nevertheless encountered disbelief and suspicion. In 1788, Knigge remarked that 'so much depends on the influence of money': luxury abounded, needs grew, the price of food and supplies increased constantly.[35] Such criticism had deep religious roots, but it became particularly loud in the era of industrialization, which revolutionized how goods were produced and circulated. While Adam Smith and his disciples sang the praises of a liberal market economy that would dramatically transform people's lifestyles, habits and mentalities, others were not quite so optimistic. To early socialist Wilhelm Weitling, who expressed his opposition in strongly religious terms, an expansive 'commercial spirit' was harmful and destructive; it fermented 'all mean, selfish and corruptive feelings' and debased man to a calculating 'machine'.[36] Karl Marx famously detested capitalist greed, and his friend and co-author Friedrich Engels, the son of a textile entrepreneur, condemned trade as an indecent business that displayed its brutal *Habsucht* (greed) openly.[37]

It was not only those on the side of workers allegedly exploited by greedy capitalists who argued against the new market practices. Conservatives, too, found it difficult to embrace a growth-driven economy that threatened to undermine the traditional social and religious order. Among Protestants and Catholics alike, anti-capitalist views were often mixed with antisemitic ones. Drawing on pertinent biblical notions and images, they saw the figure of the

---

[34]See, among others, Hermann Klencke, *Die Mutter als Erzieherin ihrer Töchter und Söhne*, 10th edn (Leipzig: Kummer, [1870] 1895), 567–73.
[35][Knigge,] *Practical Philosophy*, 111.
[36]Brodbeck, *Herrschaft*, quote 904.
[37]Karl Marx and Frederick Engels, 'Outlines of a Critique of Political Economy (1843/44)', in Marx and Engels, *Collected Works*, vol. 3 (New York: International Publishers, 2005), 442–67, here 445; Karl Marx, 'Economic and Philosophic Manuscripts of 1844: Estranged Labour', in ibid., 293–305, here 294.

Jew as the embodiment of capitalist 'greed'. In 1892, the Catholic Bavarian priest Georg Ratzinger, hiding behind a pseudonym, declared that 'the Jewish mode of doing business and acquiring wealth' relied on 'exploiting the labour of others' and privileged 'gamble and speculation' over 'honest and productive work'. Twenty years earlier, a professor from Freiburg had maintained that 'love for money is of Jewish origin' and 'has become the first and most vigorous passion and an insatiable addiction. While the Gentile earns money in order to live, the Jew lives in order to earn money.'[38]

According to sociologist Georg Simmel, however, this attitude was by no means 'Jewish' or confined to Jews, but dominated all strata of late nineteenth-century European society. As he wrote in 1899, the 'cultural and psychological setup' of the modern economy had placed money at the 'center of all interest and concern'. Instead of being used as a means to an end, money had become an end in itself. This also changed the face of avarice. People 'who reuse a dead match, who tear out empty pages, who do not throw away a tiny piece of string and look everywhere for a lost needle' were not avaricious in Simmel's opinion, because they did not think in terms of money. What mattered to them emotionally was the object's substance and material worth, not its cash value. They deeply cared for the practical merit and usefulness of certain things, whereas to a truly avaricious person, things were worthless and insignificant.[39]

Simmel's observation recalls the parable of the lost coin: the woman who lost it cared not so much about its monetary as its emotional value and material quality. She obviously loved possessing that coin; her pleasure, however, was not that of Scrooge McDuck counting his riches. As philosopher Arthur Schopenhauer claimed in 1819, pleasure was not always pleasure. An avaricious man felt no real pleasure; it was not enjoyment that drove him, but an abstract, passionate greed for money that substituted objects for 'actual', that is, sensual, delight.[40]

When Schopenhauer attributed that kind of asensual lust, or *Gier*, to senior persons apparently no longer capable of indulging in bodily pleasures, he was purposefully evoking the well-known literary trope of the old miser. Simmel, by contrast, did not limit abstract greed for money to a certain age group or gender but instead emphasized its particularity to the era of

---

[38]Olaf Blaschke, 'Antikapitalismus und Antisemitismus: Die Wirtschaftsmentalität der Katholiken im Wilhelminischen Deutschland', in *Shylock? Zinsverbot und Geldverleih in jüdischer und christlicher Tradition*, ed. Johannes Heil and Bernd Wacker (Munich: Fink, 1997), 114–46, quotes 122, 121 (Robert Waldhausen alias Georg Ratzinger) and 117 (Joseph Haegele).
[39]Georg Simmel, 'Über Geiz, Verschwendung und Armut', *Ethische Kultur* 7, no. 42 and 43 (1899): 332–5; 340–1, quotes 333–4; Simmel, *Philosophie*, ch. 3 II.
[40]Arthur Schopenhauer, *The World as Will and Representation*, trans. and ed. Judith Norman, Alistair Welchman and Christopher Janaway, vol. 2 (Cambridge: Cambridge University Press, 2018), 654.

advanced capitalism. In his account, a timeless anthropological pattern was transformed into a historically specific emotional practice, one that had become ubiquitous and characterized the mindset and behaviour of 'most men' of his time.

Varieties of greed, varieties of capitalism

Was Simmel right? Were greed and avarice for money, as he reported around 1900, the defining, constitutive and dominant features of the modern economic system? Was his statement supported by facts and figures? Or, as so many others before him, was he motivated by moral concerns, mistaking singular occurrences for general trends?

Simmel himself invited such questions by distinguishing between those types of avarice that were tied to the practical or utility value of things, and 'abstract' avarice that had no regard for things, only money. This distinction highlighted that people might engage in multiple money-related emotional practices, depending on income and social status. Those who had little to spend could not afford to hoard or save money: they had to protect and stretch their limited means, as Simmel's examples showed.

The same holds true for periods of economic downturn and depression. Twice during the first half of the twentieth century, many European societies experienced severe wartime restrictions with sharp cuts to household spending and the consumption of basic goods. Under such conditions, avarice seemed a sage approach to rationing scarce supplies. A similar observation can be made about Western societies after 1970, as they became increasingly aware that essential resources, such as energy supplies, were getting more expensive, harmed the environment or were at risk of running out altogether. Reducing private consumption and one's carbon footprint were perceived as a matter of responsible choice, rather than signs of avarice in the Kantian sense.

Greed and avarice have thus attracted a wide range of opinions which vary depending on the emotional economy in which the production, circulation and consumption of goods have been embedded. Capitalism as it has developed since the early modern period has by no means favoured a singular, uniform attitude. As Max Weber claimed in his famous reflections on the Protestant ethic, greed was not at its origin and core. To him, the common association of capitalism with greed seemed 'naïve' and 'childish'. On the contrary, the spirit of capitalism might actually restrain the 'irrational impulse' of greed or, at the very least, rationally temper it.[41]

---

[41] Max Weber, *The Protestant Ethic and the Spirit of Capitalism*, trans. Talcott Parsons (New York: Scribner's Sons, 1930), 17.

The same applied to avarice: hard work and thrift, as promoted by Calvinists, Puritans and Quakers, could well be conducive to amassing and circulating capital. Although excessive avarice prevented money from circulating and being exchanged for things that brought pleasure, a true capitalist, in Marxist terms, was hardly an ascetic non-consumer: to him, abstract love of money would be 'sheer tomfoolery'. What mattered was keeping it flowing and using it as investment capital.[42]

Although he was no Marxist, John Maynard Keynes concurred. The British economist also preferred consumption to saving as it stimulated the economy, while hoarding money hampered production and commerce.[43] Writing in 1936, Keynes had been an eyewitness to both the biggest crisis in the capitalist economy to date and the advent of consumer society as it first developed in the US. Consumer societies relied on citizens spending rather than hoarding money. They encouraged them to delight in things – to acquire goods and services not only out of need, but out of joy too. They thus emphasized capitalism's emotional pay-off, elevating pleasure as a major goal as well as a crucial driving force behind human behaviour.[44]

Such pleasure, however, was distinctly not about money, but about commodities to be consumed even if money was not immediately to hand. Were the necessary funds not readily available, they could be borrowed and paid back in instalments. There was no need to postpone the satisfaction of a desire simply because one could not afford it at that particular moment. Instant gratification became the new leitmotif of the ultra-modern consumer society, and America paved the way once again with generous loan packages and creative marketing strategies.[45]

As many European visitors confirmed, Americans had long departed from an emotional economy that condemned greed as a dangerous and socially disruptive vice. When the French aristocrat Alexis de Tocqueville toured

---

[42]Karl Marx, 'A Contribution to the Critique of Political Economy', in Marx and Engels, *Collected Works*, vol. 29 (New York: International Publishers, 1987), 279–440, here 381–3; Karl Marx, *Capital: A Critical Analysis of Capitalist Production*, vol. 1, in ibid., vol. 35 (New York: International Publishers, 1996), 593.

[43]John Maynard Keynes, *The General Theory of Employment, Interest and Money* (London: Macmillan, [1936] 1960), 108, rejected the form of saving whose sole purpose is 'to satisfy pure miserliness, i.e. unreasonable but insistent inhibitions against acts of expenditure as such'; he claimed that 'the principle of saving, pushed to excess, would destroy the motive to production' (363), in contrast to Smith, *Wealth of Nations*, 304, who regarded 'every frugal man a public benefactor'.

[44]Eva Illouz, *Cold Intimacies: The Making of Emotional Capitalism* (Cambridge: Polity Press, 2007).

[45]Frank Trentmann, ed., *The Oxford Handbook of the History of Consumption* (Oxford: Oxford University Press, 2012); Victoria De Grazia, *Irresistible Empire: America's Advance through Twentieth-Century Europe* (Cambridge, MA: Belknap, 2005); Robert Laurence Moore and Maurizio Vaudagna, eds, *The American Century in Europe* (Ithaca, NY: Cornell University Press, 2003).

the United States in the early 1830s, he was fascinated by the country's democratic spirit. Yet he was somewhat taken aback by Americans' unbridled

> love of wealth; the passion for wealth is therefore not reprobated in America, and provided it does not go beyond the bounds assigned to it for public security, it is held in honour. The American lauds as a noble and praiseworthy ambition what our own forefathers in the middle ages stigmatized as servile cupidity.[46]

A century later, democracy and greed (framed as ambition) had united in harmonious partnership, as captured by Keynes's famous quip: 'it is better that a man should tyrannize over his bank account than over his fellow-citizens'. If 'dangerous human proclivities' such as lust for dominance or violence 'can be canalised into comparatively harmless channels by the existence of opportunities for money-making and private wealth', liberal democracy had much to gain. If not, such proclivities 'may find their outlet in cruelty, the reckless pursuit of personal power and authority, and other forms of self-aggrandisement' which were hardly compatible with democratic principles.[47]

In the second half of the twentieth century, neoclassical economics redoubled their attempts to reframe greed as rational self-interest and liberate it from its 'medieval' moral shackles. The esteemed notion of the *homo oeconomicus* who relentlessly pursues the perfectly rational goal of maximizing individual gains ennobled and normalized a type of conduct that had been sharply criticized in earlier times.[48] Under the auspices of neoliberalism, and especially since the 1980s, money-making has become a highly praised activity in Western economies. Its spirit was best captured by Gordon Gekko, the hero of Oliver Stone's 1987 film *Wall Street*, in his address to a shareholders' meeting:

> The point is, ladies and gentlemen, that greed – for lack of a better word – is good. Greed is right. Greed works. Greed clarifies, cuts through, and captures the essence of the evolutionary spirit. Greed, in all of its forms – greed for life, for money, for love, knowledge – has marked the upward surge of mankind. And greed – you mark my words – will … save … the USA. Thank you very much.[49]

---

[46]Alexis de Tocqueville, *Democracy in America*, ed. Isaac Kramnick (New York: Norton & Co., [French Orig. 1835/40] 2007), 542.
[47]Keynes, *General Theory*, 374.
[48]See Chapter 8 in this volume.
[49]Sighard Neckel, 'Der Gefühlskapitalismus der Banken: Vom Ende der Gier als "ruhiger Leidenschaft"', *Leviathan* 39, no. 1 (2011): 39–53, quote 41.

This mindset was not limited to Wall Street, but quickly found acceptance on Main Street, too, and indeed, all over the world. Considerable segments of the population were captivated by the new credo of financial capitalism as more and more citizens reinvented themselves as shareholders. The near-collapse of the system in 2007/8 yielded much soul-searching and finger-pointing. Suddenly, everyone identified greed as the major culprit, above all the greed of bankers sarcastically rebranded as 'banksters'. The German media repeatedly described the situation using the terms 'greed' and 'greedy', converting self-interest into a despicable trait that led bankers to take irrational risks and jeopardize the common good.[50]

So, greed has reappeared as a cause for public concern, and a small group of key economic players bear the blame. Greed has once again been labelled a thoroughly negative passion, and even economists and business school professors have begun to examine the influence of current economics teaching on a (newly despised) 'culture of greed'.[51] One question that is still mostly unexplored concerns the socioeconomic structures that helped turn greed into an esteemed emotional practice in the first place. Equally overlooked is the fact that it was not just a small number of bankers or managers who acted with excessively acquisitive energy during the global financial crisis. When the CEO of a major bank promised shareholders a 25 per cent rate of return, those shareholders held out their hands rather than sounding the alarm.[52]

What about avarice, then, which has also been the subject of an intense public debate in many European societies over the past decades? In 2002, a major electronics chain used the slogan '*Geiz ist geil*' (being stingy is hot) to market its goods. In the Netherlands, the phrase was '*gierig maaket gelukkig*' (greed makes you happy), testifying once more to the close semantic ties between greed and avarice. A few years later, the slogan was dropped following pronounced criticism from religious and civil-society actors. German Catholics launched a counter-campaign with the slogan '*Geiz ist gottlos*' (being stingy is godless). Other critics called the slogan economically misleading, since a stingy mentality ran counter to the cherished values of fair trade and quality workmanship on which the German economy prided itself. In caring only about the lowest price, bargain-hunters disregarded quality, durability and service, and proved themselves indifferent to utility

---

[50]Frank Nullmeier, 'Vom Neid zur Gier? Über den Wandel deutscher Sozialstaatsdebatten', *Tel Aviver Jahrbuch für deutsche Geschichte* 38 (2010): 270–86, esp. 282; Maik Herold, 'Gier am Finanzmarkt? Eine Emotion und ihre Instrumentalisierung im aktuellen Krisendiskurs', in *Emotionen und Politik*, ed. Karl-Rudolf Nolte (Baden-Baden: Nomos, 2015), 249–69.

[51]Long Wang, Deepak Malhotra and J. Keith Murnighan, 'Economics Education and Greed', *Academy of Management Learning & Education* 10, no. 4 (2011): 643–60.

[52]Georg Meck, 'Ackermanns gefährliche 25 Prozent', *Frankfurter Allgemeine Zeitung*, 2 July 2013, http://www.faz.net/aktuell/finanzen/was-treiben-die-banken/was-treiben-die-banken-8-ackermanns-gefaehrliche-25-prozent-12240743.html (accessed 22 December 2022).

costs and working conditions in the countries that produced the goods. Avaricious consumers were thus asocial in their singular objective: saving money and buying cheap.[53]

Even though the chain no longer uses the slogan, others do. They are frowned upon by those better off, who increasingly turn their backs on exploitative production. Meanwhile, major fashion retailers have been named and shamed for their cost-cutting measures, as have supermarkets that sell chicken or pork at a price that no farmer can sustain under normal circumstances. But many customers choose to support businesses that openly prey upon their 'proclivity' for avarice, even though penny-pinching has long been condemned as morally questionable and reproachable. They thus conform perfectly to the ideal of economic man and woman: self-interested and indifferent to anything other than immediate monetary gains.

Contemporary societies are nevertheless typically characterized by contradictory trends. Wealthy businesspeople, particularly in the US, donate fortunes to charity, debunking the popular stereotype of the money-addicted rich. Less well-off people likewise open their wallets and generously give money in response to humanitarian crises. In the face of growing concern about natural resources being or becoming scarce, calls for more economical – that is, resource-friendly – practices abound. Saving water and energy, repairing rather than throwing away, sharing belongings and accepting social responsibility as consumers for how goods are produced have become hallmarks of a strong and strengthening movement in Western societies in recent years. Such practices are not only meant to eradicate greedy and avaricious feelings regarding money, they also aim to build a new moral and emotional economy that places global justice and responsibility – both socially and ecologically defined – at its core.[54]

If and to what extent such an economy can be compatible with global capitalism remains to be seen. In its long history, capitalism has developed many historical and regional variations, accompanied by different emotional practices. Against this background, new forms and combinations seem possible – especially when they are incentivized by market forces that react to and mirror emerging consumer sensibilities and feelings about money.

---

[53] Anselm Waldermann, 'Geiz war geil', *Spiegel*, 29 May 2007, http://www.spiegel.de/wirtschaft/werbeslogans-geiz-war-geil-a-485489.html; Thomas Tjiang, 'Ist Geiz noch geil?', http://www.ihk-nuernberg.de/de/IHK-Magazin-WiM/WiM-Archiv/WIM-Daten/2005-05/Berichte-und-Analysen/Ist-Geiz-noch-geil-.jsp (both accessed 22 December 2022).
[54] Frevert, *Kapitalismus*; Ute Frevert, 'Moral Economies, Present and Past: Social Practices and Intellectual Controversies', in *Moral Economies*, ed. Ute Frevert (Göttingen: Vandenhoeck & Ruprecht, 2019), 13–43.

CHAPTER TEN

Hans in Luck, or the Emotional Economy of Happiness in the Modern Age

Happiness is neither a modern emotional concept nor is it fundamentally or essentially linked to capitalism. Since ancient times, the quest for happiness, along with the knowledge that it is difficult to achieve and maintain, has exercised countless people. Classical poets and philosophers pondered it, as did authors in the Middle Ages and the Renaissance, who wrote about the precarious combination of felicity and chance, luck or fortune shared by most Indo-European languages, and concluded that a person is unable to be the master of his or her own happiness. Accordingly, they stressed the importance of morality, virtue and/or ritual practices so that the gods, or God, would look mercifully upon humans and generously grant them what they desired most: the state and feeling of happiness.[1]

Modernity put an end to man's dependence on God's unfathomable will. Since the eighteenth century, happiness has been treated both as a secular promise and as a moral–political right owed to all people, regardless of age, gender, class, religion or nationality. For proponents of the Enlightenment, man was his own creator and society his enabler. Modern revolutions heralded an age of happiness for everyone, and proclaimed an end to misery as old structures of power were overthrown. The new citizens forged through

---

This chapter is a thoroughly revised version of the article published under a similar title in *History of European Ideas* 45, no. 3 (2019): 363–76, doi:10.1080/01916599.2018.1534448.
[1]Martha C. Nussbaum, *The Fragility of Goodness: Luck and Ethics in Greek Tragedy and Philosophy* (Cambridge: Cambridge University Press, 1986); Darrin M. McMahon, *Happiness: A History* (New York: Grove Press, 2006), 19–139.

the events of 1776, 1789, 1848 or 1917 would enjoy utmost happiness in societies built anew by the revolutionaries. Happiness for each and every citizen was the battle cry for political change.

At the same time, capitalist industrialization pledged to make people's lives easier and more comfortable, and thus to increase their happiness. The development of consumer societies during the twentieth century ushered in new normative ideas and expectations. Having and owning 'things' was marketed as the path to personal happiness, as the slogan 'Shop yourself happy' promised. By buying 'happy' perfumes and other goods with similar names, consumer–citizens could supposedly procure a sense of contentment, elation and delight.

This chapter traces the history of happiness as it unfolded during the modern age, focusing mainly on European and North American countries, where the trends and developments were most pronounced and, through capitalist expansion, impacted on other regions as well. But the West also produced counter-trends and critiques that have left their mark on how happiness has been conceptualized, imagined and framed. Some were inspired by decidedly non-Western sources, like the small Himalayan kingdom of Bhutan. Others had their roots in the Continent, as in the case of the popular fairy tale *Hans in Luck*.

Lessons from Bhutan, behavioural economics and beyond

When the new ruler of Bhutan announced in 1972 that he planned to focus on 'gross national happiness' (GNH) rather than on 'gross domestic product' (GDP), few cared. As one of the poorest countries in the world, Bhutan did not figure on the global map. At most, the royal missive was seen as a tactic to divert attention from Bhutan's economic shortcomings. Thirty years later, things had changed dramatically. In 2004, the king invited international scholars to learn from Bhutan's experience and discuss various ways to improve national happiness. A year later, a follow-up conference took place in Canada, with 400 philosophers, economists and social scientists in attendance. More reunions were to come, and met with growing interest among academics, politicians, NGO activists and the media alike.[2] In 2005, the *New York Times* reported on the Canadian event, concluding that 'Bhutan's example is serving as a catalyst for far broader discussions of national well-being'.[3]

---

[2] For the conference proceedings, see https://www.bhutanstudies.org.bt/category/conference-proceedings/page/3/ (accessed 20 February 2023).
[3] Andrew C. Revlin, 'A New Measure of Well-Being: From a Happy Little Kingdom', *New York Times*, 4 October 2005, available online: https://www.nytimes.com/2005/10/04/science/a-new-measure-of-wellbeingfrom-a-happy-little-kingdom.html (accessed 22 December 2022).

What Bhutan had actually done, beyond coining a new term, was to change how well-being and development were examined, elaborated and measured. Instead of focusing exclusively on levels of income and investment, GNH deliberately included other variables as well. As defined by the country's 2008 constitution, these were: good governance, sustainable socioeconomic development, the preservation and promotion of Buddhist culture and environmental conservation.[4]

This broader concept of happiness has travelled the globe. Since 2012, the United Nations has regularly published 'World Happiness Reports', based on national citizens' feedback about their levels of subjective well-being. Such testimonies are then augmented by objective data on material wealth, personal security and social solidarity. Northern European countries like Norway, Denmark, Iceland, Finland and Sweden usually rank highest, followed by Australia, New Zealand and Canada. In 2016, the Organisation for Economic Cooperation and Development (OECD) decided 'to redefine the growth narrative to put people's well-being at the center of governments' efforts'.[5]

Even the OECD, whose member states boast high GDPs, has come to acknowledge that economic growth is not necessarily synonymous with happiness and well-being. The older assumption that well-being and contentment increase in tandem with available income has been reassessed by behavioural economists who have provided ample empirical data that complicate the correlation.[6] They have also drawn attention to what LSE professor Paul Dolan has called 'purpose'. In Dolan's view, what people experience and report as happiness is greatly influenced by whether they think that they have done something meaningful.[7] This supports what the president of the Center for Bhutan Studies and GNH Research, Dasho Karma Ura, said about the nature of happiness: 'People feel happy when they see something ethical' or 'have done something right and brave and courageous' that has reinstated them as a 'meaningful actor'.[8]

This is by no means a new insight. As early as 1838, John Stuart Mill took offence at what he thought of as reductionist views on human nature and

---

[4]Kai Schultz, 'In Bhutan, Happiness Index as Gauge for Social Ills', *New York Times*, 17 January 2017, available online: https://www.nytimes.com/2017/01/17/world/asia/bhutan-gross-national-happiness-indicator-.html; https://www.theguardian.com/world/2012/dec/01/bhutan-wealth-happiness-counts (both accessed 22 December 2022).
[5]http://worldhappiness.report/ed/2017/ (accessed 22 December 2022).
[6]Bruno S. Frey and Alois Stutzer, *Happiness and Economics: How the Economy and Institutions Affect Well-Being* (Princeton: Princeton University Press, 2002); Bruno S. Frey, *Happiness: A Revolution in Economics* (Cambridge, MA: MIT Press, 2008). See also Robert Skidelsky and Edward Skidelsky, *How Much Is Enough? Money and the Good Life* (New York: Other Press, 2012), esp. ch. 4.
[7]Paul Dolan, *Happiness by Design: Change What You Do, Not How You Think* (New York: Hudson Street Press, 2014).
[8]Schultz, 'In Bhutan'.

desire. Mill's teacher, Jeremy Bentham, had famously considered the 'greatest happiness of the greatest number' as the goal of politics and the yardstick of social progress.[9] Yet he had, according to Mill, falsely painted 'man' as being exclusively interested in material comforts. Bentham's disciple, in contrast, held 'man' to be a 'most complex being', driven by far more factors than personal utility. Above all, he was actuated by emotional ideals, 'the sense of *honour*, and personal dignity' among them, as well as 'the love of beauty', order, power and moral action.[10] Human behaviour, Mill concluded, was not necessarily dictated by egoism or self-love.

Instead, motives of altruism, compassion, fairness and civility ranked highly, as German philosopher Arthur Schopenhauer affirmed in 1840. How else could one explain the numerous contemporary movements and associations that tirelessly campaigned for the abolition of slavery or fought against the violence inflicted upon children, animals or prisoners? In those cases, morality had a 'direct and immediate influence' upon happiness.[11] Acting on behalf of the less fortunate obviously induced a feeling of contentment and serenity. Purposeful moral action gave people pleasure, even if the action itself was far from pleasurable.

Happiness in this instance retained the moral dimension and religious connotation that it had possessed in the pre-Enlightenment era. Closely tied to notions of virtue and decency, happiness was not to be achieved without a strong commitment to being a good person who lived in harmony with moral and civic laws. Yet even harmony would not guarantee happiness. As Immanuel Kant famously stated in 1784, human beings were not made to live the life of Arcadian shepherds. Although man 'wishes to live comfortably and pleasantly', his 'unsocial sociability' compelled him to turn 'sloth and passive contentment into labour and trouble' and thus develop his capacities. In Kant's view, individual lives and human history were governed by the natural forces of opposition and discord. Happiness was therefore a question of hope, not part of nature's plan. At best, men could and should strive to render themselves 'worthy of happiness' by obeying the categorical imperative.[12]

The French liberal thinker Benjamin Constant argued along similar lines, explicitly disavowing happiness as the only and ultimate ambition of

---

[9] J.H. Burns, 'Happiness and Utility: Jeremy Bentham's Equation', *Utilitas* 17, no. 1 (2005): 46–61.

[10] John Stuart Mill, 'Bentham', *The London and Westminster Review* (August 1838): 467–506, quotes 486, 490.

[11] Arthur Schopenhauer, *On the Basis of Morality*, trans. Arthur Brodrick Bullock (London: Swan Sonnenschein, 1903), 277, 279, *passim*; Arthur Schopenhauer, *The Wisdom of Life and Other Essays*, trans. Bailey Saunders and Ernest Belfort Bax (Washington: Dunne, 1901), 35.

[12] Immanuel Kant, 'Idea of a Universal History on a Cosmo-Political Plan', *The London Magazine* 10 (July–December 1824): 385–93, here 387 (Proposition the Fourth); Immanuel Kant, *Critique of Pure Reason*, trans. Werner S. Pluhar (Indianapolis: Hackett, 1996), 736–7.

mankind. Echoing Kant, he referred to 'the better part of our nature, that noble disquiet which pursues and torments us, that desire to broaden our knowledge and develop our faculties. It is not happiness alone, it is to self-development that our destiny calls us'.[13] Consequently, neither Constant nor Kant accepted happiness as a moral benchmark. Not everyone could agree on what happiness actually meant; one person's happiness might be another's misery. Taking the idea of individual autonomy seriously meant rejecting happiness, logically and empirically, as the common object of people's goals and actions. Under no circumstances, then, could it ever serve as the foundation of universal morality or as a guideline for politics.[14]

Reviewing the various reflections on happiness, three caveats come to mind. First, they emanated from a small number of intellectuals, predominantly philosophers. Alongside the names already mentioned, many more joined the debate, lending it further nuance and diversity.[15] Second, all these authors who wrote about happiness were intellectual elites who loved to engage each other in ongoing intertextual dialogue. The extent to which their arguments ever left the closed circuit of learned discourse is unclear. Even if some managed to build a reputation beyond academia and shaped educational programmes and political agendas, as Kant did, they can hardly be considered representative of everyone's feelings about what happiness was and why it mattered.

This does not mean that there was no relation at all between low and high, popular and elite. The more a certain notion of happiness was reiterated – in the family, in school, at church – the more likely it was that ordinary people would adopt and integrate it into their own mindset and worldview in some way. People are not born with fixed moral norms and emotions, though from an early age they are taught to take them for granted. To write a history of happiness therefore entails digging deeper into educational and religious practices and reconstructing, with the help of media like prayer books, fables, family journals, advice manuals, popular songs, political

---

[13]Benjamin Constant, 'The Liberty of the Ancients Compared with That of the Moderns (1819)', in Benjamin Constant, *Political Writings*, ed. Biancamaria Fontana (Cambridge: Cambridge University Press, 1988), 327.

[14]Wolfgang Freising, *Kritische Philosophie und Glückseligkeit: Kants Auseinandersetzung mit dem Eudämonismus seiner Zeit* (Lüneburg: Schmidt-Neubauer, 1983); Cornel Zwierlein, 'Das Glück des Bürgers: Der aufklärerische Eudämonismus als Formationselement von Bürgerlichkeit und seine Charakteristika', in *Bürgerlichkeit im 18. Jahrhundert*, ed. Hans-Edwin Friedrich, Fotis Jannidis and Marianne Willems (Tübingen: Niemeyer, 2006), 71–113, esp. 106 ff.

[15]For a wider, although far from complete, panorama of authors, see McMahon, *Happiness*. Peter N. Stearns, *Happiness in World History* (New York: Routledge, 2021), promises a global account from the agricultural age to contemporary times, from the US to parts of Africa and China. See also Mark Seymour, 'Global Happiness: From Providential Moments to Hedonic Treadmills?', in *The Routledge History of Emotions in the Modern World*, ed. Katie Barclay and Peter N. Stearns (London: Routledge, 2022), 29–45.

anthems and party manifestos, people's expectations of what happiness was and how it felt.

Third, such an endeavour has to be attentive to differences in social class, age and gender, as well as to cultural and linguistic variations. How happiness is defined, in a broader or narrower sense, as a thin or a thick concept, has consequences for how people use the term and in what contexts. In today's English-speaking world, happiness is generally understood as a thin concept, as in 'I am happy to be here' or 'I am happy to draft this chapter'. In German, *glücklich (sein)* carries a far stronger meaning. It comes with moral baggage and a kind of exuberance that defies generalization and routinization. Furthermore, the German language does not distinguish between *Glück (haben)* as fortune or luck, and *Glück* as a happy state of being. Until the eighteenth century, people chose to differentiate between *Glück* and *Glückseligkeit*. *Glück (fortuna)*, which shares its linguistic roots with the Lower Saxon and English *luck*, the Swedish *Lycka* and the Danish *Lykke*, referred to incidents that could be neither predicted nor controlled by man. *Glückseligkeit (felicitas)*, in contrast, was perceived as a state of lasting joy.[16] When *Glückseligkeit* fell into disuse during the nineteenth century, it burdened *Glück* with an ambiguity that other languages managed to avoid.

What also disappeared was the eighteenth-century attempt to link *Glück* as *fortuna* to moral values and higher principles. In 1788, a major encyclopaedia emphasized that luck was not completely accidental. Instead, it lay in the hands of a superior power and was granted by God's special providence. Since man was not in a position to influence such providence, his only option was to pray, work hard and put his complete trust in God.[17] Within such an emotional economy, God might benevolently and generously return the favour, grant man *Glück* and even allow him to experience true happiness or *Glückseligkeit*.

Hans in Luck: different readings

In some ways, this emotional economy can be glimpsed in the fairy tale *Hans im Glück (Hans in Luck)*, published by the Grimm brothers in the early nineteenth century. Still to this day, the tale has held a spot in people's collective memory, forged through bedside readings and the Grimm stories' enduring popularity, despite the ever-growing corpus of modern children's literature. Translated into numerous languages, the tales continue to find

---

[16]Johann Georg Krünitz, *Oeconomische Encyklopädie*, vol. 19 (Berlin: Pauli, 1788), 205–10, 222–32.
[17]Ibid., 208–9.

ardent fans and followers, although (or because) their connection to the realities of modern life seems less and less evident.[18]

At first glance, this pertains too to *Hans in Luck*, which can be read as a late document of a traditional society on the verge of disappearing. It was a society organized according to temporal cycles and largely structured by non-monetary economic exchange. The bartering of goods and services followed principles of individual utility that, in certain cases, diverged greatly from 'objective' material worth. So it is with Hans, a young man who has served seven years as the apprentice and helping hand of a master in an unknown trade. He has the choice to stay on, since his master is satisfied with his work and conduct. But Hans longs to go home and be with his mother, whom he has not seen for a long time. When he leaves the job, his master pays him a huge sum of gold, enough to make his fortune. Tiring on his journey, however, Hans soon exchanges the gold for a horse. He then becomes dissatisfied with the horse and trades it for a cow. Thus it continues until Hans is left with nothing but a 'light and merry heart'.

Hans feels happy and indeed expresses it vividly: "'How happy am I!' cried he: "no mortal was ever so lucky as I am."'" His various desires have all been satisfied, and, although what he desired possessed less material value each time, every single wish was fulfilled and brought him pleasure. Though the pleasure did not last, Hans is convinced that he has made profitable trades and got the best from them.[19]

In the tale's 1823 English translation, happy Hans was turned into lucky Hans, or *Hans in Luck*, which might be interpreted as a deliberate critique and revision of the original. The translator obviously did not believe that Hans was happy, but chose to present his adventures as a series of lucky incidents, in the sense of *fortuna*. This was not altogether a misrepresentation of the tale. Hans indeed considers himself lucky to have met all those seemingly generous men who talked him into trading valuable for less valuable goods and thus contributed to his growing happiness. Our hero is indeed driven by the search for happiness and '*Seelenfreude*', joy of mind, as the Grimm brothers put it. While coincidence and luck do play a role in his encountering the owners of the horse, the cow, the pig, the goose and the grindstone, he feels utterly happy about these exchanges; each greatly enhances his subjective well-being which reaches its peak after he accidentally drops his last possession into a deep river.

His actions were clearly at odds with conventional opinion around 1800. Even in a pre-capitalist economy, in which most people achieved little more than basic subsistence, Hans's choices would have irked some. One could, of

---

[18]Hans-Jörg Uther, 'Hans im Glück (KHM 83): Zur Entstehung, Verbreitung und bildlichen Darstellung eines populären Märchens', in *The Telling of Stories: Approaches to a Traditional Craft*, ed. Morten Nøjgaard et al. (Odense: Odense University Press, 1990), 119–64.

[19]*German Popular Stories*, trans. from *Kinder und Haus-Märchen*, collected by M.M. Grimm (London: Baldwyn, 1823), 1–9, quote 9. *Hans in Luck* was the first story printed in that volume.

course, choose poverty over riches, as Franciscan monks did. One could also give money to the poor, following both religious and secular norms of charity. But it was hardly possible to find any virtue or positive morality in Hans's transactions. They served the greed of those who tricked him, and were founded on fraud and delusion. Furthermore, they left him where he had started seven years earlier: without the means to support himself or his ageing mother, and without any savings to establish a household and family of his own.

Such judgements, however, fail to take into account what the tale is about: happiness, rather than luck. For Hans, happiness extends beyond economic concerns and is not based on abstract material value. Instead, it reflects the pleasure he receives from actual consumption: riding a horse instead of going by foot, enjoying milk and cheese from a cow, bacon and ham from a pig. In the long run, these purchases leave him empty-handed but in the short run, they make him happy, and that is what he desires most. In this regard, Hans both embodies and opposes the credo of the modern world. He is never content with what he possesses; he always wants to increase his happiness, thus acting in accordance with Thomas Hobbes's definition of felicity as the 'continuall successe in obtaining those things which a man from time to time desireth, that is to say, continuall prospering'.[20] And yet, Hans's prospering unfolds only in his imagination and in his own emotional experience, since each successive purchase holds less and less material value.

Hans is plainly not quite a citizen of the modern world in pursuit of the capitalist ideal of accumulating greater riches with every investment. The goods that he desires are selected according not to their exchange value but to their subjective utility, which Hans defines on the spot, without any laboured reflection or calculation. Yet his decisions to sell and buy are not wholly spontaneous and hedonistic; they do serve an ultimate goal, which goes beyond self-interest: what matters most to Hans is that he reaches home as quickly as possible to embrace his mother, something which will make both happy.

Hans's behaviour seems more in keeping with a pre-modern, pre-capitalist order that knew and cared little about individual advancement or social mobility. Its emotional economy was organized in a circular and reciprocal way that recognized different kinds of utilities and left room for moral commitments to God and kin. In such an economy, material possessions were not all that mattered. Indeed, their value might diminish quickly, depending on unforeseen and unforeseeable circumstances. Considering the contingencies of the situation, it could even be rational to forgo riches altogether and to instead prioritize what was of real value: personal relations, and a son's obligation to take care of his mother. Material wealth might

---

[20] *Hobbes's Leviathan*. Reprint of the edition from 1651, with an essay by the late W.G. Pogson Smith (Oxford: Clarendon, 1962), 48.

help, but it could not be relied upon. Even without his gold or grindstone, Hans, a healthy young man, was essentially capable of making his fortune anew, while showering his mother with filial love and comfort. Planning for the future might be futile anyway, since the future was not something that could be calculated or commanded. It appeared far more sensible to insist on present-day happiness and to try to sustain it by maintaining one's sense of optimism and trust in God. Hans was free to choose optimism over pessimism, hope over fear, trust over distrust. He used his freedom to achieve happiness.

How did children and adults interpret the fairy tale? Did they take Hans for a simpleton whose actions should be ridiculed and dismissed? Or did they envy him because, after seven years of strenuous work and dependence, he indulged his temporary freedom to take his life into his own hands and to decide for himself what made him happy? Did they see Hans as a radical dropout, an 'anti-hero' and 'archetypical fool'?[21] How did they think his mother reacted when her son returned, happy-hearted but empty-handed? Did Hans strike them as the antipode of modern possessive individualism and an inhabitant of an older and vanishing world, organized by altogether different emotional economies?

Unfortunately, next to nothing is known about how the tale was received. Even its origins are murky. It was first published in a journal in 1818 by the young classicist August Eduard Wernicke, who pretended that it came 'out of the mouth of the people'. If this was really the case is unclear. Wernicke framed the story as a moral lesson, placing great emphasis on the connection between Hans's lack of calculation and his ensuing poverty. When Wilhelm Grimm later included it in his collection of fairy tales, he did not fully endorse such criticism. He painted Hans in lighter colours, as an amiable fellow who, without harming anyone, somewhat naively and spontaneously chose to follow his own desires. This version of *Hans in Luck* came to rank among the dozen most popular tales and was reprinted over and over again, both as part of the Grimms' collection and on its own. It was also published with various illustrations, the first by George Cruikshank in 1823. In these illustrations, Hans was usually depicted as a happy figure whose body language and gestures demonstrated the joy he felt at bartering his riches.[22]

Such visual representations invite an analysis of Hans's search for *Seelenfreude* as an early comment on the modern history of happiness – one

---

[21] Maria Tatar, *The Hard Facts of the Grimms' Fairy Tales* (Princeton: Princeton University Press, 1987), 100–1. As to the Grimms' overall reception, see *The Reception of Grimms' Fairy Tales: Responses, Reactions, Revisions*, ed. Donald Haase (Detroit: Wayne State University Press, 1993).

[22] Uther, Hans im Glück, 126 ff.; Marion Schmaus, 'Von "Hans im Glück" und anderen Glückssuchern. Erzähllogik und Hermeneutik in den Märchen der Brüder Grimm', literaturkritik.de 12 (2012): 1–13.

that both reflects and relativizes conventional values and lifestyles. It can be perceived partly as an affirmation of middle-class mores and practices, but also as a subversive criticism.

Who is responsible for happiness?

For contemporaries, Hans's obsession with happiness would not have come as a surprise. Happiness was in the air; a huge number of books, articles, songs and plays in the eighteenth century focused on exactly this theme. In German-speaking countries, the quest for *Glückseligkeit* reached its peak between 1780 and 1810, with lectures on morality, sermons, comedies and advice manuals suggesting the best and proven ways of being happy. Even catechisms for children changed their traditional structure. Instead of starting with a list of commands and prohibitions, they addressed their young readers' feelings and experiences of felicity.[23]

In France, Voltaire and Diderot declared that being happy was the primary need and sole duty of humans. The American Declaration of Independence proclaimed people's inalienable right not only to life and liberty but also to the 'pursuit of Happiness'. This was very much in line with the general trend of emphasizing the individual person and his (rather than her) quest for subjective and objective well-being. In the eyes of the Founding Fathers it was clearly not sufficient to promise and grant people personal safety and the freedom to acquire, possess and use property. They should also be able to pursue happiness, whatever that meant for them. Nobody could ever ensure, of course, that they would achieve it. What mattered was that the road to happiness was open for anyone to take, as it was for Hans. All formal obstacles had to be removed. Critically, this meant that the state should refrain from interfering in people's lives.[24]

Both French philosophers and the American Founding Fathers firmly located happiness at the level of the individual man and citizen. He alone was the one who could decide which kind of happiness to choose, and there was no suggestion that the decisions had to be morally framed or restricted. A person should seek happiness for his own sake, independent of social institutions. What mattered most was his subjective feelings, his own state of mind and *Seelenfreude*. Such a radical individualization of happiness was not only consistent with the Enlightenment emphasis on man's ability to think and reason for himself, without being brainwashed by religion,

---

[23]Zwierlein, 'Glück des Bürgers', esp. 99, 105.
[24]Howard Mumford Jones, *The Pursuit of Happiness* (Ithaca, NY: Cornell University Press, 1953); Jeffrey Barnouw, 'The Pursuit of Happiness in Jefferson and Its Background in Bacon and Hobbes', *Interpretation* 11 (1983): 225–48; McMahon, *Happiness*, ch. 6.

superstition or politics; it also went hand in hand with the new interest in, and appreciation for, feelings and sensibility.

The pursuit of happiness came with two political options. For proponents of enlightened absolutist rule like Christian Wolff, a professor at Halle University in the early eighteenth century, it was the task of the state to actively create the conditions that would enable its subjects to become and remain happy.[25] Government should thus conform to the model of a well-ordered police state that aimed to secure its subjects' safety and welfare through, among other things, health policies, insurance schemes and a great many legal regulations and formal prescriptions.[26] Such regulations introduced normative ideas of how people should run their lives and think (and feel) about their future happiness. These clearly clashed with the emphasis on individual autonomy that was on the rise during the late eighteenth century.

By 1800, such paternalistic state intervention was increasingly unwelcome. There was mounting pressure on the government to restrict itself to just a few crucial functions: ensuring the rule of law, guaranteeing the security of individual property and monopolizing violence, both internally and in the protection of the state's external borders. *Glückseligkeit*, so the argument went, could not and should not figure as a legitimate state concern, though the state ought to ensure that people were not prevented from seeking it, in whatever form.[27] Liberal concepts came close to what American revolutionaries had envisaged in the 1770s. Both shared the idea of happiness as a dynamic object to strive for that defied any binding definition. What mattered was the pursuit of a goal that each person identified for themselves, in freedom and with autonomy. A generally accepted definition of happiness of religious or political provenance was thus off the table – happiness meant whatever each individual understood it to mean. It came neither, as Kant emphasized, in the form of divine pardon nor as the gift of a well-run state administration. It came from within and was felt by people who strove for self-improvement and self-perfection.[28]

---

[25]Christoph Link, 'Die Staatstheorie Christian Wolffs', in *Christian Wolff (1679–1754): Interpretationen zu seiner Philosophie und deren Wirkung*, ed. Werner Schneiders, 2nd edn (Hamburg: Meiner, 1986), 171–92; Clemens Schwaiger, *Das Problem des Glücks im Denken Christian Wolffs. Eine quellen-, begriffs- und entwicklungsgeschichtliche Studie zu Schlüsselbegriffen seiner Ethik* (Stuttgart: Frommann-Holzboog, 1995).
[26]Marc Raeff, *The Well-Ordered Police State: Social and Institutional Change through Law in the Germanies and Russia, 1600–1800* (New Haven: Yale University Press, 1983); Andre Wakefield, *The Disordered Police State: German Cameralism as Science and Practice* (Chicago: University of Chicago Press, 2009); *The Production of Human Security in Premodern and Contemporary History*, ed. Cornel Zwierlein, Rüdiger Graf and Magnus Ressel (= *Historical Social Research* 35, no. 4 (2010), Special Issue no. 134).
[27]Cornel Zwierlein, 'Glück und Sicherheit in der Politik der Aufklärung und in der Gegenwart', in *Glück*, ed. André Holenstein et al. (Berne: Haupt, 2011), 53–81, esp. 61–2.
[28]Freising, *Kritische Philosophie*; Zwierlein, Glück des Bürgers, 106 ff.

Such happiness was never easy to reach even if, in principle, it could be achieved by everybody, regardless of wealth, rank, gender or age. In order to pursue and, hopefully, obtain it, many active steps were required. Those steps linked happiness to work, competition and contest – what Kant in 1784 referred to as 'antagonism'. In his view, true happiness was out of the question for Arcadian shepherds. Their supposedly blissful state of harmony amounted to nothing but boredom, stagnation and waste of talent. Ambitiously striving for happiness, overcoming obstacles and convincing others to contribute to one's own happiness was what made the human species – and history – advance.

In Kant's reflections on universal history, one might detect some semblance of the story of Adam and Eve and their expulsion from paradise. The final judgements, however, were fundamentally different. In contrast to the Old Testament, Kant viewed the disappearance of Arcadia in a positive light. Additionally, his interpretation lacked any reference to sin and transgression. There was no desire to return and reconcile. On the contrary, only antagonism and its inherent dynamics enabled cultural progress and moral development. This was an altogether different type of happiness from the one experienced in paradise. Instead of idleness and the absence of effort, post-Arcadian happiness involved constant work and hardship – the very things from which Hans tried to escape, at least temporarily, after seven years of toil.

Kant's teachings became enormously influential during the nineteenth century, especially in Germany. His ethics of duty and virtue, which placed happiness in a subordinate position and radically severed its connection to effortless luck, were enshrined in school curricula and academic syllabi. Otto von Bismarck's 1851 lament (in a melancholic letter to his wife), 'We are not in this world in order to be happy and to enjoy ourselves but to fulfil our duty', was quoted extensively and immortalized as a motto in innumerable friendship and autograph books.[29] The emphasis on duty rather than happiness found many eloquent proponents who turned it into a moral principle, a symbol of national superiority and a goal of higher education. In 1794, renowned philosopher Johann Gottlieb Fichte wrote that happiness could not be disconnected from the 'moral nature of man': 'Not, *That which produces happiness is good*; – but, *That only which is good produces happiness*. Without morality, happiness is impossible.'[30] In a similar vein, Friedrich Wilhelm Foerster, a best-selling author and pedagogue in the early twentieth century, fought against the 'madness of believing that we are here in this world to find happiness'. A nobler conception of life, as he

---

[29] *Fürst Bismarcks Briefe an seine Braut und Gattin*, ed. Herbert Bismarck, 4th edn (Stuttgart: Cotta, 1914), 264–7, quote 264. See Ute Frevert, 'Vom Glück der Pflicht', in Frevert, *Gefühle in der Geschichte* (Göttingen: Vandenhoeck & Ruprecht, 2021), 71–90.
[30] Johann Gottlieb Fichte, *The Vocation of the Scholar*, trans. William Smith (London: Chapman, 1847), 23 (original emphasis).

saw it, required 'not happiness, but purification and perfection'. Enjoyment and pleasure – which Hans cherished dearly – did not play a major role.[31]

Happiness through work: the bourgeois gospel

It would be misleading to trace all those statements back to Kant exclusively. They also found support in the Protestant work ethic as it had developed since the Reformation and which marked many aspects of people's inner as well as outer lives. The ethic suited the developing capitalist economic system and anti-aristocratic mindset of the middle classes, serving to buttress the latter's claim to political emancipation and participation in government. Aristocrats were generally criticized for wasting their time and talent on upper-class passions and distractions in lieu of pursuing serious careers. The bourgeoisie, in contrast, prided itself on unceasing work and productive economic activity. As industrial entrepreneurs, they not only filled their own pockets and provided for their families, but offered employment and resources to others, too. As doctors, lawyers, engineers, teachers, scholars and scientists, they served mankind and advanced the domains of knowledge, health and technology. For them, unlike members of the aristocracy, joy and happiness could be derived from their own efforts and achievements, as well as how these benefited others.

The gap between the aristocracy and the bourgeoisie, between pleasure and work, was particularly stark in countries like France and Germany with strong and lasting traditions of absolutist rule that favoured and privileged nobility. It was less pronounced in Britain, whose upper social stratum was far more mixed. Instead of closing ranks against the rising middle classes, the aristocracy there represented itself as a relatively 'open elite'. Consequently, social mores and lifestyles tended to converge rather than remain segregated.[32] Pleasure and enjoyment became acceptable pursuits despite their aristocratic connotations, and quickly entered middle-class households. This was reflected in writings on happiness by political philosophers as they adopted a more democratic and less moralizing tone.

The Continental bourgeoisie also did not shy away from savouring various forms of entertainment. Indeed, the middle classes were inventive in creating ambitious cultural spaces, from coffee houses to restaurants, art clubs, museums, theatres and concert halls. Music in particular was thought to fill its listeners with utmost joy and elation, whether chamber music or symphonies, opera or romantic songs. In order to truly enjoy music, however,

---

[31]Friedrich Wilhelm Foerster, *Lebensführung* (Berlin: Reimer, 1917), 11.
[32]Eric Hobsbawm, 'The Example of the English Middle Class', in *Bourgeois Society in Nineteenth-Century Europe*, ed. Jürgen Kocka and Allan Mitchell (Oxford: Berg, 1993), 127–50.

one had to first learn and recognize its theory and structure. The same was true for the visual arts, theatre and literature. Even dining was a serious art, not light entertainment (which was as taboo as light happiness). Culture and the pleasure that it brought had to be earned and practised; it demanded individual effort and sustained long-term investment.

Not even the family was what it promised to be: a sphere of mutual joy, private ease and happiness. Admittedly, the saying 'Home Sweet Home – happiness alone' graced sofa cushions in countless middle-class households. It can be traced back to Friedrich Schiller and his much-revered 1799 'Song of the Bell'. According to the poet, happiness would not be found in a 'hostile life' in which man was surrounded by enemies and competitors. Instead, it reigned supreme in 'matters of family' that were governed by 'the housewife so modest, the mother of children'.[33] At home, the father and husband was supposed to relax and revel in true love and tenderness. In this function, family represented both the counterpart to and the civilizational core of civil society. It offered men the promise of happiness in a safe haven, protected from the turmoil of the market, work and politics. For women, family provided a space in which they could live up to their 'natural essence and determination', which was to make others happy.

Yet family ideals and practices had a laborious underbelly. For women, family was a sphere of hard work, care and concern. Making a husband and children happy called for multiple skills and perpetual efforts that took a toll on women's health and vitality (not least the significant risk of dying in childbirth). Nevertheless, those efforts had to be hidden behind a veil of positive emotions and uplifting spirits. Women's work for their families was not regarded as such; instead, it was supposed to be a token of love.

Men were thus driven to think about the home as a happy, work-free space. Still, this did not necessarily mean that it was the only space for them to experience happiness. Contrary to Schiller's negative depiction of life outside the family, many middle-class men obviously enjoyed their professional and public lives in 'hostile' environments. First-person accounts such as diaries, letters and autobiographies reveal how much pleasure and comfort men actually drew from their work, and from the social interaction and status it involved.

Under certain circumstances, then, work felt like and created happiness. Under other circumstances and for other people, it did not. Modern industry as it came to characterize and dominate the capitalist mode of production made it increasingly difficult to conceive of work as a source of individual happiness. The early twentieth-century assembly line, based

---

[33] Marianna Wertz, 'Friedrich Schiller's "The Song of the Bell"', *Fidelio* 10, no. 1–2 (2005): 36–45, quotes 42. On nineteenth-century family ideals and practices, see Ute Frevert, *Women in German History: From Bourgeois Emancipation to Sexual Liberation* (Oxford: Berg, 1989), 61–147; Leonore Davidoff and Catherine Hall, *Family Fortunes: Men and Women of the English Middle Class 1780–1850* (London: Hutchinson, 1987).

on the division of labour, became its most conspicuous symbol. Work processes were increasingly fragmented; creative work, such as that of Schiller's bell founders, was in short supply, and so was the happiness that stemmed from it.

Since the early days of the Industrial Revolution, this development attracted fierce criticism. Some observers condemned what they called alienation, the growing distance between a producer and his product. In his 1845 book *The Conditions of the Working-Class in England*, the young German entrepreneur and socialist Friedrich Engels famously contrasted the moral and physical deprivation that he detected among industrial workers with the happy, comfortable and quasi-idyllic life those people had apparently led in rural villages before taking up factory employment in Manchester.[34] In his later life, Engels acknowledged that the division of labour would not disappear from the modern world, and thus other remedies to heal or make up for the deficiencies inherent in dissociated and mechanized work processes would be necessary.

Around 1900, industrial psychologists began to turn their attention to the problems of monotony and fatigue. Side by side with entrepreneurs, they launched the 'struggle for joy in work' and advocated compensatory measures like sports, social outings, competitions and more respectful communication between workers and bosses. For trade unionists, such endeavours were futile and barely scratched the surface of workers' miserable lot. They campaigned instead for higher wages and shorter working hours.[35] The lower classes could obtain happiness, if at all, away from work. Consequently, the labour movement's political lexicon did not include any terms related to enjoyment whatsoever and focused instead on activity, pursuit, gains and, above all, struggle. Socialists did not fight for happiness but for freedom, equality and justice.

Tellingly, in 1865, Karl Marx's answer to the question 'what is your idea of happiness' was a laconic 'to fight'. Living in misery was an admission of 'submission'.[36] The father of socialism thus conformed to and confirmed the basic lesson of his liberal middle-class upbringing: men should not be subject

---

[34]Frederick Engels, 'The Conditions of the Working-Class in England', in Marx and Engels, *Collected Works*, vol. 4 (New York: International Publishers, 1975), 233–689, here 333–5 (with a sudden Kantian twist at the end, when Engels criticizes such a 'cozily romantic' existence as 'not worthy of human beings', ibid., 335).

[35]Sabine Donauer, *Emotions at Work – Working on Emotions: The Production of Economic Selves in Twentieth-Century Germany*, PhD thesis, Freie Universität Berlin 2013, available online: (http://www.diss.fu-berlin.de/diss/receive/FUDISS_thesis_000000100445). See Chapter 8 in this volume.

[36]*Familie Marx privat: Die Foto- und Fragebogen-Alben von Marx' Töchtern Laura und Jenny. Eine kommentierte Faksimile-Edition*, ed. Izumi Omura et al. (Berlin: Akademie-Verlag, 2005), 234–5. Filling out questionnaires that asked for one's favourite virtue, flower or colour, or personal maxims and mottos, was a pastime of the European middle classes in the nineteenth century.

to anyone and achieved happiness when they stood up for their principles and convictions. In this sense, the labour movement was not the antithesis of a bourgeois–capitalist system of values, but its product.

Back to pleasure

A more categorical opposition emerged out of the artistic culture of Romanticism, with writers such as Friedrich Schlegel cherishing the 'spirit of pleasure' as much as the 'right to idleness'. In a similar vein, French utopian socialists called for the liberation of the passions and praised the transformational power of hedonistic love.[37] In his early days, Marx allowed himself to dream of a communist society that came close to paradise. By abolishing the division of labour, it would provide the social and material conditions in which happiness could finally be achieved. Everyone would be free

> to do one thing today and another tomorrow, to hunt in the morning, fish in the afternoon, rear cattle in the evening, criticise after dinner, just as I have a mind, without ever becoming hunter, fisherman, shepherd or critic.[38]

While Marx still believed in creative activity (including fighting) as the foundation of happiness, his son-in-law, Paul Lafargue, loudly and provocatively extolled laziness in a deliberate counterpoint to what he considered the plague of his time: the addiction to work. In his view, revolutionary socialists should strive to undermine the capitalist morality that sought 'to reduce the producer to the smallest number of needs' and 'suppress his joys and his passions'.[39]

Lafargue was by no means the last person to condemn capitalism and its social structures for obstructing desire, pleasure and happiness. The twentieth century repeatedly yielded criticisms of, and counter-proposals to, what was perceived as the repression, alienation and commodification of human beings under capitalism. Starting with the youth and life-reform

---

[37] From Schlegel's *Lucinde* (1799), quoted in Walter Benjamin, *The Arcades Project*, trans. Howard Eiland and Kevin McLaughlin (Cambridge, MA: Belknap Press of Harvard University Press, 1999), 379; *Fourier: The Theory of the Four Movements*, ed. Gareth Stedman Jones and Ian Patterson (Cambridge: Cambridge University Press, 1996).
[38] Karl Marx and Frederick Engels, *The German Ideology*, in Marx and Engels, *Collected Works*, vol. 5 (New York: International Publishers, 1976), 74.
[39] Paul Lafargue, *The Right to Be Lazy and Other Studies*, trans. Charles H. Kerr (Chicago: Kerr, 1907), 4. Perhaps unsurprisingly, Lafargue's answer to the question about happiness, in 1868, was 'un bon dessert', while his idea of misery was being cold ('avoir froid') (*Familie Marx privat*, 339).

movements around 1900, which included zealous followers of Friedrich Nietzsche and Stefan George, this outlook gathered steam with the hippy culture of the 1960s, the hedonistic arm of the student movement and the New Age groups of the 1980s. All sought happiness in liberation from the bourgeois norms of possessiveness and careerism. They tried to find it in new forms of community as well as in individual transgression, thrill-seeking and drug use. They also discovered psychotherapy, in its many old and new forms, as a means to overcome individual barriers, inhibitions and depression.[40]

For the young members and supporters of these counter-movements, the Kantian doctrine of duty and virtue clearly no longer held sway. They were not interested in morality but in happiness, conceived as the individual maximization of fulfilled desire. Nor were they keen on sublimating desire and transforming it into culture-creating labour, as their parents and grandparents had done and as Sigmund Freud had shrewdly analysed. Instead, happiness, experienced with relish, became a legitimate end in itself. Such emancipation from 'bourgeois' morality was felt both as personally liberating and as a way to finally change society for the better. Since revolutions could no longer be relied upon to bring about true happiness, as socialist countries had proven, subversion seemed to offer a more practicable and successful option.

There were simultaneously other forces at work that profoundly transformed the way people thought and felt about happiness. In hindsight, the subcultural celebration of desire and enjoyment was a sideline to a broader development that shaped society as a whole. Since the early twentieth century, and especially after 1945, the emergence of modern consumer culture has reinvented citizens as pleasure- and happiness-seeking customers. Individual happiness, the kind promised by the advertising industry, could be achieved by buying more and newer goods. Armed with the latest findings of applied psychology, advertisers continuously promoted new venues and arenas of happiness: from the 'Strength through Joy' programmes of Nazi-era tourism to the pleasures of personal travel in private cars; from exultation over a cup of coffee made with real beans to the lure of state-of-the-art espresso machines; from romantic campsite moments to the luxuries of a Caribbean beach hotel. Consumption guaranteed happiness, no matter whether it was

---

[40]Sven Reichardt, *Authentizität und Gemeinschaft: Linksalternatives Leben in den siebziger und frühen achtziger Jahren* (Berlin: Suhrkamp, 2014); *Das alternative Milieu: Antibürgerlicher Lebensstil und linke Politik in der Bundesrepublik Deutschland und Europa 1968–1983*, ed. Sven Reichardt and Detlef Siegfried (Göttingen: Wallstein, 2010); Joachim C. Häberlen and Jake P. Smith, 'Struggling for Feelings: The Politics of Emotions in the Radical New Left in West Germany, c.1968–84', *Contemporary European History* 23, no. 4 (2014): 615–37; Joachim C. Häberlen, 'Feeling Like a Child: Dreams and Practices of Sexuality in the West-German Alternative Left during the Long 1970s', *Journal for the History of Sexuality* 25, no. 2 (2016): 219–45.

the purchase of a tennis racket, a perfume or a diamond ring, though the steady increase in spending was not incidental.[41]

The happiness to be achieved through consumption is characterized, first, by the absence of work. The sole purpose of work is to enable the acquisition of worldly goods and services; the concept of 'gainful employment' expresses this with perfect clarity. Second, happiness is a private rather than public affair. It occurs in intimate spaces, not in society, let alone in the political arena. Today, Aristotle's claim that happiness is located in the polis seems as strange as Wolff's conviction that the state is responsible for citizens' happiness. Third, happiness is defined as personal enjoyment and pure pleasure, it has no relation to shared moral convictions and objectives. In a 1998 survey, Germans were asked to define what happiness meant to them. They had to choose between two possible answers: 'To me happiness means fulfilling all my wishes', and 'To me happiness means doing my duty'. Only 19 per cent of respondents chose the second option – an outcome that would make Kant, Fichte and Foerster turn in their graves.

This trend demonstrates an unfaltering enthusiasm for individual freedom and autonomy. Dissociating happiness from duty or work helps to thoroughly individualize and privatize it. No longer subject to a general morality, the individual is free to pursue her own goals and live her own life. Individualism comes with baggage and burdens, though. In the absence of general norms and obligations, new expectations arise, producing new patterns of conformity. As consumers, people follow trends and hypes, thus subscribing to visions of happiness that are far less unique and individual than promised. Furthermore, the pursuit of those modes of happiness imposes high psychological as well as material demands. The Caribbean beach hotel costs far more than a tent at a camping ground.

Psychologically, the emphasis on happiness gives rise to all kinds of uncertainties. If you are the proverbial architect of your happiness, you have only yourself to blame when happiness does not present itself. How do you know that you are truly happy, rather than just feeling fine? What is the difference between being happy and having fun (which seems to be the standard expectation in contemporary life)? People looking for help and guidance in this arena consult therapists and philosophers, or they buy self-help books, the number of which has skyrocketed. Professors of psychology eagerly offer their advice on shopping in a way that optimizes the shopper's happiness: 'Money can buy many, if not most, if not all of the things that

---

[41] Frank Trentmann, *Empire of Things: How We Became a World of Consumers, from the Fifteenth Century to the Twenty First* (London: Allan Lane, 2016), part 2. As to Nazi politics of happiness (compared to those in Switzerland), see Isabelle Haffter, *Politik der 'Glückskulturen': NS-Deutschland und die Schweiz, 1933–1945* (Berlin: De Gruyter, 2021).

make people happy, and if it doesn't, then the fault is ours.'[42] Their advice is gladly taken, and books like *Happy Money* sell millions of copies in many languages. Although advice literature has been around since the nineteenth century, it has grown exponentially since the mid-twentieth century, in two areas in particular: love and happiness.

What does Hans do next?

What would Hans in Luck have thought of this development? His story unfolds at the beginning of the modern era that promoted individual happiness in its various shapes and guises. Hans's choices could be interpreted as belonging to an older, distinctly pre-modern emotional economy that neither cared much about planning and providing for the future, nor privileged the exchange value of goods over their use value. Accordingly, Hans favoured instant gratification, spontaneous joy and gratitude and, last but not least, filial love and commitment to one's family.

On the other hand, Hans might be viewed as an early individualist who deliberately defies norms around how to make one's fortune and achieve success. He is the one who defines what his happiness means and when it arises, and he radically frees himself from social expectations and prescriptions. Yet he is hardly a born anarchist, since he has complied with collective norms by serving his master diligently, loyally and continuously for seven years. Still, as soon as his term is over he acts in a quasi-anarchical way that disregards any long-term economic calculation. Instead of following the logic of reason, he gives in to impromptu intuitions and incentives. Each of them makes him objectively poorer. Subjectively, though, Hans experiences ever greater happiness.

As such, the story could also be read as an early critique of the new, thoroughly modern emotional economy that was slowly starting to change people's preferences and references. Hans does not believe in the concept of accumulating riches, and his material transactions fall desperately short of advancing his material well-being. They do not even live up to their original promises, but Hans does not seem to mind. His values simply defy the capitalist logic, since he is not at all interested in the exchange value of marketable goods.

With that attitude, would Hans be a ready adherent of revolutionary slogans that promised him greater happiness as soon as he bought into the rhetoric of radical upheaval? At first glance, yes, since in his interactions with

---

[42]Elizabeth W. Dunn, Daniela T. Gilbert and Timothy D. Wilson, 'If Money Doesn't Make You Happy Then You Probably Aren't Spending It Right', *Journal of Consumer Psychology* 21, no. 2 (2011): 115–25; see also Elizabeth Dunn and Michael Norton, *Happy Money: The Science of Happier Spending* (New York: Simon & Schuster, 2013).

others Hans could be easily manipulated and talked into making idealistic decisions that, upon closer inspection, served others' interests more than his own. So we might very well imagine Hans enjoying the festival of happiness organized by French revolutionaries in the early 1790s, or believing in the Bolshevik notion of vigorous new men who would build a healthy and happy socialist society in the 1920s by putting behind them the perversions of capitalist morality.

Yet it is hard to believe that Hans in Luck would retain his optimism after decades of revolutionary propaganda that continuously and conspicuously failed to deliver on its promises. In lieu of alternatives, he might join subversive cultural movements that tried to entice him into a happy paradise of liberated sexuality, shared material possessions and mind-altering substances. But equally, he might become an aficionado of capitalist consumer culture. In fact, Hans did abandon the sphere of productive labour after seven years of toil, and found happiness in reaping the benefits. He was shopping for the best bargains, in a manner of speaking, and everything he bought or exchanged made him ecstatically happy. He might thus qualify as a prototype of the modern consumer who bought what was marketed as an experience of happiness.

The tale of Hans in Luck thus invites many diverse and even contradictory historical representations and interpretations. One thing, however, is indisputable: Hans's search for happiness and *Seelenfreude* is not concerned with, or limited by, moral prescriptions and social conventions. He cares neither for morality nor for the opinion of others (not even that of his mother) and how they might regard his regressive transactions. Instead, Hans is preoccupied with his own feelings, and he repeatedly considers himself a happy person. Usually it is the narrator's voice that delivers the final verdict and accords happiness to the hero – all's well that ends well. In this story, Hans himself reflects on what he is doing; he is his own narrator. This, too, might make him look like the prototype of a modern person: conscious of his emotions and on the hunt for pleasures whose shelf-life is getting shorter and shorter.

Two centuries later, these modern men and, by now, women, find themselves in a dizzying situation. On the one hand, happiness still figures as the most cherished and sought-after item on people's personal wish lists. On the other, insecurities concerning what real happiness might feel like abound. Individualization and the pluralization of lifestyles have transformed happiness into something multifaceted and highly diverse. Many try to shop their way to it, others attempt to return to the 'simple things' as the apparent source of innocent pleasure.

At the same time, happiness has, once again, become the gold standard of well-being. Schools have introduced curricula on happiness; companies like Coca-Cola have founded 'Happiness Institutes' in various countries in order to uncover strategies and attitudes that might enhance our zest for life.

Governments work closely with think tanks that pursue empirical 'happiness research' and make policy suggestions to shift priorities. Interestingly, the most advanced research units go far beyond measuring the cognitive dimension of life satisfaction (which is what forms the basis of the World Happiness Reports). Nor do they simply evaluate people's daily emotions, good and bad. Instead, they deliberately include a 'eudaimonic dimension' that concerns the notion of a good life.[43] By explicitly invoking ancient Greek concepts (that thrived well into the eighteenth century), happiness in this view refers 'to people's perception of the meaningfulness (or pointlessness), sense of purpose, and value of their life'.[44]

Such references take heed of what contemporary Buddhist intellectuals and Western behavioural economists have recently emphasized and what European philosophers had already confirmed in the early nineteenth century: purpose and meaning matter. How we define it, though, is up to us. While absolutist rulers and religious institutions have long imposed their normative views on people, liberal-democratic societies take citizens to be the makers of their own fortunes and happiness. The state, as liberal thinkers have maintained since around 1800, is neither responsible nor authorized to determine what human happiness is and how it is to be achieved. All it can do is clear the way and facilitate people's search for their own happiness, a lesson that Soviet-style regimes learned in 1989/90. Meanwhile, the search goes on.

---

[43] See, for example, the publications of the Happiness Research Institute that advises the Nordic Council of Ministers. Nordic countries, which rank highest in World Happiness Reports, take a close and continuous interest in improving their citizens' well-being: https://www.happinessresearchinstitute.com/happinessresearch (accessed 22 December 2022).
[44] *Subjective Well-Being: Measuring Happiness, Suffering, and Other Dimensions of Experience. A Report by the National Research Council*, ed. Arthur A. Stone and Christopher Mackie (Washington: National Academies Press, 2013), 19.

CHAPTER ELEVEN

Emotions and Material Culture: Say It with Flowers

Capitalism not only tapped into people's emotional economies by changing the way they experienced work, affecting their habits of spending and saving money and influencing their idea and expectations of happiness, it also left a deep imprint on the emotional meaning of things. When goods could be afforded by ever larger segments of the population thanks to centralized manufacturing and mass production, this had a bearing on both their positional and their emotional value. Just as certain goods or things were given the power to speak of and to people's social aspirations, they acquired the power to denote complex emotional attachments and purposes.

Those attachments are and were often genuinely personal, due to the way commodities such as clothes or furniture are appropriated in capitalist material culture. As individual possessions, commodities might work to beautify and enrich the buyer's life. They might even, as with fancy cars, replenish his or her vitality and project a particular image of the self.[1] Presented as gifts, material objects transcend the realm of self-fashioning and foster social relationships. Through marketing and use, some gift items have come to carry specific emotional messages. As Sally Holloway has analysed, the Georgian culture of courtship comprised love tokens such

---

This chapter is a revised and expanded version of the article 'The Emotional Language of Flowers', in *Feelings Materialized: Emotions, Bodies, and Things in Germany, 1500–1950*, ed. Derek Hillard, Heikki Lempa and Russell Spinney (New York: Berghahn, 2020), 202–21.
[1]Deborah Lupton, *The Emotional Self: A Sociocultural Exploration* (London: Sage, 1998), 137 ff.

as flowers, portrait miniatures and locks of hair, which emphasized the intimacy of the relationship. It also invented the printed Valentine card.[2]

These days, the cult of Valentine's Day in its global iteration includes more than cards.[3] Above all, it is about flowers. In fact, flowers have come to occupy a central position in material culture and how it shapes and mediates emotions. This position has developed over time and with the help of powerful agents in industry and advertising. As the commercial slogan 'Say it with flowers' suggests, flowers speak an emotional language that is specific and diverse at the same time. Roses and daffodils, violets and chrysanthemums, lilies and carnations all embody, represent and express different emotions. Compared with other goods, flowers seemingly convey emotional messages in a direct manner. As gifts, they define an emotion-based relationship between giver and receiver. Even outside gift cultures, they are meant to communicate feelings, moods and sentiments, whether as articles of fashion, as decorative objects in private and public spaces, as ornaments in paintings and porcelain or as signs of political affiliation and communication.[4]

To apply Clifford Geertz's terms, flowers can be theorized as symbols that 'give meaning' and 'objective conceptual form' to emotions. They do this in two ways: by offering a model *of* reality and 'shaping themselves to it', and/or by constituting a model *for* reality which entails shaping real emotions to be like or as flowers.[5] While flowers figure predominantly as representations of feelings, they themselves mould and model feelings in given contexts – by privileging certain ones over others, or by highlighting positive affect in contentious political encounters. Flowers have indeed become crucial emotional players: they mobilize emotions in social relationships and thus actively influence or even transform those relationships.

---

[2]Sally Holloway, *The Game of Love in Georgian England: Courtship, Emotions, and Material Culture* (Oxford: Oxford University Press, 2018), esp. 108–16; see also Stephanie Downes, Sally Holloway and Sarah Randles, eds, *Feeling Things: Objects and Emotions through History* (Oxford: Oxford University Press, 2018); Hillard, Lempa and Spinney, eds, *Feelings Materialized*.
[3]On the South Asian adoption of the Valentine cult, see Christiane Brosius, 'Love in the Age of Valentine and Pink Underwear: Media and Politics of Intimacy in South Asia', in *Transcultural Turbulences: Towards a Multi-Sited Reading of Image Flows*, ed. Christiane Brosius and Roland Wenzlhuemer (Berlin: Springer, 2011), 27–66.
[4]See, for a global overview, Jack Goody, *The Culture of Flowers* (Cambridge: Cambridge University Press, 1993). As for Japan and its infatuation with cherry blossoms, see Emiko Ohnuki-Tierney, *Flowers That Kill: Communicative Opacity in Political Spaces* (Stanford: Stanford University Press, 2015), 25–56. For paintings, see Andreas Honegger, *Die Blumen der Frauen: Blumensymbolik in Gemälden aus 7 Jahrhunderten* (Munich: Sandmann, 2011); Suzanne L. Marchand, *Porcelain: A History from the Heart of Europe* (Princeton: Princeton University Press, 2020), 216–17.
[5]Clifford Geertz, *The Interpretation of Cultures* (New York: Basic Books, 1973), 93.

This transformative power can be studied on several levels: in private, intimate relations as well as in politics and at the workplace. Starting around 1800 in Europe, flowers were increasingly used to imbue people's interactions and communications with emotions. In an age that dramatically changed the way individuals conceived of themselves and their relationships with others, flowers served as a gift or accessory with positive emotional value. Emotions were made visible, tradeable and negotiable through the language of flowers, which invited and enabled a multitude of social and political practices.

To start with, flowers played an important role in political communication as party emblems or gifts that sent emotive messages from giver to receiver, bestowing a humane glow on both. Flowers in this setting served to emotionalize and personalize politics in the modern era of mass political participation. Flowers intensified emotional communication between friends and lovers in the private sphere, too. They were supposed to convey a set of pleasant feelings, speaking a language that had to be taught and learnt. Consequently, specific genre and advice books for this very purpose proliferated during the nineteenth and twentieth centuries, just as the production and consumption of flowers was growing at an exponential rate. It was further hastened by the invention and commodification of emotional festivals like Mother's Day and St Valentine's Day – celebrations that point to the gendered structure of customs around flowers. In most cases, it was men who bought and gave flowers to women, not the other way around. The practice was facilitated by the common conviction that women bore a certain resemblance to flowers, and vice versa. The modern age worked to draw clear lines between men and women, and masculinity and femininity, and it enlisted flowers to both confirm and romanticize the distinction.

Political flower power

On 19 July 2017, Prince William and his wife Kate, Duchess of Cambridge, arrived in the German capital for an official visit. Many Berliners gathered in front of the Brandenburg Gate to get a glimpse of the royal couple, or perhaps even a handshake. Women especially were smitten with the Duchess and astutely commented on what she was wearing: a coatdress that looked both 'serious' and 'feminine'. In addition to its elegance, the colour caught everyone's attention: a fabulous blue, neither dark nor light but *kornblumenblau*, as one woman expertly observed.[6]

Her observation was correct, the dress was indeed the colour of the cornflower. But likely very few people in Berlin's centre that day were aware of the political symbolism. Cornflowers had acquired a particular emotional

---

[6]*Tagesspiegel*, 20 July 2017, 9.

significance in late nineteenth-century Germany. They were widely known as the favourite flower of the nation's first emperor, and citizens rushed to gift him cornflower-related items on every occasion. In the 1870s, the cornflower was designated the *Kaiserblume*, the emblematic flower of the new empire. As Eva Giloi has shown, a veritable cult around cornflowers and cornflower memorabilia emerged that outlasted Wilhelm I.[7]

Nowadays the cult seems to have been largely forgotten – except, perhaps, by a few protocol experts in the British Foreign Office. Considering that the Duchess of Cambridge chooses her outfits very carefully so as to include references to national styles and traditions, it is not altogether improbable that politics was behind her choice of coatdress. It might have been intended to convey a message of sympathy: look, we (the British) know about your (the Germans') history, we appreciate your traditions and pay them respect. With Brexit looming, such a message could not fail to be appreciated by those who grasped its meaning.

Around 1900, the cornflower conveyed other messages. Linked to the oft-recounted story of the young Prussian Prince Wilhelm consoling his mother, Luise, during the dark days of Napoleonic conquest, it signified vulnerability as much as a child's love and trust. As a wildflower that blossomed in fields and meadows, it spoke of modesty rather than regal magnificence.[8] The narrative of 1806 served to remind the emperor and his devoted citizens of the humiliation Prussia had suffered at the hands of France, and of the seemingly ongoing threat posed by their neighbour. In this context, the cornflower represented national perseverance and ultimate victory against all odds. As such, it was held in high esteem during the imperial era. Veterans' associations used it in their efforts to raise funds and welfare organizations staged so-called cornflower days in order to collect donations for social causes.[9]

The practice of attaching sentimental value to flowers and instrumentalizing them for political ends was not a Prussian–German invention. Napoleon I, Luise's French counterpart and foe, had created a similar tradition for himself. During his lifetime, he became known as *'Père la Violette'*, with narratives weaving private issues – his love affair with Josephine de Beauharnais and her passion for violets – into political visions of renewed power and imperial regalia following the defeat in 1813.

---

[7]Eva Giloi, *Monarchy, Myth, and Material Culture in Germany 1750–1950* (Cambridge: Cambridge University Press, 2011), 161–6.

[8]Ibid., 163. The story of Wilhelm and Luise and the cornflower has different versions; in some Wilhelm consoles his mother, in others it is Luise who comforts her son (see, e.g., Emmy Giehrl, 'Kornblumen', *Deutsche Revue über das gesamte nationale Leben der Gegenwart* 22, no. 1 (1897): 121–3).

[9]Eva Schöck-Quinteros, 'Blumentage im Deutschen Reich: Zwischen bürgerlicher Wohltätigkeit und Klassenkampf', *Ariadne* 39 (2001): 44–51. See also Siegfried Becker, 'Kornblumen: Zur politischen und kulturellen Symbolik in den Nationalitätenkonflikten Österreich-Ungarns', *Hessische Blätter für Volks –und Kulturforschung* 34 (1998): 69–114.

Even after Napoleon was finally exiled to St Helena, his followers chose to wear violets on their lapels as a symbol of loyalty and a sign of mutual recognition.[10]

Attributing political meaning to flowers stemmed in fact from a longer tradition. Since ancient times, lilies had adorned royal coats of arms and palatial spaces. The modern era not only challenged the rule of kings and queens, opening politics up to ordinary citizens but also added sentiment to symbolism. For French aristocrats in danger of being decapitated under the guillotine, red carnations became symbols of impassioned resistance.[11] After the Bourbons returned to the throne in 1814, white (or silver) lilies reappeared on the political stage as an emblem of the royalist camp which took vicious revenge on Napoleon's henchmen.[12]

The red carnation was also adopted as a party flower, albeit in different settings. From 1890 onwards, crimson carnations were worn by men and women who supported the socialist movement and its struggle against capitalist exploitation. The 1889 International Socialist Workers Congress in Paris designated 1 May an occasion to advance the global campaign for the eight-hour working day. In Germany, where the socialist movement was legally constrained and politically suppressed until 1890, public rallies and red flags were not permitted. In their place, supporters donned red carnations, thus inaugurating a tradition that continues to this very day.[13] In the GDR, everyone participating in May Day celebrations wore a red carnation on their lapel. Even after the demise of state socialism, left-wing politicians and citizens gather every year in early January to lay the flowers on the graves of communist leaders like Rosa Luxemburg, Karl Liebknecht, Wilhelm Pieck, Walter Ulbricht and others, in continuation of a GDR propaganda event.[14]

---

[10]Karl Gottlieb Bretschneider, *Der vierjährige Krieg der Verbündeten mit Napoleon Bonaparte in Rußland, Teutschland, Italien und Frankreich in den Jahren 1812 bis 1816*, vol. 2 (Annaberg: Freyerische Buchhandlung, 1816), 434; Karl Reimer, 'Parteiblumen', *Innsbrucker Nachrichten*, 3 May 1900, 1–2. Napoleon III continued his uncle's tradition.

[11]Gabriele Tergit (alias Elise Reifenberg), *Kleine Geschichte der Blumen* (Berlin: Ullstein, 1981), 116.

[12]Reimer, 'Parteiblumen', mentions the Order of the (Silver) Lily under Louis XVIII; it was evidently given to so many followers of the royalist cause that it eventually came to figure as a party flower.

[13]Gottfried Korff, 'Seht die Zeichen, die euch gelten: Fünf Bemerkungen zur Symbolgeschichte des 1. Mai', in *100 Jahre Zukunft: Zur Geschichte des 1. Mai*, ed. Inge Marßolek (Frankfurt: Büchergilde Gutenberg, 1990), 15–39; for Austria, see Brigitte Lehmann, 'Ehrwürdige Rote Nelke', in *Die ersten 100 Jahre: Österreichische Sozialdemokratie 1888–1988*, ed. Helene Maimann (Vienna: Brandstätter, 1988), 102–5.

[14]https://www.morgenpost.de/berlin/article105890420/Rote-Nelken-fuer-Karl-und-Rosa.html; https://www.visitberlin.de/de/zentralfriedhof-friedrichsfelde (both accessed 22 December 2022). As I witnessed in 2010, carnations (which quickly sold out in florists nearby) were distributed quite unevenly among the graves of socialist heroes: the one with the most flowers was that of Rosa Luxemburg, while Walter Ulbricht's had the fewest.

The red carnation was also the favourite flower of Emperor Wilhelm II, however, so it clearly did not always reference socialism. During his thirty-year reign (1888–1918), shops and department stores displayed their patriotism in windows with garlands of carnations wound around the imperial bust.[15] Citizens sent flowers for the emperor's birthday or other festivities, thus forming an intimate bond with the royal family. This tradition, which had been popularized with Wilhelm I and his famous cornflowers but faded after the forced abdication of the Hohenzollern dynasty in 1918, was adopted again under National Socialism. Adolf Hitler was flooded with bouquets, sent or given chiefly by female admirers. Children decorated their hand-written letters to the Führer with flowers, privileging the plain alpine edelweiss (supposedly his favourite).[16] Nevertheless, the song 'Hitlers Lieblingsblume ist das Edelweiß' was banned in 1939 as 'national kitsch'.[17]

Flowers thus conveyed different messages when used as a means of political communication. Whereas citizens chose them to proclaim their emotional attachment and sympathy, politicians and heads of state liked to be photographed with bouquets that highlighted their popularity while, at the same time, testifying to their good character. With flowers in their hands, even mass killers like Hitler and Stalin looked peaceable, benevolent and kind.[18]

The variety of flower did not particularly seem to matter. In most European countries, roses were held in high regard both as personal and political gifts; they were adopted as an emblem by the Second Socialist International. In West Germany, Social Democrats used both red carnations and red roses as their party flowers. In 1986, the British Labour Party replaced the red flag of their logo with the red rose, thus paying tribute to England's national flower. For different reasons, the French Parti Socialiste adopted the red rose in 1969.

In the same year, the West German artist Joseph Beuys exhibited a *Revolutionsklavier* at the Düsseldorf Academy of Arts. His revolutionary piano was strewn with more than two hundred red carnations and roses. Three years later, at the fifth documenta exhibition of contemporary art in Kassel, Beuys used the red rose to explain the relationship between evolution

---

[15]Dirk Reinhardt, *Von der Reklame zum Marketing: Geschichte der Wirtschaftswerbung in Deutschland* (Berlin: Akademie-Verlag, 1993), 416. According to the popular writer Elsbeth Ebertin, who was born in 1880, Wilhelm II's favourite flowers were actually tea roses and mignonettes: *Die Lieblingsblumen der deutschen Kaiser und des Führers Adolf Hitler* (Weinsberg: Brot & Feierabend, 1935), 5.
[16]See the compilation of letters (often accompanied by flowers) in Bundesarchiv Berlin, NS 51, no. 63–77; Ebertin, *Lieblingsblumen*, 7.
[17]Hans-Jörg Koch, *Das Wunschkonzert im NS-Rundfunk* (Cologne: Böhlau, 2003), 366.
[18]See the propaganda photos reprinted in Ohnuki-Tierney, *Flowers That Kill*, 71–4 (Stalin), 74–8 (Hitler); Joachim Fest and Heinrich Hoffmann, *Hitler – Gesichter eines Diktators: Eine Bilddokumentation*, 2nd edn (Munich: Herbig, 1993), 58–9, 98–9.

and revolution: while the blossoming flower signified revolutionary change, it was still the product of organic development.[19]

The party that Beuys eventually helped to found did not choose the red rose as a symbol, opting instead for the yellow sunflower. Even before various local and regional initiatives merged to formally establish the Green Party in 1980, sunflowers appeared on their flyers, brochures and election posters. They signified the Greens's emphasis on nature and ecology, and sent a message of optimism, hope and grassroots enthusiasm.[20] When, in 1983, twenty-eight representatives took their seats in the newly elected federal parliament, they carried with them ailing fir trees to raise awareness of the dire state of Germany's forests. But they also brought sunflowers, signalling their commitment to ecological progress and social change. Although it has undergone several design iterations in recent years, the sunflower is still the Green Party's primary logo. Its emotional meaning is easily decoded: joy, human warmth and cheerfulness.

Codes of knowledge

The Green Party's choice of a flower as the emblem of its political goals and agenda might have seemed obvious. In general, however, there was no compelling reason why parties should use flowers for their logos, and indeed most parties did not.[21] Still, people had long adopted flowers as multi-variant symbols. Starting in the early nineteenth century, European authors drafted elaborate 'languages of flowers' that connected type and colour to specific meanings and messages. According to the booklet *Vollständige Blumensprache* (Complete Language of Flowers), published in 1850, the sunflower spoke of distant, unfulfilled love and reverence; red carnations represented lovesickness; and red roses were associated with eternal, passionate love.[22]

From around 1800, such booklets had been appearing in ever greater numbers. The French unleashed the hype and set the tone, and other countries soon followed suit. Popular French books were often quite literally adapted

---

[19]Götz Adriani, Winfried Konnertz and Karin Thomas, *Joseph Beuys* (Cologne: DuMont, 1994), 128.
[20]Roland Vogt, 'Auf der Suche nach dem Salzkorn – Symbolnutzung bei der Friedensbewegung und bei den Grünen', *Forschungsjournal Neue soziale Bewegungen* 1 (1988): 36–42; Gudrun Silberzahn-Jandt, 'Die Sonnenblume und der Müll', *Hessische Blätter für Volks- und Kulturforschung* 34 (1998): 115–26, here 120–2. The sunflower also referenced the image of the smiling sun, which originated in Denmark in 1975 and has since become the long-standing emblem of the international anti-nuclear movement.
[21]With the exception of Sweden, where most parties use flower symbols.
[22]*Vollständige Blumensprache, der Liebe und Freundschaft gewidmet, oder Bedeutung der Pflanzen und Blumen nach occidentalischer Art* (Warburg: Schilp, 1850), 29, 33, 37.

by British or German authors, and German texts quickly appeared in French and English translation. Readers, predominantly female, across the Channel and on each side of the river Rhine seemed eager to know about flowers and what they had to say, and publishers were keen to make the information available for purchase.

To explain the obsession with the language of flowers, it helps to examine the contexts in which the language was spoken. The 1850 booklet explicitly declared that it was dedicated to 'love and friendship', not to politics. Flowers predominantly mediated intimate relations between lovers, friends, parents and children, and literary texts, poems and novels presented numerous appropriate models for emulation.[23] As one late nineteenth-century author advised, his book should be used as a present for lovers only:

> Both parts can then interpret the sent or given flowers and their meaning according to what the sender wanted to say. In the gentlest way, wishes, explanations, thoughts and feelings are thus to be mutually exchanged, without letting any stranger know and interfere.[24]

The assurance implicitly referred to the popular narrative around the genre's alleged Oriental origins. From the very start, authors had drawn upon the so-called Selam tradition as described by European visitors to the Ottoman Empire. Selam, the secret language of flowers, was said to be exchanged between a male lover and the woman he courted behind the closed walls of the harem. Although scholars had cast serious doubt on whether such a practice had ever really existed, the legend's popularity persisted, since it both eroticized the code and gave it an exotic twist.[25] Endowed with this pedigree, flowers became the ideal tool to communicate finely nuanced feelings of affection, longing, hope, gratitude and devotion. In less intimate relations, they might convey something completely different. Flowers offered by an employer to a long-standing subordinate did not necessarily indicate the same feelings as flowers that a suitor gave to his potential mother-in-law.

Yet in each and every relationship flowers were thought to communicate feelings and, as such, they were highly praised and valued during the age

---

[23]Anna Ananieva, 'Getrocknete Blumen: Literarische Figurationen sentimentaler Erinnerungspraktiken zwischen modischer Chiffre und intimem Souvenir in Révéroni Saint-Cyrs *Sabina d'Herfeld*', in *Die Sachen der Aufklärung*, ed. Frauke Berndt and Daniel Fulda (Hamburg: Meiner, 2012), 389–401; Anna Ananieva and Christiane Holm, 'Phänomenologie des Intimen: Die Neuformulierung des Andenkens seit der Empfindsamkeit', in *Der Souvenir: Erinnerung in Dingen von der Reliquie zum Andenken*, ed. Birgit Gablowski (Cologne: Wienand, 2006), 156–87.
[24]M. Unterbeck, *Neueste vollständige Blumen-, Fächer- und Briefmarkensprache* (Stuttgart: Schwabacher, no date – possibly from the 1870s or 1880s), 4.
[25]Beverly Seaton, *The Language of Flowers: A History* (Charlottesville: University of Virginia Press, 1995), 61–5; Clemens Alexander Wimmer, 'Bücher über Blumensprache', *Zandera* 13 (1998): 15–25.

of sensibility and Romanticism in the late eighteenth and early nineteenth centuries. Since feelings were deemed crucial markers of a person's character and individuality, flowers came to be regarded as important means of translation. Contemporaries considered it a major challenge to cultivate their feelings in a way that rendered them readable to others. This was especially pressing for the educated middle classes, whose emotional economy aimed to distinguish them from both the aristocracy and the common people. In such a context, flowers were discovered as an instrument to both facilitate and complicate emotional communication. They could deliver discreet messages that were otherwise difficult to convey through words. Potentially, every feeling, in all its nuances, could be expressed by a particular flower – hence the extensive lists provided by many guidebooks and lexica. They referenced hundreds of different species and their attached symbolism, far more than an ordinary flower garden or florist contained.[26] The sheer number could not but overwhelm and baffle those who were intent on learning the art of giving and receiving flowers for sentimental purposes.

Even though nineteenth-century books on flowers were of limited practical value, they sold well and in numerous editions. They figured as popular gifts at Christmas or New Year, designed, as an American author put it in 1854, 'as a Table Book for the Parlor, of a sentimental character, to diversify the monotony of a long winter evening'.[27] Owning such a book signalled a family or a person's cultivation and civility, marking them as members of a higher social class and culture.

Yet the books' message was not completely irrelevant in real life. Some of their content was included in the manner books and advice manuals that proliferated throughout the nineteenth and early twentieth centuries. In such condensed form, the language of flowers did indeed influence people's behaviour and modes of communication. While earlier manuals, above all the famous *Knigge* of 1788, did not mention the flowery form of expression, later ones did. Since the 1870s, Franz Ebhardt's *Der gute Ton in allen Lebenslagen* (Appropriate Behaviour in all Circumstances) included a chapter on flowers. They were described as 'signs' and 'symbols' for 'what lives in our heart and shies away from being openly expressed and addressed'. Crediting the French and their substantial expertise, the author confirmed that the language of flowers and colours was by now well understood in Germany too.[28] Peonies, for example, were known to express love without words, while violets represented grace, lilies innocence and daisies truth and modesty.

---

[26] *Vollständige Blumensprache* listed about seven hundred different flowers. See Unterbeck, *Blumen-, Fächer- und Briefmarkensprache*, 9–68 (with an equally long list from *Adlerkraut* to *Zittergras*).
[27] Quoted in Seaton, *Language of Flowers*, 19.
[28] Franz Ebhardt, *Der gute Ton in allen Lebenslagen: Ein Handbuch für den Verkehr in der Familie, in der Gesellschaft und im öffentlichen Leben*, 13th edn (Leipzig: Klinkhardt, 1896), 191, 193. Unterbeck, *Blumen-, Fächer- und Briefmarkensprache*, 4, claimed that the language of flowers was 'by now [meaning the 1870s or 1880s] well-known and popular'.

Ebhardt's list was manageable and easy to grasp and remember. Equally clear was the advice he gave to young women: red flowers were wholly taboo since they expressed 'fiery passion', which was traditionally men's territory. Young ladies in France, he warned, would never wear red carnations, poppies or roses, flowers hardly compatible with the female sex and its 'gentle dignity'.[29] At most, ladies could claim a light, rosy red for themselves – a colour which, since the 1920s, has become typical for feminine baby clothes, toys, bed linen and room furnishings.[30]

Gendered practices

Colours were thus used as a marker of gender difference. This was most conspicuous in wedding attire, which, starting in Queen Victoria's era, was white (the colour of purity) for the bride and black (the colour of respectability) for the groom. Applied to flowers, colour became even more significant. A bouquet of red roses meant something entirely different from one of white or yellow. Such meanings were particularly crucial in interactions between men and women, where the language of flowers had the greatest import. Relevant manuals offered detailed advice to young men on how to wield it correctly and thereby avoid mistakes that might ruin a relationship before it had the chance to bloom. In addition to choosing the appropriate flower in the right colour, men had to ensure that the flowers were nicely arranged in sophisticated bouquets. It was unacceptable to offer a potted flower to a young woman, although such gifts were popular among female friends. A man's gift should only elicit short-term attention; anything else would immodestly imply that he claimed a longer presence in the life of his beloved.[31]

Flowers were not only given (usually by men) and received (by women) as tokens of affection and adoration. Both genders also wore them. Fashion dictated that women adorn their dresses and hats with flowers, fresh as well as synthetic, while men wore flowers on the lapels of their coats or suits. When Social Democrats wore red carnations as a sign of protest and solidarity in 1890, they were perfectly in line with contemporary fashions.

A lucrative industry and trade developed after French Huguenots brought the production of artificial flowers to Germany in the late eighteenth century.[32]

---

[29]Ebhardt, *Der gute Ton*, 193–4.
[30]Eva Heller, *Wie Farben wirken: Farbpsychologie – Farbsymbolik – Kreative Farbgestaltung* (Reinbek: Rowohlt, 1989), 118. Traditionally, light blue was used to dress girls while young boys were clothed in pink (just as red was predominantly taken to be a 'male' colour and blue a 'female' one) (ibid., 56).
[31]Ebhardt, *Der gute Ton*, 220, 226–7.
[32]Alfred Meiche, *Die Anfänge der Kunstblumenindustrie in Dresden, Leipzig, Berlin und Sebnitz* (Dresden: Meinhold, 1908).

It was mainly women who were employed in cottage industries for very low wages to craft flowers from silk or paper that looked as beautiful as freshly cut ones but lasted far longer.[33] Women also sold flowers, as assistants in the burgeoning florists or as volunteers during the 'flower days' that became widely popular in the early twentieth century. Organized predominantly by middle-class women with the backing of prominent institutions, the 'fair sex' (and especially its younger members) offered white daisies and blue cornflowers to local citizens. The money raised went towards social welfare projects, usually for children. Everyone, men and women of all social classes, was addressed: 'In the service of giving love' the flower should form a 'bond between all circles', decorating 'the frock-coat and the tennis clothing, the officer's uniform and the worker's hat, the elegant ladies' suit and the dress of the cleaning woman'.[34]

Women therefore figured prominently as producers, sellers and consumers of flowers. But they were not the primary buyers.[35] Still to this day, it is usually men who give flowers to women, not the other way around. Men rarely receive flowers (or for that matter sweets or perfume, other typically feminine gifts). On more formal occasions, however, male politicians, CEOs and orchestra conductors do get bouquets (that they quickly hand over to their wives, female partners or colleagues). In the era of Wilhelm I, though, gender roles were far more rigid, as the ageing emperor jokingly confirmed. At the sight of the many birthday bouquets he had been sent from far and wide, he remarked: 'it isn't right; it doesn't suit an old man like me at all – yes, if I were a pretty young woman or a little girl that would be different!'[36] More than age, gender was what mattered when it came to flowers, although royals were exempted.

There was another exception, and it concerned the manliest of men: soldiers. When German troops were mobilized in August 1914, men in military uniforms, conscripted or volunteering, were adorned with flowers as they departed for the battlefield. Women who gathered at train stations made sure that no defender of heath or hearth left without a flower. Even after the defeat in 1918, they welcomed back with garlands those who had survived the carnage. Flowers here were a symbol of life and gratitude; even citizens opposed to the war, like Käthe Kollwitz, did not hesitate to honour

---

[33]Regarding work conditions, see the 1908 and 1911 minutes of congresses organized by the Zentralverband der in der Blumen-, Blätter-, Palmen- und Putzfederfabrikation beschäftigten Arbeiter und Arbeiterinnen Deutschlands, in *Quelleneditionen zur Geschichte der deutschen Arbeiterbewegung, Projekt 2: Proletarische Frauenbewegung* (Wildberg: Belser, 1998).

[34]Quoted in Schöck-Quinteros, 'Blumentage', 46–7 (from the *Casseler Tageblatt*, 14 August 1910).

[35]It is unclear when exactly women started to buy flowers for themselves to decorate their homes. Victorian interiors showed little evidence of cut flowers (although vases were ubiquitous); potted plants prevailed. See Judith Flanders, *Inside the Victorian Home: A Portrait of Domestic Life in Victorian England* (New York: Norton & Co., 2004), 177, 180, 196.

[36]Quoted in Giloi, *Monarchy*, 162.

those who had fought it (among them, her two sons).[37] Unlike in Britain, in Germany there was no particular flower dedicated to the memory of soldiers who had fallen on the field of honour. The red poppy, still worn by British, Australian and Canadian citizens on 11 November, is not part of remembrance customs in France or Germany.[38]

Women giving flowers to departing or returning soldiers seemed, at first sight, to turn the traditional gender order on its head. Upon closer inspection, however, it remained intact. Men, as the common narrative held, went to war in order to protect women and children. In return, women had to reward them with even greater love, submission and devotedness. Flowers in the hands of women therefore implied an intimate promise: when you come back, you will find a grateful wife or yearning bride ready to welcome you into her bed. The close connection between women and flowers that sprang from a century-old tradition persisted.

This connection had been addressed by female and male authors alike with particular zeal beginning in the late eighteenth century. In 1802, the young German Romantic poet Friedrich von Hardenberg, alias Novalis, had his hero Heinrich von Ofterdingen dream of a blue flower, expressing his longing for a loving woman. Three decades earlier, in her poem 'To a Lady, with some painted Flowers', the prominent English author Anna Laetitia Barbauld compared women to flowers: 'Flowers sweet, and gay, and delicate like you; Emblems of innocence, and beauty too'. The analogy was not meant to embarrass the lady or make her 'blush': 'Your best, your sweetest empire is – to please.'[39]

Still, the analogy did make some women colour. The writer and early feminist Mary Wollstonecraft vigorously rejected it since, in her opinion, virtue 'must be acquired by *rough* toils, and useful struggles with worldly *cares*'. She remarked with contempt that to reduce women to sweet and delicate flower-like creatures was what 'the men tell us'; women should know better.[40] Mainstream attitudes, though, supported Barbauld and countless others who repeated the same message over and over again. As one magazine stated in 1848, women and flowers shared a 'natural sympathy: women are themselves flowers, gently, diligently and lovingly cultivated so that they can bring joy to their future owners through beauty and grace'.[41]

---

[37]Käthe Kollwitz, *Die Tagebücher*, ed. Jutta Bohnke-Kollwitz (Berlin: Akademie-Verlag, 1989), 844, 384, 389.
[38]Jennifer Iles, 'In Remembrance: The Flanders Poppy', *Mortality* 13, no. 3 (2008): 201–21. France adopted cornflowers as emblems of remembrance, albeit for a shorter time and with less prevalence. In New Zealand, poppies are worn for ANZAC Day on 25 April.
[39]Anna Laetitia Aikin, 'To a Lady, With Some Painted Flowers', available online: http://digital.library.upenn.edu/women/barbauld/1773/1773-painted.html (accessed 4 January 2023).
[40]G.J. Barker-Benfield, *The Culture of Sensibility: Sex and Society in Eighteenth-Century Britain* (Chicago: University of Chicago Press, 1992), quote 265.
[41]*Neubert's Deutsches Magazin für Garten- und Blumenkunde* 1 (1848): 148, quoted in Karin Hausen, '"… durch die Blume gesprochen": Naturaneignung und Symbolvermarktung', in *Fahrrad, Auto, Fernsehschrank: Zur Kulturgeschichte der Alltagsdinge*, ed. Wolfgang Ruppert (Frankfurt: Fischer, 1993), 52–78, 223–5, quote 224.

Capitalizing on the analogy, from the early twentieth century onwards florists marketed flowers more aggressively. They used the slogan 'say it with flowers' (in German: let flowers speak), implying that flowers should, above all, talk of love. The message became louder when commercial associations started to popularize 'Mother's Day'. Invented in the US before the First World War, the celebration was backed by conservative and religious groups as well as welfare associations in the 1920s. By 1930, it was widely celebrated in Germany. Unsurprisingly, the perfect gift for mothers was flowers – in all shapes, varieties and colours, but with one message: love and gratitude. Between 1933 and 1945, National Socialism transformed Mother's Day into an opportunity for political propaganda, giving special honours – including flowers – to mothers of large families.[42]

After the Second World War, the GDR, in unison with other socialist countries, opted instead to celebrate International Women's Day in early March. It was accompanied by different ideological messages but also with armfuls of flowers, mostly red carnations.[43] Starting in the early 1990s, florists again led the charge, stridently working to popularize St Valentine's Day in Germany and Continental Europe. Lufthansa's proud announcement in 2013 that the carrier had transported 1,000 tons of roses from Nairobi, Bogota and Quito to Frankfurt for sale on 14 February offers a clue as to how successful and lucrative the business has proven to be. Again, love paved the commercial way, and lovers eagerly took up the offer to express their deeply felt emotions through flowers. And again, it was and is usually men that buy and give flowers to women as a token of their affection.[44]

The profound gendering of most practices and interactions involving flowers was not beyond critique. Like Mary Wollstonecraft, who had taken offence to the analogy between flowers and women, feminists in the 1970s opposed Mother's Day and its flowery ornamentation for camouflaging the discrimination women faced in society and politics. International Women's Day as it was routinely practised in the Eastern bloc attracted similar criticism, even though it was originally initiated by women demanding female suffrage. Around 1900, socialists in many European countries and in the US

---

[42]Hausen, 'Blume', 69, 74–6; Karin Hausen, 'Mothers, Sons, and the Sale of Symbols and Goods: the "German Mother's Day" 1923–1933', in *Interest and Emotion: Essays on the Study of Family and Kinship*, ed. Hans Medick and David Warren Sabean (Cambridge: Cambridge University Press, 1984), 371–413; Irmgard Weyrather, *Mutterkreuz und Muttertag: Der Kult um die 'deutsche Mutter' im Nationalsozialismus* (Frankfurt: Fischer, 1993).
[43]Temma Kaplan, 'On the Socialist Origins of International Women's Day', *Feminist Studies* 11, no. 1 (1985): 163–71; *Internationaler Frauentag: Tag der Frauen seit 75 Jahren*, ed. Gudrun Hamacher (Frankfurt: Vorstand der IG Metall, 1985).
[44]https://lufthansa-cargo.com/-/lhc-press-media-details-2013-page4-6-wc (accessed 4 January 2023). Among the gifts given on Valentine's Day, flowers came top in 2020/21.

had started to campaign for social and political rights. Rose Schneiderman, a textile worker and trade union organizer from New York, painted the following picture in 1912: 'What the woman who labors wants is the right to live, not simply exist [...] The worker must have bread, but she must have roses, too.' Addressing 'women of privilege', she claimed that 'even the humblest worker' had a right to 'the sun and music and art', wilfully choosing the rose to symbolize the difference between sheer existence and true life.[45]

The quote about bread and roses was quickly popularized in poems and songs, and second-wave feminism adopted it as a key slogan (while keeping its distance from communist-style appropriations). Yet the 1960s also saw a movement to break down gender divisions when it came to flowers. In 1967, Scott McKenzie landed a global hit with his song 'San Francisco' and its opening line: 'If you're going to San Francisco be sure to wear some flowers in your hair.' It appealed to people of all genders, and was received enthusiastically by a generation that set out to replace war (in Vietnam) with peace, sexual constraints with libertinage and gender hierarchy with equality. Flowers had symbolic value: the 'hippies' wished to 'blossom freely like flowers' so that 'the world will be saved by this now free generation'.[46]

But flowers were not just used to adorn one's hair and clothes. Following the prompt of poet Allen Ginsberg in 1965, flowers were also given to policemen and soldiers. 'Flower Power' was supposed to send a peaceful, cheerful and non-violent message of anti-war sentiment. In October 1967, during the March on the Pentagon, a young man placed carnations into the barrels of military policemen's rifles, a scene which was captured and immortalized in an iconic photograph.[47] Seven years later, the gesture was repeated in Lisbon, when a young Portuguese woman handed a red carnation to a rebellious soldier. Soon after, Lisbon was flooded with red carnations and the military revolt was baptized the 'carnation revolution', *revolução dos cravos*.[48]

To summarize: starting in the late eighteenth century, flowers were strongly associated with emotions. Poems, novels, lexicons, paintings, picture books and advice manuals all emphasized this relationship in great detail and with exceptional ingenuity. Directed, above all, at lovers, they

---

[45]Sarah Eisenstein, *Give Us Bread But Give Us Roses: Working Women's Consciousness in the United States, 1890 to the First World War* (London: Routledge, 1983), quoted 32.
[46]Bennett M. Berger, 'Hippie Morality – More Old than New', *Trans-action* 5 (1967): 19–27, quote 20. See Allen Ginsberg, 'Demonstration as Spectacle or Example, as Communication, or How to Make a March/Spectacle', in *The Portable Sixties Reader*, ed. Ann Charters (London: Penguin Classics, 2002), 208–12.
[47]https://www.worcesterart.org/exhibitions/kennedy-to-kent-state/ (accessed 4 January 2023).
[48]Kenneth Maxwell, 'Portugal: "The Revolution of the Carnations", 1974–75', in *Civil Resistance and Power Politics: The Experience of Non-violent Action from Gandhi to the Present*, ed. Adam Roberts and Timothy Garton Ash (Oxford: Oxford University Press, 2009), 144–61.

marketed and popularized an emotional language that was well received by the educated middle classes, particularly among women. Flowers herewith turned into powerful symbols of femininity and gentility. With the untiring assistance of commercial enterprises, these symbols reached ever more households, especially on Mother's and Valentine's Day. Statistically, the average German currently spends around 150 euros per year on flowers and flowerpots, an amount that is rising.[49] A fifth of the sum is spent on bouquets bought for Mother's Day, and a growing percentage goes towards Valentine's Day. Flowers have thus retained their deeply gendered meanings, although men also occasionally receive flowers as a token of professional or political recognition.

Throughout the modern period, flowers have served as material representations of emotions, imbuing the latter with colour, shape and smell. They have helped bring emotions to the fore, giving them an audible voice. Their work does not stop at representation, however; they also assist the promotion of emotions in private and public communication. Though they rose to prominence in the age of sensibility and Romanticism, flowers have outlived those eras and cultures, stabilizing emotions as a crucial mode of social interaction in both intimate and more formalized relationships. In the early twentieth century, florists embarked on an aggressively successful marketing drive that capitalized on the symbolism of flowers, further contributing to the public visibility and prominence of emotions. Flowers, as a mass commodity, put emotions centre stage and acted as material proof of that position.[50]

They did (and do) so in distinct social contexts: among individuals who either were or wanted to be in a special relationship with another; among members of communities that shared certain political goals and values; as signs of personal allegiance and dedication in the case of citizens sending flowers to monarchs and heads of state; or as tokens of respect, gratitude and appreciation among friends, neighbours and colleagues. Contexts and practices are crucial for the emotional language of flowers to function and flourish. Removed from these contexts, meanings shift and symbolic references collapse.

As an overall trend, the extensive and various use of flowers in private and public communication testifies to a growing emotionalization that arose in European and North American societies around 1800. The emotional

---

[49] ZVG_Jahresbericht_2022_Web_221214.pdf (derdeutschegartenbau.de): 19; https://www.zeit.de/news/2022-02/11/privathaushalte-geben-monatlich-zwoelf-euro-fuer-blumen-aus (both accessed 4 January 2023).
[50] On the commodification of emotions, see Eva Illouz, *Consuming the Romantic Utopia: Love and the Cultural Contradictions of Capitalism* (Berkeley: University of California Press, 1997); *Emotions as Commodities: Capitalism, Consumption and Authenticity*, ed. Eva Illouz (London: Routledge, 2017).

language of flowers became part of an elaborate code for highlighting, addressing and sharing feelings: love, above all, and affectionate attachment but also longing, grief, sorrow and solidarity. Negative feelings, such as anger, rage, envy or jealousy, were implicitly left out and made taboo. In certain cases, as in the Flower Power movement, flowers were even deliberately employed to highlight positive feelings in political actions that might otherwise have provoked resentment and violence.

At the same time, earlier attempts to formalize and thus restrict the emotional coding of flowers have not been successful. In contemporary Western culture and society, people tend to use flowers as they wish. While red roses still symbolize passionate love, red carnations have all but lost their political relevance, except to a small number of citizens and at a small number of events. The pluralization of lifestyles and the dissolution of political milieus all contributed to the language of flowers becoming less fixed and more polysemic and individualized. Reviving a mandatory flower alphabet, grammar or syntax seems out of the question. People still use flowers to communicate feelings, but they increasingly do so free from prescribed rules. Capitalist market societies both enable and benefit from this freedom. As the popular slogan 'Express your feelings by giving flowers' pertains to an infinite number of relations and situations, it generously increases the volume of sales and profits – not to mention the environmental damage – made by the thriving international flower industry.[51]

---

[51] As to the environmental problems caused by those industries, see Yi-Chen Lan et al., 'Life Cycle Environmental Impacts of Cut Flowers: A Review', *Journal of Cleaner Production* 369, no. 1 (2022), available online: https://doi.org/10.1016/j.jclepro.2022.133415.

PART THREE
Politics of Emotion

CHAPTER TWELVE

Emotional Politics in Europe's Long Nineteenth Century

Looking at Europe from the 1780s to the First World War, one cannot help noticing massive and fundamental political changes. To start, there was the 1789 revolution, which profoundly transformed the political landscape in France and had strong repercussions in other parts of Europe and beyond. In 1848, many countries were experiencing considerable revolutionary turmoil, and even though activists stopped short of reaching their ambitious goals, they left a long-lasting imprint on political structures and processes. Even tradition-bound monarchies gradually accepted constitutions that forced them to share power with newly assertive citizens. Rather than being confronted with passive and (more or less) obedient subjects, European kings and queens increasingly had to come to terms with people who were pleading for a new political contract between rulers and ruled. Buzzwords such as parliamentary representation, universal suffrage and democratization were swiftly gaining momentum, as were notions of national identification. New players entered the field, as parties, associations and media attempted to mobilize and organize those who felt empowered to voice their opinions and take part in political deliberations. Old players were confronted with new rules and competing claims as to who could legitimately participate in political debates and decision-making. As a consequence, politics was redefined as a multi-layered process with a growing multitude of participants whose expectations were as diverse as their experiences.

What role, if any, did emotions play in this development? Although the question has rarely been asked, there is no lack of evidence to help

---

This chapter is a revised and expanded version of the article 'In Public: Emotional Politics', in *A Cultural History of the Emotions in the Age of Romanticism, Revolution, and Empire*, ed. Susan J. Matt (London: Bloomsbury, 2019), 157–74.

answer it. Revolutionaries of 1789 and 1848 zealously talked about the new feelings engendered by the overthrow of the *ancien régime*. Liberal activists agonized over politics becoming an arena of passionate party struggle. Conservatives evoked traditions of loyalty and dynastic reverence, while monarchs engaged in sophisticated emotional politics to uphold bonds of faithful adherence. Republicans in turn invented their own mechanisms to foster political allegiance and took great care to create emotionally charged national symbols and material culture.

All in all, processes of politicization and democratization brought about and mobilized collective emotions that had hitherto not played a significant role on the political stage. Even if early modern kings and princes had been keen to proclaim their intention to rule with love instead of fear, their concept of loving relations was light-years away from nineteenth-century notions of love of country, king or queen, empire and nation. In a similar vein, trust entered the political lexicon as a powerful term that was accompanied by tight restrictions, and in many ways it replaced or curtailed older notions of loyalty and fidelity.

To analyse how and why the importance of emotions in politics grew over the long nineteenth century, one has to distinguish between various political actors, spaces and media. Revolutionaries conceived other strategies from those of embattled monarchs to win or reclaim the hearts of citizens. Men (and, increasingly, women) of different social classes and political leanings harboured their own ideas of how to define relations with the state and its personnel. Palaces elicited emotions and emotional practices distinct from those of city squares and streets, just as the emotional styles of party meetings and parliamentary sessions diverged.[1] Finally, the media underwent an equally strong tidal change that affected both the quality and quantity of political information and opinion-making. If one only considers the huge proliferation of newspapers (which often had more than one daily edition) around 1900, the extent to which they were able to influence the political mass market becomes apparent.[2]

Politics, as a whole, learnt to experiment with diverse languages of emotions, in oral, written and visual form. The more political actors addressed citizens in the age of franchise reform, the more they relied on enlisting emotions in order to attract and retain public support. When Max Weber warned in 1919 that politics 'is an activity conducted with the head, and not with other parts of the body or soul', he found himself in the midst of a new revolution. Passions were rising on all sides. Yet Weber was hardly eschewing passion altogether; he knew from first-hand experience that

---

[1] See Ute Frevert et al., *Feeling Political: Emotions and Institutions since 1789* (Cham: Palgrave Macmillan, 2022).
[2] As to the notion of a 'political mass market', see James Retallack, 'The Authoritarian State and the Political Mass Market', in *Imperial Germany Revisited: Continuing Debates and New Perspectives*, ed. Sven Oliver Müller and Cornelius Torp (New York: Berghahn, 2011), 83–96.

dedication to politics 'can only be generated and sustained by passion'.[3] This was true for the men and, to a lesser extent, the women who held or sought political office. It also pertained to the far larger constituencies who were discovering politics not as a personal ambition but as a civic commitment.

Emotional politics before, during and after 1789

In an effort to trace emotions in politics, one might start with Ancient Greece and Aristotle's reflections on how to move an audience with emotional rhetoric. Considering the participatory structure of Athenian politics, orators were indeed well advised to create 'suitable temperaments' and steer emotional energies towards certain objects and goals.[4] When the democratic element was lost in later times, rulers no longer had to deliver engaging speeches in order to rally support and consent. Nevertheless, as the Florentine politician, diplomat and political philosopher Niccolò Machiavelli pointed out in the early sixteenth century, princes should strive to be both loved and feared by their subjects; as the default, fear generally proved to be a more stable mechanism of rule than love.[5]

During the reign of absolutism, European monarchs increasingly chose to discard Machiavelli's recommendation, at least in theory. Prussia's Friedrich II, who became king in 1740, wrote long treatises refuting him. Fear, he claimed, would only produce crowds of slaves who would do what was requested of them and nothing more. Love, in contrast, could incite subjects to 'great achievements' that enhanced the state's power and glory. Yet the king did very little to put theory into practice. Even though he graciously accepted his subjects' tokens of reverence, his rule relied on strict obedience rather than on emotional compliance and commitment.[6]

Friedrich died three years before the French Revolution violently turned the tables of emotional politics. Obedient subjects reinvented themselves as assured citizens who took pride in claiming political rights and asserting sovereign power over their own – and the nation's – fate and well-being. The nation's 'will and desire' of which the Paris-based writer Germaine de

---

[3]Max Weber, 'The Profession and the Vocation of Politics', in *Weber: Political Writings*, ed. Peter Lassman and Ronald Speirs (Cambridge: Cambridge University Press, 1994), 309–69, quote 353.
[4]Amélie Oksenberg Rorty, ed., *Essays on Aristotle's Rhetoric* (Berkeley: University of California Press, 1996); Cheshire Calhoun and Robert C. Solomon, eds, *What Is an Emotion?* (New York: Oxford University Press, 1984), 48; William V. Harris, *Restraining Rage: The Ideology of Anger Control in Classical Antiquity* (Cambridge, MA: Harvard University Press, 2001).
[5]Niccolò Machiavelli, *The Prince*, ed. W.J. Cornell (Boston: Bedford, 2005), 90–3.
[6]Ute Frevert, *Gefühlspolitik: Friedrich II. als Herr über die Herzen?* (Göttingen: Wallstein, 2012), 50, *passim*.

Staël spoke so highly in 1789 was expressed with 'a sincere and impartial enthusiasm' and went hand in hand with 'generous sentiments' that aimed to engender a new solidarity or 'fraternity' among citizens.[7] Fraternal bonds and feelings were henceforth to unite the French people regardless of social class and religion – with the exception of women and slaves, who were initially omitted from the national project.

Imagining and presenting the nation as a band of brothers who had emancipated themselves from an omnipotent father drew on various conceptions of fraternity that were circulating at the time: monastic, pietist and masonic. All placed great emphasis on brotherly love and friendship as the glue that bound men of different social origins together and formed a new unity of companions who thought and felt alike.[8] Politicized during the revolutionary events, fraternity became the rallying cry of civic assemblies and was demonstrated by emotional practices like walking arm in arm or publicly embracing each other.[9]

Such practices were widely appreciated by those who fervently sought to set democratic achievements on safe and stable grounds. Remodelling free citizens' sentiments, habits, principles and actions proved to be a major task.[10] For Maximilien Robespierre, a revolutionary society would craft its 'masterpiece' by creating a rapid 'instinct' in men that told them how to do what was morally (or rather, politically) good without having to engage in protracted reasoning.[11] Emotions were supposed to do the job of directing people's political opinions and judgements. But how could one instil such emotions, instincts and intuitions? And how could one make sure that they remained aligned with revolutionary politics, especially as the latter became widely and ferociously contested among the various groups

---

[7]William M. Reddy, 'Sentimentalism and Its Erasure: The Role of Emotions in the Era of the French Revolution', *Journal of Modern History* 72, no. 1 (2000): 109–52, here 110, 134.

[8]Wolfgang Schieder, 'Brüderlichkeit', in *Geschichtliche Grundbegriffe*, ed. Otto Brunner, Werner Conze and Reinhart Koselleck, vol. 1 (Stuttgart: Klett-Cotta, 1972), 554–81, here 552–66; Catherine Brice, ed., *Frères de sang, frères d'armes, frères ennemis: La fraternité à Italie* (Rome: Collection de l'École Française de Rome, 2017); Lynn Hunt, *The Family Romance of the French Revolution* (Berkeley: University of California Press, 1992), 12–13, ch. 3.

[9]Schieder, 'Brüderlichkeit', 565–6; Reddy, 'Sentimentalism', 140.

[10]As the Temporary Commission on Republican Surveillance put it in 1793, 'there is nothing, absolutely nothing in common between the slave of a tyrant and the inhabitant of a free state; the customs of the latter, his principles, his sentiments, his action, all must be new', quoted in Lynn Hunt, *Politics, Culture, and Class in the French Revolution* (Berkeley: University of California Press, 1984), 29.

[11]Sophie Wahnich, 'Sentiments et émotions dans l'élaboration des savoirs politiques instinctifs', *Revue Suisse d'Histoire* 61, no. 1 (2011): 22–38, quote 32; Sophie Wahnich, *Les Émotions, la révolution française et le présent* (Paris: CNRS Éditions, 2009); Sophie Wahnich, 'Les Émotions collectives comme émotions sacrées et souveraines pendant la Révolution française 1789-1794', in *Histoire des émotions collectives: Épistémologie, émergences, experiences*, ed. Damien Boquet, Piroska Nagy and Lidia Zanetti Domingues (Paris: Classiques Garnier, 2022), 353–82.

of self-proclaimed revolutionaries? New symbols like the cockade, hymns, cults and festivals seemed helpful, as did political assemblies, speeches and rallies. The latter, however, were in increasing danger of being split along party lines.[12]

To avert this, republicans placed a strong emphasis on national identification and patriotic feelings. Ever since Abbé Sieyès famously proclaimed that the third estate – comprising those who did not belong either to the clergy or to the aristocracy – was the nation itself, it became the deliberate focus of patriotism and related propaganda efforts. When the Jacobin deputy Joseph Fouché visited the provinces in 1793, he reported on the powerful emotional appeal of the 'happy festival of a general and fraternal reunion around the tree of liberty': 'Such sweet tears ran from every eye, because the love of the fatherland lives in every heart.' The following sentence was equally telling: 'Send arms to the citizens of Clamecy, they are ready to shed their blood in its defense.'[13]

Love of nation and fatherland not only materialized in joyous, tearful outbursts of fraternal feeling for other members of the nation. It was also expressed in acts of sacrifice such as going to war and protecting the nation from outside enemies. The nation here acquired a quasi-religious aura; it was clearly more than the sum of its parts and promised transcendence and progress. By embodying the cherished values of liberty and equality, it assumed a historical mission to serve humanity and foster social improvement around the globe. To be a citizen of the French nation, therefore, meant to commit oneself without restraint to the universal task. Lack of commitment was suspected to be a sign of treason and was punished with severe sanctions that ranged from public humiliation to radical exclusion.[14]

Such expectations exercised a great deal of emotional pressure on men as well as on the smaller number of women who, despite widespread male resistance, strove to be active members of and participants in the political nation. Especially during the Reign of Terror, accusations of treason were omnipresent. The fanatic moralization and emotionalization of politics did its best to turn even the most eager *ami du peuple* into an alleged enemy of the national cause. As the immediate threat of foreign military invasion, which had rallied citizens to concerted acts of collective sacrifice, receded, Robespierre's camp attempted to purify and regenerate the nation through violent purges sold as radical justice. Overextending their case, the Jacobins quickly lost out to more moderate factions that reduced the pressure on people to display (and question) heart-felt, utterly sincere emotions towards the revolutionaries' goals. Depoliticizing the streets and clubs was in line

---

[12]Mona Ozouf, *Festivals and the French Revolution* (Cambridge, MA: Harvard University Press, 1991).
[13]Reddy, 'Sentimentalism', quote 140.
[14]Charles Walton, *Policing Public Opinion in the French Revolution: The Culture of Calumny and the Problem of Free Speech* (New York: Oxford University Press, 2009), 3–9, 193–225.

with handing politics back to those who were more concerned with citizens' private fortunes than with *bonheur commun* and the republic of virtue. From then on, happiness was to be found in a calm family life and the pursuit of self-interest, rather than in public agitation.[15]

Yet there was no way back to the times of the *ancien régime*, when politics had been largely monopolized by the ruler and his councils. Even under Napoleon's authoritarian leadership, citizens were summoned to voice their opinion in plebiscites and did so in the millions.[16] After the Bourbon monarchy was restored in 1815, the constitution limited the right to elect parliamentary representatives to a small group of wealthy taxpayers. Although the franchise was extended after the July revolution of 1830, it was still far from including the majority in the sphere of politics. Fear of the *classes dangereuses* – mainly workers, whose numbers were growing rapidly during the Industrial Revolution – prompted liberals and conservatives to restrict political deliberation to so-called reasonable and responsible citizens. Reason was associated with property and education monopolized by a group of *notables* who held enlightened opinions and made logical judgements. In no way were elections supposed to open the door to the passionate agitation of radical demagogues who preached emotional excess and fostered social division.

Instead, the 'bourgeois' monarchy installed in 1830 sought to engage citizens in a thoroughly pacified form of family romance.[17] Assuming the title 'King of the French' instead of 'King of France', Louis Philippe deliberately reached out to the people. He presented himself as a monarch whose habits, behaviour and morals were those of a 'citizen king'. Portraits showed him alongside his wife and children in a constellation that purportedly resembled the prototypical French family with a caring patriarch, loving mother and cheerful offspring. The message was clear: the king was the true representative of the French nation and embodied its fundamental virtues. If such a monarch bore responsibility for the nation's fate, politics would return to solid ground and citizens would be able to rejoice in the peaceful conduct of their private affairs.[18]

---

[15]William M. Reddy, *The Navigation of Feeling* (Cambridge: Cambridge University Press, 2001), 190–210. The *bonheur commun* was proclaimed as the 'goal of society' in the Jacobin Constitution of 1793. As to various notions of happiness, see Chapter 10 in this volume.

[16]Malcolm Crook, 'Uses of Democracy: Elections and Plebiscite in Napoleonic France', in *The French Experience from Republic to Monarchy, 1792–1824*, ed. Maire F. Gross and David Williams (New York: Palgrave, 2000), 58–71.

[17]Hunt, *Family Romance*, makes use of Freud's concept to analyse the power games of 1789 in terms of filial and parental/maternal relations.

[18]Munro Price, *The Perilous Crown: France between Revolutions, 1814–1848* (London: Macmillan, 2007).

The emotional charm of royalty

Louis Philippe was not alone in sending this message. Earlier in the century, Prussia had experienced similar tendencies of royal embourgeoisement and popularization. Queen Luise, who died young in 1810, had been heralded as a heroine of middle-class mores and intimate family life at the Berlin court. Together with her husband, Friedrich Wilhelm III, she was at the centre of public attention, and local guilds and civic associations competed jealously to host the couple for coffee and cake. Even though she readily complied, promising to 'earn and deserve the love of our subjects by politeness, attentiveness, and gratefulness', she quibbled at the inverted expectation of royals 'courting' citizens.[19]

Shortly after the French king and queen met their ends at the guillotine, such inversions actually seemed to make a lot of sense. Although local magistrates vowed that Prussians would never emulate their neighbours' insolent example, there was widespread concern that even Prussians might turn against their king. As the officer August Neidhardt von Gneisenau wrote to Friedrich Wilhelm in 1811, the monarchy needed the 'love of a people enthusiastic for its ruler' in order to be secure. Such love was to be nurtured and sustained by emphasizing the active role of subjects in 'protecting throne and state'. Due to long-standing neglect, these conservative elements were lying dormant. Once awakened, they would 'amaze the world'.[20]

Defeated and humiliated in 1807 by Napoleon and his seemingly invincible army, the Prussian king took the advice to heart, albeit reluctantly. In 1813, he emphatically appealed to 'my people' to defend the fatherland and assert Prussian honour.[21] While honour had hitherto been the exclusive property of the prince and the state he represented, it now stood as a collective good in which each Prussian participated, for better or worse. Even though Friedrich Wilhelm surely did not quite intend it, his offer to extend honour to all subjects and citizens was the first step on the long path to political democratization. Moreover, it was a move that not only used highly emotional language but also targeted a crucial emotional concept and practice. Contemporaries believed that honour, whether socially or politically defined, was firmly 'rooted in the heart' – the very organ from which emotions sprang.[22] To let citizens partake in the honour of state and

---

[19] Hubert Büschel, *Untertanenliebe: Der Kult um deutsche Monarchen 1770–1830* (Göttingen: Vandenhoeck & Ruprecht, 2006), 261; Matthias Schwengelbeck, *Die Politik des Zeremoniells: Huldigungsfeiern im langen 19. Jahrhundert* (Frankfurt: Campus, 2007), 121.
[20] *Gneisenau: Ein Leben in Briefen*, ed. Karl Griewank (Leipzig: Köhler & Amelang, 1939), 175.
[21] Karen Hagemann, *Revisiting Prussia's Wars against Napoleon: History, Culture and Memory* (New York: Cambridge University Press, 2015); Ute Frevert, *A Nation in Barracks: Modern Germany, Military Conscription and Civil Society* (Oxford: Berg, 2004), 22–30.
[22] Ute Frevert, *Emotions in History – Lost and Found* (Budapest: Central European University Press, 2011), quote 41. See also Chapter 3 in this book.

prince thus created emotional ties that far surpassed the affection subjects were traditionally expected to harbour towards their dynastic rulers. In addition, it promised a larger share of active responsibility and pride than they had previously enjoyed.

In many European countries, citizens proved eager to bear such responsibility. They were no longer satisfied with being treated like children by an omnipotent father who claimed to know best what was good for them. Still, very few went as far as exiling or killing the father. Even liberals who insisted on the necessity of a constitution did not want to abolish monarchical order. Rather, they promoted the iconic image of a citizen king and queen who consented to share power and cooperate with the 'nation' on the basis of mutual respect and adherence to the rule of law. Britain served as a role model here, especially when the young Queen Victoria ascended the throne in 1837. As a constitutional monarch, her influence on government decisions was limited; she only had the 'right to be consulted, the right to encourage, the right to warn', as Walter Bagehot put it in 1867.[23] Her symbolic power, however, was immense.

Especially after her marriage to Prince Albert in 1840, the queen's popularity grew enormously. With nine children, the royal household appeared to be the incarnation of middle-class morality and family values: loving, caring, burden-sharing, reasonably thrifty, responsible. Court scandals became a thing of the past; in their place, heart-warming portraits of the royal family flooded the country in the form of reprints on postcards and other material objects. Even though the monarchy was not uncontested, republican criticism remained on the margins of public discourse. The middle-class press, in particular, actively propagated a sense of reverence that met with widespread approval. As the 'first media monarch', Victoria was depicted, in an increasingly emotional language, both as the matriarchal centre of a well-ordered family and as a romanticized fairy-tale figure. Each member of the growing family received ample attention. Births were celebrated as much as weddings.[24] Multiple assassination attempts further strengthened the nation's attachment to the queen who, in Benjamin Disraeli's words, was regarded as 'the proper leader of the people'.[25]

The people that sent Victoria tokens of love and loyalty and took an eager interest in every trivial detail of the royal household were by no means apolitical or, as republicans believed, 'sick'. In their eyes, the queen was not

---

[23] Walter Bagehot, *The Collected Works of Walter Bagehot, vol. 4: The English Constitution*, ed. F. Morgan (London: Routledge, 1995), 112.

[24] John Plunkett, *Queen Victoria: First Media Monarch* (Oxford: Oxford University Press, 2003); Richard Williams, *The Contentious Crown: Public Discussion of the British Monarchy in the Reign of Queen Victoria* (Aldershot: Ashgate, 1997); Antony Taylor, *'Down with the Crown': British Anti-monarchism and Debates about Royalty since 1790* (London: Reaktion Books, 1999).

[25] Benjamin Disraeli, *Coningsby*, 2nd edn, vol. 3 (London: Colburn, 1844), 101.

removed from politics but at its very heart. Her direct political power limited by the (uncodified) constitution, she was assigned a symbolic and emotional power that helped to integrate diverse political opinions. Furthermore, it served the larger goal of epitomizing the global achievements and claims of the British Empire. Her jubilees, above all the 'golden' and 'diamond' in 1887 and 1897 respectively, marked the heyday of British glory and were deliberately staged as triumphant events. The millions of citizens who witnessed the royal procession or read about it in the newspaper were invited to feel included and to genuinely participate in that glory. Victoria personified everything that was laudable about British civilization – achievements which would be generously exported to other regions around the world.

Personification was a crucial part of what the constitutional monarch did in and for politics. At a time when politics was becoming more multi-layered and bureaucratic, the focus on queen or king offered a way for people to access politics without getting lost in procedural intricacies and complexities. In positive terms, it allowed emotions to be bound to abstractions like monarchical rule, empire or national endeavours that by themselves could scarcely be loved, adored or worshipped. Personified by the royal leader, such abstractions were brought to life and embraced by large parts of the population, especially by those who shied away from getting entangled in the more mundane operations of the political process. Given Victoria's character, it was particularly easy to present her as the immaculate figurehead of British politics and as the embodiment of the empire's 'moral responsibility'.[26] But even when a monarch's personality was deemed less agreeable, they could, with the help of the press, acquire an air of serenity and gravitas that sold well to the national public.

Image management became more and more important in all European countries during the nineteenth century. It proved indispensable in newly founded nation-states like Italy, where the monarchy actively participated in the construction of national identity.[27] It was equally essential in traditionally multi-ethnic empires like Austria–Hungary, which were experiencing bouts of nationalist strife and the ongoing threat of secession after 1848. Emperor Franz Joseph, who reigned between 1848 and 1916, played a crucial role here. Having ascended to the throne in the midst of a revolution that strove to end absolutist rule in Vienna, the young emperor, who harboured strictly anti-constitutional views, was never popular among liberal-minded citizens, let alone with the growing social-democratic movement. Yet he soon became iconic for bridging the rift between the various lands of the Habsburg Empire. Emphasizing his strong attachment to Catholicism and his position as the

---

[26]*The Times*, 17 July 1897, 13.
[27]Catherine Brice, *Monarchie et identité nationale en Italie (1861–1900)* (Paris: Éditions EHESS, 2010).

commander of a multi-national army, Franz Joseph sought to strengthen the two major forces that could fight nationalism and prevent the empire's dissolution.

The cult of personality that developed during the last decades of his long reign expressed itself in quasi-religious forms. In 1908, 80,000 children from all parts of the country were sent to Schönbrunn palace to congratulate the 'lonely' emperor on the sixtieth anniversary of his reign. Having lost many members of his family to sickness, suicide and assassination, Franz Joseph was venerated as the uncontested father of the fatherland who worked incessantly for the unity and well-being of his 'children'. Even social democrats could not but acknowledge, albeit grudgingly, that monarchical sentiments had perhaps never been stronger or more pervasive:

> It is altogether false to assume that our era bears a levelling tendency and minimizes monarchical grandeur and sublimity through parliamentary and constitutional mechanisms. When, in all times, have princes ever been worshipped in such devout humility as today?[28]

What was new about the modern 'worship' of princes was not the degree of humility, but the number of people who openly and willingly showed it. Archives of the nineteenth century store hundreds of thousands of letters that were sent to kings and queens. They spoke of love, gratitude and devotion, and they were written by men and women of all ages and from all social classes. Those who wrote letters or sent poems and presents did not do so for any material gain; at most, they asked for a signed photograph to proudly display in the family's living room.[29] Such outpouring of 'dynastic sentimentality', as Otto von Bismarck called it, was indeed a novel experience that was by no means a given.[30] After the revolutions of 1848 had been crushed in Vienna, Budapest, Munich, Berlin and elsewhere, monarchical rule lost some of its unquestioned legitimacy and recognition. The monarch's decision to take sides and dispatch troops against liberal and democratic forces had politicized his authority, which no longer existed above and beyond the urgent question of 'how the state should be governed in the future'. Instead, as the German political economist Lorenz von Stein

---

[28] *Arbeiter-Zeitung*, 14 August 1908. See Lawrence Cole and Daniel Unowsky, eds, *The Limits of Loyalty: Imperial Symbolism, Popular Allegiances, and State Patriotism in the Late Habsburg Monarchy* (New York: Berghahn, 2007); Daniel Unowsky, 'Creating Patriotism: Imperial Celebrations and the Cult of Franz Joseph', *Österreichische Zeitschrift für Geschichtswissenschaften* 9, no. 2 (1998): 280–93.

[29] Eva Giloi, '"So Writes the Hand That Swings the Sword": Autograph Hunting and Royal Charisma in the German Empire, 1861–1888', in *Constructing Charisma*, ed. Edward Berenson and Eva Giloi (New York: Berghahn, 2010), 41–51; Eva Giloi, *Monarchy, Myth, and Material Culture in Germany 1750–1950* (Cambridge: Cambridge University Press, 2011).

[30] Otto von Bismarck, *Gedanken und Erinnerungen* (Berlin: Propyläen, 1990), 222, 224.

observed in the 1850s, the monarchy had become, 'even among the masses, an object of reflection, discussion, and investigation'.[31]

While von Stein spoke and wrote in favour of a bipartisan social monarchy that cared particularly for the lower classes and would in turn attract their strong support, the organized labour movement was less enthusiastic. Even though some of its leaders approved of monarchical rule (albeit bound and limited by a constitution), most did not. Still, in their own homes, social democrats sometimes chose to hang portraits of Ferdinand Lassalle and August Bebel, the founders of the party, next to a picture of the emperor.[32] In Bavaria or Saxony, allegiance to local dynasties vastly outranked sympathy for the Prussian rulers, who, despite ascending the imperial throne in 1871, never quite succeeded in presenting themselves as German.[33]

Nevertheless, even the house of Hohenzollern gradually learnt how to deal with popular sentiment in post-revolutionary times. For Wilhelm I, German emperor from 1871 to 1888, the learning curve was particularly steep. Widely despised and exiled as a military firebrand during the 1848 revolution, he later turned into a beloved fatherly figure whose death at the age of 91 was mourned by millions. When he was seriously wounded by an assassin in 1878, the palace was flooded with telegrams, letters and presents from all segments of the population wishing him well. Wilhelm jokingly called the assassin his 'best doctor', referring not to his physical health but to the surge in popularity that he enjoyed as a result of the assassination attempt. Rather than being heralded as a martial hero and military commander-in-chief, his vulnerability and frailty won people's hearts.[34]

That these hearts had to be won in order to sustain monarchical rule was the lesson learnt against the backdrop of what Wilhelm had, in the 1860s, condemned as 'misleading press' and 'party fervour'.[35] The throne was to recapture public opinion, and it could do so through emotional politics. As a Prussian king, Wilhelm renounced traditional forms of collective homage and invented new ceremonies like the coronation. His birthdays were made into local and national events, celebrated by middle-class dignitaries as well

---

[31]Lorenz von Stein, *Das Königthum, die Republik und die Souveränetät der französischen Gesellschaft seit der Februarrevolution 1848*, 2nd edn (Leipzig: Wigand, 1855), 12.

[32]Werner Blessing, 'The Cult of Monarchy, Political Loyalty and the Workers' Movement in Imperial Germany', *Journal of Contemporary History* 13, no. 2 (1978): 357–75; Gerhard A. Ritter and Klaus Tenfelde, *Arbeiter im Deutschen Kaiserreich 1871–1914* (Bonn: Dietz, 1992), 602.

[33]As reported by the police, workers' opinions on the monarchy were by no means positive in the republican city of Hamburg: Richard J. Evans, *Kneipengespräche im Kaiserreich: Die Stimmungsberichte der Hamburger Politischen Polizei 1892–1914* (Reinbek: Rowohlt, 1989), 322–40.

[34]Carola Dietze, 'Terror in the Nineteenth Century: Political Assassinations and Public Discourse in Europe and the United States, 1878–1901', *Bulletin of the German Historical Institute* 40, no. 1 (2007): 91–7; Giloi, *Monarchy*, 157–85, 209.

[35]*Kaiser Wilhelms des Großen Briefe, Reden und Schriften*, ed. Ernst Berner, vol. 2 (Berlin: Mittler, 1906), 30, 39, 41.

as by the army and in schools. His favourite cornflower became an emblem of personal attachment; citizens wore and gave them to one another (and to the king) on his birthday.[36] Textbooks invariably included personal interest stories about the royal family; all students knew the poem 'The Emperor is a kind and decent man', which was not only recited but also set to a popular melody and sung, and thus stuck in everybody's memory. The words roused a recurring motive of monarchical sentiments: to be close to the king, to see him face to face and possibly to hold his hand.[37]

Such 'learnt' longings were not limited to children. Many adults of both genders and all ages shared the desire to entertain a 'personal relationship' with the monarch. While conservatives saw this as confirming the 'indissoluble loyalty' of subjects, liberals emphasized the voluntary affection of a 'free citizenry'.[38] Freedom, though, always harboured the possibility of a change of opinion. This is why the historian and public intellectual Heinrich von Treitschke repeatedly warned that 'the intimate trust of a people in its rulers must constantly be earned afresh'.[39]

To do this, the monarch and his councillors happily leaned on the new channels of communication and media. Following in his English grandmother Victoria's footsteps, the German emperor Wilhelm II, who ruled from 1888 to 1918, deployed photography and film to reach out to the public and to portray himself as a monarch in touch with his people. He was constantly in the news, inaugurating patriotic monuments, visiting cities, opening military celebrations or meeting with other monarchs. Above all, he loved to give speeches. Nicknamed the 'talking emperor', he used every opportunity to address diverse audiences in highly emotional language. Occasionally, he forgot that journalists, who had their own agendas and interests, were present. The press, as Wilhelm soon found out, could not be relied on as an obedient tool of monarchical politics. Liberal, Catholic and socialist dailies that had been multiplying since the 1880s and sold millions of copies (some printing several issues per day) often selectively quoted the emperor's speeches to pinpoint flaws and rebuke his views. Creating scandal proved a convenient way to sell even more copies and win over readers. Due to repressive press laws concerning *lèse-majesté*, journalists usually refrained from directly insulting the monarch. But, if they aligned with liberal or left-wing party politics, they certainly did not shy away from openly criticizing Wilhelm's behaviour and attacking his politics.[40]

---

[36]See Chapter 11 in this volume.
[37]Eckhard John, '"Der Kaiser ist ein lieber Mann": Schulische Liedsozialisation im Kaiserreich', in *Good-bye Memories? Lieder im Generationengedächtnis des 20. Jahrhunderts*, ed. Barbara Stambolis and Jürgen Reulecke (Essen: Klartext, 2007), 25–41.
[38]Schwengelbeck, *Politik*, quotes 267–8.
[39]Heinrich von Treitschke, *Politics*, vol. 2 (New York: Macmillan, 1916), 75.
[40]Martin Kohlrausch, 'The Workings of Royal Celebrity: Wilhelm II as Media Emperor', in *Constructing Charisma*, ed. Berenson and Giloi, 52–66; Martin Kohlrausch, *Der Monarch im Skandal: Die Logik der Massenmedien und die Transformation der wilhelminischen Monarchie* (Berlin: Akademie-Verlag, 2005); Jörg Requate, *Journalismus als Beruf* (Göttingen: Vandenhoeck & Ruprecht, 1995).

Mass mobilization and party politics

The press was one of several factors that thoroughly influenced the emerging political mass market in the nineteenth century. As that market expanded with the extension of the right to vote, new forms of political mobilization and organization developed, creating further opportunities for emotional politics and putting emotions centre stage.

In many Continental European countries, mass mobilization started around 1848. Revolutionary news from Paris travelled fast, sparking a wave of protests and petitions to kings and parliaments (in places where they already existed). People gathered in local squares and on the streets, listened to self-proclaimed orators and continued the debate in pubs and assemblies of all kinds. New associations were formed every day, and older ones became highly politicized spaces where men, and sometimes women, expressed opinions and fought to defend them against competing ones. Millions were initiated into political life and set out to redefine and transform politics.[41]

Constant communication was at the heart of the politicizing process. People talked and listened, read leaflets and newspapers, circulated rumours, drafted petitions, wrote letters and articles. In cities like Berlin and Vienna, speeches were held on every corner at every hour. It was the era of the orator, whose rhetoric determined the success or failure of ideas and viewpoints. To capture people's attention, appeals to their emotions proved particularly helpful. How the audience was addressed – as brothers, fellow citizens, friends – set the tone for what was to follow. One strategy was to empower listeners and spectators as political actors and whip up the public mood. The new-born citizen was supposed to cast off his passive status as subject and proudly voice his own thoughts and feelings. Imbued with patriotic fervour, he would then seek like-minded others with whom he could collaborate to bring about change. Another strategy aimed to emotionally divide the political field into friends and enemies. While friends could be trusted and loved, enemies were to be suspected, feared, despised or hated. At both extremes, such strategies could, and did, verge on the fanatic. While fanaticism had hitherto been defined as a religious phenomenon, it now extended to politics.

This became evident not only in spontaneous gatherings but also in parliamentary assemblies, which were institutionalized during the constitutionalist phase of the 1848 revolutions. As had happened in France after 1789, competing factions quickly upped the oratory pressure and fought each other with fierce words and emotional zeal. Parliamentarians did not hesitate to exchange insults, and more than once instigated duels in order to honourably settle a case. They shouted, screamed, threatened and

---

[41] Ute Frevert, 'Feeling Political in Demonstrations: Street Politics in Germany, 1832–2018', in Frevert et al., *Feeling Political*, 341–71.

sought to seduce their audience. They hammered their fists, waved their arms, rose from their seats and rushed to the rostrum. They shed tears, they were enraged, they jubilated. And their emotional outbursts were observed: by journalists who later reported on what they had seen and heard, and by spectators who had come to witness first-hand how the new politics was practised. Rather than silently watching from the gallery what was happening below, visitors likewise chose to be vocal and either cheered or howled down the speakers. Parliamentary assemblies thus resembled and were perceived as battlefields, with words and voices as sharp as weapons, accessorized with body language that not only expressed strong emotions but also helped to impress them upon others.[42]

At times, passions ran so high that violence erupted. Assassination attempts were not unheard of. Elderly gentlemen, professors and businessmen felt emotionally overwhelmed and deeply troubled by the heated style of political communication. They tended to blame democrats and socialists for kindling passions and stoking social discontent. But this was only half true. Even though left-wingers were more closely attuned to popular moods and better equipped to use them to boost their political claims, liberals and conservatives quickly learnt to rally the wider public as well. Especially during elections, they developed increasingly sophisticated strategies to mobilize voters, again by issuing fervently emotional appeals and promises.

'Practising democracy' by attracting citizens to the ballot box and making them support a party's political agenda necessitated passionate campaigning by those seeking election.[43] Winston Churchill, who undertook his first campaign in 1899, thoroughly enjoyed

> the succession of great halls packed with excited people until there was not room for one single person more – speech after speech – meeting after meeting – three even four in one night – intermittent flashes of Heat & Light & enthusiasm – with cold air and the rattle of a carriage in between.[44]

He always appreciated a 'splendid fight', though only ones that abided by the rules and were fought with words rather than fists. Indeed, when Conservative supporters in Birmingham turned in fury against the Liberal politician David Lloyd George in 1902 and physically threatened him, Churchill was outraged.[45]

---

[42]See, for example, the first-hand account by Heinrich Laube, *Das erste deutsche Parlament*, 3 vols (Aalen: Scientia, [1849] 1978).
[43]Margaret L. Anderson, *Practicing Democracy: Elections and Political Culture in Imperial Germany* (Princeton: Princeton University Press, 2000).
[44]Martin Gilbert, *The Will of the People: Winston Churchill and Parliamentary Democracy* (Toronto: Vintage Canada, 2006).
[45]Ibid., 16, 25. See also, for Britain, Frank O'Gorman, 'Campaign Rituals and Ceremonies', *Past & Present* no. 135 (1992): 79–115; for the US, Richard Franklin Bensel, *The American Ballot Box in the Mid-Nineteenth Century* (Cambridge: Cambridge University Press, 2004), esp. 287–95.

The emotionalization of politics as it occurred in parliamentary sessions and during election campaigns was not applauded by everybody. When the republican lawyer Léon Gambetta took the floor of the French National Assembly in the 1860s and 1870s, sweeping away friends and foes alike with his passionate oratory, he was frequently criticized for the profusion of emotions in his speeches. Detractors reprimanded Gambetta for behaving irresponsibly, and were threatened by the prospect of him becoming a plebiscitary tribune of the people. Those who favoured his politics tried to defend him against such allegations, maintaining that reason and emotion were not, in his case, opposed but rather strategically complemented one another.[46] Politics, so the argument went, needed both careful reasoning and strong passions. As Max Weber put it in 1919, politicians had to be passionate as well as responsible, and to act with a sense of proportion that helped to merge 'hot passion and cool judgment [...] together in a single soul' without privileging one over the other.[47]

In the popular opinion of the times, this sense of proportion pertained only to men. The majority of people, including women, held politics to be a male business. It demanded strong nerves and equally sturdy egos that would not collapse under pressure. Considered emotionally frail and delicate, women were not deemed capable of participating in the 'passionate battles' fought over political affairs. If they did, they would supposedly either be defeated by more passionate and determined men, or lose their 'sweet femininity' and turn into despicable viragos. Politics, too, would suffer from women engaging in party strife and verbal sparring matches; since they were seen to be strong in sentiments but weak in passions, women would temper politics down to a babbling brook rather than raise it to an energetic, powerful current. Great deeds, as conventional wisdom had it, came out of 'great passions' and thus demanded genuinely passionate men rather than overly sensitive women.[48]

For this and other reasons, women were neither allowed to vote in political elections nor to participate in party politics. Party membership, which rose consistently in the latter half of the nineteenth century, remained an exclusively male privilege and was zealously guarded against feminist demands for inclusion. Parties did increasingly learn to integrate and enlist their members' wives, sisters and daughters, albeit on supposedly non-political grounds. Socialist parties in particular evolved into complex organizations with a myriad of branches and activities open to all family members, from cradle to grave. Getting children and wives involved in

---

[46]Paula Cossart, 'L'émotion: un dommage pour l'idée républicaine: Autour de l'éloquence de Léon Gambetta', *Romantisme* 119 (2003): 47–60; Yves Déloye, 'Le Charisme controlé: Entre grandeur et raison: La posture publique de Léon Gambetta', *Communications* 69 (2000): 157–72.
[47]Weber, 'Profession', 353.
[48]Frevert, *Emotions in History*, 115–19.

party festivals, choirs and volunteer work meant politicizing even those who could not and would not be part of direct political deliberation and decision-making. And it formed lasting emotional bonds between the families in question, who viewed each other as belonging to a fast-growing and ultimately victorious political movement. Those bonds were fostered by common symbols and practices, such as waving flags and singing songs that were emotionally charged and that connected the individual person to the higher goals of the political community.[49]

From its very beginning, the labour movement had invented and employed strong emotional language in order to strengthen internal cohesion and provide shelter against external repression. Robert Owen's cooperative movement was no less keen on emphasizing warm fraternal relations among its members than the friendly societies that played a significant role in the making of the English working class.[50] In Germany, the first workers' political organization, formed in 1848, carried fraternity in its very name and chose two clasped brotherly hands as its main (and enduring) emblem. As brothers, party members were not only supposed to love and help but also to trust each other. As one organizer warned in 1862, if workers did not learn to overcome mutual suspicion and establish 'fraternal trust', they would never achieve their political ambitions.[51]

Trust, defined as the ability to believe in and rely on the cooperating person's goodwill, kindness and benevolence, became a major political buzzword that accompanied the development of constitutionalism, party politics and democratization. Trust, in liberal opinion, was to govern the relations between rulers and ruled and to enable power-sharing: rulers trusting their former subjects, who were becoming self-confident citizens; citizens trusting the government that they had themselves helped to install by sending elected representatives to parliament. Unlike traditional notions of loyalty, modern trust was considered mutual, conditional and relatively short-term.[52]

In order for the people to trust the government, certain prerequisites had to be in place, above all parliamentary control. In order for voters to trust their representatives, the latter had to stick to their political agenda and keep the promises they had made before the election. Periodically, such compliance had to be tested and affirmed (or not) in a new round of voting.

---

[49]Ritter and Tenfelde, *Arbeiter*, 818–35; Wolfgang Ruppert, ed., *Die Arbeiter* (Munich: C.H. Beck, 1986).
[50]*The Owenite Socialist Movement: Pamphlets and Correspondence*, ed. Gregory Claeys, 10 vols (London: Routledge, 2005); Edward P. Thompson, *The Making of the English Working Class* (Harmondsworth: Penguin, 1968), 456–88, 857–87.
[51]Frolinde Balser, *Sozial-Demokratie 1848/49–1863: Die erste deutsche Arbeiterorganisation 'Allgemeine Arbeiterverbrüderung' nach der Revolution* (Stuttgart: Klett, 1962); Ute Frevert, *Vertrauensfragen: Eine Obsession der Moderne* (Munich: C.H. Beck, 2013), 172.
[52]See Chapter 2 in this volume.

Even hereditary monarchs were well advised, as Treitschke reminded them, to bid for the people's trust, which in the age of political mass mobilization and participation was no longer a given.

Trust thus proved to be both a highly attractive and utterly deceptive emotional disposition. It was appealing because it secured the smooth functioning of political cooperation and communication. Its downside lay in the fact that it was inherently unstable and constantly endangered. When betrayed, trust could and would be withdrawn, with profoundly negative consequences for the trusting and the trusted alike. This is why political parties and associations were so eager to build multiple layers of trust with and among their members and supporters. Integrated networks of mutual trust not only stabilized and streamlined organizational structures, they also helped, through the ongoing practice of trust-building rituals, to bind people more permanently to an organization. Even if political goals and dreams, as in the case of the socialists, would not be achieved during a person's lifetime, and even if members were at times disappointed with the performance of their leaders, such networks and practices were able to stand on their own.

In an age that was becoming increasingly obsessed with the image of allegedly unbound and unstructured 'masses', the task was hardly a trivial one. Just as liberals and conservatives had feared the *classes dangereuses* in the first half of the nineteenth century, later decades witnessed a growing anxiety about political masses. In 1895, Gustave Le Bon published a treatise on *La Psychologie des foules*, which was immediately translated into English and German, among other languages. The book drew on the author's observations of what had happened in the French capital under military siege in 1870/1, especially during the months of the Paris Commune. For Le Bon, this had been a lesson in demagoguery that emotionally manipulated and channelled the discontent widespread among the working classes. In his view, the 'masses' were easy prey for gifted orators who knew how to excite them. Emotional contagion travelled fast, and exaggerated feelings often triggered violent actions. Especially when the masses were anonymous, as in demonstrations or spontaneous gatherings, they proved highly suggestible and reacted strongly to visual incentives like flags, banners and posters.[53]

On the one hand, these anonymous masses posed a threat to a civil society that had developed a close-knit web of diverse groups, associations and parties to organize and integrate its newly empowered citizens. On the other hand, they provided the dynamic base from which emerging social and political movements recruited their followers. This held particularly true for

---

[53]Gustave Le Bon, *The Crowd: A Study of the Popular Mind* (Whitefish: Kessinger, [French Orig. 1895] 2003); Susanna Barrows, *Distorting Mirrors: Visions of the Crowd in Late 19th Century France* (New Haven: Yale University Press, 1981); Joop van Ginneken, *Crowds, Psychology, and Politics, 1871–1899* (New York: Cambridge University Press, 1992); Jean-Jacques Courtine, 'La Voix du people: Les émotions, le langage et la foule à l'aube de l'ère des masses', in *Histoire des émotions*, ed. Boquet, Nagy and Zanetti Domingues, 91–105.

the new brand of nationalism that had been flourishing in many European countries since the 1870s. In Britain, it bore the name jingoism, referring to a popular song in which 'true Britons' pledged to take up arms and fight the Russian Bear, if necessary. Already during the revolutionary and Napoleonic era, wars had become highly politicized events that were intimately bound up with patriotic feelings and national interests.[54] Even in countries which did not have compulsory conscription and relied on a professional army, military conflict usually sparked a fire of popular enthusiasm that increasingly verged on open chauvinism. 'Sentiments of national honour', as Evelyn Baring, Earl of Cromer and Britain's Consul-General in Egypt after 1883, put it, were 'stung to the quick' whenever colonial or intra-European conflicts arose. Politicians would do well not 'to run absolutely counter to the impulse of the national imagination'. Instead, they should seek to march ahead of the crowd and 'guide it'.[55]

This is precisely what the French general Georges Boulanger attempted in the 1880s. Seeking revenge for the defeat France had suffered at the hands of German forces in 1870/1, the decorated officer and war minister put himself at the forefront of an ascending political movement that sought to restore national honour and return the country to monarchical rule. Parading on a black horse through the streets of Paris, Boulanger was the chosen idol of many who were disappointed with the Third Republic. *Boulangisme*, as the movement was called, drew on popular sentiments that converged on the exaltation of the French nation as the most cherished object of identification. Several songs hailed the general as the nation's saviour, and tens of thousands of Parisians joined in the refrain '*C'est Boulanger qu'il nous faut*'.[56]

The idealized hero guiding the misled nation back to honour and glory could be associated both with traditional monarchy and with the modern form of charismatic leadership that was gaining momentum in the process of nineteenth-century politicization. As Max Weber observed first-hand, charisma held even more affective power than dynastic sentimentalism.[57] This power was grounded in personal trust and the belief that the charismatic leader embodied values, feelings and visions of the future similar to those of the people he guided. At the same time, the leader depended on his followers,

---

[54]Linda Colley, *Britons: Forging the Nation, 1707–1837* (New Haven: Yale University Press, 1992); *Nationalist and Racialist Movements in Britain and Germany before 1914*, ed. Paul Kennedy and Anthony Nicholls (London: Macmillan, 1981).

[55]Evelyn Baring Earl of Cromer, *Modern Egypt*, vol. 2 (London: Macmillan, 1908), 109–10. For the US, see Nicole Eustace, *1812: War and the Passions of Patriotism* (Philadelphia: University of Pennsylvania Press, 2012).

[56]Patrick Hutton, 'Popular Boulangism and the Advent of Mass Politics in France, 1886–90', *Journal of Contemporary History* 11, no. 1 (1976): 85–106.

[57]Max Weber, *Economy and Society*, ed. Guenther Roth and Claus Wittrich, vol. 1 (Berkeley: University of California Press, 1978), 241–2.

who added collective force to his ideas and made it possible for them to be put into action. In return, charismatic men speaking on behalf of the nation offered citizens the chance to actively participate in the national project of self-purification and self-elevation. Ultimately, everybody would benefit and feel honoured by the arrangement.

From tradition to charisma

Socializing national honour was one important way to emotionally rally people behind a political cause. Once the nation found itself ennobled as sovereign during the French Revolution, each citizen theoretically had a part in its newly ascribed honour and glory. Patriotism, the love of the fatherland, became redefined as the love of the nation. Such love stemmed from, and was translated back into, fraternal feelings that male citizens were supposed to espouse for one another as free and equal members of the united and indivisible nation. Fraternity implied mutual assistance and solidarity, and was accompanied by strong bonds of trust. Trust, unlike loyalty, was not assured but had to be built and stabilized through cooperation and communication.

Although it depended on a multitude of prerequisites, trust proved to be another influential means of emotionally enriching the world of politics as it developed during the long nineteenth century. Gradually replacing older notions of subjects' unconditional fidelity, trust heralded a political system that was based on a novel calibration of power. Even in those European countries where monarchical power was less bound by constitutional constraints, politics was no longer confined to what was decided in palaces and cabinets. As citizens demanded and eventually succeeded in obtaining political representation, the importance and visibility of parliamentary politics grew. Parties and other political associations sought to organize and channel public opinion, and they achieved this by enlisting members and followers through intensely emotional rhetoric and practice. Warm and trusting relations within an organization stood side by side with a deep distrust of those outside, whose interests and motives were deemed hostile and treacherous.

Insofar as politicization arose alongside a growing sense of political fragmentation and exclusionary polarization, reminders of the 'nation' as one and indivisible mounted. Monarchy, which had persisted in most European countries, now took on new tasks. First, it reinvented itself as an integrative element of politics that promised to rise above party factions and embody the nation as a whole. From Louis Philippe, who ascended the French throne in 1830, to Wilhelm II, the last German emperor, virtually all monarchs imagined and portrayed themselves as *roi citoyen* or *Volkskaiser*. They tried or pretended to be in touch with their citizens, and took great care to endear themselves to populations who would otherwise be driven apart by political strife and controversy. With the help of new forms of media, they made themselves visible and approachable; people were offered the chance to follow, in intimate detail, their queen's or king's or emperor's actions and whereabouts. Furthermore, they were invited to address royals directly, send them poems and presents, congratulate them on their birthdays and mourn their passing.

Second, this kind of intense communication served the task of rendering government 'intelligible' to the 'vacant many', as Walter Bagehot had phrased it in 1867. While 'the nature of a constitution, the action of an assembly, the play of parties, the unseen formation of a guiding opinion, are complex facts, difficult to know and easy to mistake', the actions of the monarch were 'easy ideas' that effortlessly captured the 'attention of the nation'. By appealing to 'diffused feeling' rather than 'to the understanding' of complicated 'impersonal' laws and mechanisms, a monarchy could, thirdly, strengthen people's personal attachment. The best of all monarchical worlds that the English journalist observed in his time was 'a *family* on the throne' that 'brings down the pride of sovereignty to the level of petty life' and 'sweetens politics' by speaking to men and women's 'bosoms'.[58]

Nevertheless, sweetening politics was not synonymous with abolishing the taste for participation altogether. While nineteenth-century monarchies fared rather well when it came to mastering the complex emotional tasks before them, they did not depoliticize citizens or turn them into passive spectators of royal weddings and state visits. The limits of political legitimacy and dynastic attachment became obvious during and after the First World War. By the 1920s, many Continental European countries had abolished monarchical rule. Revolutions in Saint Petersburg, Berlin, Munich, Vienna and Budapest once again turned the tables, as royal families were executed or sent into exile. Even if monarchical sentiment survived in some pockets of society (as it had done in republican France), it could no longer mobilize or integrate larger parts of the population.[59]

This did not mean, however, that citizens became indifferent to emotional and personalized politics. The more fragmented and polarized the political culture was, and the more a nation had suffered military defeat and alleged dishonour, the more citizens were drawn to charismatic leaders who promised renewed glory and national regeneration. Such leaders based their appeals not on traditional sources of legitimacy, but on strong affective ties

---

[58]Bagehot, *English Constitution*, 78, 81–2.
[59]Arne Hofmann, 'Obsoleter Monarchismus als Erbe der Monarchie: Das Nachleben der Monarchie im Monarchismus nach 1918', in *Das Erbe der Monarchie: Nachwirkungen einer deutschen Institution seit 1918*, ed. Thomas Biskup and Martin Kohlrausch (Frankfurt: Campus, 2008), 241–60; Stephan Malinowski, *Die Hohenzollern und die Nazis: Geschichte einer Kollaboration* (Berlin: Propyläen, 2021), chs 1 and 2; Stephan Malinowski, *Nazis and Nobles: The History of a Misalliance* (Oxford: Oxford University Press, 2020), chs 2 and 3.

to those who trusted them and shared their visions of the future. In Italy, Benito Mussolini set the populist precedent. Dismantling the constitution, outlawing parties and abolishing parliament, the self-proclaimed Duce quickly installed himself as the sole focus of political allegiance (though he allowed the monarchy to continue).[60]

Meanwhile in Germany, the 26-year-old journalist Joseph Goebbels was despairing over the fate of his country. After Wilhelm II had been forced to abdicate in 1918, the republic of Weimar found it hard to establish itself against fervent resistance fuelled by right-wing and communist parties. Official attempts to endow republicanism with positive emotions and foster people's attachment to democratic values and practices were given too little time to sink in.[61] As extremists from both left and right whipped up antagonistic feelings of hatred and contempt towards the republican state, its supporters dwindled in number. Many turned their backs on party politics altogether, blaming it for fracturing the nation's unity and gnawing at Germany's strength. Some joined *Bünde* that offered strong ties of emotional belonging.[62] Others, like young Goebbels, dreamt of a leader with a 'firm hand'. In the summer of 1924, he confided in his diary that 'Germany is longing for the One' who would save the broken and humiliated nation. Fomenting 'enthusiasm and complete devotion' on his path to power, such a figure would help the people to overcome internal ruin and external weakness. In Goebbels's imagination, this man would resemble the late Otto von Bismarck rather than the kings and emperors Bismarck had served as Prussian prime minister and German chancellor. A few months later, the desperate journalist met the hero he yearned for: Adolf Hitler, who would soon commence a new chapter of emotional politics.[63]

---

[60]Christopher Duggan, *Fascist Voices: An Intimate History of Mussolini's Italy* (London: Bodley Head, 2012); Stephen Gundle, Christopher Duggan and Giuliana Pieri, eds, *The Cult of the Duce: Mussolini and the Italians* (Manchester: Manchester University Press, 2013).
[61]Manuela Achilles, 'With a Passion for Reason: Celebrating the Constitution in Weimar Germany', *Central European History* 43, no. 4 (2010): 666–89.
[62]See Herman Schmalenbach, 'Die soziologische Kategorie des Bundes', *Die Dioskuren* 1 (1922): 35–105.
[63]*Die Tagebücher von Joseph Goebbels*, ed. Elke Fröhlich, part I, vol. 1 (Munich: Saur, 1987), 34.

CHAPTER THIRTEEN

Love and Hate, Faith and Despair under National Socialism

On 8 August 1934, Bernhard Rust, the German minister of science, education and national culture, gave a talk in Munich. He spoke at the Circus Krone, where on 30 October 1923 Adolf Hitler had called for a 'national revolution' against the government in Berlin. 'From this place', Rust reminded his audience, all of them members of the National Socialist Teachers League and the Hitler Youth, 'the star went forth into the night' – a star that, like the one in the Christmas tale, presaged the advent of a new era, a 'German resurrection'. With Hitler's appointment as chancellor the previous year, the resurrection had now officially begun. According to the minister, 'love' for the Führer and 'boundless faith in him have uplifted our people. This is how they march outdoors day after day, hour by hour. Singing in rhythm.'

Rust was not a particularly rousing speaker; his rhetoric did not excite the audience or get their blood rushing. Yet even this man, who was trained as a classical philologist and patterned the facial hair on his upper lip after that of his great role model, knew how to summon pithy sayings and catchy images in order to get his point across. He made use of a religious vocabulary that was deliberately cast in military language, repeatedly extolling the 'national community marching together' and the 'columns of young boys

---

This chapter partly draws on an article published as 'Faith, Love, Hate: The National Socialist Politics of Emotions', in *Munich and National Socialism: Catalogue of the Munich Documentation Centre for the History of National Socialism*, ed. Winfried Nerdinger and Hans-Günter Hockerts (Munich: C.H. Beck, 2015), 479–86.

marching today'. Furthermore, he kept emphasizing 'faith': the faith of the Führer in his people, and that of the people in the Führer and the path he had mapped out for them. The speech concluded with a personal credo: 'I have faith in German youth' – a youth who would be raised 'in the camp and in the column'.[1]

Love and faith, marching and singing, column and camp: these terms fed a programme of educational and cultural indoctrination whose emotional content was as blatant as it was volatile. The German populace – children and adolescents in particular – had to be mobilized and instructed in the practice of feeling. Emotions like affection and trust, but also pride and fanaticism, disgust and hate, were acknowledged and valued as political assets. Skilful propaganda campaigns and the art of ceremony, drawn from a tried and tested arsenal of religious and military rituals and semantics, worked to evoke these emotions and keep them alive.

Yet, the regime and its propaganda apparatus were aware of the downsides of emotional politics. Passions could become unruly; once inflamed, they might start a wildfire that would be difficult to extinguish. The object of feelings might conceivably shift; emotions could become erratic. It was not easy to stabilize or institutionalize them. An overly obvious or predictable targeting of emotions risked habituation and might result in disinterest, reticence and avoidance. All in all, a politics of emotion was a double-edged sword; it could sharpen the blade but it might also dull it. For this very reason, National Socialism banked on a specific order of emotions associated with camp and column, marching and singing. Within that order, emotions were not only created and rehearsed but also channelled, brought into line and fenced in.

Charisma and propaganda: the appeal to emotions

National Socialism did not invent the politics of emotions. Since early modern times at the latest, it had been a commonplace that political rule could not afford to disregard emotions.[2] Around 1920, Max Weber sought to theorize the affective dimension of politics in his famous typology of

---

[1] Ulf Pedersen, *Bernhard Rust: Ein nationalsozialistischer Bildungspolitiker vor dem Hintergrund seiner Zeit* (Braunschweig: Forschungsstelle für Schulgeschichte und Schulentwicklung, 1994), quotes 273, 275, 278, 279. Alfred Rosenberg, a major ideologue of the Nazi movement, described the 'lifestyle' of the German nation at the time as that of a 'marching column' (*Gestaltung der Idee*, ed. Thilo von Trotha (Munich: Eher, 1936), 303). As to the regime's strategies to 'win over the young', see Richard J. Evans, *The Third Reich in Power 1933–1939* (New York: Penguin, 2005), 261–90.
[2] See Chapter 12 in this volume.

legitimate authority. Defined as 'the probability that a command with a given specific content will be obeyed by a given group of persons', authority demanded assent and the probability of 'compliance'. Compliance could be acquired through violence (or the threat of violence), but it functioned better when it was obtained voluntarily. This required communication: people needed to be convinced of the legitimacy of rule. A ruler hoping for 'devotion' rather than mere consent had to go further still: instil trust and win the favour of his followers.

For authority to be successful and to assert itself, it was crucial to mobilize and enlist the enduring affection, admiration and love of the ruled. This could be done either by calling on the time-honoured character of authority, on its traditional form and 'sanctity', or through the arrival of a charismatic leader who, by virtue of their personal magnetism, would win over the hearts of the people. Hardest of all to sustain was that type of rule whose legitimacy was based on statutory regulations and bureaucratic procedures. In reality, as Weber was quick to point out, none of these ideal types ever appeared in pure form. Usually, people had a variety of reasons for emotionally accepting a particular kind of authority and complying with it more or less devotedly.[3]

Weber illustrated his abstract reasoning with some historical examples. The archetypal charismatic personality he had in mind was Kurt Eisner, the 'demagogically' talented leader of the Bavarian Revolution in November 1918 and the state's first premier, who was murdered in 1919 by a right-wing assassin. He might have also mentioned Adolf Hitler, who since 1919 had been putting his rhetorical talents to work in the German army's 'anti-Bolshevik education' office, and, from 1920, as a professional orator for the newly founded National Socialist German Workers' Party (NSDAP). It is just as likely, though, that the sociologist might have simply dismissed the First World War veteran as one of the many 'barefoot prophets' who roamed the country in the 1920s, stirring up the very same hopes for salvation that they promised to fulfil.[4] Back then, Hitler was still a long way from embodying charismatic authority; the 'personal devotion', 'hero worship' and 'trust' he was met with came from just a small group of dedicated followers.[5]

There was, however, one subject he had studied and executed expertly: propaganda. Using Allied and German war propaganda as his guide, Hitler developed a concept of 'political advertising' as the 'art' of emotional persuasion. As he wrote in *Mein Kampf* (published in 1925), propaganda had to be consciously and specifically 'brought home to the masses'. Given that 'the overwhelming majority of the nation are so feminine in their disposition

---

[3]Max Weber, *Economy and Society: An Outline of Interpretive Sociology*, ed. Guenther Roth and Claus Wittich (Berkeley: University of California Press, 1978), 53, 212–15, 242–5, 226.
[4]Ulrich Linse, *Barfüßige Propheten: Erlöser der zwanziger Jahre* (Berlin: Siedler, 1983).
[5]As to Hitler's early successes as an orator and the enthusiasm of his audiences, see Ian Kershaw, *Hitler: 1889–1936: Hubris* (London: Allen Lane, 1998), chs 4–7.

and outlook that their thought is ruled by sentiment rather than by sober deliberation', the art of propaganda had to 'find its way in the appropriate psychological form to capture the attention and, further, the hearts of the masses': 'it must be directed towards the feelings [of the public] and less towards their so-called reason'.[6]

In many respects, Hitler's remarks recalled the observations shared by the French physician Gustave Le Bon in his 1895 book *The Crowd: A Study of the Popular Mind*. Le Bon also viewed crowds as 'feminine' and highly excitable. 'Like women', a crowd 'goes at once to extremes' and makes the individual behave as a 'creature acting by instinct': 'He possesses the spontaneity, the violence, the ferocity, and also the enthusiasm and heroism of primitive beings.' Politicians who had to contend with the 'voice of the masses' needed to learn how to influence and guide these instincts, possibly through a rhetoric of 'affirmation, repetition, and contagion': 'To know the art of impressing the imagination of crowds is to know at the same time the art of governing them.'[7]

Whether Hitler was familiar with Le Bon's book (which had been translated into German in 1908) has not been established.[8] But he probably had read the article by neurologist Julius Roßbach about the 'soul of the masses' which was printed in a Munich newspaper in 1919 and which cited Le Bon extensively.[9] Unlike Le Bon and Roßbach, though, Hitler did not stop at observation and analysis; he put findings into practice. The many years of street and beer hall politics gave him plenty of time to train, test and correct his public appearances. The rhythm of his speech, his choice of words, the modulation and volume of his voice – all of this was meticulously rehearsed, until it permeated his very bearing. Furthermore, Hitler had an outstanding talent for reading the mood of the public and adapting himself to it. His audience's facial expressions told him whether or not he was being understood. As he stated in *Mein Kampf*,

> a great and popular orator will always let himself be led by the broad masses so that from them will emotionally flow just the word he needs and that in its turn will go straight to the hearts of his listeners.[10]

---

[6]Adolf Hitler, *Mein Kampf: Eine kritische Edition*, ed. Christian Hartmann et al. (Munich: Institut für Zeitgeschichte, 2016), vol. 1, 489, 497, 499, 501, 507; vol. 2, 1193. See also Gerhard Paul, *Aufstand der Bilder: Die NS-Propaganda vor 1933* (Bonn: Dietz, 1990).
[7]Gustave Le Bon, *The Crowd: A Study of the Popular Mind* (Whitefish: Kessinger [French Orig. 1895] 2003), 36, 44, 56, 80, 141.
[8]This is contrary to Jacques Courtine's allegation ('La Voix du peuple: Les émotions, le langage et la foule à l'aube de l'ère des masses', in *Histoire des émotions collectives: Épistémologie, émergences, expériences*, ed. Damien Boquet et al. (Paris: Classiques Garnier, 2022), 92–105, here 94). Le Bon did, however, influence Sigmund Freud who, in 1921, published his *Group Psychology and the Analysis of the Ego*: https://www.gutenberg.org/ebooks/35877 (accessed 5 March 2023).
[9]Kershaw, *Hitler: 1889–1936*, 156, 652–3.
[10]Hitler, *Mein Kampf*, vol. 2, 1193.

Whether and how the strategy worked depended on the time and place. Hitler knew only too well that meetings first thing in the morning found people in a different mental state than in the evening, when 'human willpower' and the 'energy to resist' had become so weakened that the speaker had an easier time winning over the public. Certain rooms were better suited to arousing particular moods and feelings, as Catholic churches, with their twilight atmosphere and aroma of incense, attested. In any event, both mass meetings and words properly spoken and enriched by memorable images proved far more effective than any written text. A 'mass gathering' generated a 'mass suggestion' that turned an individual into 'a member of a community'. He felt 'gripped by the tremendous force of the suggestive intoxication and enthusiasm of three or four thousand others' and left the meeting fortified, invigorated and encouraged.[11]

He also left in an organized and orchestrated manner. Rather than being emotionally overwhelmed, chaotic, confused or wild, National Socialists followed a rigid choreography characterized by marches, columns and song. According to Hitler, in party meetings 'blind discipline' had to prevail; the 'authority of the chairman' was not to be disputed. Though they had been seized by 'waves of enthusiasm' during a gathering, party members would exit calmly and 'march in rows of four through the town singing *Oh Germany in High Esteem*'. Passion and fanaticism – a concept that had a thoroughly positive ring in the National Socialist vocabulary – were expressed in an orderly fashion and responded obediently to a Führer who was showing them the path to take.[12]

March, column and song: here they were again, in close proximity to intoxication and enthusiasm. Their original home was in the military, which Hitler had witnessed and appreciated first-hand. The military signified discipline, order, allegiance, leadership and obedience. It also stood for the emotional values that National Socialism championed: honour and absolute loyalty. Symbols and affective signs of these values were abundant, on flags, banners, uniforms, decorations and in music. And yet, military affiliation was based on compulsion; most soldiers were in service not because they wanted to be, but because they had to. The Nazi movement, by contrast, had no such means of coercion at its disposal prior to 1933. It needed to recruit supporters and followers, whose commitment had to be maintained during prolonged periods of political failure and marginalization. A vigorous, powerful, strong-willed emotional language was therefore of the utmost importance in ensuring enduring allegiance. It always proved more difficult, Hitler was convinced, 'to shake faith than knowledge. Love is less subject to change than respect. Hatred is more lasting than aversion.'[13]

---

[11]Ibid., 1203.
[12]Ibid., 1221–3; as to fanaticism and its positive connotation, see ibid., vol. 1, 877–8, 903.
[13]Ibid., 879.

In order to guarantee emotional devotion and enlist the 'fanaticism' of the 'broad masses' as the 'driving force which can bring about the most tremendous revolutions on this earth', the Führer did more than apply his personal talents as a gifted speaker and propagandist. He also deployed all the methods he had copied from the military and the Catholic Church, as well as from the new mass movement of the late nineteenth and early twentieth centuries: social democracy. Over and over again, Hitler returned to the 'strong attractive power' of the 'Marxist movement', to which he could relate on 'emotional grounds':

> In Berlin, after the War, I witnessed a mass demonstration of Marxists in front of the Royal Palace and the Lustgarten. A sea of red flags, red armbands and red flowers was sufficient to give that rally of about 120,000 persons an outward appearance of tremendous strength. I could myself feel and understand how easily the average man succumbs to the suggestive magic of such a grandiose piece of theatre.[14]

Community formation and devotion

By 1 May 1933, Berlin's Lustgarten belonged at last to the National Socialists. Under a sea of swastika flags, a gigantic youth rally took place with Hitler and the ageing President Paul von Hindenburg in attendance. At the same spot where 200,000 people had protested Hitler's appointment as chancellor just three months earlier, the Führer was now celebrating his triumph.

The Lustgarten was too small, though, for the proper May Day festivities, which had to be moved to the Tempelhof airfield where 1.5 million people gathered. Propaganda Minister Joseph Goebbels, who was responsible for organizing this 'masterpiece' of a 'mass demonstration', recorded the achievement in his diary: 'It is nearly impossible to survey this enormous mass of people. Glittering and shining, searchlights pass over the crowd. All one sees is the grey masses, standing shoulder to shoulder.' After Hitler's speech, which invoked the 'new ethos' of work and the unity of the people, the audience was seized by 'a fantastic rapture of enthusiasm':

> Devoutly and powerfully, the Horst Wessel Song chimes up into the eternal night sky [...] It is no longer just a phrase: we have become a single nation of brothers. And the one who guided us on this path is riding now, standing upright in the car, back to the Chancellery on Wilhelmstraße, through a Via Triumphalis of living human bodies that has formed around him.

---

[14]Ibid., 879, 889; vol. 2, 1243.

And then, abruptly, his next sentence: 'Tomorrow we will occupy the trade union offices. No resistance is anticipated.'[15]

On occasions when resistance was encountered, it was brutally suppressed. The regime treated its opponents with anything but gentleness. The distinction between friend and foe was rigid and extreme: enemies, whether politically, racially or socially defined, were marked for annihilation. But who was considered a friend? Were only 'Old Fighters' that had joined the party in the 1920s included, or also the new supporters who filled the ranks after 1933? Should the nearly 12 million voters who cast their ballots for the Nazi Party in the last free election of November 1932 be counted? Or the more than 17 million who opted for the NSDAP in the elections of March 1933, which were already overshadowed by terror? What about those still standing on the sidelines? After all, in March 1933 the NSDAP had only received 44 per cent of the vote; the majority of the electorate had supported other parties. How could they be won over to the 'national revolution'?

Compared to the years before 1933, the regime could unquestionably use many more means to effect general consent and compliance. Terror was one, but it alone would not do the job. As Goebbels frequently remarked, National Socialists were not looking for obedient slaves who could be kept in line with fear and 'at the point of the bayonet'.[16] Rather, they aimed to win the people's 'hearts' and gain their 'love' through positive incentives: they provided work and dispensed financial benefits, they removed civil servants critical of the party and filled their positions with grateful supporters. In foreign affairs, they pursued a policy of strength which went down well with many citizens: both the reintroduction of military conscription in 1935 and the invasion of the demilitarized Rhineland a year later met with widespread approval.

In 1936, Denis de Rougemont, a Swiss citizen who was working at the University of Frankfurt as a French lecturer, recounted the 'euphoria' triggered by the news that German troops were now stationed along the Rhine. As a witness to history schooled in psychoanalysis, he found 'that the stimulation of these "liberated" populations is vaguely obscene: it occurs to me that "befreien" ("liberate") is related to "freien" which means as much as "marry". The reoccupation of the Rhineland is a kind of sexual act, just as much as a political one.'[17] The Austrian communist and psychoanalyst Wilhelm Reich also diagnosed sexual undercurrents and

---

[15]*Die Tagebücher von Joseph Goebbels*, ed. Elke Fröhlich, part I, vol. 2 (Munich: Saur, 1987), 413–15.

[16]Bernd Sösemann, *Propaganda: Medien und Öffentlichkeit in der NS-Diktatur*, vol. 2 (Stuttgart: Steiner, 2011), 754 (quote Goebbels): 'It may be nice to have authority over bayonets, but it is even nicer to have authority over hearts!'

[17]*Travels in the Reich 1933–1945: Foreign Authors Report from Germany*, ed. Oliver Lubrich (Chicago: University of Chicago Press, 2010), 85.

overtones in *The Mass Psychology of Fascism*. His book, which was brought out by a Danish publisher in 1933 and soon confiscated and banned in Germany, posited a connection between the repression of 'drives' and 'human feelings'. Fascism, Reich argued, created a space for the orgiastic longing of the masses – a longing suppressed both within the authoritarian nuclear family and in the Christian churches. Repressed sexuality sought 'substitute gratifications' and found them in the 'libidinous mechanism' of the uniform or in the 'erotically provocative effect of rhythmically executed goose-stepping'.[18]

Other observers likewise claimed to sense sexual or erotic vibrations in the communication between the Führer and his people. Hitler's early statements on the feminine disposition of the masses, along with his remarks about propaganda as an act of overcoming that made men and women fall under the 'dominating power of a strong will', added fuel to such associations. So did accounts of ecstatic behaviour at mass meetings and rallies. Rougemont was himself present on 11 March 1936 when Hitler spoke in Frankfurt's Festhalle. After a four-hour wait in the crowd, the time had come:

> The arc-lights in the hall are turned out as illuminated arrows are lit up on the vaulted ceiling, pointing to a door on the level of the first balcony. A spotlight picks out a small man dressed in brown, bareheaded, smiling ecstatically, standing on the threshold. Forty thousand people, forty thousand arms have been raised in a single movement. The man comes forward very slowly, saluting with a slow gesture, like a bishop, to a deafening thunder of rhythmic *Heils* [...] They are all standing rigidly to attention, motionless and shouting in time, their eyes glued to the illuminated spot, to that face with its ecstatic smile, and tears run down their faces in the darkness.[19]

Although the Swiss visitor buried his hands in his pocket, he, too, experienced 'a special sort of shiver and heartbeat', a 'sacred horror'. Standing next to him were young girls and militiamen from the Labour Service, alongside shabbily clothed women and workers. Apparently, the women did not behave any differently from the men. Both genders were affected 'to their core'. In the crowd, they seemed equally receptive to strong emotional impressions and equally likely to be moved to tears. The reserve men were generally taught to cultivate melted away; in the dark, they wept and abandoned themselves to the Führer.

For all his shivering, Rougemont remained 'lucid' enough to see through the 'liturgy' of the rally. He observed carefully which choreographic strategies were deployed to elicit the desired effects. Nothing was left to

---

[18] Wilhelm Reich, *The Mass Psychology of Fascism*, trans. Vincent R. Carfagno (London: Souvenir Press, 1972), 31–2.
[19] *Travels in the Reich*, ed. Lubrich, 86–7.

chance. Each of Hitler's public appearances was meticulously staged and planned with military precision. The immense swelling of the propaganda apparatus shows how important this instrument of mass mobilization was even after the Nazis had seized power.[20] Without having read Max Weber's explanations of charisma, Hitler was well aware of the fragility of the aura that he had acquired during the 'years of struggle'. As much as he banked on the love and faith of the 'masses' to stabilize his power, he could not count on their permanence. A charismatic leader of the kind that many people had been longing for since the 1920s needed at some point to deliver, to prove himself in order to retain their recognition, 'personal devotion' and 'trust'.[21] The more powerful and strong-willed he appeared as an agitator and visionary, the more omnipotent an image he projected. The more promises he made, the greater the hopes and expectations pinned on the new ruler to turn these visions and promises into reality.

For precisely this reason, propaganda was assigned an even more important role after 1933. Not only had it 'seized power for us', Goebbels stated in 1935; it would also 'maintain us in power'. In order to satisfy comrades and supporters, and to persuade 'the millions of people who are still keeping a distance', the party had to reach their 'soul'. To that end, rhetoric was not enough. Propaganda must continue to 'beat the drum', albeit in a cleverly timed rhythm. Non-stop drumming would have a dulling effect; what mattered was a healthy mix of enthusiasm and information. Nuances were crucial, as was moderation: 'One does not have to organize a cultic celebration every time five National Socialists get together.' The Catholic Church set the precedent: it did not read 'a High Mass with a Te Deum every day, but only on certain holidays'.[22]

Emotional practices and rhythmic synchronization

National days took up a great deal of space in the regime's calendar. Carefully and extravagantly staged, they were part of an avalanche of assemblies that washed over the German populace every year like clockwork: from mass

---

[20]Sösemann, *Propaganda*, vol. 2; Mathias Friedel, 'Goebbels' Propagandisten in Hessen', in *Medien im Nationalsozialismus*, ed. Bernd Heidenreich and Sönke Neitzel (Paderborn: Schöningh, 2010), 53–82.

[21]Klaus Schreiner, '"Wann kommt der Retter Deutschlands?" Formen und Funktionen von politischem Messianismus in der Weimarer Republik', *Saeculum* 49, no. 1 (1998): 107–60; Ludolf Herbst, *Hitlers Charisma: Die Erfindung eines deutschen Messias* (Frankfurt: Fischer, 2010).

[22]Quotes from a speech by Joseph Goebbels to 4,000 'propagandists' at the Nuremberg Party Rally on 16 September 1935, in Sösemann, *Propaganda*, vol. 2, 753–9; Goebbels, *Tagebücher*, vol. 2, 515.

parades on the anniversary of the 'national uprising', through the Heroes' Commemoration Day, May Day celebrations and Nuremberg Party Rallies to the Thanksgiving Festival on the Bückeberg in Northern Germany. In between were crammed a large number of additional festivities, from Mother's Day to the solstice, Hitler's birthday to the Day of the Movement, a commemoration of the Munich Beer Hall Putsch on 9 November 1923. One-time events like the 1936 Olympic Games were organized for both domestic and foreign audiences in accordance with the rules used in the art of propaganda.[23]

When it came to choreographing mass scenes, nobody was a match for Goebbels and his staff. Whether the setting was the Munich Feldherrnhalle, the newly built Olympic Stadium in Berlin or the Party Rally Grounds in Nuremberg, everywhere crowds were on the march, in orderly formations or standing to attention. They epitomized not dull monotony but curbed enthusiasm and dedicated loyalty. A sophisticated architecture of light and sound amplified the impression of unity and purpose. Blazing torches and domes of light, as devised by the architect Albert Speer, created a sublime festive mood; the collective singing of hymns aroused deep feelings of community and a 'zest for life' reflected in 'joyous and cheerful faces'.[24]

Communal singing also conveyed a feeling of active participation: one was not merely a spectator or listener who passively received authoritative messages, but an active designer and creator. Through singing, inner feelings of pride, power, happiness and joy were produced, even rage and hatred if required. These connected the individual to other singers: joint singing synchronized the feelings of the multitude. Just as soldiers worked up courage before a battle by singing aloud, National Socialism's 'Old Fighters' used the same method to banish fear and, simultaneously, to demonstrate strength and uniformity. Singing, in combination with marching in lockstep, gave the human (male) body a steady rhythm and lent it a powerful and determined aura.

---

[23] Reinhard Rürup, ed., *1936 – Die Olympischen Spiele und der Nationalsozialismus: Eine Dokumentation* (Berlin: Stiftung Topografie des Terrors, 1996); Frank Eckhardt, 'Olympia im Zeichen der Propaganda', in *Medien*, ed. Heidenreich and Neitzel, 235–51. On the choreography of festival days, see Peter Reichel, *Der schöne Schein des Dritten Reiches: Faszination und Gewalt des Faschismus* (Munich: Hanser, 1991), esp. 114 ff., 208 ff., 262 ff.; on their integrative function see Dietmar von Reeken and Malte Thießen, eds, '*Volksgemeinschaft' als soziale Praxis* (Paderborn: Schöningh, 2013).

[24] Quoted from Wolfgang Stumme, *Was der Führer der Einheit vom Singen wissen muß* (Wolfenbüttel: Kallmeyer, 1937), 5; 'Musikerziehung – Menschenerziehung', *Musik und Volk* 2 (1934/35): 181–5; Anne Niessen, '*Die Lieder waren die eigentlichen Verführer!' Mädchen und Musik im Nationalsozialismus* (Mainz: Schott, 1999); Stephan Marks, *Warum folgten sie Hitler? Die Psychologie des Nationalsozialismus* (Düsseldorf: Patmos, 2007); Richard Klopffleisch, *Lieder der Hitlerjugend* (Frankfurt: Lang, 1995), esp. 236–50.

After 1933, marches and songs became daily events, as Minister Rust had mentioned in 1934 and Rougemont described in his *Journal d'Allemagne* of 1938:

> At first we used to run to the window every time the street echoed to the sound of singing. It was either a black or brown group marching along three in a row, or else a formation of the Hitler Youth, the Jungvolk or the League of German Girls. Plump young girls, or very young boys. But we were already familiar with the rhythm of the songs – a phrase, then silence for four paces [...] You simply take no notice any more.[25]

Yet such familiarity, which Rougemont experienced as early as one month after his arrival in Frankfurt, posed a problem. Routinization neither agreed with the Führer's charisma nor suited the nation's 'soul'. There was a danger of wearing thin the capacity for enthusiasm among the young, who were the most important resource and addressee of National Socialist emotional politics. Never-ending marches and songs were bound to become monotonous at some point even for the most avid *Pimpf* (as the 10–14-year-old boys in the junior division of the Hitler Youth were called). As important as rituals were for imprinting moods and recalling emotions, it was crucial to guard against the effects of becoming habituated and numb.

The same held true for rhetorical figures and emotive concepts. The constant and omnipresent talk of love for the Führer; the banners on streets and in factories admonishing everyone to be loyal and trust the regime; the school curriculum that in every subject was obliged to elucidate the value of honour – this unrelenting barrage made it easy for feelings of weariness and surfeit to set in. The regime that took great care to monitor people's 'moods', 'desires' and 'emotional attitudes' left it to the Ministry of Propaganda to influence those attitudes and inspire 'confidence in the Führer'.[26] Goebbels certainly did have an intuitive sense of how to reach out to the public, and he warned against overdoing it. But even he could not prevent occasional feelings of emotional exhaustion and resignation.

What Goebbels recommended and commissioned in response was the production of light entertainment films as well as dance music and music request programmes on the radio. Cutting back on cult aspects in favour of 'normal' daily life undoubtedly helped avoid emotional overkill.[27] Moreover, whether consciously or unconsciously, Nazi propagandists exploited a proven means for generating emotions: expressing feelings through verbal

---

[25]*Travels in the Reich*, ed. Lubrich, 81.
[26]*Meldungen aus dem Reich 1938–1945: Die geheimen Lageberichte des Sicherheitsdienstes der SS*, ed. Heinz Boberach, vol. 1 (Herrsching: Pawlak, 1984), 69–72.
[27]Jörg Koch, 'Das NS-Wunschkonzert', in *Medien*, ed. Heidenreich and Neitzel, 253–71; Hans Sarkowicz, '"Nur nicht langweilig werden ...": Das Radio im Dienst der nationalsozialistischen Propaganda', in ibid., 205–34. On film, see the overview by Rainer Rother, 'Nationalsozialismus und Film', in ibid., 125–44.

communication and body language actively worked to create and sustain those feelings. Just as communal singing could call up – depending on the melody and rhythm – vitality and belonging, sadness or anger, activities like collective marching, outstretched arm movements, speaking in chorus and shouting *Sieg Heil* produced emotions that were only felt as such via bodily synchronization and rhythmic repetition.

Along with the column, the camp was a major site for practising and experiencing collective emotions. When Rust praised it in 1934 as the perfect place to learn National Socialist values and visions, it was by no means the concentration or extermination camp he had in mind. Rather, he was alluding to the camp life of the Hitler Youth. Familiar to children and adolescents from the pre-1933 Free Youth and Young Workers' movements, the camp had been appropriated by the post-1933 Staatsjugend for their own purposes. They held weekend camps, three-week summer camps, music education camps, rural training and labour service camps, and many others. The camp taught self-leadership and discipline but also, and above all, camaraderie, mixed with a shot of adventure and campfire romanticism. Most children and young people got something out of these experiences: girls in particular enjoyed escaping parental supervision and 'taking to the road'. After the war, if anything about National Socialism was fondly recollected it was the camp, together with the companionship and community spirit it had offered.[28]

Even Sebastian Haffner, who emigrated to Britain in 1938, was unable to resist the pull of the camp community. When, as a young legal intern, he was required to report for duty at a training camp that inculcated in its students the worldview of the military and National Socialism, he experienced this demand as a crude impertinence. All the same, he observed first-hand how compulsion could be transformed into bliss:

> It was a pleasure to go for a cross-country run together in the morning, and then go naked into the communal hot showers together, to share the parcels that one or other received from home, to share, too, the responsibility for misdemeanours that one of your comrades had committed, to help and support one another in a thousand little ways. We [...] had boyish battles and fights. We were all the same. We floated in a great comforting stream of mutual reliance and gruff familiarity.[29]

---

[28] Arno Klönne, *Jugend im Dritten Reich: Die Hitler-Jugend und ihre Gegner* (Munich: dtv, 1990), esp. 57, 81–2; Dagmar Reese, *Growing up Female in Nazi Germany: Social History, Popular Culture and Politics in Germany* (Ann Arbor: University of Michigan Press, 2006); Melita Maschmann, *Account Rendered: A Dossier of My Former Self* (Lexington, KY: Plunkett Lake Press, 2013), 19, 35–6; Renate Finckh, *Mit uns zieht die neue Zeit* (Baden-Baden: Signal, 1978), 74–81, 101, *passim*; Bernhard Haupert and Franz Josef Schäfer, *Jugend zwischen Kreuz und Hakenkreuz* (Frankfurt: Suhrkamp, 1991), 146 ff.

[29] Sebastian Haffner, *Defying Hitler: A Memoir*, trans. Oliver Pretzel (London: Phoenix, 2003), 231.

Clearly, even critical minds that rejected Nazi ideology and its rhetoric of community could become infected by the emotional practices of the camp. Outside the camp, though, they quickly recovered their sense of detachment and were able to observe from a distance exactly how the National Socialist politics of emotions operated.

Hatred, *Volkszorn* and their Jewish targets

This was especially true for citizens who, due to their Jewish background, were made to feel the negative effects of this emotional politics. The regime not only emphasized inclusive emotions like joy, pride, faith and trust, it also preached hatred and disgust towards those it considered enemies or traitors of the nation. Like fanaticism, hate was given a profoundly positive connotation during the Third Reich: National Socialists could and did harbour 'heroic hatred', an emotion derived from their 'sense of duty and responsibility to protect imperilled values'. In contrast, 'Marxist *class* hatred' or Jewish 'hatred of religion' were feelings apparently born out of 'cowardice' and 'envy' and proved anything but heroic or noble.[30]

Made into objects of hatred and disgust, shame and humiliation, Jews watched in bewilderment as people turned these feelings into deeds or practised the art of withholding empathy and looking away.[31] As a general rule, such actions were condoned by state institutions and party organizations alike. From early on, the Nazi state had imposed harsh legislation against Jewish Germans, and the NSDAP and related associations encouraged their members to openly harass and intimidate them. Violence erupted long before November 1938. Synagogues were set on fire, shops were boycotted. Shaming processions took place in many towns and cities, usually targeting Jewish men who went out with non-Jewish women. When Jews complained, they were punished yet again. In March 1933, the Jewish lawyer Michael Siegel entered a police station in the centre of Munich with the intention of pressing charges against Stormtroopers who had demolished his client's shop windows. Instead, he was beaten up and paraded through the streets barefoot, with his trousers cut short and a sign around his neck stating: 'I will never again complain to the police.'[32]

---

[30]*Meyers Lexikon*, 8th edn, vol. 5 (Leipzig: Bibliographisches Institut, 1938), 899.
[31]See Peter Fritzsche, 'The Management of Empathy in the Third Reich', in *Empathy and Its Limits*, ed. Aleida Assmann and Ines Detmers (Basingstoke: Palgrave, 2016), 115–27; Aleida Assmann, 'Looking Away in Nazi Germany', in ibid., 128–48.
[32]Ute Frevert, *The Politics of Humiliation: A Modern History* (Oxford: Oxford University Press, 2020), 61. As to antisemitic violence before 1938, see Michael Wildt, *Hitler's Volksgemeinschaft and the Dynamics of Racial Exclusion: Violence against Jews in Provincial Germany, 1919–1939* (New York: Berghahn, 2012), chs 3–7; Marion A. Kaplan, *Between Dignity and Despair: Jewish Life in Nazi Germany* (New York: Oxford University Press, 1998), ch. 1.

Practices of humiliating and terrorizing Jewish citizens were thus already well under way in the early days of the Nazi regime. The orders for some actions, like the first nationwide boycott in April 1933, came from above. In most cases, however, local party members felt empowered to act all on their own. They were convinced that they were 'working towards the Führer' and complying with his wishes.[33] Jews were continuously scapegoated and bore the blame for any and everything that went wrong. Whenever there was criticism from abroad concerning, for instance, the violation of the Versailles treaty regulations in 1935 and 1936, the propaganda apparatus claimed that the 'international Jewry' was responsible and promised retaliation. In the summer of 1938, when the Czechoslovakia crisis caused widespread concern that there would be an impending war, Jews were again condemned as warmongers. Local Nazis in a small village published the following leaflet:

> In the last critical weeks, the Jew had the firm intention of hounding a part of the peoples of the world into a frightful war. The German nation was to be defeated and obliterated. Millions of people were to be slaughtered and murdered. Towns and villages of the German Gaue were to be destroyed. More than hundreds of thousands of German families would have faced unspeakable suffering. That was the will of the Jews [...] Our unshakeable will is: in a short time, Windsbach must be Jew-free.[34]

By then, hate speech had infiltrated many towns and villages, not to mention larger cities. The ground was well prepared for what was to come in early November, when a young Jewish man and Polish citizen shot a German diplomat in Paris to draw attention to the ongoing expulsion of Polish Jews from the Reich. The Ministry of Propaganda advised the press to give the assassination 'the greatest attention' and to emphasize that it 'was certain to have the most serious consequences for Jews in Germany'. Local Nazis began rioting against Jewish shops, synagogues and people on the spot. As the news broke on the evening of 9 November that the diplomat had died from his wounds, the party leadership was gathered for dinner in Munich at the annual commemoration of the Beer Hall Putsch of 1923. Hitler had an intense conversation with Goebbels and then left, whereupon Goebbels delivered a fanatical half-hour long hate speech. It was met, as he noted in his diary, with thunderous applause: 'They all immediately dashed to the telephones. Now the people will act.'[35]

---

[33] Kershaw, *Hitler 1889–1936*, ch. 13.
[34] Wildt, *Hitler's Volksgemeinschaft*, quote 237.
[35] Goebbels, *Tagebücher*, vol. 6, 178–83; *NS-Presseanweisungen der Vorkriegszeit*, vol. 6.3: 1938 (Munich: Saur, 1999), 1050.

Who were 'the people'? In actual fact, it was mostly loyal party members and Stormtroopers who took the call and rushed to action. The SS or *Schutzstaffel* (protection squadron) received explicit orders to keep out of the affair, and the police were told to ensure that the pogrom unfolded in an orderly fashion. They were not to hinder the 'demonstrations' but to intervene whenever non-Jewish property was endangered. Similar commands were given to the local fire brigades. They, too, should only do their jobs when fires threatened to spread to neighbouring buildings. And so they did.

When synagogues were torched that night, when Jewish shops and apartments were raided, families terrorized and men arrested, it was officially attributed to what Goebbels called *Volkszorn*, the wrath of the people. The minister claimed that it was a spontaneous, quasi-automatic reaction to the murder in Paris. At the same time, he was well aware that this wrath had to be built up and 'released', as he put it, through propaganda. Radio programmes, films and newspaper articles did just that. In his inflammatory speech in Munich, Goebbels had made it clear that the party would have to 'organize and execute' everything. But it should under no circumstances 'appear outwardly as originator of the demonstrations'.[36] The regime tried to attribute the violence it unleashed to the entire nation, whose feelings were purportedly deeply hurt by the Paris events and who reacted with an immediate emotional outburst that, Goebbels claimed, was utterly understandable and justified. The Führer, the party and the people were, so it seemed, feeling and acting as one. This was emotional politics at its most effective.

How did the victims see it? 1938 has often been called the fateful year for German Jews, on the grounds that persecution took a new and radical turn. But was this really so? Reading Victor Klemperer's extensive diaries raises some doubts.[37] The professor of Romance languages meticulously noted and commented on each and every incident of antisemitism, over which he became increasingly depressed. The son of a rabbi, Klemperer had converted to Protestantism in 1912. He was married to a non-Jewish woman and did not consider himself Jewish in a religious or cultural sense, but that did not spare him from being targeted by the racial politics of the Third Reich. Nevertheless, he insisted on being 'more German than the Nazis'. For him, the 1935 Nuremberg Laws that deprived him of his German

---

[36]*Nuremberg Trial Proceedings*, vol. IV, 18 December 1945, available online: https://avalon.law.yale.edu/imt/12-18-45.asp (accessed 29 January 2023). As to the pogroms in small towns and villages, see Wildt, *Hitler's Volksgemeinschaft*, 238–46; Alan E. Steinweis, *Kristallnacht 1938* (Cambridge, MA: Harvard University Press, 2009).
[37]Victor Klemperer, *I Shall Bear Witness: The Diaries of Victor Klemperer, 1933–41*, trans. Martin Chalmers (London: Weidenfeld & Nicolson, 1998); Victor Klemperer, *To the Bitter End: The Diaries of Victor Klemperer, 1942–1945*, trans. Martin Chalmers (London: Weidenfeld & Nicolson, 1999).

citizenship were a slap in the face. He further lost his professorship at Dresden University, and he feared being expelled from his beloved house and garden. The terror of 9 November, however, was barely mentioned in his diaries. For him, it was just one more step in the direction of driving Jews out of the country, which had been the officially stated goal since 1933.

Klemperer stayed and survived, protected partly by his marriage and partly by the Allied air raid on Dresden in February 1945, which allowed him to escape. Others did what the Nazis expected them to do and left Germany for good. Before November 1938, 150,000 of the 550,000 German Jews had already left; the largest number had done so in 1933, directly after the Nazis came to power. Between November 1938 and September 1939 another 90,000 Jews emigrated – in 'normal' years the figure had been around 20,000. Those who remained were too old or too poor to leave; almost all of them were later deported and murdered.

For those who departed after 9 November 1938, that day made all the difference. At least this is how they remembered it shortly after fleeing the country. In August 1939, the *New York Times* announced a competition organized by three Harvard faculty men. They asked recent German immigrants to write about 'My Life Before and After January 30th, 1933', and more than 250 people responded over the next few months. The great majority were Jews for whom the November pogrom had provided the conclusive reason to arrange the emigration most had dreaded.[38]

'A date that I shall never forget'; 'the preceding sufferings, privations, humiliations and horrors cannot be compared with what happened on this single night'; 'the high point of Hitler's Jewish policy'; 'it was generally recognized that the situation was coming to a head, but what happened in November was worse than we ever imagined': this is how people remembered the acts of violence. Although they had expected things to get worse after 1933, they could not have envisioned what occurred on 9 November and the days that followed: 30,000 Jewish men were arrested and taken to concentration camps; 400 were murdered or committed suicide; 1,400 synagogues, prayer halls and schools went up in flames; Jewish cemeteries and graves were vandalized; thousands of shops and apartments were raided and damaged. Those who witnessed and lived through the ordeal vividly recollected the fear and utter desperation they had felt at their complete helplessness. They wrote about the police standing by or even participating in the destruction; they recalled firemen watching as synagogues were burnt to the ground. They were, in short, devastated and lost all hope that there was any future for Jews in the German racial state. Even Klemperer now felt an urgent need to leave Germany for the United States.

---

[38] Uta Gerhardt and Thomas Karlauf, eds, *The Night of Broken Glass: Eyewitness Accounts of Kristallnacht* (Cambridge: Polity Press, 2012); Kaplan, *Between Dignity and Despair*, 129 ff.

Perpetrators and the pleasure of humiliation

What did they write about the perpetrators? How did they perceive the behaviour of their non-Jewish neighbours, friends and colleagues? Interestingly, there was a marked tendency in the reports to distinguish between Nazis and others. Many authors mentioned that police officers, when alone with their Jewish prisoners, 'repeated apologetically that they had nothing to do with these monstrous and disgraceful acts, but after all that was how they earned their living'. Police arrest was widely preferred to Nazi prisons, as police officers generally treated the arrested men 'decently and in accordance with the rules'. A man who had been interned after the pogrom in a fire brigade training school recounted that 'the firemen had acted properly, and in some cases even generously'. But every afternoon SS men came from the nearby city of Königsberg and made the detainees 'run and sing with them'.[39]

The real culprits were thus identified as 'black- and brownshirts' – meaning SS men, Stormtroopers and NSDAP members. They were depicted as cruel, sadistic, brutish and extremely violent. The violence was not just instrumental but also pleasurable: perpetrators enjoyed terrorizing and humiliating their victims, and they mocked and ridiculed them in a way that was reminiscent of older charivari parades. Siegfried Merecki from Vienna reported that Stormtroopers and other Nazis 'made me take off my winter coat and wait. Soon a man came back with my coat. Both arms had been half cut away.' Another man

> spied my almost new, wide-brimmed felt hat. Saying that he would make it still more beautiful, he took scissors and cut the brim to pieces and made large holes in it [...] Then we were made to march down the street in rank and file and with our inside-out coats. I noticed that other prisoners' trousers had been cut short and their coat-tails cut away [...] We were taken to the police station in the Grosse Mohrengasse, where a large crowd shouted threats. In the guardroom, there were about fifty other fellow sufferers, several guards and a few SA men. When one of the guards saw our strange get-ups, he asked what kind of farce we were playing and ordered us to put our coats back on in the usual way [...] Suddenly one of the SA men there waved me into another room where there was no one. He ordered me to clean his boots. They were very clean, and I gathered that I was not the first to have this honour. I was ordered to clean them with the tail of my overcoat and then with the silk lining. I rubbed as hard as I could. Finally, he let me go unharmed.[40]

---

[39] Gerhardt and Karlauf, eds, *Night of Broken Glass*, 43, 78, 184–5, 213.
[40] Ibid., 38–9.

Other prisoners were forced to box each other and perform physical exercises for hours on end. They had to 'crawl on the floor', 'do somersaults' and sing. An Orthodox rabbi was singled out for special treatment and commanded to chant Jewish songs in front of laughing SS thugs: 'They came up to the man and, while he had to go on singing, one after another they cut off the remnants of his beard. Whenever he got so tired that he stopped singing, he was struck in the face and on the head and had to continue.'[41]

The camp and the column, marching and singing: here they were again. This time they were engaged not to turn German citizens into faithful and passionate Nazis, but to demean, degrade and terrorize Jewish outcasts.[42] Victims were made to feel that they were at the absolute mercy of their perpetrators. The latter, though, did not show mercy but instead used every means available to deprive Jews of their human dignity and self-esteem. For the Nazis, such politics of humiliation served to strengthen their own power and confirm their higher status. Debasing others and watching them suffer obviously made them feel superior. Acting as part of a larger group supplied a sense of entitlement and authority that filled them with satisfaction. Even on a one-on-one basis and without a wider audience, as experienced by Merecki, they took personal pleasure in humiliating those at their hands.

Bystanders: embarrassment and complicity

What about the bystanders who did not actively participate in the violence and humiliation? Many events took place in broad daylight for all to see; even the nightly acts of destruction were not committed without spectators. As Hugo Moses from Cologne testified, 'most of the "German people" who a day later the government said were responsible for what happened that night lay peacefully in bed' the evening of 9 November.[43] Still, when synagogues were burned and apartments noisily demolished, neighbours, friends and acquaintances were bound to see and hear.

Testimonies about their reactions proved ambivalent. An 'Old Fighter' and Stormtrooper who prided himself on his violent and hateful behaviour towards Jewish citizens in Brühl remarked condescendingly that 'all in all, the people lacked understanding and even rejected our action'. Reportedly,

---

[41]Ibid., 169, 49. See, for similar transgressions, Steinweis, *Kristallnacht*, 25–6, 77–8, *passim*.
[42]Peter Loewenberg, 'The Kristallnacht as a Public Degradation Ritual', *Leo Baeck Year Book* 32 (1987): 309–23.
[43]Gerhardt and Karlauf, eds, *Night of Broken Glass*, 21.

only the children went wild and knew no limits.⁴⁴ Encouraged by their teachers as well as leaders of the Hitler Youth, they often finished off the work of destruction.⁴⁵ Among adults, there was considerable variation. Some were compassionate and tried their best to calm the situation and console the victims, while others kept their distance, settled personal scores or looked the other way.⁴⁶

This was not a novel experience. Social relations between Jewish and non-Jewish Germans had gradually become strained after 1933. Klemperer was a good example and a careful chronicler of the estrangement. He recounted the growing antisemitism around him, mainly in institutions like students' and professional associations. At the same time, he noted 'sympathy visits' by colleagues and friends in May 1933. But even those who declared that they were not antisemites found it necessary to draw a line between 'Germans' and 'Jews'. In June 1935, Klemperer wrote that

> many otherwise well-meaning people [...] have begun to halfway acquiesce to Hitler. Their opinion: If at the cost of going backwards internally he restores Germany's power externally, then this cost is worth while. Conditions at home can always be made good later.

More and more, his 'Aryan' friends and colleagues decided to stay away or avoid contact. Still, Klemperer rarely experienced what he called 'wild anti-Semitism'. As late as March 1940, he observed: 'For my part I encounter much sympathy, people help me out, but fearfully of course.'⁴⁷

Fear certainly played a role when non-Jewish Germans severed or minimized their ties with the Jewish population. Those who still frequented Jewish shops were often photographed and publicly exposed. Denunciations abounded. Housemaids in Jewish families faced pressure to quit and seek new employment. Women who cried upon seeing the devastation of the pogrom were publicly rebuked. On 10 November 1938, Julius Streicher, Hitler's most powerful man in Lower Bavaria, gave a public speech in Nuremberg's main market square, declaring: 'We know that there are also people among us who have sympathy for the Jews, people who are not worthy of living in this city, not worthy of belonging to this people of which you are a proud part.'⁴⁸

---

⁴⁴*Die inszenierte Empörung: Der 9. November 1938. Themen und Materialien* (Bonn: Bundeszentrale für politische Bildung, 2010), ch. 3, here 33–4, available online: https://www.bpb.de/system/files/pdf/CC7XZK.pdf (accessed 19 January 2023).
⁴⁵Gerhardt and Karlauf, eds, *Night of Broken Glass*, 28, 34, 211. See also Steinweis, *Kristallnacht*, 60, 82–7.
⁴⁶Ibid., 119–27; Kaplan, *Between Dignity and Despair*, 123 ff.
⁴⁷Klemperer, *I Shall*, 15, 121, 315
⁴⁸Gerhardt and Karlauf, eds, *Night of Broken Glass*, 264. The speech was mentioned by Rudolf Bing from Nuremberg (ibid., 59).

Even citizens who did feel sympathy and compassion for Jewish people became increasingly reluctant to show it openly. Among those who recorded their life stories in 1939, several reported feeling abandoned:

> so many friends we had known for decades sooner or later turned their backs on us. We had the feeling that they were not at first entirely convinced that what they were doing was correct, but they gradually changed their minds. They learned that the party's recipes were the right ones for the German people and the fatherland. It was very painful for us to see and feel this.

For some, 9 November vastly accelerated the process: now 'Jews were avoided even by Aryans who had not previously done so'.[49]

Others, however, emphasized that 'decent' people everywhere were appalled by the pogrom. In a number of cases, 'Aryan' business partners had sent a warning before the events. Many observed what they called a 'vexed uneasiness'; several sensed 'a deep feeling of depression and shame' that gripped the public. Fritz Rodeck, a journalist from Vienna, wrote: 'I have spoken with people from all occupations and social classes, with workers, businessmen and intellectuals, Nazi supporters and Nazi opponents: I have not found a single person who approved of these events but many who were filled with the deepest revulsion.' After Rodeck had been

> robbed of everything and stripped of all my assets, a large number of Aryan acquaintances made what amounted to condolence visits to me, brought me gifts, offered me money and helped me in every conceivable way. They were all ashamed and deeply depressed [...] There were Aryan women who said, weeping: 'We are not to blame for this! Forgive us!'

The journalist concluded: 'For me it is a true satisfaction to be able to testify that even in National Socialist Greater Germany there are still decent people; there are still good human beings.'[50]

Can this conclusion be taken at face value? Or did it conceal a latent message? Forty-five-year-old Hugo Moses gave a hint at the end of his report:

> If I constantly emphasize that with few exceptions my earlier Aryan friends and acquaintances were good and generous to us right up until our departure, that means that in their hearts a large part of the German

---

[49]Ibid., 82, 42.
[50]Ibid., 85, 59, 219. Physician Hertha Nathorff from Berlin 'heard a few passers-by remarking sadly about these events; but most of them just walked timidly and quietly through the streets' (ibid., 149). Such conduct might have been an expression of shame.

people did not approve or participate in the anti-Semitic pogrom. Were it otherwise, I could not write these lines today on my way to the land of freedom without concern for the lives of those dear to me. Then those unfortunate fellow Jews who are now still having to maintain their miserable existence in Germany would certainly no longer be alive.[51]

This was the crucial point. The belief in the German people's ultimate decency and humanity served an end, or rather several ends. In Rodeck's case, it upheld the memory of a life that was not entirely based on illusions. Institutions and politics might fail, but people could still be decent. If so, there would be something worth clinging to in a new, unsettling and dizzying life across the ocean. If so, one's whole identity would not have to be completely obliterated.

Moses's case was different. Here, the person writing had not yet arrived on American shores; he was still making his way there on a ship from Europe and the events he recounted were very recent. Furthermore, he was deeply worried about those left behind, family and friends who had not yet emigrated and perhaps never would. The thought that Germany was full of fervent Nazis and Jew-haters was, under these circumstances, simply unbearable. Holding on to the belief that a 'large part of the German people' was decent and good assuaged his fears and let him hope that things would not get worse.

Yet they did get worse for the Jews who remained in Europe. Most Germans grew accustomed to looking the other way when they saw Jews being marched to railway stations and deported eastwards. Goebbels's propaganda machine continued to work efficiently after November 1938. Films like *Jud Süß* and *The Eternal Jew*, both released in 1940, whipped up antisemitic feelings of disgust and repulsion. Even if 'wild antisemitism' and vehement hatred were limited to party members, Stormtroopers and SS men – and, not to forget, the Hitler Youth, who had played an inglorious role in the pogrom – 'quiet' antisemitism and indifference were widespread. Many people just did not care what happened to their Jewish former fellow citizens, and indeed profited in material terms from their expulsion.

The regime's emotional politics was therefore eventually successful. It probably did not achieve the goal of winning over the millions of Germans who, for religious, moral or political reasons, were not enamoured with the Führer and his party; according to Goebbels, they amounted to 10 per cent of the population in 1935.[52] But it taught them some important lessons: first, they learnt that the regime would not hesitate to carry out its most radical promises and threats. The targets of official hatred and contempt were made to feel the consequences, without mercy or exception. One could

---

[51]Ibid., 34.
[52]Sösemann, *Propaganda*, vol. 2, 754, 757.

only hope not to be among them. Second, the violent exclusion of Jews ultimately forged stronger bonds among non-Jewish Germans, whether active perpetrators or embarrassed bystanders. The latter, who passively allowed the repression to happen and sometimes felt shame as a result of it, were no less complicit than those who carried it out.

The historian Hans Mommsen, who was born in 1930, remembered that his father Wilhelm, a professor of history at Marburg University, had taken him and his twin brother to the city's burnt-down synagogue on 10 November 1938. Wilhelm Mommsen, who had been raised in a liberal family and had himself held liberal political views during the Weimar Republic, turned ashen and seemed paralysed at the sight of it.[53] Yet two years later, he joined the NSDAP. Although he was never at the forefront of National Socialist historiography, he did bow to völkisch interpretations of history and officially subscribed to the politics of the racial state. He might have had various reasons for complying: protecting his economically insecure professional status, pride in Hitler's foreign policy achievements, satisfaction at the dismantlement of the Treaty of Versailles, which had been considered an injustice and a national humiliation by the vast majority of German citizens after the First World War. Even liberal-minded men and women who counted themselves – as Wilhelm Mommsen's doctoral supervisor Friedrich Meinecke did – among the 'opposition', rejoiced when German troops entered Paris in June 1940 and forced the French to acknowledge defeat at the very site where Germany had signed the armistice in 1918.[54]

When Klemperer learnt of the German victory, he was devastated:

> Meanwhile everything has become even more gloomier. France! The boundless German triumph [...] The language, the gestures in the Forest of Compiègne! [...] On language I note: the ruthless, lightening-fast changes of tone. In autumn France was a chivalrous nation, only led astray by England, and it was courted. Then, during the offensive, in ever-increasing measure 'Jew ridden', 'N[*****] ridden', 'decadent', 'sadistic'

---

[53]Personal communication. See also Hans Mommsen's 1999 interview http://hsozkult.geschichte.hu-berlin.de/beitrag/intervie/hmommsen.htm (accessed 19 January 2023).

[54]In June 1940, 77-year-old history professor Friedrich Meinecke congratulated his son-in-law Carl Rabl both on his birthday and on his achievements 'as a member of the mighty force that is now punishing France for the peace of Versailles. I, too, am full of admiration for what our army does surpassing all expectations.' In early July, he wrote to his Austrian colleague Heinrich Ritter von Srbik that the preceding weeks had 'deeply moved' him and filled him with 'pride and joy'. Having kept an oppositional distance from the Nazi regime because of its 'negative sides', he was now prepared to 'relearn' and consider 'reconciliation' (Friedrich Meinecke, *Ausgewählter Briefwechsel*, ed. Ludwig Dehio and Peter Classen (Stuttgart: Koehler, 1962), 192–4). Meinecke, who had co-founded the German Democratic Party in 1918, clearly appreciated the 'national' dimension of Nazi rule far more than the regime's antisemitic and anti-liberal politics.

... Pictures of bestialised negroes, reports of stomachs slit open, mutilated corpses etc.⁵⁵

He also reported people's expectation that England would be the next military target, and 'the absolute certainty of speedy final success even before autumn'. Nationalist sentiment skyrocketed, as Klemperer noted with bewildered incomprehension, even among Jewish Germans – 'were they not affected as Jews, they would be Nazis'.⁵⁶

Numbness versus love and decency: emotional politics and its effects

Klemperer himself did not share those sentiments. Instead, he closely observed the regime's emotional politics and how the people around him reacted to what they heard and saw. Shortly after the war, he published his notebook on the *Lingua Tertii Imperii*. In it, he described how National Socialism had 'corrupted and poisoned' various emotional concepts and practices, from heroism to pride, bravery and loyalty. In the eyes of the philologist, the language of the Third Reich was characterized by the 'preference for everything to do with emotions and instinct'. While emotion was 'not itself the be-all and end-all', it served as 'a means to an end': the regime's taking 'possession of the people only through emotional effect'. Ultimately, however, the language of emotions had to 'surrender to a state of numbing dullness without any freedom of will or feeling; how else would one have got hold of the necessary crowd of executioners and torturers?' The 'perfect group of followers' felt nothing at all, it simply followed.⁵⁷

Was Klemperer's diagnosis of a collective mindset bereft of 'any feeling' correct? Undoubtedly, the regime's officials, be they bureaucrats or camp guards, police officers or SS men, carried out their cruel work like a well-oiled machine and neither felt nor exhibited effusive enthusiasm in its course. Yet they had all been inculcated with the principle summoned by Heinrich Himmler, minister of the interior and *Reichsführer* of the SS, in 1943: to be 'honest, decent, loyal and comradely only to those who belong to our own blood, and to nobody else'. They were not meant to care about foreign populations under German rule. Compassion with Russian forced labourers, in particular, clearly betrayed the duty to serve and protect one's own 'people and blood'. Pitilessness and rigour were also needed to fight

---

⁵⁵Klemperer, *I Shall*, 329.
⁵⁶Ibid., 329–30 (concerning Curt Feder, a former district court judge).
⁵⁷Victor Klemperer, *The Language of the Third Reich: LTI – Lingua Tertii Imperii: A Philologist's Notebook*, trans. Martin Brady (London: Athlone Press, 2000), 2, 221, 223, 228. See also Horst Dieter Schlosser, *Sprache unterm Hakenkreuz* (Cologne: Böhlau, 2013).

internal enemies who sought to 'destroy the mood of the German people' and undermine their resilience in the wake of Allied aerial bombings. Those 'defeatists' deserved neither mercy nor deference. If the 'fate of the nation' demanded it, drastic measures like beheadings had to be taken, without regard for social or personal attachments.

A 'particularly difficult chapter', Himmler added, was 'the extermination of the Jews'. Purportedly, German-style 'tact' required that nobody ever speak about it in public. 'It gave each of us a chill; yet, we realized that we would do it again next time when ordered and necessary.' Moving from words to deeds was anything but easy. Addressing his subordinates, the SS leader confidentially broke the silence:

> Most of you know what it means when 100 corpses are lying there or 500 or 1000. But we have stuck it out and have remained decent (*anständig*) with a few exceptions of human weaknesses. This has made us tough and firm (*hart*), and it counts as a glorious chapter of our history which will, however, never be written up [...] We had the moral right and the duty towards our people to kill that other people before they murdered us. All in all, we can say that we fulfilled this hardest task for the love of our people. And we have taken on no defect within us, in our soul, in our character.[58]

Himmler's speech contradicts Klemperer's claim that a 'numbing dullness' prevailed among the 'perfect group' of Nazi followers. It rather testified that love of *Volk* and Führer was and remained a strong motivating force. That force was by no means confined to SS men; 'love of Germany' had drawn the young Melita Maschmann and many others to National Socialism.[59] Love for Hitler as Germany's saviour had been kindled and supported by propaganda and cultish practices that proved particularly formative for children and adolescents.[60] This love sometimes even outlasted the end of the war. Klemperer himself mentioned one of his former students who had joined the party early. When they met again in 1946, he confronted him with the regime's 'atrocious crimes' that were now apparent for all to see. After a long pause the younger man answered Klemperer 'very quietly': 'I accept all that. The others misunderstood him, betrayed him. But I still believe in HIM, I really do.'[61]

---

[58] https://www.1000dokumente.de/index.html?c=dokument_de&dokument=0008_pos&st=de (accessed 19 January 2023).
[59] Maschmann, *Account Rendered*, 26, 211. Maschmann, who became a high-ranking leader of the League of German Girls (BDM), insisted that hate (against enemies or foreign powers) initially played no role at all and was only exhibited during the war.
[60] Ian Kershaw, *The 'Hitler Myth': Image and Reality in the Third Reich* (Oxford: Clarendon Press, 1987).
[61] Klemperer, *Language*, 118.

Love, faith, hate: these and other emotions were injected and hammered into racially defined Germans under National Socialism. Never before in the nation's history had the state clamped down so forcefully on people's feelings and devised such comprehensive mechanisms in order to generate emotions, keep them alive and align them with its political goals. While hate speeches and images did not reach every part of the population, they nevertheless managed to effectively quell empathy and breed indifference to the suffering of the regime's victims.

Stoking existing feelings of aversion towards alleged enemies, as well as national pride and trust in the Führer, served the goal of obtaining the consent and affective commitment of actual and future citizens. At the same time, the regime generated and channelled emotions through practices of active mobilization. Marching in file, collective singing and leisure camps ensured that emotions were both produced and controlled on command and on purpose. This happened in youth organizations as well as among Stormtroopers and the SS, not to mention the National Socialist Teachers League, whose members had heard the education minister speak in 1934 at Munich's Circus Krone and were inspired to send schoolchildren to raid and demolish Jewish shops four years later.

CHAPTER FOURTEEN

Emotional Styles and Political Cultures in East and West Germany

Totalitarian regimes like National Socialism – or Italian Fascism and the Soviet Union under Stalin – developed an emotional politics with a strong focus on children and adolescents, who would embody the future generation of ideologically committed and passionately fanatic citizens. In schools and youth organizations, they were taught the essentials of political love and hatred, of unlimited trust in the leader and loyal comradeship with one another. They also learnt who their enemies were and how they deserved to be treated. Those lessons were apparently well received; at least this is what contemporaries witnessed in daily encounters with 'contaminated' youngsters and schoolchildren who wilfully and enthusiastically participated in hateful practices of violent exclusion.

What happened when fascism and National Socialism were defeated after the Second World War? Where did the passion go? Melita Maschmann, who had joined the Hitler Youth as a 15-year-old in 1933 and remained a dedicated party official until the very end, needed a decade to come to terms with her former self and to emotionally distance herself from that time.[1] Victor Klemperer's student still believed in the godlike Führer long after

---

This chapter is a starkly revised and widely expanded version of the article 'Emotional Styles in Post-War German Politics', in *The Oxford Handbook of German Politics*, ed. Klaus Larres, Holger Moroff and Ruth Wittlinger (Oxford: Oxford University Press, 2022), 33–44.

[1] See Melita Maschmann, *Account Rendered: A Dossier of My Former Self* (Lexington, KY: Plunkett Lake Press, 2013). The book was published in German in 1962 and had several editions. See Helen Epstein, 'I was a Nazi, and Here's Why', *The New Yorker*, 29 May 2013, available online: https://www.newyorker.com/books/page-turner/i-was-a-nazi-and-heres-why (accessed 29 January 2023).

the latter's suicide in April 1945. Others, like young Günter Schabowski, immediately found a new object of desire and adoration.[2]

Born in 1929, Schabowski held a leadership position in the Hitler Youth. After the military capitulation, he stayed in the Soviet-occupied zone and launched his career as a socialist.[3] He joined the Free Trade Union Movement as well as the Free German Youth (FDJ) and became a member of the governing Socialist Unity Party (SED) in the German Democratic Republic (GDR). An editor of the party's 'central organ', the *Neues Deutschland* newspaper, he divided the world into good socialists and bad capitalists. While the socialist fatherland commanded each person's commitment and love, capitalist countries should be hated and despised. Asked, in 1968, by a West German visitor 'with raised eyebrows' if a state could really be 'loved' by its citizens, he proclaimed that this was indeed the case, but only when that state was a socialist one and had been created by and for the people.

It was no accident that the visitor from the West had asked this very question. Seeing the effort that was put into celebrating the nineteenth anniversary of the GDR's founding, she must have sensed a deep divide. While the Federal Republic (FRG) marked the date of its founding with little aplomb, the GDR did so with much fanfare, including parades and supposedly voluntary labour stints 'in the state's honour'. Schoolchildren, workers and millions of members of mass organizations were called upon to participate in the event and make it a roaring success. Schabowski explained to his incredulous interlocutor that this was all done in the name of 'affection, trust, and love' for a state that guaranteed the future security of its citizens and the 'new happiness of the socialist community of man'.[4]

Whether the West German sceptic was convinced by the East German's argument is not known. Living in a country that made only sparse use of national symbols and very rarely appealed to people's patriotic feelings, she probably remained critical of the sight of citizens – among them crowds of children and adolescents – marching through the streets, waving flags, chanting, singing and promising their loyalty to the regime. If she happened to belong to the generation that came of age in 1968, she might have been even more hesitant. Rudi Dutschke, the charismatic leader of the West German student movement, had grown up in East Germany and left in 1961,

---

[2]Günter Schabowski rose to prominence on 9 November 1989, when, as a leading GDR politician, he gave a slightly mistaken answer to a journalist's question about when the GDR would finally grant its citizens the right to free travel. His answer that a new regulation to grant visas for private trips would come into effect 'immediately' raised expectations and made crowds of people take to the streets, with the result that the Berlin Wall opened, against all odds, that very night.

[3]Dorothee Wierling, 'The Hitler Youth Generation in the GDR: Insecurities, Ambitions and Dilemmas', in *Dictatorship as Experience: Towards a Socio-Cultural History of the GDR*, ed. Konrad H. Jarausch (New York: Berghahn, 1999), 307–24.

[4]Günter Schabowski, 'Kann man einen Staat lieben? Anmerkungen zu einer skeptischen Frage', *Neues Deutschland*, 7 October 1968, 9.

disillusioned and frustrated by the lack of what he envisioned as democratic socialism. Three days before the wall was built in Berlin, he registered as a political refugee. The West, though, was by no means his promised land or paradise. The 'extra-parliamentary opposition' (APO) that formed in the Federal Republic and of which Dutschke was part thoroughly distrusted the state and its political personnel. In 1968, APO members were in no mood to celebrate the founding of the Federal Republic; they were busy passionately fighting the Emergency Acts, impending legislation which they thought would curtail fundamental rights and maximize governmental power.[5]

This chapter looks at post-war German political cultures with a special interest in their emotional patterns and practices. How did governments, parties and social movements enlist emotions in their political activities? Were they copying the emotional styles that had been developed and enacted during the Third Reich, or did they move away from them?[6] How did West and East differ, and why? Were there competing styles and claims to emotions among and within the two German states? Drafting a particular emotional style, I will argue, was a major challenge and component of state-building in the FRG as well as in the GDR. How those styles emerged and developed, became accepted or contested, reveals a great deal about political cultures and how they conceptualize the relationship between citizens and those who embrace politics as a 'vocation', in Max Weber's terms.[7] It also explains, at least in part, the current discourse on the 'emotionalization' of politics, which will be discussed at the chapter's end.

Reason and emotion

In 1943, the US government commissioned and funded four short films produced by Walt Disney. One was called *Reason and Emotion*, and it received an Oscar nomination a year later.[8] Its first part introduced the audience to contemporary perceptions of what an emotion was and how it related to reason. Every man and woman, so the story went, must resist the temptations of emotion, personified for men by a primitive, uncultured caveman and for women by a voluptuous, pleasure-seeking sybarite. Reason, in contrast, was depicted as a balding, bespectacled man in a suit and a spinster governess. Even though none of the four types of gendered

---

[5]Frank Biess, *German Angst: Fear and Democracy in the Federal Republic of Germany* (Oxford: Oxford University Press, 2020), 184–94.
[6]On the concept of emotional style, see Benno Gammerl, 'Emotional Styles – Concepts and Challenges', *Rethinking History* 16, no. 2 (2012): 161–75.
[7]Max Weber, 'The Profession and Vocation of Politics [1919]', in *Weber: Political Writings*, ed. Peter Lassman and Ronald Speirs (Cambridge: Cambridge University Press, 1995), 309–69.
[8]Tracy Louise Mollett, *Cartoons in Hard Times: An Animated Short of Disney and Warner Brothers in Depression and War 1932–1945* (New York: Bloomsbury, 2017), 130–3.

personification were very appealing, reason should, the film argued, maintain the upper hand. Putting emotions in the driver's seat would harm society and even endanger civilization. Since one could not live entirely without emotions, however, rational reflection was needed to keep them in check.

The film's second half adapted the lesson to the politics of the time. In Nazi Germany, the audience was told, emotion had taken over, fuelled by incessant propaganda and a monstrous leader who knew no bounds on his path to global destruction. Under the threat of Germany's vanquishing power, Americans should not lose their heads (or courage), but keep battling. The film ends on an optimistic note, with the reasonable fellow in a suit steering a fighter jet. He is not alone in the plane, though: his co-pilot turns out to be the good-natured caveman, who provides the just cause with emotional energy and moral support. Together, they lead the nation to ultimate victory.

The propaganda film highlighted a widespread concern about the appropriate relationship between reason and emotion, not only but particularly in politics. Preceded by developments in the arts, where a 'new sobriety' (*Neue Sachlichkeit*) had succeeded Expressionism, the interwar period had witnessed manifold attempts to keep political emotions at bay. In his inaugural address of March 1933, President Franklin D. Roosevelt tried to garner support for his New Deal politics by shielding citizens from the abounding emotion of fear. Fear was aptly defined as 'nameless, unreasoning, unjustified terror which paralyzes needed efforts to convert retreat into advance'.[9] By this time, Germany was already in the firm grip of National Socialism, which propelled and enlisted a host of other 'unreasoning' emotions, from national honour and pride to feelings of racial superiority and antisemitic disgust.[10] As the Disney film portrayed it ten years later, in the midst of a new war, pride had taken the lead, transforming the German people into fanatics and mobilizing them against a world of perceived enemies, democratic and undemocratic, in Europe and beyond.

It would be misleading, though, to identify democratic regimes with emotional styles that favoured sobriety and restraint, and to paint undemocratic regimes as indulging in a politics of emotional overwhelm and excess. In the modern age of mass participation, politicians across different parties and systems deliberately appealed to people's emotions in order to

---

[9] Franklin D. Roosevelt: 'The only thing we have to fear is fear', https://www.archives.gov/education/lessons/fdr-inaugural (accessed 19 January 2023). See also Ira Katznelson, *Fear Itself: The New Deal and the Origins of Our Time* (New York: Norton & Co., 2013); Wolfgang Schivelbusch, *Three New Deals: Reflections on Roosevelt's America, Mussolini's Italy and Hitler's Germany, 1933–1939* (New York: Picador, 2007); David M. Kennedy, *Freedom from Fear: The American People in Depression and War, 1929–1945* (New York: Oxford University Press, 1999).

[10] See Chapter 13 in this volume; as for antisemitic feelings, see the special issue by Uffa Jensen and Stefanie Schüler-Springorum, eds, 'Gefühle gegen Juden', *Geschichte und Gesellschaft* 39, no. 4 (2013).

market their politics and win support. They did so in times of peace, but even more so in times of war, or when gearing up for military conflict. They enacted emotional politics and they reflected on whether doing so was good or bad, helpful or harmful, effective or flawed. Furthermore, they closely observed what competitors did, and, as the Disney film shows, they sought to learn from each other, through imitation or negation.

They also tried to uncover people's sentiments and determine how they received certain political messages. Expertise in observing national opinion had first been developed in the US, where Gallup polls started in 1935. Two years later, the United Kingdom followed suit, conducting 'mass observations' on a grand scale. Gathering information about citizens' feelings, dispositions and inclinations turned out to be of great value. Politicians used this data when preparing for election campaigns; economic players incorporated it into public relations and marketing strategies. The more companies, parties and government agencies knew about what citizen–consumers desired and abhorred, feared and loved, the better they could target, tailor and sell their goods, services and politics.

Such interest was by no means restricted to the interwar or war periods. The triumph of polling opinions, attitudes and feelings continued after 1945, easily crossing political and ideological borders. While the Federal Republic mostly relied on private organizations to conduct large-scale surveys, the GDR drew on an increasingly dense spy network to report on whether and how state socialism was succeeding in conquering the hearts and minds of the East German populace. The lesson had been learnt: mass politics had to appeal to people's emotions, and these emotions needed to be acutely monitored and worked upon.

Sobriety over collective pathos

Yet one cannot help but notice the tone of unease that often went along with acknowledging this lesson. To many political actors and observers, the relationship between reason and emotion was highly ambiguous. Not everyone believed in the power and legitimacy of charisma, and more than a few distrusted the appeal to people's feelings (which was often tantamount to actively shaping and moulding those feelings). Even Hitler's description of the 'feminine' masses who could only be reached with emotional communication bore traces of condescension and contempt. The feminine, as it was constructed in contemporary gender discourses, contained both lustful seduction on the one hand, and threats of emasculation on the other. Emotional politics thus made attractive promises but it also proved dangerous to the 'reasoning powers' over which men apparently had special dominance.[11]

National Socialism had taken great pains to ensure that these masculine powers – and ensuing privileges and prerogatives – did not succumb to feminine influence. Positions of political authority were filled with men and, unlike during the Weimar Republic, there were no female representatives in the (largely ineffective) parliament. Meanwhile, visual media eagerly published photographs of women cheering for the Führer, ecstatically waving and blowing kisses when he passed through their hometowns. This generated the enduring myth of women as Hitler's most passionate supporters and idolizers.[12]

After the war, a similar but gender-neutral narrative was added to the legend about women having been charmed by Hitler's charisma and falling under his erotic spell. Now it was the entire nation that was supposed to have been conquered and seduced, misled and betrayed. The GDR found a quick and easy way to exculpate its citizens by putting all the blame on a quantifiable group of militarists, imperialists and fascists. That group was squarely located in West Germany; its members were purportedly working tirelessly to bring about a third World War against communism. For its part, the East German population was collectively absolved of guilt and responsibility, and ought to show their gratitude in turn by committing themselves unequivocally to the new socialist state.[13]

Things did not go quite as smoothly and homogeneously in West Germany, where there was no such generous offer of forgiveness or amnesia. Confronted with the monstrous crimes and atrocities of the Nazi regime, people reacted defensively. As the Heidelberg philosopher Karl Jaspers mentioned in his early post-war lectures on *The Question of German Guilt*, 'there are some who admit guilt, including their own, and many who hold themselves guiltless but pronounce others guilty'.[14] Some blamed the regime at large and tried to exonerate its main figure; others held Hitler alone

---

[11] Adolf Hitler, *Mein Kampf: Eine kritische Edition*, ed. Christian Hartmann et al. (Munich: Institut für Zeitgeschichte, 2016), vol. 1, 507. See Chapter 13 in this volume for further evidence.

[12] See, for example, Ernst Bloch, 'Die Frau im Dritten Reich (1937)', in Bloch, *Vom Hasard zur Katastrophe: Politische Aufsätze 1934–1939* (Frankfurt: Suhrkamp, 1972), 129–36. As to the post-war rehearsal of that myth, see Maruta Schmidt and Gabi Dietz, eds, *Frauen unterm Hakenkreuz* (Berlin: Elefanten Press, 1983), 7–8 (with concurrent quotes from the West German journalist Joachim Fest and GDR historian Jürgen Kuczynski).

[13] As to communist views on people's shared responsibility for Nazism and ensuing strategies of blaming and absolving, see Jeffrey Herf, *Divided Memory: The Nazi Past in the Two Germanys* (Cambridge, MA: Harvard University Press, 1997), chs 1, 3–5; Ralph Giordano, 'Der verordnete Antifaschismus', in Giordano, *Die zweite Schuld oder Von der Last, Deutscher zu sein* (Hamburg: Rasch & Röhring, 1987), 215–28.

[14] Karl Jaspers, *The Question of German Guilt*, trans. E.B. Ashton (New York: Capricorn Books, 1961), 27. Jaspers held his lectures at Heidelberg University in the winter term of 1945/46. He had spent the Nazi period in a kind of 'inner emigration' as he tried to protect his Jewish wife.

responsible, emphasizing their own innocence. Emigrants like Theodor W. Adorno, who returned to Frankfurt first in 1949 and then permanently in 1953, were taken aback by people's denial of their involvement and liability. In 1959, Adorno saw 'cold forgetting' coupled with 'dissatisfaction' and 'rage' against Allied re-education as key traits of the West German zeitgeist.[15] Foreign visitors who toured Germany in the early years following capitulation likewise reported on a widespread mood of apathy, malaise and resentment. Such resentment had as its object both the Nazi regime and current efforts to convince the population of the charms of democracy.[16]

This was especially the case for the younger generation, who had lived under the powerful spell of National Socialist propaganda and education during their formative years. It was no coincidence that many post-war surveys and polls focused on young people, be they refugees or not, urban or rural dwellers, employed or unemployed, male or female. In 1957, the sociologist Helmut Schelsky presented a synthesis of these enquiries under the catchy title *Die skeptische Generation*. Writing about blue- and white-collar workers aged between 14 and 25, Schelsky described them as politically passive and neutral. They were interested neither in big ideas nor in intimate attachments to leaders or groups. War and post-war experiences had dealt a heavy blow to young people's inclination to identify with and commit to political ideologies or regimes. Instead of faithfully believing in grand promises and ideals, they sought to stabilize and secure their personal and private lot. Unlike former generations, who either indulged in romanticism or embraced political imaginaries, members of the sceptical generation harboured a 'sober' sense of reality. They appreciated and emphasized family relations and were career-minded. Overall, they shied away from joining organizations; if they did so, they followed material and strategic motives rather than enthusiastically engaging with dogmas and bold visions for the future.[17]

Politically, young people – and women in particular – kept their distance. Older age groups within the cohort turned their back on politics 'silently and without argument'. This was, as Schelsky saw it, their reaction to what they had personally and collectively experienced under National Socialism and after. Those who were born during the war and had been too young to be 'seduced' or manipulated by the regime were more outspoken about their radical reluctance to get involved, and widely subscribed to the popular 'Count me out!' sentiment. They had 'borrowed', in Schelsky's terms, their

---

[15]Theodor W. Adorno, 'The Meaning of Working through the Past', in Adorno, *Critical Models: Interventions and Catchwords*, trans. Henry W. Pickford (New York: Columbia University Press, 1998), 89–103, quotes 98–9.
[16]Anna M. Parkinson, *An Emotional State: The Politics of Emotion in Postwar West German Culture* (Ann Arbor: University of Michigan Press, 2015), 5–23.
[17]Helmut Schelsky, *Die skeptische Generation: Eine Soziologie der deutschen Jugend* (Düsseldorf: Diederichs, 1963), 7, 73–83.

political scepticism from the adult generation and fully endorsed the overall approach of 'functional dispassion' (*Sachlichkeit*).[18]

For Alexander and Margarete Mitscherlich, who both taught at the newly founded Sigmund Freud Institute in Frankfurt, such emphatic dispassion or 'objectivity' shielded Germans from honestly confronting their recent past. As the two psychoanalysts wrote in 1967, people simply chose to forget their ardent love for the Führer in order to avoid feelings of guilt and shame. Becoming 'apolitically conservative', they lost any interest in creating, organizing and structuring politics. Instead, they dedicated their energy to producing and consuming, thus achieving the Federal Republic's economic 'miracle'. The only emotional continuity between pre- and post-1945 was, as the Mitscherlichs saw it, the massive fear and hatred of communism.[19]

Anti-communism indeed built an emotional bridge between totalitarian and democratic politics in the West. The ways the 'red peril' was characterized proved strikingly similar. Election posters commissioned by conservative parties (CDU/CSU) in 1949 and 1953 showed demonizing images immediately reminiscent of the visual language used and popularized by the Nazis. Communism appeared as a dark-skinned monster with Asian features and greedy claws that threatened the white-skinned German mother and child.[20]

Apart from those continuities, however, and in stark contrast to the GDR, West Germany's political culture in the 1950s turned out to be remarkably unemotional. Sobriety characterized the style of Bonn's first political representatives, Konrad Adenauer and Theodor Heuss. Both eschewed big words and heroic gestures; both preferred factual arguments to fiery or overwhelming speeches. When President Heuss called for 'a new national feeling' in his 1949 inaugural address, he quickly added that this feeling should be marked by modesty, devoid of any 'haughty hubris'.[21] Speaking on the radio on New Year's Eve, Heuss did not miss the opportunity to stress

---

[18]Ibid., 355, 362.
[19]Alexander and Margarete Mitscherlich, *The Inability to Mourn: Principles of Collective Behavior*, trans. Beverley R. Placzek (New York: Grove Press, 1975), ch. 1. See Paul Nolte, 'Von der Gesellschaftsstruktur zur Seelenverfassung: Die Psychologisierung der Sozialdiagnose in den sechziger Jahren', in *Psychoanalyse und Protest: Alexander Mitscherlich und die 'Achtundsechziger'*, ed. Tobias Freimüller (Göttingen: Wallstein, 2008), 70–94. As a critique, see Parkinson, *Emotional State*, ch. 3.
[20]Election Posters 1949–1998, http://www.bpb.de/lernen/grafstat/150415/wahlplakate-1949-1998 (accessed 29 January 2023); Elizabeth Heineman, 'The Hour of the Woman: Memories of Germany's "Crisis Years" and West German National Identity', in *The Miracle Years: A Cultural History of West Germany, 1949–1968*, ed. Hanna Schissler (Princeton: Princeton University Press, 2001), 21–56; Eric D. Weitz, 'The Ever-Present Other: Communism in the Making of West Germany', in *Miracle Years*, ed. Schissler, 219–232; Biess, *German Angst*, ch. 3.
[21]Dolf Sternberger, ed., *Reden der deutschen Bundespräsidenten Heuss/Lübke/Heinemann/Scheel* (Munich: Hanser, 1979), 5–10, quote 10.

his commitment to the 'spirit of realistic objectivity' and 'sobriety'.[22] When Chancellor and Foreign Minister Adenauer was selecting a West German national anthem in 1952, he did not make his decision with a view to possible emotional effects but with consideration of 'foreign policy pragmatism': after all, the embassies abroad needed a hymn to honour guests.[23] At home, Adenauer adopted a paternal tone and spoke in flat, unemotional terms, as in this typical end-of-year interview: 'In 1961, we want to work hard and be diligent, conscientious, and loyal as ever.'[24]

Advocating sobriety instead of emotionally charged pathos, Heuss and Adenauer followed, probably unknowingly, the advice of sociologist Theodor Geiger. In 1950, Geiger, who had first fled to Denmark then to Sweden during the Nazi period, wrote the preface for a collection of essays that sought to rethink democracy as a 'sober' and 'rational' project. Highly averse to any ideologies that enlisted 'collective pathos' and 'community emotionalism', he considered such inherently aggressive and belligerent pathos – be it for the cause of nation, class or church – a 'public menace'. Referring to fascism and communism, but also to religious fanaticism, Geiger put his faith instead in democratic education. It would have to protect citizens from any 'cult of emotionality' and teach them 'to leave their feelings at home when they move into the sphere of public life'. What was needed was

a shift of emphasis in favor of the intellectual powers, a systematic intellectualization of the individual and his training in emotional asceticism [...] The *homo intellectualis* must be led to victory over the *homo sentimentalis*.[25]

Geiger knew very well that the word 'intellectualization' would likely 'make many readers shy away. They sense the threat of a crippling of the emotions, an inner impoverishment, a kind of barbarization.' Yet he certainly did not

---

[22]Reinhard Kiehl, ed., *Alle Jahre wieder* (Düsseldorf: My Favourite Book, 2001), 49 (*Sachlichkeit*), 51 (*sachlich, Nüchternheit*), 68 (*Nüchternheit*).
[23]*Heuss – Adenauer, Unserem Vaterlande zugute: Der Briefwechsel 1948–1963* (Berlin: Siedler, 1989), 109–14, quote 112.
[24]Edgar Wolfrum, 'Konrad Adenauer: Politik und Vertrauen', in *Charismatische Führer der deutschen Nation*, ed. Frank Möller (Munich: Oldenbourg, 2004), 171–91, quote 184. According to Social Democrat Carlo Schmid, Adenauer 'sometimes felt like a kind of tutor. Many Germans accepted this, and, according to general opinion, saw him as a father figure' (Carlo Schmid, 'Ein Denkmal seiner Zeit', *DIE ZEIT*, 21 April 1967, 3). See also Mitscherlich and Mitscherlich, *Inability*, 13.
[25]Theodor Geiger, *On Social Order and Mass Society*, ed. Renate Mayntz (Chicago: Chicago University Press, 1969), quotes 187–8, 217, 222, 236, italics in the original. Geiger died in 1952, and his essays on 'Die Gesellschaft zwischen Pathos und Nüchternheit' were published posthumously in 1960. See Paul Nolte, *Die Ordnung der deutschen Gesellschaft: Selbstentwurf und Selbstbeschreibung im 20. Jahrhundert* (Munich: C.H. Beck, 2000), 311–13.

mean that a person should 'be weaned away from his emotions'. As he saw it, they had a legitimate place in private life, among family and friends. The public sphere, though, should be kept free of 'emotions and irrational ideas'.[26]

Geiger spoke the language of many West Germans who judged emotions to be thoroughly private affairs that had no right mingling with politics. On this, politicians from all mainstream parties agreed. When Gustav Heinemann, the first Social Democratic federal president, was asked in 1969 whether he loved his state, the answer was short and crisp: 'No, I don't love states, I love my wife. That's all.'[27] Such pointed sobriety – which bluntly contradicted Günter Schabowski's statement from 1968 – was mirrored in state architecture. In 1969, the Federal Constitutional Court moved into a new modernist building that combined functional design and multiple glass features with a dedicated absence of ornamental glory and pride. When Adenauer's successor, Ludwig Erhard, eventually commissioned a proper residence, he made sure that it defied all 'hubris'. The *Kanzlerbungalow* of 1966 was a transparent flat roof construction in the style of classical Modernism, designed by Sep Ruf.[28]

Counter-currents and countercultures

Nonetheless, there were counter-currents to such transparency and 'functional dispassion' (Schelsky). Erhard's successor, Kurt Georg Kiesinger of the CDU, found the residence uncomfortable and redecorated it with cosier furnishings. While Adenauer had been known, according to the *New York Times* journalist Cyrus Sulzberger, for his 'wooden face' that seldom showed a 'restrained half-smile', Heuss appreciated the 'motives of the soul' as much as he understood 'objective' concerns.[29] In 1960, social democrat Carlo Schmid cautioned against an overdose of 'rational thinking' that

---

[26]Geiger, *On Social Order*, 192.
[27]Hermann Schreiber, *Gustav Heinemann: Portrait of a President* (Hamburg: Fischer, 1969), 79. The journalist portrayed Heinemann as a politician of 'sobriety' (*Nüchternheit*) who kept his distance from any sort of collective emotions.
[28][Günther Kühne], 'Bundesverfassungsgericht in Karlsruhe', *Bauwelt* 48 (1969): 1714–22; *Kanzlerbungalow*, ed. Stiftung Haus der Geschichte der Bundesrepublik Deutschland and Wüstenrot-Stiftung (Munich: Prestel, 2009); Philipp Nielsen, 'Building Bonn: Affects, Politics, and Architecture in Postwar West Germany', in *Architecture, Democracy, and Emotions: The Politics of Feeling since 1945*, ed. Till Großmann and Philipp Nielsen (London: Routledge, 2019), 39–57.
[29]Cyrus L. Sulzberger, *A Long Row of Candles: Memoirs and Diaries, 1934–1954* (New York: Macmillan, 1969), 762 (quote from 1952); Kiehl, *Alle Jahre*, 49.

might make people 'wither and become wooden'. In his view, excessive 'practicality' threatened to overwhelm the 'powers of the soul'.[30]

Such critical reflections resonated with what the Mitscherlichs stated about the eagerness of West Germans to rebuild the economy while indulging in 'psychic immobilism' and 'political apathy'.[31] Evoking the 'powers of the soul' also questioned the claim to absolute rationality that underlay Cold War strategic planning and decision-making.[32] It even bore some resemblance to what Herbert Marcuse, another German emigré, wrote and preached in the US to a growing international audience of students.

As a preeminent theorist of the New Left, Marcuse criticized advanced capitalist societies for their alienating and objectifying tendencies. People, he argued, had become but mere extensions of commodities who 'find their soul in their automobile, hi-fi set, split-level home, kitchen equipment'.[33] Philosophers, sociologists and especially psychoanalysts, who enjoyed a good reputation during the 1960s, repeatedly warned of the emotional and political costs of such commodification. In addition to emptying and depoliticizing the public sphere, it put a grave psychological burden on each individual, generating new, structurally embedded pathologies. Against this backdrop, Marcuse understood why students seemed to be obsessed with the issue of individual authenticity and fought 'against the evils of repression and the need for being oneself'. Yet the goal of 'self-actualization' could prove equally repressive, since such 'private and personal rebellion' weakened the 'power of the intellect' to engage in a 'more authentic' opposition.[34]

The 1968ers who found inspiration in Marcuse's texts did not in fact exclusively put their trust in brainpower. They also considered themselves part of what sociologist Talcott Parsons referred to as an 'expressive revolution' against the dominance of rationality and discipline.[35] Emotions were no longer outlawed and frowned upon, but ennobled as incubators and resources of subversive action. While the Easter March movement against nuclear weapons and rearmament had privileged rational argument and

---

[30]Carlo Schmid, 'Der Mensch im Staat von morgen', in Schmid, *Politik muß menschlich sein* (Bern: Scherz, 1980), 9–30, quotes 12–13. Such warnings could also be heard from intellectuals who, in the tradition of Weimar's 'conservative revolution', attacked modern industrial society and technology (and, not to forget, democracy) for their 'soullessness' and 'cold rationality' (Armin Mohler, *Was die Deutschen fürchten* (Stuttgart: Seewald, 1965), 195).
[31]Mitscherlich and Mitscherlich, *Inability*, 8, 27.
[32]Paul Erickson et al., *How Reason Almost Lost Its Mind: The Strange Career of Cold War Rationality* (Chicago: Chicago University Press, 2013).
[33]Herbert Marcuse, *One-Dimensional Man: Studies in the Ideology of Advanced Industrial Society* (London: Routledge, 1964), 9.
[34]Herbert Marcuse, 'Repressive Tolerance', in Robert Paul Wolff, Barrington Moore and Herbert Marcuse, *A Critique of Pure Tolerance* (Boston: Beacon Press, 1965), 81–117, here 113–15.
[35]Talcott Parsons, 'Religion in Postindustrial America: The Problem of Secularization', *Social Research* 41, no. 2 (1974): 193–225, esp. 221–2.

information, the APO of the late 1960s invented and propagated a different emotional style. The group openly expressed and experimented with emotions such as anger, outrage, hatred and fear.[36] Their passionate rhetoric took heart from a counterculture that owed as much to earlier life reform movements as to the hippies and Flower Power protests of their own times. To many young leftists, Marcuse's warning about the allegedly apolitical credo of self-actualization missed the point. Joining consciousness-raising groups, listening to and understanding one's own feelings and those of others was meant to raise the level of empathy, solidarity and commitment to the political struggle.[37] Emotions thus acquired a new dignity and valence as signs of subjectivity, authenticity and *Betroffenheit* (concern or dismay). Furthermore, they were perceived as a means to address, invite and encourage supporters through expressive action.

While older political generations were shocked and appalled by the new emotional style, it quickly spread beyond student and counterculture milieus. Strengthened by the therapeutic turn, new political actors, from feminists to the environmental and peace movements, embraced it.[38] They found their own reasons to cast doubt on the alleged rationality – or rather reasonability – of socioeconomic developments and political decision-making. The women's movement unmasked rationality as a technique of patriarchal domination and, by coining the slogan 'the personal is political', helped emotions to leak from the private sphere into politics. Environmentalists attacked the inherent contradictions of economic rationality that ruthlessly exploited natural resources and that they feared would ultimately destroy

---

[36] Holger Nehring, 'Angst, Gewalterfahrungen und das Ende des Pazifismus: Die britischen und westdeutschen Proteste gegen Atomwaffen, 1957–1964', in *Angst im Kalten Krieg*, ed. Bernd Greiner, Christian Th. Müller and Dierk Walter (Hamburg: Hamburger Edition, 2009), 436–64; Michael Geyer, 'Cold War Angst: The Case of West-German Opposition to Rearmament and Nuclear Weapons', in *Miracle Years*, ed. Schissler, 376–408; Belinda Davis, 'Provokation als Emanzipation: 1968 und die Emotionen', *Vorgänge* 42, no. 4 (2003): 41–9; Biess, *German Angst*, chs 6 and 7.

[37] Sven Reichardt, *Authentizität und Gemeinschaft: Linksalternatives Leben in den siebziger und frühen achtziger Jahren* (Berlin: Suhrkamp, 2014), ch. 2; Timothy Scott Brown, *West Germany and the Global Sixties: The Anti-Authoritarian Revolt, 1962–1978* (Cambridge: Cambridge University Press, 2013); Joachim Häberlen, *The Emotional Politics of the Alternative Left: West Germany, 1968–1984* (Cambridge: Cambridge University Press, 2018); Joachim Häberlen et al., eds, *The Politics of Authenticity: Countercultures and Radical Movements across the Iron Curtain, 1968–1989* (New York: Berghahn, 2020).

[38] As to the influence of the psychotherapeutic turn, which reached West Germany in the 1970s, see Nikolas Rose, *Inventing our Selves: Psychology, Power, and Personhood* (Cambridge: Cambridge University Press, 1996); *Das beratene Selbst: Zur Genealogie der Therapeutisierung in den 'langen' Siebzigern*, ed. Sabine Maasen et al. (Bielefeld: Transcript, 2011); Eva Illouz, *Saving the Modern Soul: Therapy, Emotions and the Culture of Self-Help* (Berkeley: University of California Press, 2008); Maik Tändler, *Das therapeutische Jahrzehnt: Der Psychoboom in den siebziger Jahren* (Göttingen: Wallstein, 2016). See also, with a focus on psychoanalysis, Anthony D. Kauders, 'West German Psychoanalysis in Post-Analytic Times: Navigating Demands for Self-Actualization, Self-Governance, and Social Change, 1968–1990', *Geschichte und Gesellschaft* 48, no. 2 (2022): 197–219.

human and non-human life. Anti-nuclear activists emphasized the long-term effects of nuclear waste, which were strategically downplayed by the nuclear industry and its political lobby. Finally, the peace movement condemned the flawed rationality of the Cold War and the monstrous capacities of destruction that the two major power blocs had created and that threatened to set the world alight. Such rationality hardly seemed compatible with what Enlightenment thinkers had once praised as the 'highest of the mental faculties': reason, which drew 'on all of them (understanding, memory, judgment, imagination)'.[39]

Distrusting the hobbled politics of contemporary rationality went along with revaluing emotional sincerity and authenticity, affective solidarity and moral sensibilities. Ridiculed and discarded by traditional political players, those sensibilities were favoured by the new political groups that formed in the late 1970s, first locally and then, from 1980, fused and consolidated in an official party, the Greens (*Die Grünen*). When they first entered the federal parliament in 1983, party members carried sunflowers (symbolizing a healthy and happy future) and marred fir branches to draw attention to the looming ecological crisis. Even though the Greens could not change the procedures and protocols of parliament, they did represent a new current on the political stage. What is more, rather than quickly falling apart or losing momentum, as many had predicted, the new party survived and broadened its appeal. Over the years, it managed to gain respect and recognition for its unorthodox agenda and customs (including sporting long hair, beards and hand-knitted sweaters) even from those who had initially greeted it with contempt.[40]

The 'emotional element' in the GDR

Just as West Germany's political class was irritated by the emergence of groups that called themselves *bunt* (colourful), alternative or green, the GDR regime was finding it difficult to make sense of similar trends east of the river Elbe. Intellectuals, academics and artists, often shielded by the Protestant Church, increasingly challenged official politics from the 1970s onwards. The message sounded remarkably familiar: as 'rational management' had failed to solve contemporary conflicts and problems at home and abroad, people sought to retrieve 'the emotional element' by emphasizing human vulnerability, sensibility and subjectivity.[41]

---

[39]See Erickson et al., *Reason*, 8, ch. 1.
[40]Silke Mende, '*Nicht rechts, nicht links, sondern vorn*': *Eine Geschichte der Gründungsgrünen* (Munich: Oldenbourg, 2011).
[41]*Schiller auf den Bühnen sozialistischer Länder*, ed. Verband der Theaterschaffenden der DDR (Weimar: VT, 1985), esp. 57–9 (intervention by Helmut Pollow). See Mary Fulbrook, *Anatomy of a Dictatorship: Inside the GDR, 1949–1989* (Oxford: Oxford University Press, 1995), 151–242.

Emotional subjectivity was not something the regime had hitherto taken into account. Instead, they had put their faith in the manipulative power of mass rallies, marches, festivals, flags and collective singing – practices that drew on traditions of the socialist labour movement as well as on long-established Soviet strategies of securing public approval. Passionate appeals abounded. Children and adolescents, in particular, were targeted, at school and in the mass organizations of the Young Pioneers and the Thälmann Pioneers, as well as in the FDJ. Although membership was voluntary, participation was astonishingly high. Some joined for strategic reasons, while others were attracted by the leisure and group activities. With memories of the war still fresh, many children happily embraced the message that the socialist state safeguarded peace and security. In 1950, 9-year-old Rosa Albrecht from Rostock wrote to GDR President Wilhelm Pieck and thanked him for his care and help:

> Do you remember when bombs were falling in 1942 and many fathers had to go to war? And some children lost their parents? But now we all fight for peace, us Young Pioneers included. Now we can have a good night's rest and are not tired when we are going to school at 8 am because we are not woken up by bombs and sirens as during the terrible war.

Thirteen-year-old Egon Krenz (who in October 1989 briefly succeeded Erich Honecker as head of state) also addressed Pieck and expressed his gratitude for the outcome of the first parliamentary elections in 1950:

> Now we children in the GDR can look forward to a happy future without war and crisis. The war has done great harm to our family. I lost my father at the age of four, our house was reduced to rubble shortly before the breakdown. Today we live as *Neubürger* in the GDR. My mother who as a war widow receives only 55 Marks thus voted for the candidates of the National Front and for peace. We as young pioneers stand in the first row of the world peace front.[42]

Such passionate acclaim and support was invited and welcomed by the government, which from the very start counted on children and young people

---

[42]Federal Archives Berlin, DA 4 no. 1135: letters to Pieck by Rosa Albrecht and Egon Krenz, both from 16 October 1950. The term *Neubürger*, new citizen, was GDR speech for refugee or expellee (Krenz's family had lived in Kolberg, which after 1945 became part of Poland). In the first parliamentary elections held in October 1950, only candidates of the National Front (an alliance of parties and associations dominated by the SED) were listed on the ballot paper, so Mrs Krenz did not actually have a choice.

as 'bearers of hope' for the socialist future.⁴³ But the regime also sought to enlist the older generation, through organizational efforts, ideological appeals and emotional language.⁴⁴ Time and again, the authorities stressed citizens' 'unshakable trust' in the state and its representatives. Equally important was the declaration of 'indissoluble friendship' with socialist 'sister countries', especially the Soviet Union.⁴⁵ Stalin was hailed as 'the best friend of the German people'; opulent celebrations took place to mark his seventieth birthday in 1949. When he died four years later, the poet and future minister of culture Johannes R. Becher published a pompous ode to the 'Eternal Survivor' who had guaranteed the world 'never-ending happiness'.⁴⁶

Bertolt Brecht's reaction to Stalin's death proved somewhat more reserved, although he, too, joined the official chorus of mourners. Still, the famous author and theatre director was well aware that this chorus did not represent the general opinion. The continuous stream of people leaving for West Germany proved that trust in the East German state was indeed far from unshakeable. Brecht's recommendation was that the government be sensitive to the 'mood' and 'worries' of citizens. Furthermore, it should improve and professionalize its public 'appeal' through popular media programmes and festive events, with a particular emphasis on 'choral and individual singing, lectures, and political speeches'.⁴⁷ Two days before his death in 1956, Brecht told his colleague Erwin Strittmatter: 'You know I have to say one thing: we have neglected emotions.' Strittmatter commented: 'This from someone who always provoked the audience with sentences such as: "Don't stare so romantically!"'⁴⁸

While in his concept of epic theatre the young Brecht had fully subscribed to the mantra of distance, restraint and reflection, the older Brecht warmed to the idea that people's emotions needed to be properly addressed and directed towards a common political cause. Nevertheless, despite the significant effort of the GDR government to emotionally integrate and mobilize citizens, the

---

⁴³Dorothee Wierling, *Geboren im Jahr Eins: Der Jahrgang 1949 in der DDR: Versuch einer Kollektivbiographie* (Berlin: Links, 2002); Dorothee Wierling, 'Mission to Happiness: The Cohort of 1949 and the Making of East and West Germans', in *Miracle Years*, ed. Schissler, 110–25; Juliane Brauer, *Zeitgefühle – Wie die DDR ihre Zukunft besang: Eine Emotionsgeschichte* (Bielefeld: Transcript, 2020).
⁴⁴Mary Fulbrook, *The People's State: East German Society from Hitler to Honecker* (New Haven: Yale University Press, 2008), emphasizes the 'participatory' character of the GDR dictatorship.
⁴⁵Stefan Heym, 'Je voller der Mund, desto leerer die Sprüche – Leben mit der Aktuellen Kamera', in *So durften wir glauben zu kämpfen ... – Erfahrungen mit DDR-Medien*, ed. Edith Spielhagen (Berlin: Vistas, 1993), 93–100, esp. 95.
⁴⁶Johannes R. Becher, 'Dem Ewig-Lebenden', *Neues Deutschland*, 7 March 1953, 4.
⁴⁷Bertolt Brecht, *Schriften zur Politik und Gesellschaft* (Frankfurt: Suhrkamp, 1967), 325, 330–1.
⁴⁸'Die Masse schrie "hurra"!', *Der Spiegel*, 2 November 1992, 279.

results were less than convincing. To many, the slogans sounded empty and repetitive and the constant marching and flag-waving felt tedious and forced. The generational shift from Walter Ulbricht to the younger Honecker in 1971, though at first greeted with high expectations, did not change the pattern of publicly voiced enthusiasm and frustration levelled in private. GDR politics increasingly appeared stale, dogmatic and frozen in time. Even among children and adolescents, the promises and visions of a better future vanished into oblivion.

This became particularly obvious when perestroika, championed by the new Soviet leader Mikhail Gorbachev, opened the door to greater dynamism in the Eastern bloc. For the young dissidents who had focused, as in the Federal Republic, on topics such as environmental pollution or disarmament and peace, the perceived rupture between a liberalizing Soviet Union and a toughening regime in East Berlin deepened the sense of political distrust. When the government was found to have rigged local elections in 1989, distrust grew into a wave of protests that finally brought the regime down.[49]

9 November 1989 was undoubtedly the most emotional moment in contemporary German history. The opening of the hermetically closed and militarily guarded wall came as a huge surprise for East Berliners, and indeed everybody. The following months brought an intensely creative atmosphere of both wishful thinking and strategic planning. All hopes of keeping the failed state alive and reforming it from within died out by March 1990, when GDR citizens voted against further experiments and for a swift reunification of the two Germanies.

Post-1989 passionate politics

Political culture has changed considerably since 1990. The party system has diversified, first with the formation of a leftist party that attracted many former GDR citizens and SED members, then, more recently, with the success of a right-wing movement that summons far more supporters in the former East than the West.[50] While mainstream parties have moved closer to each other on issues like European integration, economic globalization, welfare and migration, left- and right-wing populism have become the choices of those who have felt abandoned or estranged by what they perceived as denationalization. According to an election poll from September 2017, 95 per cent of voters for the far-right Alternative for Germany (AfD) were

---

[49]Ilko-Sascha Kowalczuk, *End Game: The 1989 Revolution in East Germany* (New York: Berghahn, 2022).
[50]In 2017, the AfD entered the Bundestag for the first time, with 12.6 per cent of the general vote (East Germany 21.9 per cent, West Germany 10.7 per cent). Die Linke received 9.2 per cent of the overall vote (East 17.8; West 7.4). In 2021, the AfD got 10.3 per cent altogether, with 18.9 per cent in the East and 8.2 per cent in the West.

worried about a 'loss of German culture' due to the arrival of Muslim migrants and refugees.[51] Consequently, election campaigns have gathered emotional steam, with strategic outbursts of resentment and accusations not previously experienced in the Federal Republic, where sobriety, combined with fairness, had been the dominant feature since 1949, in clear contrast to National Socialism.[52]

Admittedly, the emergence of the extreme right is not peculiar to Germany. It has happened in many European as well as non-European countries. Due to historical experiences, though, it has sent shock waves through Germany's political class and media. Many fear for the stability of a political system with parties that agree to form coalition governments and protect the consensus of civilized restraint and mutual respect. The AfD is seen to undermine this consensus by conducting an 'anti-politics' which rejects democratic procedures and violates the norms of decent, non-violent behaviour.[53] At the same time, they epitomize the trend towards the emotionalization of politics by bringing hate speech, expressive rage and a sharp distinction between foes (to antagonize) and friends (to love and trust) into the political arena.

Even if right-wingers indeed introduced a new and forcefully emotional tone into politics, they did not start the trend. Populism is not the cause of politicians' growing inclination to appeal to people's emotions and citizens' increasing tendency to express themselves in emotional terms. Nor have such inclinations been restricted to totalitarian regimes with a firm monopolistic grip on people's attitudes and feelings. As this chapter has discussed, emotions have also been incorporated into the politics of liberal democracy. A century ago, Max Weber stated that modern politics needed politicians who paired 'cool' judgement and a 'realistic' sense of responsibility with 'hot' passion.[54] Public demand for the display of such (controlled) passion increased greatly in the age of mass media. The emergence and proliferation of visual media influenced the move towards personalized and personalizing politics, just as

---

[51]'Umfragen zu AfD', https://www.tagesschau.de/wahl/archiv/2017-09-24-BT-DE/umfrage-afd.shtml (accessed 25 January 2023).
[52]As to election campaigns before 1990, see Thomas Mergel, *Propaganda nach Hitler: Eine Kulturgeschichte des Wahlkampfs in der Bundesrepublik 1949–1990* (Göttingen: Wallstein, 2010).
[53]Paula Diehl, 'Antipolitik und postmoderne Ringkampf-Unterhaltung', *Aus Politik und Zeitgeschichte* 67 (2017): 25–30; Melanie Amann, *Angst für Deutschland* (Munich: Droemer, 2017).
[54]Weber, Profession and Vocation of Politics, 353, 369. See also Hinnerk Bruhns, '"Politics as a Vocation": A Contribution to Germany's Democratization in 1919?', *Journal of Classical Sociology* 19, no. 4 (2019): 316–30; Felix Heidenreich and Gary S. Schaal, eds, *Politische Theorie und Emotionen* (Baden-Baden: Nomos, 2012); Paul Hoggett and Simon Thompson, eds, *Politics and the Emotions: The Affective Turn in Contemporary Political Studies* (New York: Continuum, 2012); Karl-Rudolf Korte, ed., *Emotionen und Politik* (Baden-Baden: Nomos, 2015).

it emphasized the element of entertainment and, consequently, the quest for emotional profiling. Since the 1960s, spin doctors, pollsters and campaign managers have creatively worked to improve politicians' public images and enhance their likeability. These new techniques privilege strategies of personalization and 'sentimentalization' more than they strengthen rational and informed debate.[55] They not only assist the process of stripping politics of content and criticism but also pave the way for different sorts of populism.[56]

Although most citizens reportedly favour fact-based discourse and sober argumentation, they also cherish heated controversies and passionate speech. Above all, they value 'authenticity' – which is why politicians are systematically trained in the art of communication, with a particular focus on emotion management and 'authentic' performance. Authenticity had been a leftist battle cry of the 1960s, meant to resist and overcome forces of alienation and commodification. Fifty years later, it saw a revival, albeit in a sanitized form.[57] Authenticity now implies being true to and honest about one's individuality and values. According to a widely shared consensus, truth and honesty seem to come from people showing their genuine emotions and thus allowing others to feel what they feel.[58]

The quest for authenticity clearly supports the 'emotional element' of democratic politics. It also mirrors the trend towards valorizing emotions as a crucial asset and resource in people's lives. That trend started in Western countries during the 1960s and was strengthened by the expansion of therapeutic culture. Enthroning emotions as prime bearers of an authenticity that allegedly could not be manipulated by external forces, psychotherapy in its multiple forms did a lot to change the way people thought about themselves and how they interacted with the world around

---

[55] Wolfgang Streeck, 'Merkel: Ein Rückblick', *Frankfurter Allgemeine Zeitung*, 16 November 2017, 11.
[56] See William Davies, 'How Feelings Took over the World', *The Guardian*, 8 September 2018; Karolina Wigura and Jaroslaw Kuisz, 'Populists Understand the Power of Human Emotion: Europe's Liberals Need to Grasp It, too', *The Guardian*, 11 December 2019; Cas Mudde, *Populist Radical Right Parties in Europe* (Cambridge: Cambridge University Press, 2007); Jan-Werner Müller, *What Is Populism?* (London: Penguin, 2017); Benjamin Moffitt, *The Global Rise of Populism: Performance, Political Style, and Representation* (Stanford: Stanford University Press, 2016); Jesse Prinz, 'Emotion and Political Polarization', in *The Politics of Emotional Shockwaves*, ed. Ana Falcato and Sara Graça da Silva (Cham: Springer, 2021), 1–25.
[57] As to the sixties and the spirit of 'authenticity', see Marshall Berman's 2009 preface to the second edition of his book *The Politics of Authenticity: Radical Individualism and the Emergence of Modern Society* (London: Verso, 2009). The book that first came out in 1970 was about eighteenth-century Paris, where the author sought to find the roots of his generation's attempt to renew democracy and change the world for the better. See also Häberlen, *Emotional Politics*, and Häberlen et al., eds, *Politics of Authenticity*.
[58] See Chapter 6 in this volume.

them. This found expression in the new social movements of the 1970s and 1980s, which organized collective protest around shared feelings of fear, sorrow or anger.

Politically, there are of course major differences between those movements and recent populism, especially on the right. Yet they converge in that they speak an emotional language and challenge politics and politicians to take their worries and desires seriously. With an interesting twist, the rallying slogan of the late 1960s originally coined by the leftist students' movement and second-wave feminism, 'The personal is political', has seen an unexpected renaissance. Connecting personal experience to larger social, cultural and political developments has now become the emotional style of the extreme right.

Still, it is one emotional style among several that populate the political field with varying degrees of intensity and antagonistic thrust. Liberal democracy, as it has developed in (West) Germany over the course of more than seven decades, has lived with many forms of emotional expression, from marked restraint to exuberance. It has also seen multiple actors exploring different styles, from governments and parties to social movements, NGOs and grassroots initiatives. And it has seen different emotions mobilized for the sake of political action, from trust and love to fear and *thymos* ('wrath' or 'rage' in Greek), which is currently being monopolized by völkisch groups.[59] Historically speaking, it is this very variety of actors, styles and feelings that both adds to the vibrancy of democratic politics and distinguishes it from the homogenized mode of emotional politics practised by totalitarian regimes.

---

[59]Ute Frevert, *The Power of Emotions: A History of Germany from 1900 to the Present* (Cambridge: Cambridge University Press, 2023), 33–4.

NAME INDEX

Abdullah (King of Saudi Arabia) 114
Adenauer, Konrad 314–6
Adorno, Theodor W. 133, 313
Akerlof, George 199
Akihito (Tenno) 114
Albert (Prince Consort) 266
Albrecht, Rosa 320
Alcuin of York 204
Alexander III of Macedon (Alexander the Great) 42
Anders, Günther 2–3
Aquinas, Thomas 121
Arendt, Hannah 2, 49
Aristotle 204, 236, 261
Arnim, Achim von 73
Arrow, Kenneth 39
Asquith, Herbert 98–9
Aston, Louise 172

Bagehot, Walter 266, 278
Baier, Annette 39
Balzac, Honoré de 210
Banks, Carl 202
Barbauld, Anna Laetitia 252
Baring, Evelyn (Earl of Cromer) 276
Barrett, Lisa Feldman 24
Baudouin, Paul 111
Beauharnais, Josephine de 244
Bebel, August 269
Beccaria, Cesare 126
Becher, Johannes R. 321
Beethoven, Ludwig van 201
Bell, Daniel 178
Bell, Johannes 109
Benedetti, Vincent 95
Bennigsen, Adolf von 75–6
Bennigsen, Elisabeth von 75–6
Bentham, Jeremy 222
Berger, Peter 7, 86

Bergk, Johann Adam 126–7
Bergson, Henri 26
Berman, Marshall 324
Bernstein, Leonard 6
Beuys, Joseph 246–7
Bing, Rudolf 299
Bismarck, Otto von 75, 95–6, 230, 268, 279
Bluntschli, Johann Caspar 92–3
Boguslawski, Albert von 68
Boltanski, Luc 163, 181
Bosch, Robert 53
Boulanger, Georges 276
Bourdieu, Pierre 64
Brady, James 78
Braidley, Benjamin 53–4
Braithwaite, John 121
Brandt, Willy 115
Brecht, Bertolt 321
Brinvilliers, Marquise de (Marie-Madeleine Marguerite d'Aubray) 147
Brooke, Rupert 98
Brown, Gordon 134
Burke, Edmund 57, 124
Byron, George Gordon (Lord) 152–3

Calvin, John 206
Camphausen, Wilhelm 95
Carlyle, Thomas 12, 34
Carmer, Johann Heinrich von 127
Catherine (Kate) (Duchess of Cambridge) 243–4
Catherine II (Empress of Russia) 154
Charles V (Holy Roman Emperor) 42
Chiapello, Ève 163, 181
Churchill, Winston 98, 111, 272
Cicero, Marcus Tullius 204
Clark, Kenneth 157, 162

NAME INDEX

Clausewitz, Carl von 100
Clemenceau, Georges 109
Clinton, Bill 114
Constant, Benjamin 222–3
Cooper, Anderson 21
Cottrell, Leonard 156–7
Cruikshank, George 227

Damasio, Antonio 24, 33
Defoe, Daniel 123–4
Dehmel, Richard 108
Deleuze, Gilles 24, 26
Demos, Virginia 23
Descartes, René 194
Dickens, Charles 151, 202
Diderot, Denis 228
Disraeli, Benjamin 266
Dolan, Paul 221
Dönniges, Helene von 75
Dönniges, Wilhelm von 75
Dutschke, Rudi 308–9

Ebert, Friedrich 110, 130
Ebhardt, Franz 249–50
Eisenhower, Dwight D. 113
Eisner, Kurt 283
Ekman, Paul 23, 25
Elias, Norbert 15–18, 121
Elizabeth I (Queen) 154
Engels, Friedrich 163, 168–70, 172, 178, 211, 233
Erhard, Ludwig 316
Erikson, Erik 41, 45

Falkenhagen, Oswald 75
Febvre, Lucien 14–15, 17–19, 65, 112
Feder, Curt 303
Fest, Joachim 312
Fichte, Johann Gottlieb 230, 236
Foerster, Friedrich Wilhelm 154, 230, 236
Forsyth, Jenny 123
Foucault, Michel 127, 157
Fouché, Joseph 263
Frank, Hans 160
Franz Joseph (Emperor of Austria) 267–8
Freud, Sigmund 16, 18, 194, 210, 235, 264, 284

Friedrich II (King of Prussia) 90, 125, 261
Friedrich Wilhelm III (King of Prussia) 265
Fröbel, Friedrich 45
Fugger (family) 42, 205

Gambetta, Léon 273
Garve, Christian 90
Gaulle, Charles de 18, 65, 111–12
Gay, Peter 18–19
Geertz, Clifford 242
Geiger, Theodor 315–6
George, Stefan 235
Giddens, Anthony 58
Gilligan, Carol 154
Giloi, Eva 244
Ginsberg, Allen 254
Gneisenau, August Neidhardt von 265
Goebbels, Joseph 111, 279, 286–7, 289–91, 294–5, 301
Goethe, Johann Wolfgang (von) 185
Goleman, Daniel 20, 158, 181
Gorbachev, Mikhail 322
Gracián, Baltasar 42
Grey, Edward 98–9
Grimm, Jacob 224–5, 227
Grimm, Wilhelm 224–5, 227
Gürtner, Franz 82

Häberlen, Joachim 27
Haffner, Sebastian 292
Hardenberg, Friedrich von (Novalis) 252
Hardin, Shena 121
Harkort, Friedrich 170
Hauptmann, Gerhart 172
Havelock, Henry 104
Heine, Heinrich 172
Heinemann, Gustav 316
Heinrich IV (German Kaiser) 115
Hellpach, Willy 173
Heuss, Theodor 314–6
Hicks, John R. 191
Himmler, Heinrich 303–4
Hindenburg, Paul von 286
Hirschman, Albert O. 170, 209
Hitler, Adolf 59, 111, 246, 279, 281–6, 288–91, 294, 296, 299, 302, 304, 311–12

NAME INDEX

Hobbes, Thomas 90, 226
Hochschild, Arlie Russell 8
Hoffmann, Leonard 80
Höhn, Johanna 145
Holloway, Sally 241
Holtei, Karl von 150, 152–3
Homer 11
Honecker, Erich 320, 322
House, Edward 109
Hübner, Karl Wilhelm 172
Hugo, Victor 96, 155
Huizinga, Johan 13–15, 17–18
Hume, David 140, 143–4, 159, 209
Hunt, Lynn 148
Hutcheson, Francis 6, 50, 61, 63–4, 140

Illouz, Eva 185–6
Itzig, Moritz 73
Izard, Carroll E. 21, 23

James, William 22, 175
Jaspers, Karl 312
Johnson, Samuel 142, 149, 153
Jünger, Ernst 100
Justi, Heinrich von 207

Kagan, Jerome 33
Kahneman, Daniel 196–7
Kant, Immanuel 28, 126, 148, 153, 161, 208, 222–3, 229–31, 236
Karma Ura, Dasho 221
Kennedy, John F. 113
Key, Philip Barton 78
Keynes, John Maynard 191–7, 199, 214–15
Khrushchev, Nikita 113
Kiesinger, Kurt Georg 316
Klemperer, Victor 295–6, 299, 302–4, 307
Knigge, Adolph Freiherr von 209, 211
Kollwitz, Hans 102
Kollwitz, Käthe 101–2, 106–9, 172, 251
Kosegarten, Ludwig Gotthard 140
Koselleck, Reinhart 26
Kraepelin, Emil 174
Krenz, Egon 320
Krupp, Alfred 56, 171
Kuczynski, Jürgen 48, 312

La Bruyère, Jean de 147
Lafargue, Paul 234
Lange, Carl 22
Laqueur, Thomas W. 150
Lassalle, Ferdinand 75, 269
Latzko, Andreas 105
Lawrence, Thomas Edward 104
Le Bon, Gustave 29, 275, 284
Leibniz, Gottfried Wilhelm 90
Lessing, Gotthold Ephraim 142–3, 157
Levenstein, Adolf 173–4
Levy, Sara 73
Lewis, Helen Block 135
Liebknecht, Karl 245
Lipmann, Otto 175
Lipps, Theodor 140
List, Heinrich 160
Lloyd George, David 99, 103, 272
Locke, John 56
Lorenz, Max 93
Louis Philippe (King of the French) 264–5, 277
Louis XIV (King of France) 96
Louis XVI (King of France) 57
Louis XVIII (King of France) 245
Luhmann, Niklas 40
Luise (Queen Consort of Prussia) 95, 244, 265
Luther, Martin 42, 44
Luxemburg, Rosa 245

MacDonald, Ramsay 99
Machiavelli, Niccolò 42, 205, 261
Mandeville, Bernard 206
Mann, Thomas 74
Marcuse, Herbert 317–18
Margalit, Avishai 122
Marx, Karl 163, 168–70, 178, 211, 233–4
Maschmann, Melita 304, 307
Massumi, Brian 24–6
Matt, Susan 184
Mayo, Elton 177–8, 180–1
McKenzie, Scott 254
Meinecke, Friedrich 302
Mendelssohn, Moses 143
Merecki, Siegfried 297–8
Mill, John Stuart 189, 221–2
Miller, William 117

NAME INDEX

Mitscherlich, Alexander 314, 317
Mitscherlich, Margarete 314, 317
Moede, Walther 175
Mohammad Reza Pahlavi (Shah of Iran) 113
Molènes, Alexandre de 151
Molière 207, 210
Mommsen, Hans 302
Mommsen, Wilhelm 302
Montesquieu (Charles de Secondat, Baron de Montesquieu) 169
Moses, Hugo 298, 300–1
Müller, Hermann 109
Münsterberg, Hugo 175–6
Mussolini, Benito 279

Napoleon I (Emperor of the French) 95, 244–5, 264–5
Napoleon III (Emperor of the French) 94–6, 245
Nathorff, Hertha 300
Newton, Isaac 194
Nicholas II (Tsar) 97
Nicolai, Friedrich 149–50
Nicolson, Harold 110
Nietzsche, Friedrich 26, 45–6, 66, 208, 235
Nixon, Richard 113
North, Douglass C. 198
Novalis (Hardenberg, Friedrich von) 252
Nussbaum, Martha 119, 122

O'Neill, Onora 60
Obama, Barack 114
Owen, Robert 274

Parsons, Talcott 317
Pestalozzi, Johann Heinrich 145–6, 149
Pétain, Philippe 111–12
Pieck, Wilhelm 49, 245, 320
Plato 121–2, 204
Plessner, Helmuth 47–8, 133
Polo, Marco 42
Pufendorf, Samuel 90
Putin, Vladimir 113
Putnam, Robert D. 46

Rabl, Carl 302
Racowicza, Janko von 75

Ratzinger, Georg 212
Reddy, William 27
Reich, Wilhelm 287–8
Renan, Ernest 96
Ricard, Samuel 169–70
Riehl, Wilhelm Heinrich 93
Robert, Ludwig 72
Robespierre, Maximilien 262–3
Rodeck, Fritz 300–1
Roosevelt, Franklin D. 310
Rose, Nikolas 180
Rosenberg, Alfred 282
Rosenberg, Hans 17
Roßbach, Julius 284
Rougemont, Denis de 287–8, 291
Rousseau, Jean-Jacques 142–3
Ruf, Sep 316
Rust, Bernhard 281, 291–2

Samuelson, Paul 191
Sartre, Jean-Paul 97
Srbik, Heinrich Ritter von 302
Schabowski, Günter 308, 316
Schachter, Stanley 22–3
Schelsky, Helmut 313, 316
Schiller, Friedrich 232–3
Schlegel, Friedrich 234
Schmalenbach, Herman 47
Schmid, Carlo 115, 315–6
Schmoller, Gustav 189–90, 195
Schneiderman, Rose 254
Schopenhauer, Arthur 154, 162, 212, 222
Schumpeter, Joseph 187–8, 193, 195
Schwarz, Matthäus 205
Sedgwick, Eve Kosofsky 25
Sévigné, Madame de (Marie de Rabutin-Chantal) 147
Shakespeare, William 205, 207
Shebbeare, John 124
Sherrington, Charles 181
Shiller, Robert 199
Sickles, Daniel 78
Siegel, Michael 293
Siemens, Carl von 53
Siemens, Werner von 53
Sieyès, Emmanuel Joseph (Abbé) 263
Simmel, Georg 40, 44, 51, 63–5, 86, 119, 138, 212–13

Simon, Herbert 196
Sinclair, Upton 172
Singer, Jerome 22–3
Singer, Tania 156
Smith, Adam 8, 140–3, 161, 169, 188–9, 208, 211
Smith, Thomas 205–6
Sombart, Werner 195
Speer, Albert 290
Staël, Germaine de 261–2
Stalin, Josef 246, 307, 321
Stearns, Carol 18–19
Stearns, Peter 18–19
Stein, Lorenz von 268–9
Stern, Clara 2
Stern, William 2, 175
Stone, Oliver 215
Streicher, Julius 299
Strittmatter, Erwin 321
Sulzberger, Cyrus 316

Thackeray, William 152–3
Thaw, Harry Kendall 79–80
Tocqueville, Alexis de 214
Tomkins, Silvan 22–3, 25, 32, 120
Treitschke, Heinrich von 89–91, 93, 116, 270, 275
Trotha, Adolf von 110
Tversky, Amos 196

Ulbricht, Walter 245, 322

Vattel, Emer de 90–1, 116
Veblen, Thorstein 188–9, 198–9
Victoria (Queen) 250, 266–7, 270
Vincke, Georg von 75

Virchow, Rudolf 158
Voltaire 228

Wagner, Cosima 45
Wagner, Richard 45–6
Watson, John 184
Weber, Marianne 66
Weber, Max 9, 12–15, 17, 35, 64, 66–7, 98, 102, 167–8, 173–5, 186, 187, 193, 206, 213, 260, 273, 276, 282–3, 289, 309, 323
Wedgwood, Josiah 186
Weitling, Wilhelm 211
Welcker, Carl 68
Welskopp, Thomas 179
Werner, Anton von 96
Werner, Ruth 48
Wernicke, August Eduard 227
Wettstein-Adelt, Minna 158
Wharton, Francis 78
White, Stanford 79
Wilhelm I (King of Prussia, German Kaiser) 95, 244, 246, 251, 269
Wilhelm II (German Kaiser) 97, 246, 270, 277, 279
William (Prince of Wales) 243
Wilson, Woodrow 109
Witkop, Philipp 102
Wolff, Christian 44, 51, 229, 236
Wollstonecraft, Mary 252–3
Wundt, Wilhelm 190
Wurmser, Léon 118–19

Zedler, Johann Heinrich 43–4
Zola, Émile 155